DOOMSDAY CLOCK
PART 1

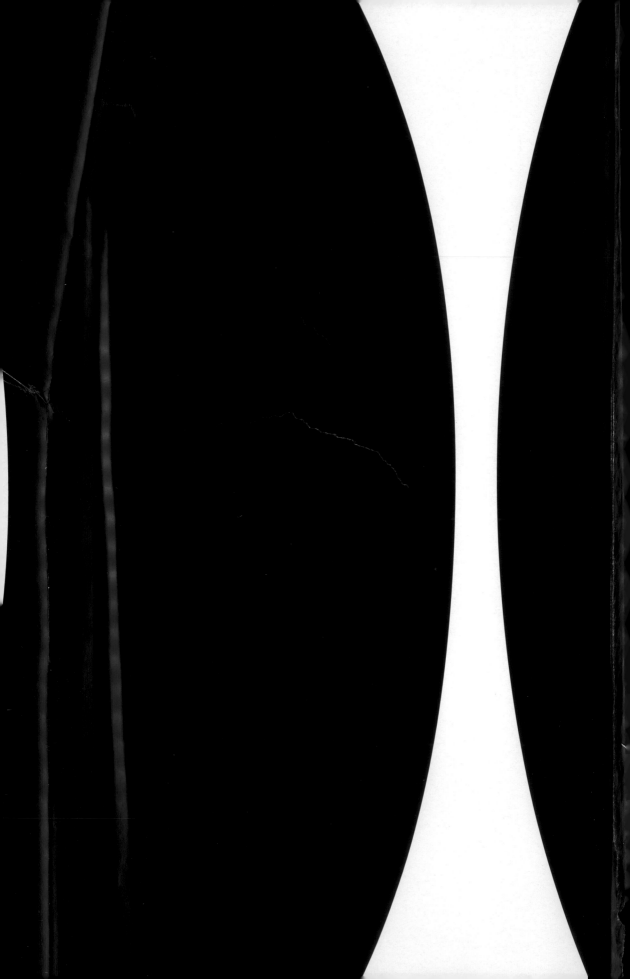

DOOMSDAY CLOCK
PART 1

GEOFF JOHNS
writer

GARY FRANK
illustrator

BRAD ANDERSON
colorist

ROB LEIGH
letterer

AMIE BROCKWAY-METCALF
original issue back matter design

GARY FRANK and
BRAD ANDERSON
collection cover artists

Watchmen created by
Alan Moore and Dave Gibbons.

Superman created by
Jerry Siegel and Joe Shuster.
By special arrangement
with the Jerry Siegel family.

Publisher's Note: The doomsday clock is a symbol created in 1947 by the Science and Security Board of the academic journal *Bulletin of the Atomic Scientists,* in response to the world's growing geopolitical insecurities and rising fear of nuclear war. The time on the clock — the proximity to midnight — indicates the view of the Science and Security Board regarding the likelihood of a global catastrophe. Initially, the clock was set to 11:53 p.m., but in 1953, with both the U.S. and the Soviet Union testing thermonuclear devices, the clock reached 11:58 p.m., its most ominous reading since its inception. By 1968 the situation had improved with the signing of the first Strategic Arms Limitation Treaty (SALT I) by the U.S. and the Soviet Union, and the clock eased back to 11:48. However, the two countries' jockeying for power and the apparent failure of a second round of SALT negotiations in 1984 pushed the clock forward to three minutes before midnight, where it remained for the duration of WATCHMEN'S initial publication. In 1991 the clock was set at 11:43 p.m., the farthest from midnight that it had ever reached up to that point, in recognition of the signing of the SALT II accords by the U.S. and the Soviet Union. In 2007, however, the Science and Security Board decided that the clock should also reflect the risk of climate change and life science technological issues. The clock returned to three minutes to midnight in January 2015 due to "[un]checked climate change, global nuclear weapons modernizations, and outsized nuclear weapons arsenals." The doomsday clock moved to two and a half minutes until midnight in 2017, and two minutes until midnight in 2018, where it remains now.

BRIAN CUNNINGHAM Editor – Original Series
AMEDEO TURTURRO Associate Editor – Original Series
JEB WOODARD Group Editor – Collected Editions
ROBIN WILDMAN Editor – Collected Edition
STEVE COOK Design Director – Books
AMIE BROCKWAY-METCALF Publication Design
KATE DURRÉ Publication Production

BOB HARRAS Senior VP – Editor-in-Chief, DC Comics
PAT McCALLUM Executive Editor, DC Comics

DAN DiDIO Publisher
JIM LEE Publisher & Chief Creative Officer
BOBBIE CHASE VP – New Publishing Initiatives & Talent Development
DON FALLETTI VP – Manufacturing Operations & Workflow Management
LAWRENCE GANEM VP – Talent Services
ALISON GILL Senior VP – Manufacturing & Operations
HANK KANALZ Senior VP – Publishing Strategy & Support Services
DAN MIRON VP – Publishing Operations
NICK J. NAPOLITANO VP – Manufacturing Administration & Design
NANCY SPEARS VP – Sales
MICHELE R. WELLS VP & Executive Editor, Young Reader

DOOMSDAY CLOCK PART 1

DC Comics, 2900 West Alameda Ave., Burbank, CA 91505
Printed by LSC Communications, Kendallville, IN, USA. 8/30/19. First Printing.
ISBN: 978-1-77950-120-2

Library of Congress Cataloging-in-Publication Data is available.

PEFC Certified

This product is from sustainably managed forests and controlled sources

PEFC/29-31-337   www.pefc.org

**Dedicated to
Len Wein**

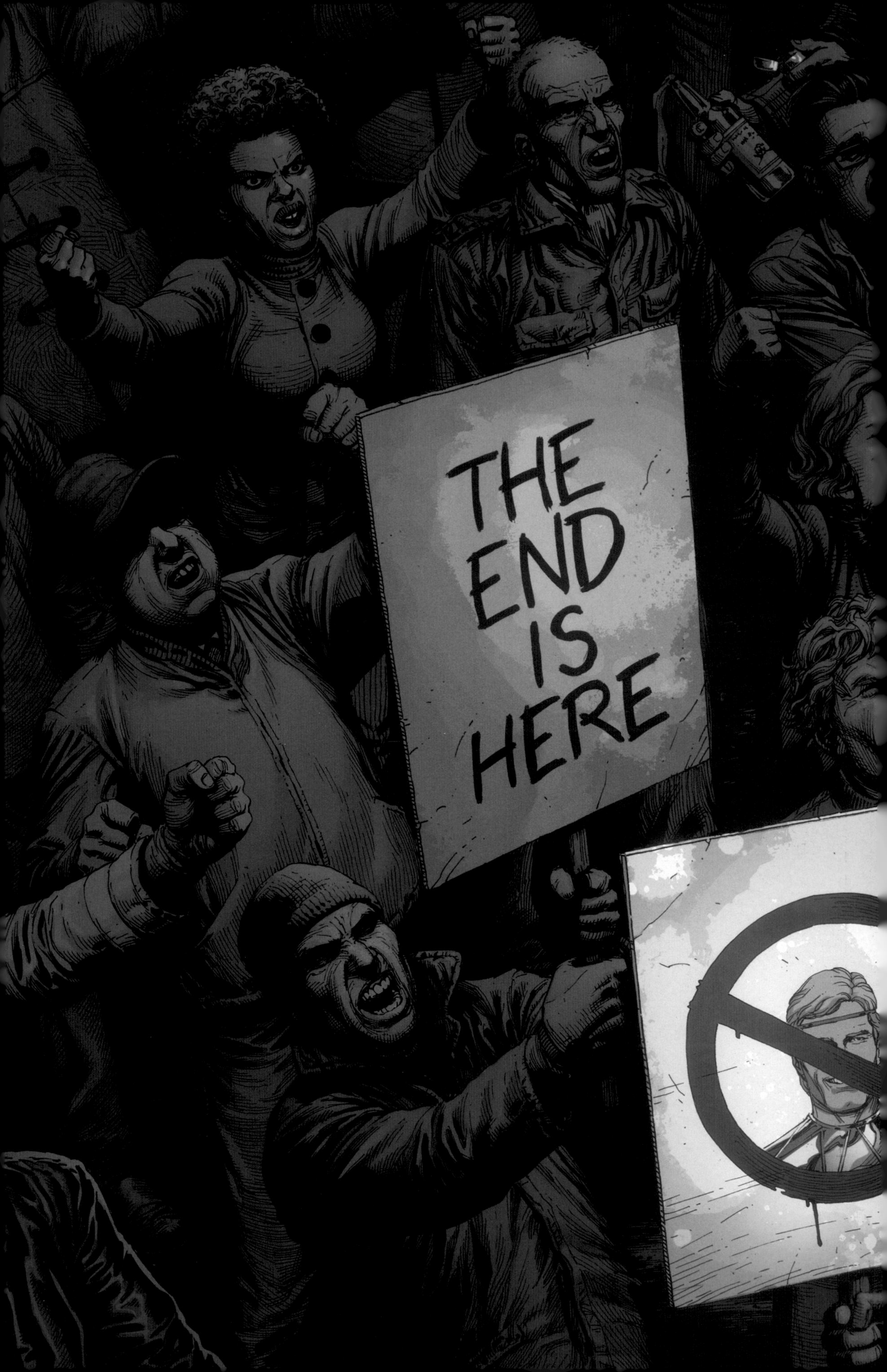
THE END IS HERE

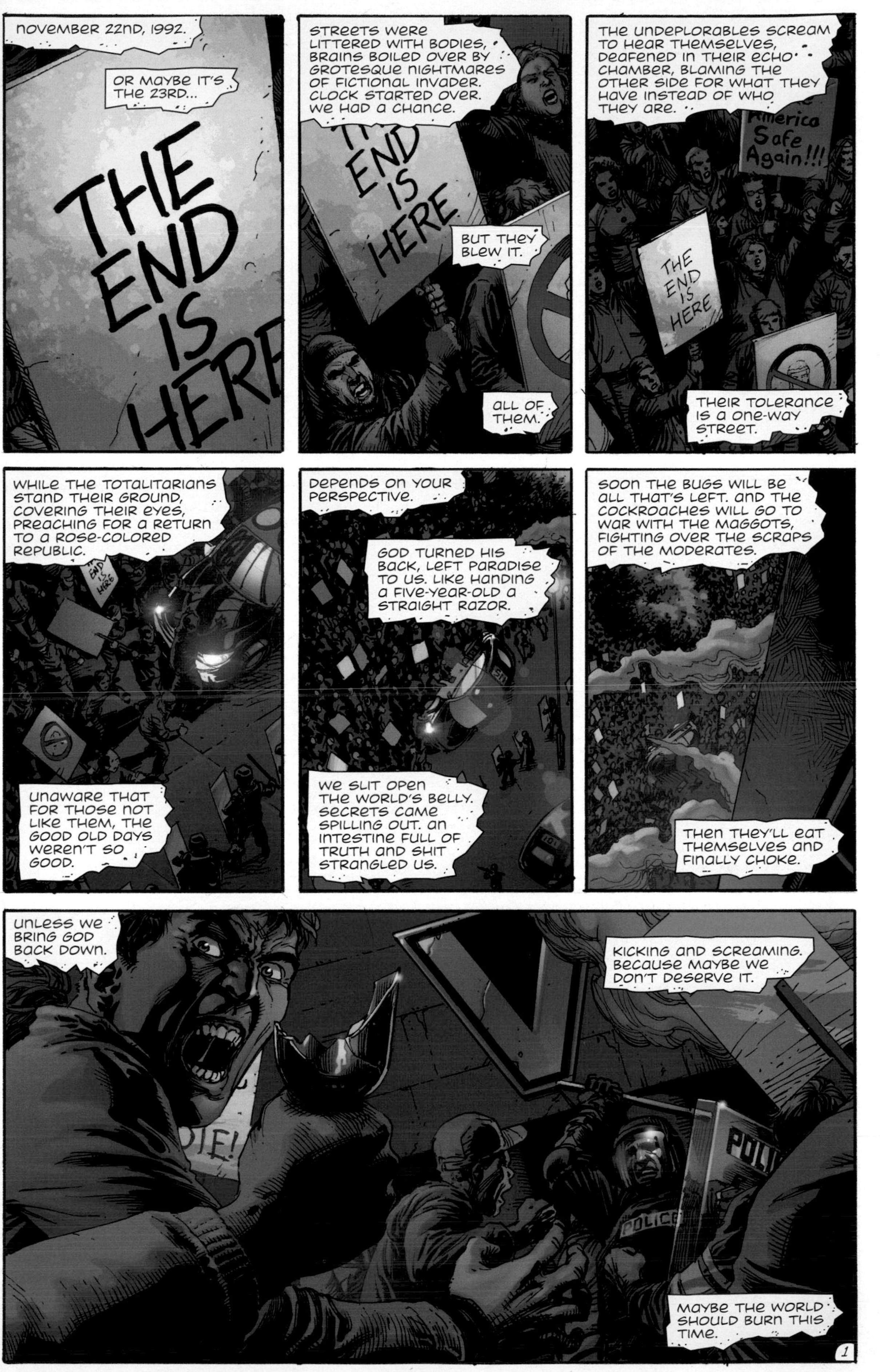
NOVEMBER 22ND, 1992.
OR MAYBE IT'S THE 23RD...
THE END IS HERE
STREETS WERE LITTERED WITH BODIES, BRAINS BOILED OVER BY GROTESQUE NIGHTMARES OF FICTIONAL INVADER. CLOCK STARTED OVER. WE HAD A CHANCE.
THE END IS HERE
BUT THEY BLEW IT.
ALL OF THEM.
THE UNDEPLORABLES SCREAM TO HEAR THEMSELVES, DEAFENED IN THEIR ECHO CHAMBER, BLAMING THE OTHER SIDE FOR WHAT THEY HAVE INSTEAD OF WHO THEY ARE.
America Safe Again!!!
THE END IS HERE
THEIR TOLERANCE IS A ONE-WAY STREET.
WHILE THE TOTALITARIANS STAND THEIR GROUND, COVERING THEIR EYES, PREACHING FOR A RETURN TO A ROSE-COLORED REPUBLIC.
UNAWARE THAT FOR THOSE NOT LIKE THEM, THE GOOD OLD DAYS WEREN'T SO GOOD.
DEPENDS ON YOUR PERSPECTIVE.
GOD TURNED HIS BACK, LEFT PARADISE TO US. LIKE HANDING A FIVE-YEAR-OLD A STRAIGHT RAZOR.
WE SLIT OPEN THE WORLD'S BELLY. SECRETS CAME SPILLING OUT. AN INTESTINE FULL OF TRUTH AND SHIT STRANGLED US.
SOON THE BUGS WILL BE ALL THAT'S LEFT. AND THE COCKROACHES WILL GO TO WAR WITH THE MAGGOTS, FIGHTING OVER THE SCRAPS OF THE MODERATES.
THEN THEY'LL EAT THEMSELVES AND FINALLY CHOKE.
UNLESS WE BRING GOD BACK DOWN.
KICKING AND SCREAMING. BECAUSE MAYBE WE DON'T DESERVE IT.
DIE!
POLI
POLICE
MAYBE THE WORLD SHOULD BURN THIS TIME.

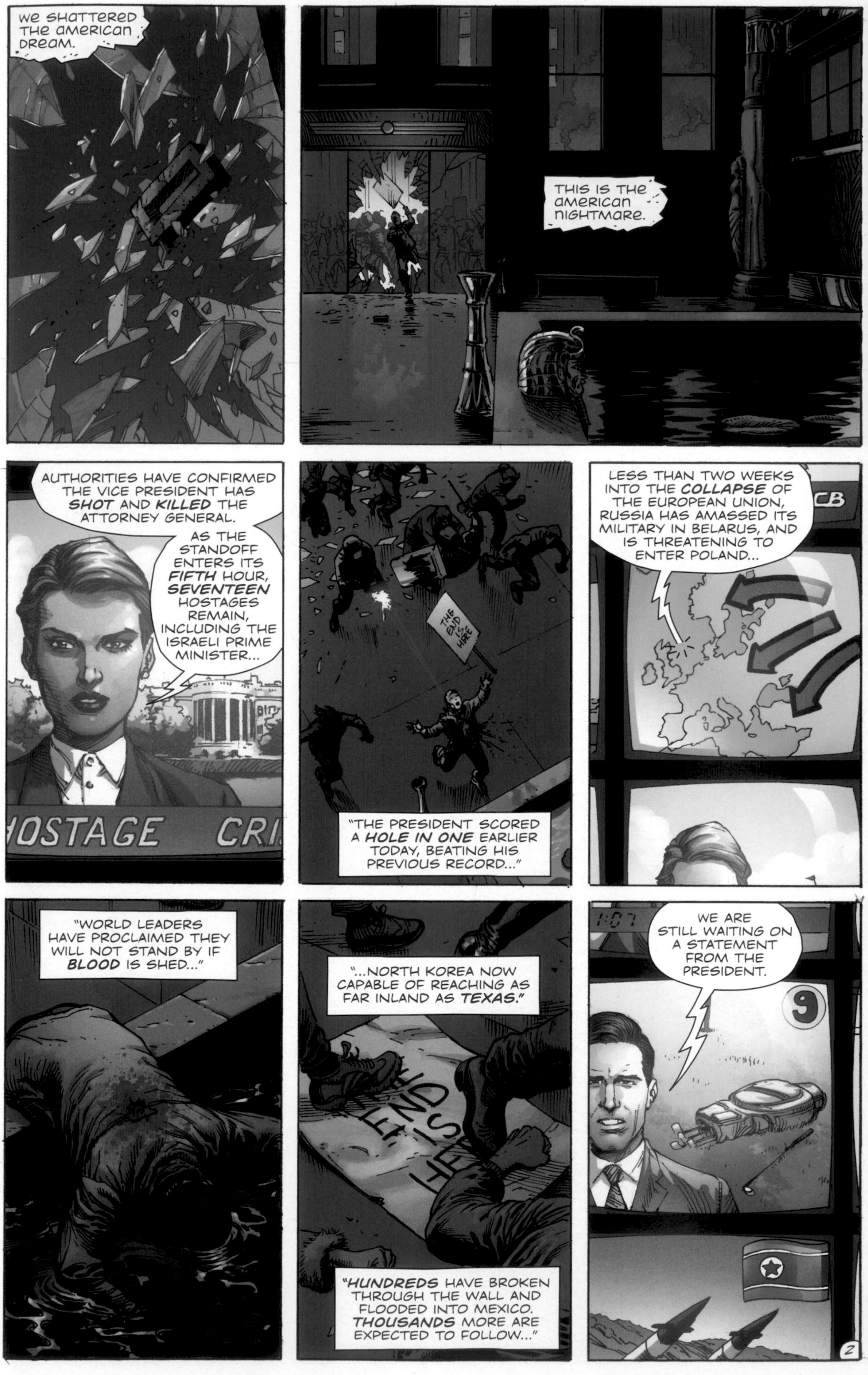
WE SHATTERED THE AMERICAN DREAM.
THIS IS THE AMERICAN NIGHTMARE.
AUTHORITIES HAVE CONFIRMED THE VICE PRESIDENT HAS SHOT AND KILLED THE ATTORNEY GENERAL.
AS THE STANDOFF ENTERS ITS FIFTH HOUR, SEVENTEEN HOSTAGES REMAIN, INCLUDING THE ISRAELI PRIME MINISTER...
HOSTAGE CRI
THE END IS HERE
"THE PRESIDENT SCORED A HOLE IN ONE EARLIER TODAY, BEATING HIS PREVIOUS RECORD..."
LESS THAN TWO WEEKS INTO THE COLLAPSE OF THE EUROPEAN UNION, RUSSIA HAS AMASSED ITS MILITARY IN BELARUS, AND IS THREATENING TO ENTER POLAND...
"WORLD LEADERS HAVE PROCLAIMED THEY WILL NOT STAND BY IF BLOOD IS SHED..."
"...NORTH KOREA NOW CAPABLE OF REACHING AS FAR INLAND AS TEXAS."
"HUNDREDS HAVE BROKEN THROUGH THE WALL AND FLOODED INTO MEXICO. THOUSANDS MORE ARE EXPECTED TO FOLLOW..."
WE ARE STILL WAITING ON A STATEMENT FROM THE PRESIDENT.

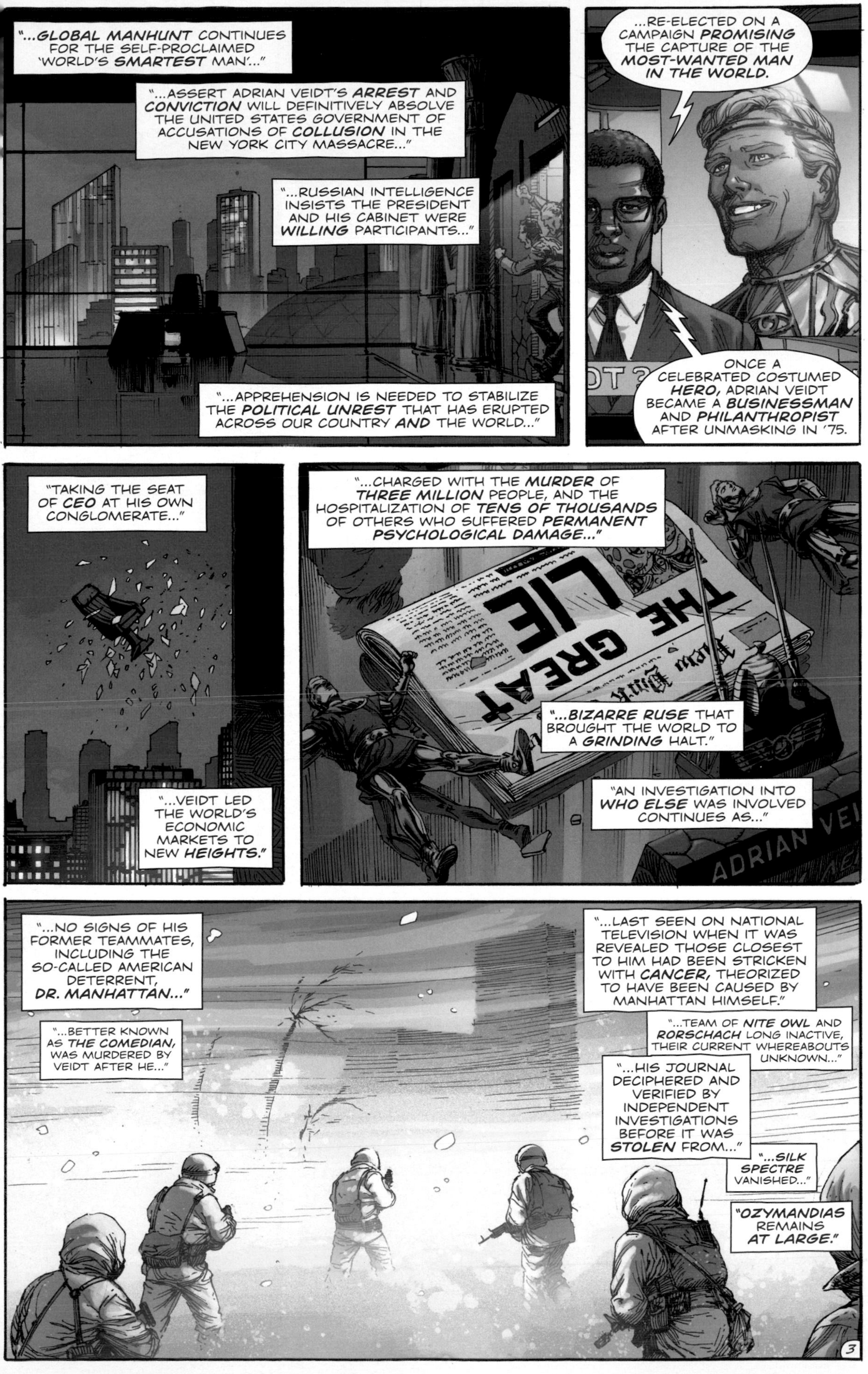
"...GLOBAL MANHUNT CONTINUES FOR THE SELF-PROCLAIMED 'WORLD'S SMARTEST MAN'..."
"...ASSERT ADRIAN VEIDT'S ARREST AND CONVICTION WILL DEFINITIVELY ABSOLVE THE UNITED STATES GOVERNMENT OF ACCUSATIONS OF COLLUSION IN THE NEW YORK CITY MASSACRE..."
"...RUSSIAN INTELLIGENCE INSISTS THE PRESIDENT AND HIS CABINET WERE WILLING PARTICIPANTS..."
"...APPREHENSION IS NEEDED TO STABILIZE THE POLITICAL UNREST THAT HAS ERUPTED ACROSS OUR COUNTRY AND THE WORLD..."
...RE-ELECTED ON A CAMPAIGN PROMISING THE CAPTURE OF THE MOST-WANTED MAN IN THE WORLD.
ONCE A CELEBRATED COSTUMED HERO, ADRIAN VEIDT BECAME A BUSINESSMAN AND PHILANTHROPIST AFTER UNMASKING IN '75.
"TAKING THE SEAT OF CEO AT HIS OWN CONGLOMERATE..."
"...VEIDT LED THE WORLD'S ECONOMIC MARKETS TO NEW HEIGHTS."
"...CHARGED WITH THE MURDER OF THREE MILLION PEOPLE, AND THE HOSPITALIZATION OF TENS OF THOUSANDS OF OTHERS WHO SUFFERED PERMANENT PSYCHOLOGICAL DAMAGE..."
THE GREAT LIE
"...BIZARRE RUSE THAT BROUGHT THE WORLD TO A GRINDING HALT."
"AN INVESTIGATION INTO WHO ELSE WAS INVOLVED CONTINUES AS..."
"...NO SIGNS OF HIS FORMER TEAMMATES, INCLUDING THE SO-CALLED AMERICAN DETERRENT, DR. MANHATTAN..."
"...BETTER KNOWN AS THE COMEDIAN, WAS MURDERED BY VEIDT AFTER HE..."
"...LAST SEEN ON NATIONAL TELEVISION WHEN IT WAS REVEALED THOSE CLOSEST TO HIM HAD BEEN STRICKEN WITH CANCER, THEORIZED TO HAVE BEEN CAUSED BY MANHATTAN HIMSELF."
"...TEAM OF NITE OWL AND RORSCHACH LONG INACTIVE, THEIR CURRENT WHEREABOUTS UNKNOWN..."
"...HIS JOURNAL DECIPHERED AND VERIFIED BY INDEPENDENT INVESTIGATIONS BEFORE IT WAS STOLEN FROM..."
"...SILK SPECTRE VANISHED..."
"OZYMANDIAS REMAINS AT LARGE."

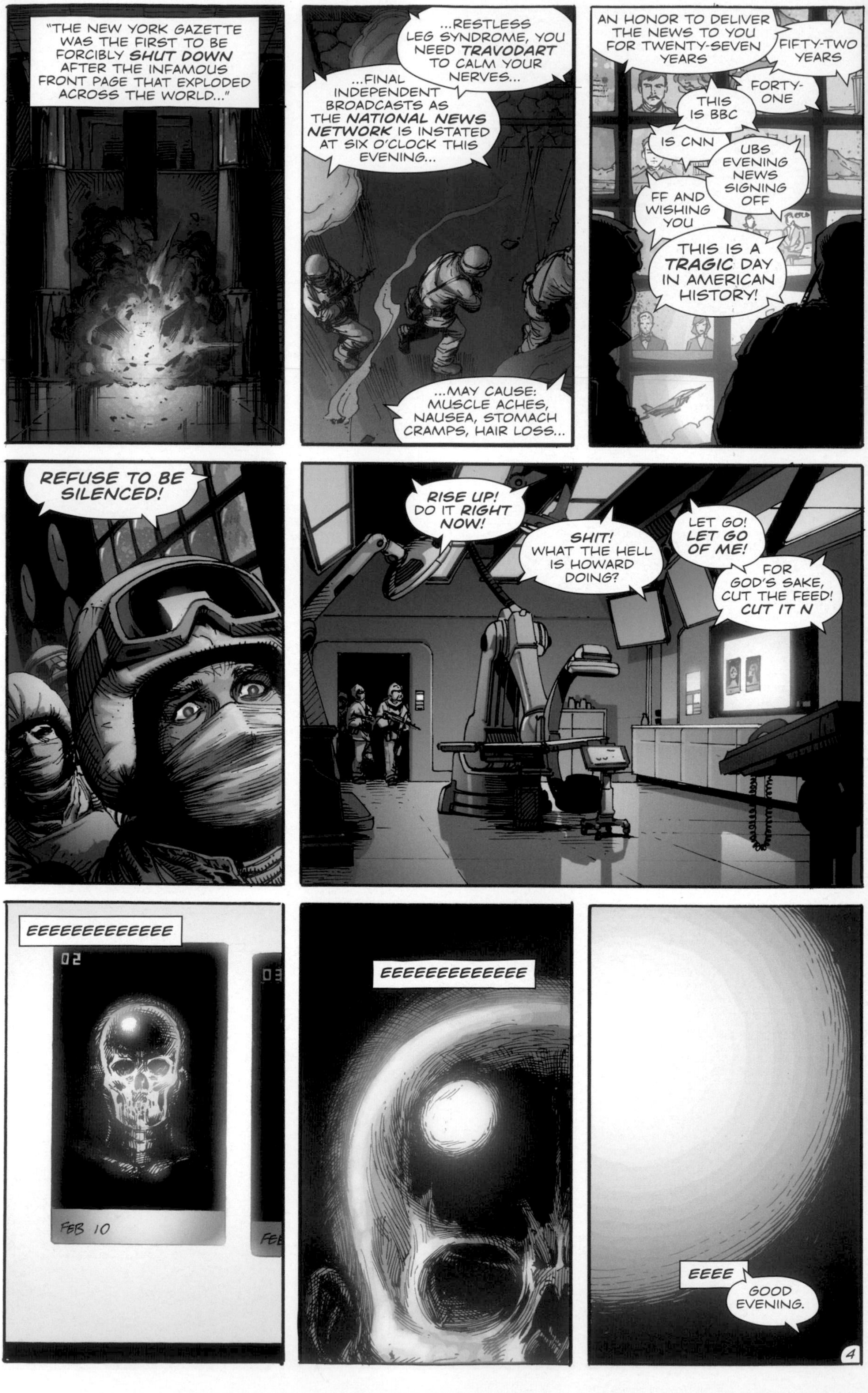

"THE NEW YORK GAZETTE WAS THE FIRST TO BE FORCIBLY SHUT DOWN AFTER THE INFAMOUS FRONT PAGE THAT EXPLODED ACROSS THE WORLD..."
...RESTLESS LEG SYNDROME, YOU NEED TRAVODART TO CALM YOUR NERVES...
...FINAL INDEPENDENT BROADCASTS AS THE NATIONAL NEWS NETWORK IS INSTATED AT SIX O'CLOCK THIS EVENING...
...MAY CAUSE: MUSCLE ACHES, NAUSEA, STOMACH CRAMPS, HAIR LOSS...
AN HONOR TO DELIVER THE NEWS TO YOU FOR TWENTY-SEVEN YEARS
FIFTY-TWO YEARS
FORTY-ONE
THIS IS BBC
IS CNN
UBS EVENING NEWS SIGNING OFF
FF AND WISHING YOU
THIS IS A TRAGIC DAY IN AMERICAN HISTORY!
REFUSE TO BE SILENCED!
RISE UP! DO IT RIGHT NOW!
SHIT! WHAT THE HELL IS HOWARD DOING?
LET GO! LET GO OF ME!
FOR GOD'S SAKE, CUT THE FEED! CUT IT N
EEEEEEEEEEEEE
02
FEB 10
03
EEEEEEEEEEEE
EEEE
GOOD EVENING.

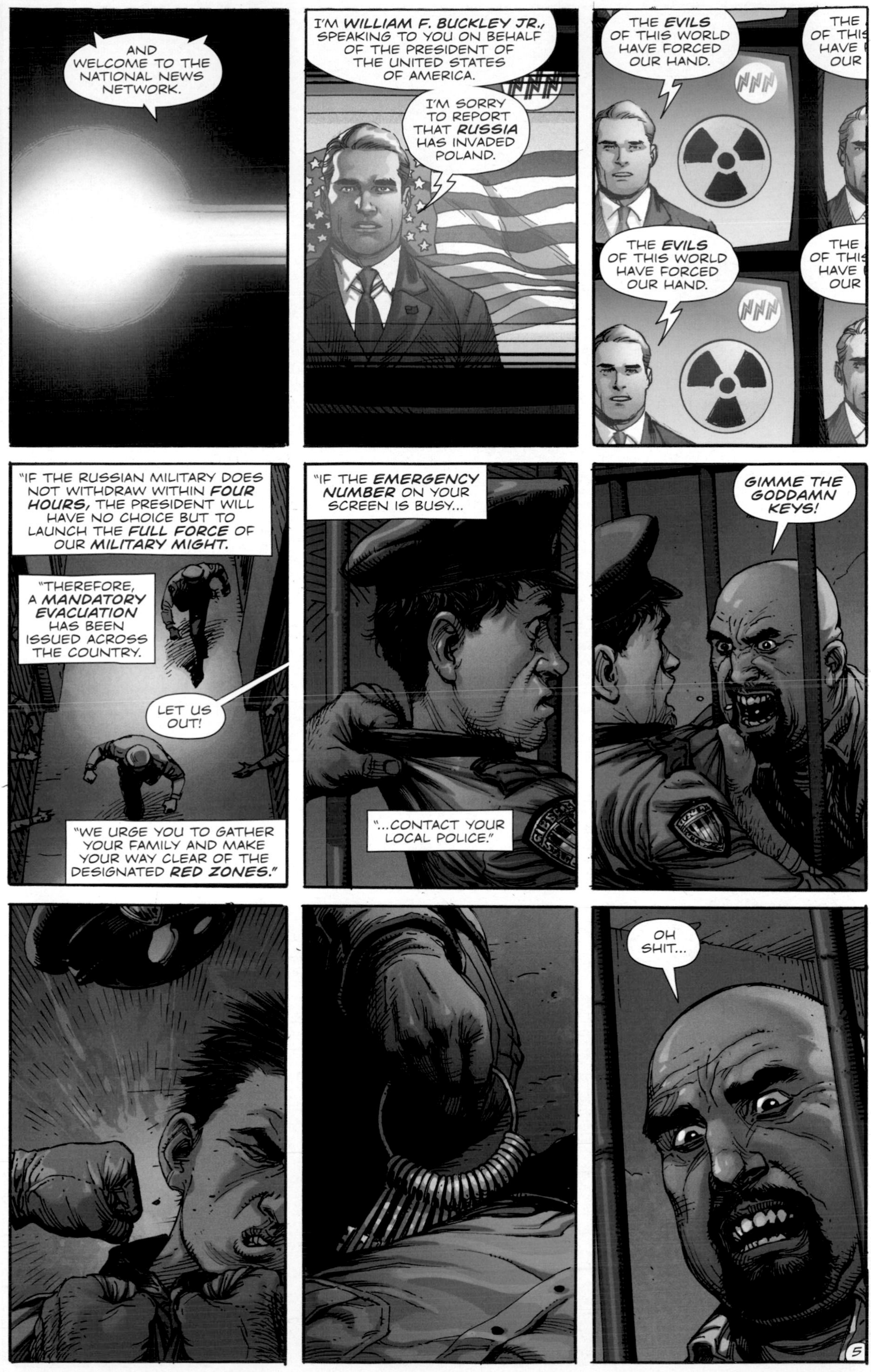
AND WELCOME TO THE NATIONAL NEWS NETWORK.
I'M WILLIAM F. BUCKLEY JR., SPEAKING TO YOU ON BEHALF OF THE PRESIDENT OF THE UNITED STATES OF AMERICA.
I'M SORRY TO REPORT THAT RUSSIA HAS INVADED POLAND.
THE EVILS OF THIS WORLD HAVE FORCED OUR HAND.
THE EVILS OF THIS WORLD HAVE FORCED OUR HAND.
"IF THE RUSSIAN MILITARY DOES NOT WITHDRAW WITHIN FOUR HOURS, THE PRESIDENT WILL HAVE NO CHOICE BUT TO LAUNCH THE FULL FORCE OF OUR MILITARY MIGHT.
"THEREFORE, A MANDATORY EVACUATION HAS BEEN ISSUED ACROSS THE COUNTRY.
LET US OUT!
"WE URGE YOU TO GATHER YOUR FAMILY AND MAKE YOUR WAY CLEAR OF THE DESIGNATED RED ZONES."
"IF THE EMERGENCY NUMBER ON YOUR SCREEN IS BUSY...
"...CONTACT YOUR LOCAL POLICE."
GIMME THE GODDAMN KEYS!
OH SHIT...

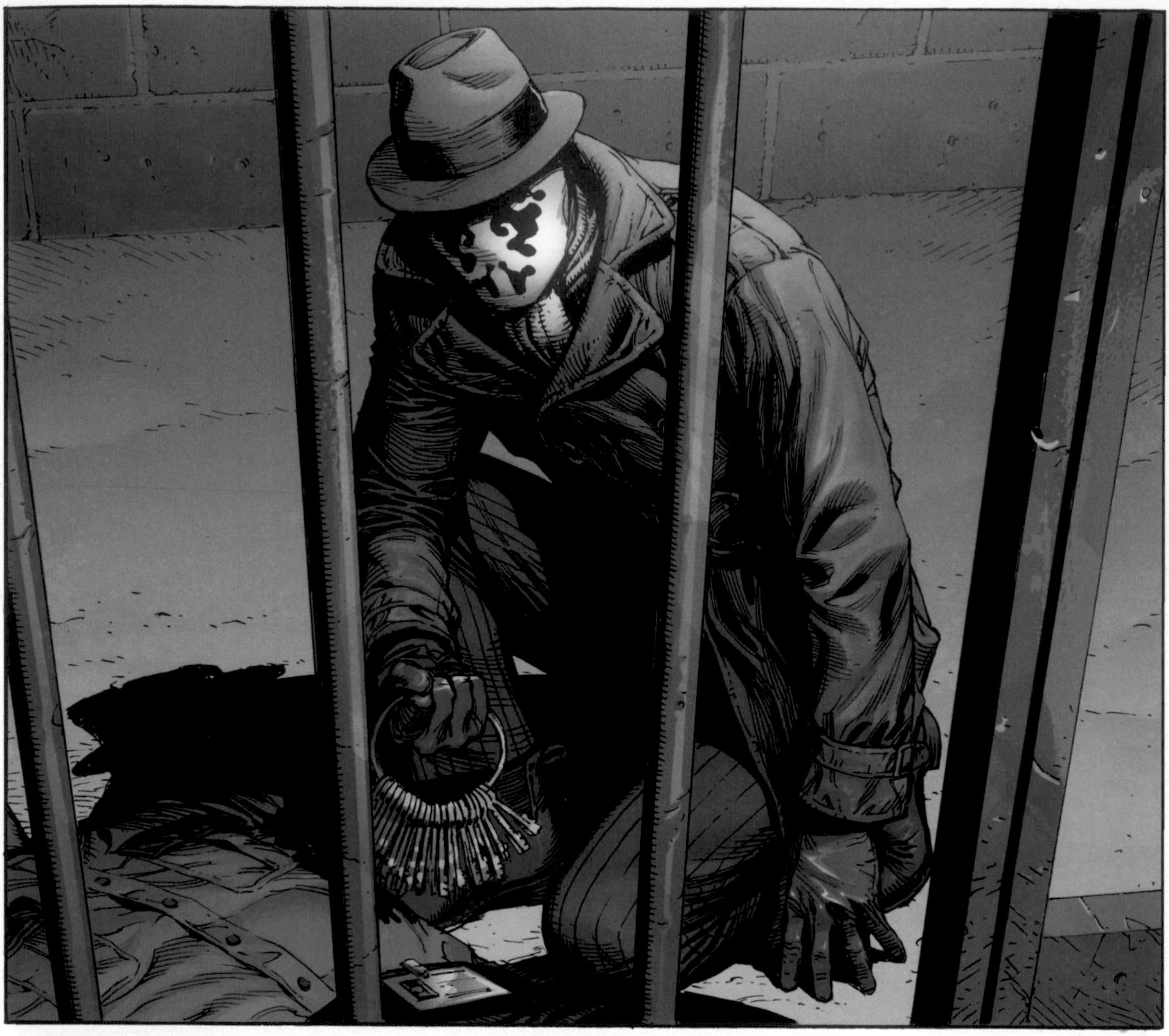

THAT ANNIHILATED PLACE

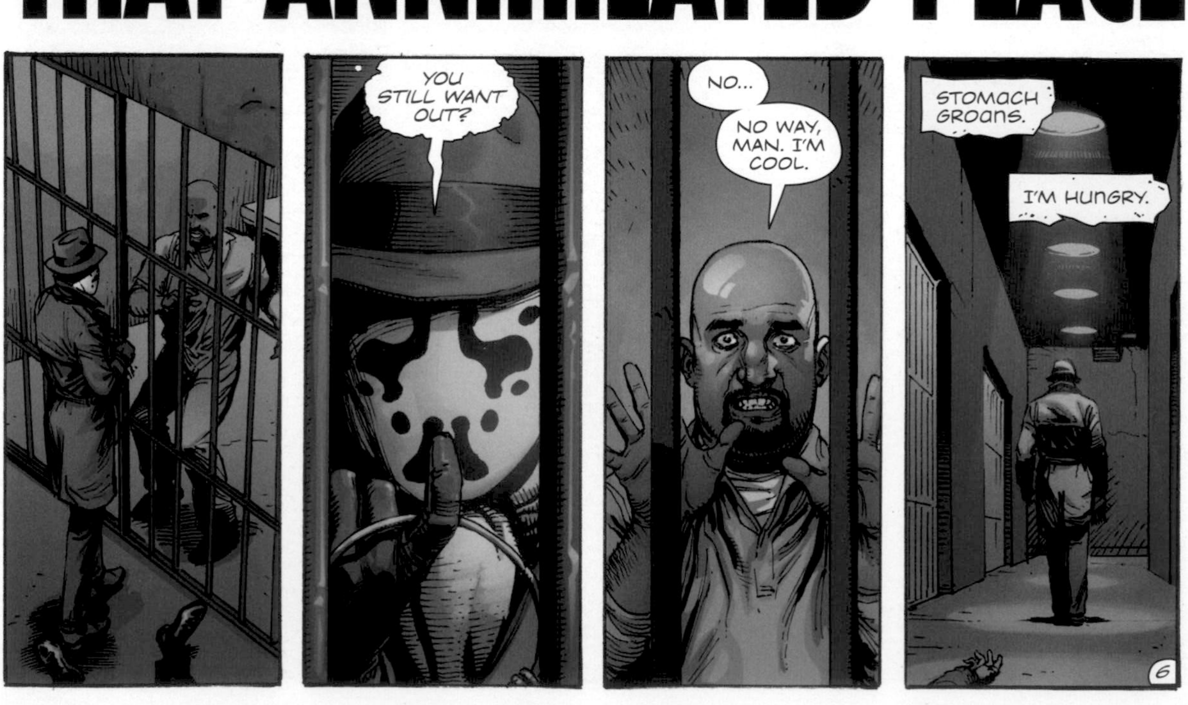

YOU STILL WANT OUT?
NO...
NO WAY, MAN. I'M COOL.
STOMACH GROANS.
I'M HUNGRY.

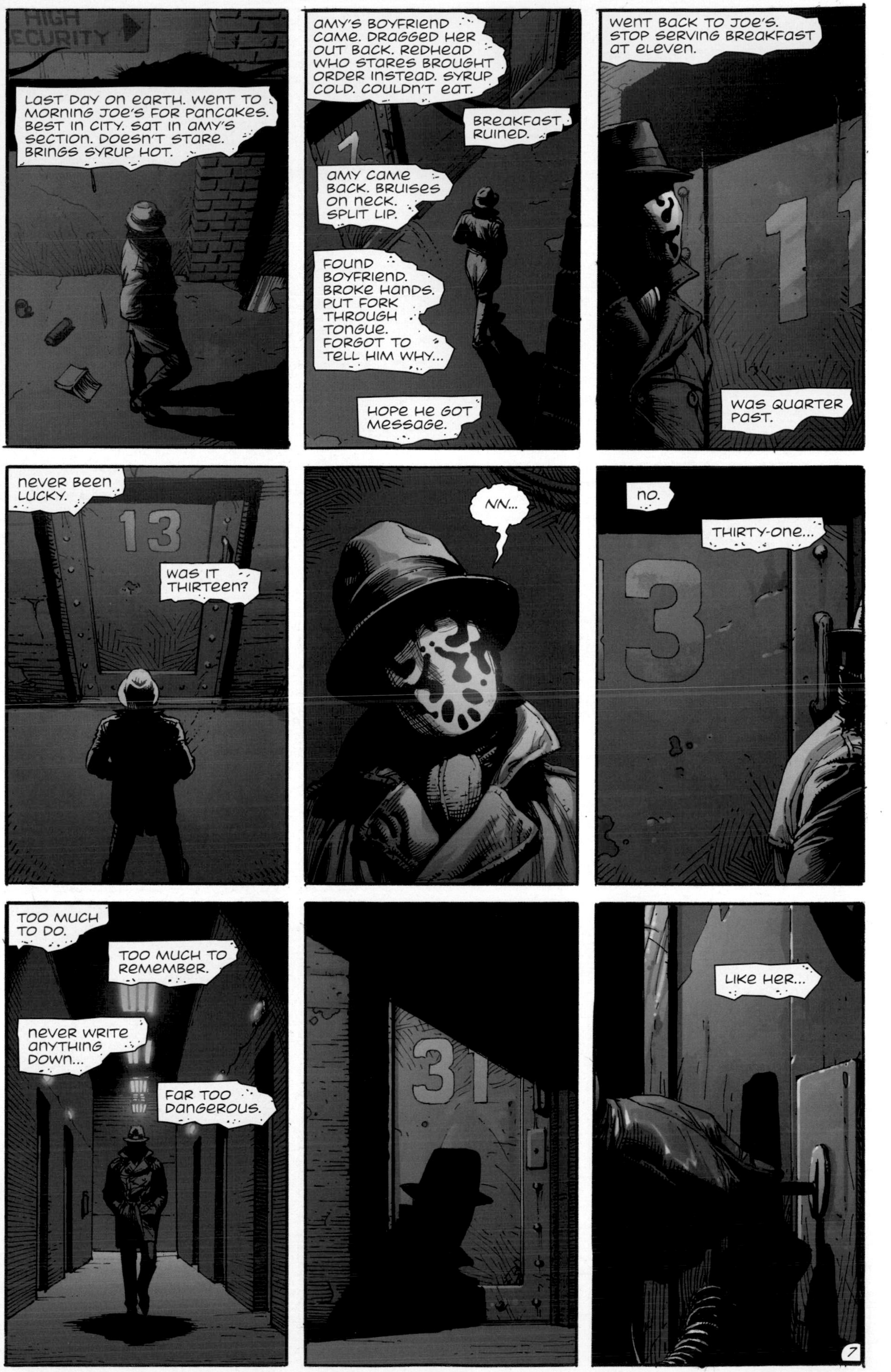
HIGH
SECURITY
LAST DAY ON EARTH. WENT TO MORNING JOE'S FOR PANCAKES. BEST IN CITY. SAT IN AMY'S SECTION. DOESN'T STARE. BRINGS SYRUP HOT.
AMY'S BOYFRIEND CAME. DRAGGED HER OUT BACK. REDHEAD WHO STARES BROUGHT ORDER INSTEAD. SYRUP COLD. COULDN'T EAT.
BREAKFAST RUINED.
AMY CAME BACK. BRUISES ON NECK. SPLIT LIP.
FOUND BOYFRIEND. BROKE HANDS. PUT FORK THROUGH TONGUE. FORGOT TO TELL HIM WHY...
HOPE HE GOT MESSAGE.
WENT BACK TO JOE'S. STOP SERVING BREAKFAST AT ELEVEN.
WAS QUARTER PAST.
NEVER BEEN LUCKY.
WAS IT THIRTEEN?
NN...
NO.
THIRTY-ONE...
TOO MUCH TO DO.
TOO MUCH TO REMEMBER.
NEVER WRITE ANYTHING DOWN...
FAR TOO DANGEROUS.
LIKE HER...

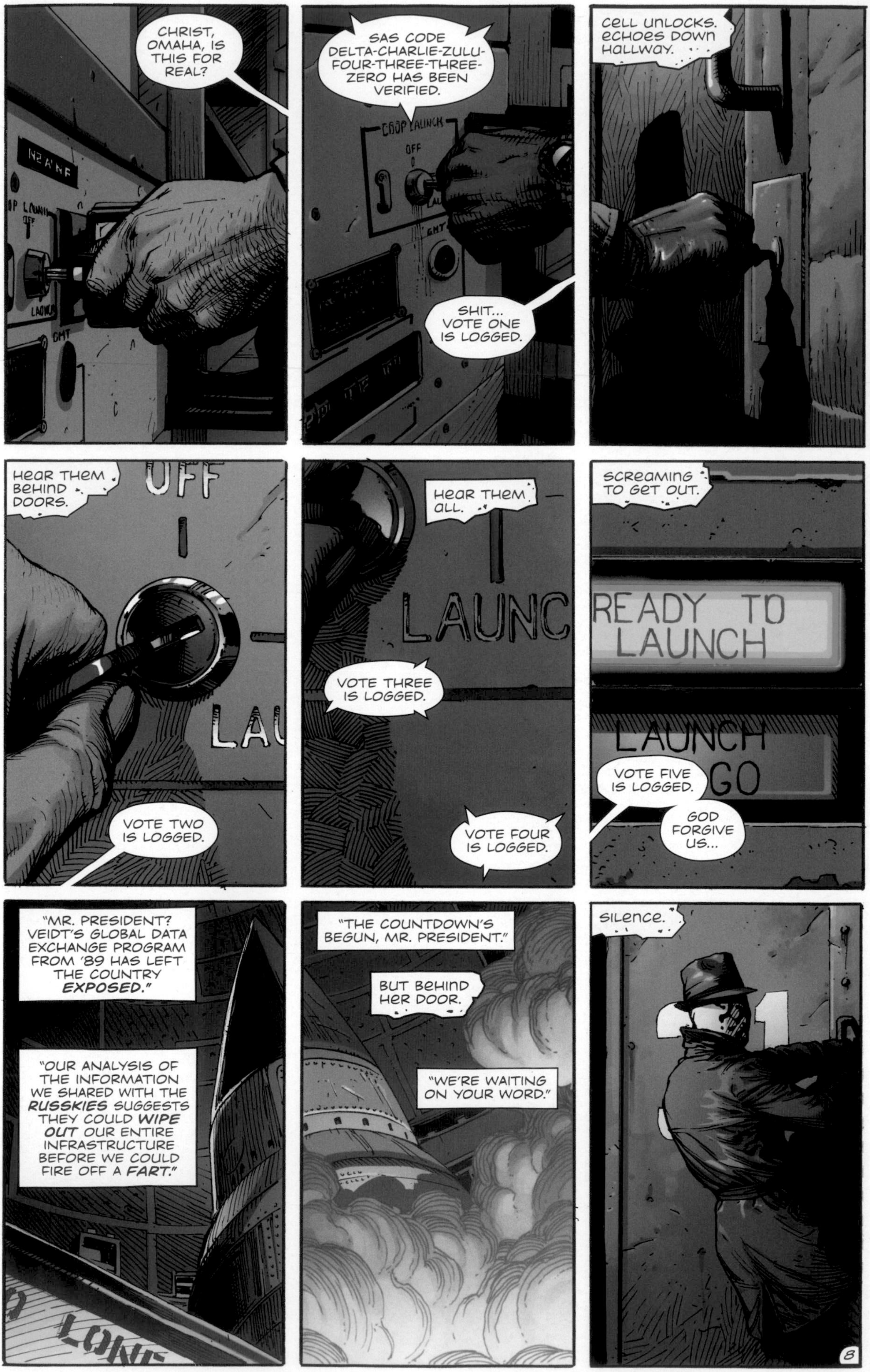
CHRIST, OMAHA, IS THIS FOR REAL?
SAS CODE DELTA-CHARLIE-ZULU-FOUR-THREE-THREE-ZERO HAS BEEN VERIFIED.
SHIT... VOTE ONE IS LOGGED.
CELL UNLOCKS. ECHOES DOWN HALLWAY.
HEAR THEM BEHIND DOORS.
VOTE TWO IS LOGGED.
HEAR THEM ALL.
LAUNC
VOTE THREE IS LOGGED.
VOTE FOUR IS LOGGED.
SCREAMING TO GET OUT.
READY TO LAUNCH
LAUNCH GO
VOTE FIVE IS LOGGED.
GOD FORGIVE US...
"MR. PRESIDENT? VEIDT'S GLOBAL DATA EXCHANGE PROGRAM FROM '89 HAS LEFT THE COUNTRY *EXPOSED.*"
"OUR ANALYSIS OF THE INFORMATION WE SHARED WITH THE *RUSSKIES* SUGGESTS THEY COULD *WIPE OUT* OUR ENTIRE INFRASTRUCTURE BEFORE WE COULD FIRE OFF A *FART.*"
"THE COUNTDOWN'S BEGUN, MR. PRESIDENT."
BUT BEHIND HER DOOR.
"WE'RE WAITING ON YOUR WORD."
SILENCE.

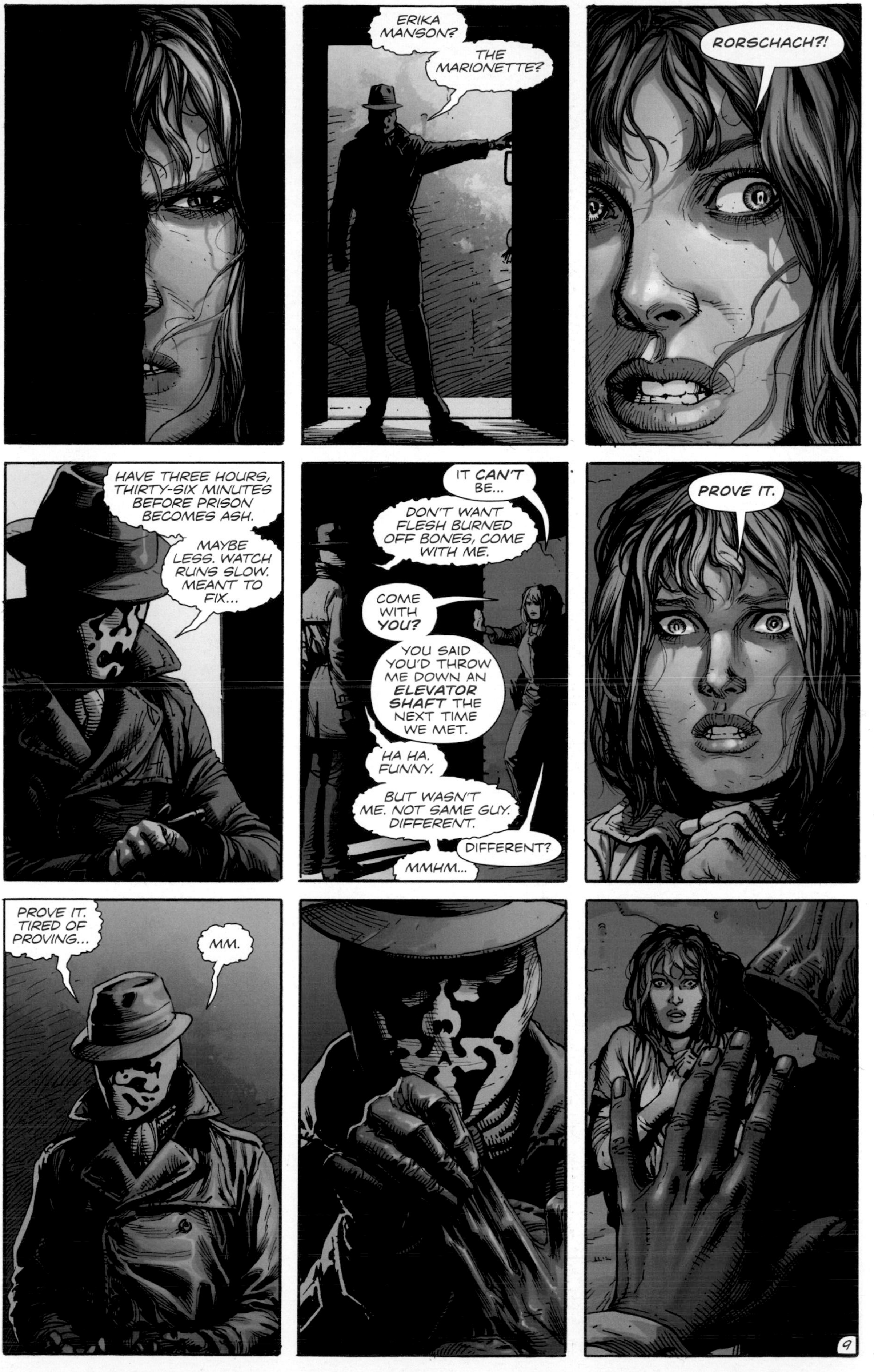
ERIKA MANSON?
THE MARIONETTE?
RORSCHACH?!
HAVE THREE HOURS, THIRTY-SIX MINUTES BEFORE PRISON BECOMES ASH.
MAYBE LESS. WATCH RUNS SLOW. MEANT TO FIX...
IT CAN'T BE...
DON'T WANT FLESH BURNED OFF BONES, COME WITH ME.
COME WITH YOU?
YOU SAID YOU'D THROW ME DOWN AN ELEVATOR SHAFT THE NEXT TIME WE MET.
HA HA. FUNNY.
BUT WASN'T ME. NOT SAME GUY. DIFFERENT.
DIFFERENT?
MMHM...
PROVE IT.
PROVE IT. TIRED OF PROVING...
MM.
9

YOU'RE OUT OF YOUR **GODDAMN MIND** DRESSING LIKE **THAT**.

RORSCHACH FINDS YOU...

I AM RORSCHACH.

WHERE'D I PUT IT...

HERE. PAYMENT.

FOR WHAT?

JOB.

IT'S STICKY.

SYRUP...

ROUGH MORNING.

HUH. YOU **DO** SOUND A LITTLE LIKE HIM FROM WHAT I REMEMBER...

SO WHERE'S THE **REAL** RORSCHACH? HE DEAD?

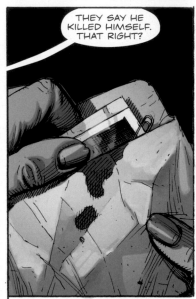

THEY SAY HE KILLED HIMSELF. THAT RIGHT?

PICTURE'S A LITTLE OLD...

BUT YOU COME WITH ME. DO JOB.

FIND OUT WHERE BOY IS.

DEAL?

10

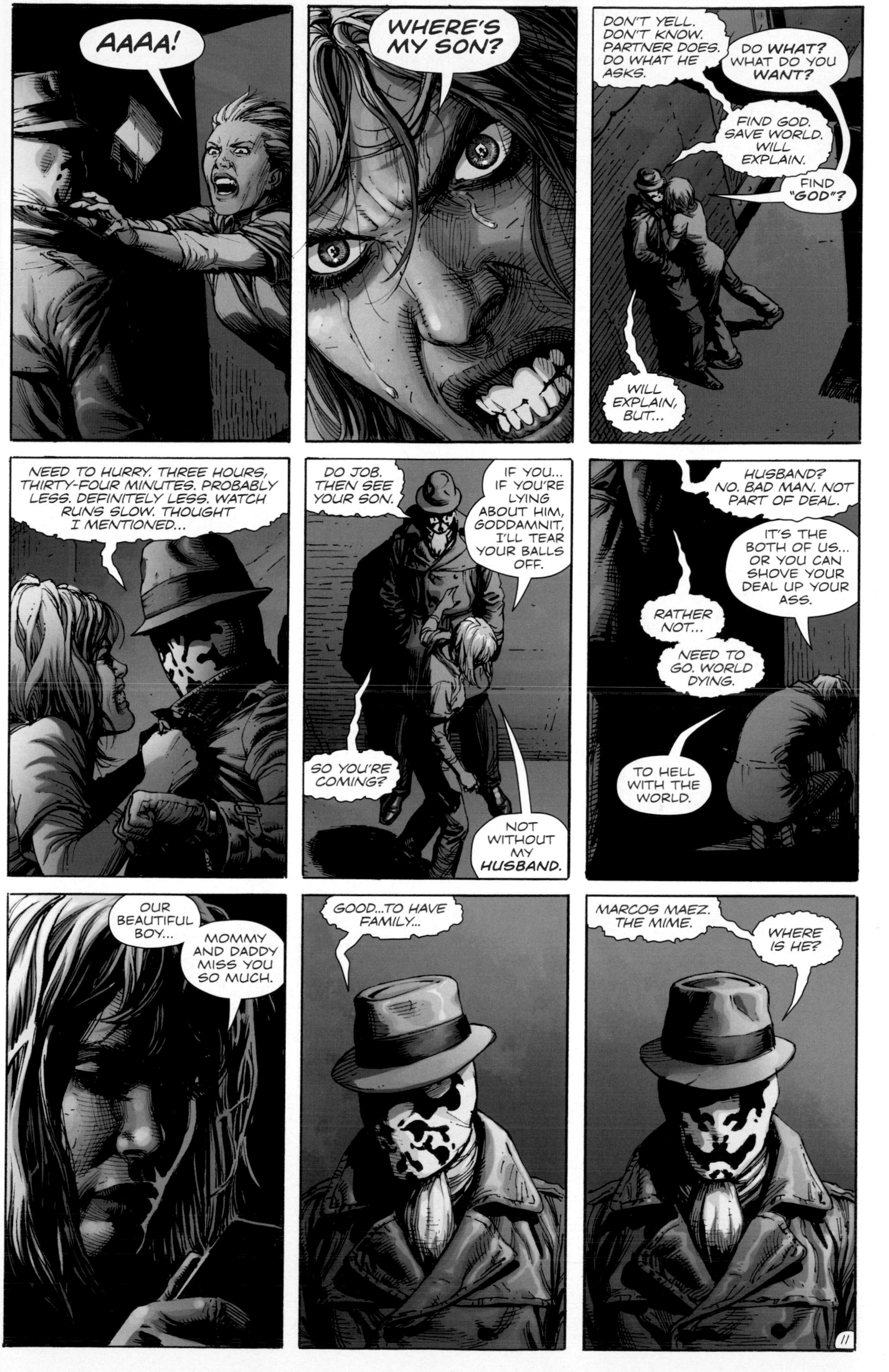
AAAA!
WHERE'S MY SON?
DON'T YELL. DON'T KNOW. PARTNER DOES. DO WHAT HE ASKS.
DO WHAT? WHAT DO YOU WANT?
FIND GOD. SAVE WORLD. WILL EXPLAIN.
FIND "GOD"?
WILL EXPLAIN, BUT...
NEED TO HURRY. THREE HOURS, THIRTY-FOUR MINUTES. PROBABLY LESS. DEFINITELY LESS. WATCH RUNS SLOW. THOUGHT I MENTIONED...
DO JOB. THEN SEE YOUR SON.
IF YOU... IF YOU'RE LYING ABOUT HIM, GODDAMNIT, I'LL TEAR YOUR BALLS OFF.
SO YOU'RE COMING?
NOT WITHOUT MY HUSBAND.
HUSBAND? NO. BAD MAN. NOT PART OF DEAL.
IT'S THE BOTH OF US... OR YOU CAN SHOVE YOUR DEAL UP YOUR ASS.
RATHER NOT...
NEED TO GO. WORLD DYING.
TO HELL WITH THE WORLD.
OUR BEAUTIFUL BOY...
MOMMY AND DADDY MISS YOU SO MUCH.
GOOD...TO HAVE FAMILY...
MARCOS MAEZ. THE MIME.
WHERE IS HE?

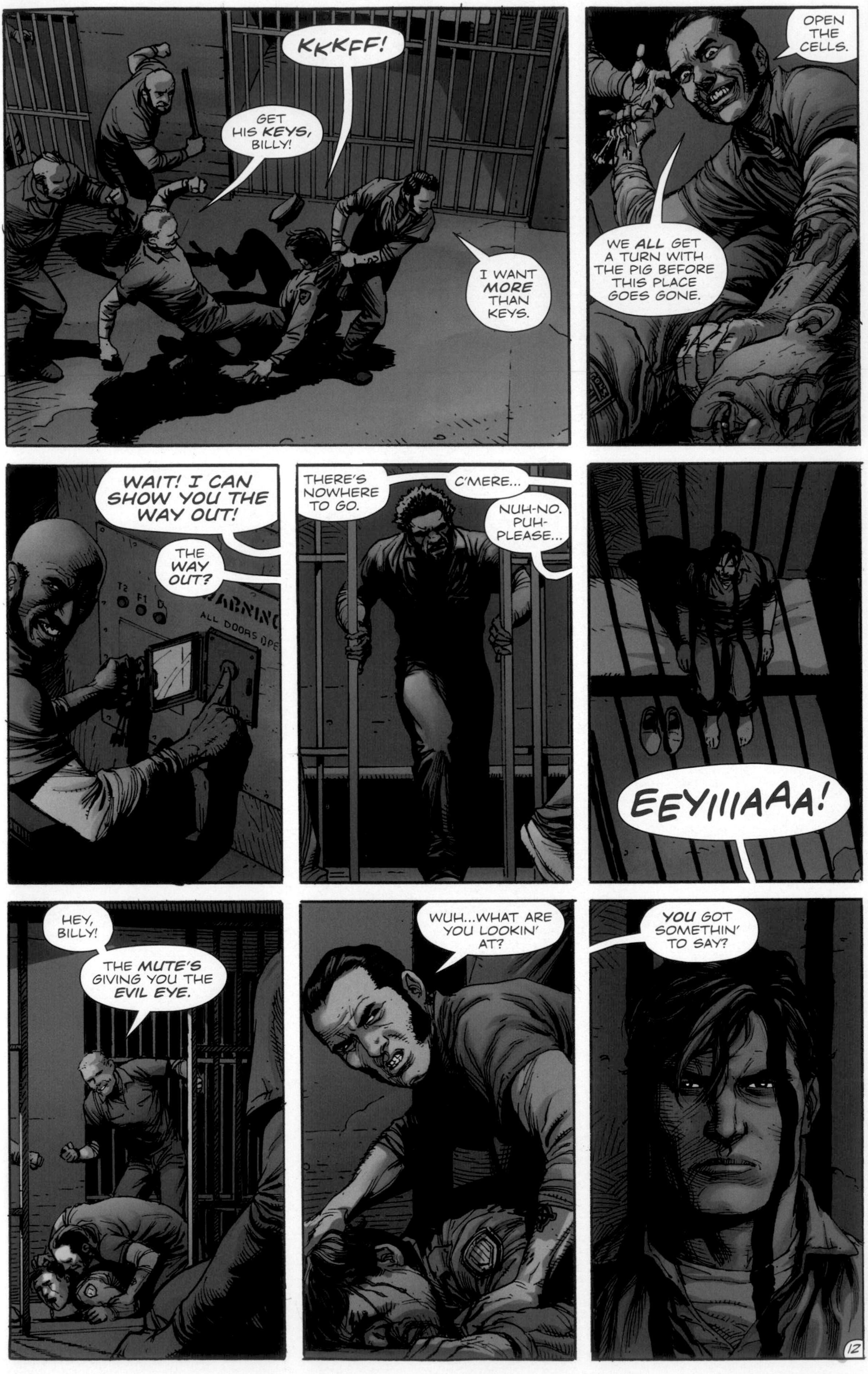

KKKFF!
GET HIS KEYS, BILLY!
I WANT MORE THAN KEYS.
OPEN THE CELLS.
WE ALL GET A TURN WITH THE PIG BEFORE THIS PLACE GOES GONE.
WAIT! I CAN SHOW YOU THE WAY OUT!
THE WAY OUT?
WARNING
ALL DOORS OPE
THERE'S NOWHERE TO GO.
C'MERE...
NUH-NO. PUH-PLEASE...
EEYIIIAAA!
HEY, BILLY!
THE MUTE'S GIVING YOU THE EVIL EYE.
WUH...WHAT ARE YOU LOOKIN' AT?
YOU GOT SOMETHIN' TO SAY?

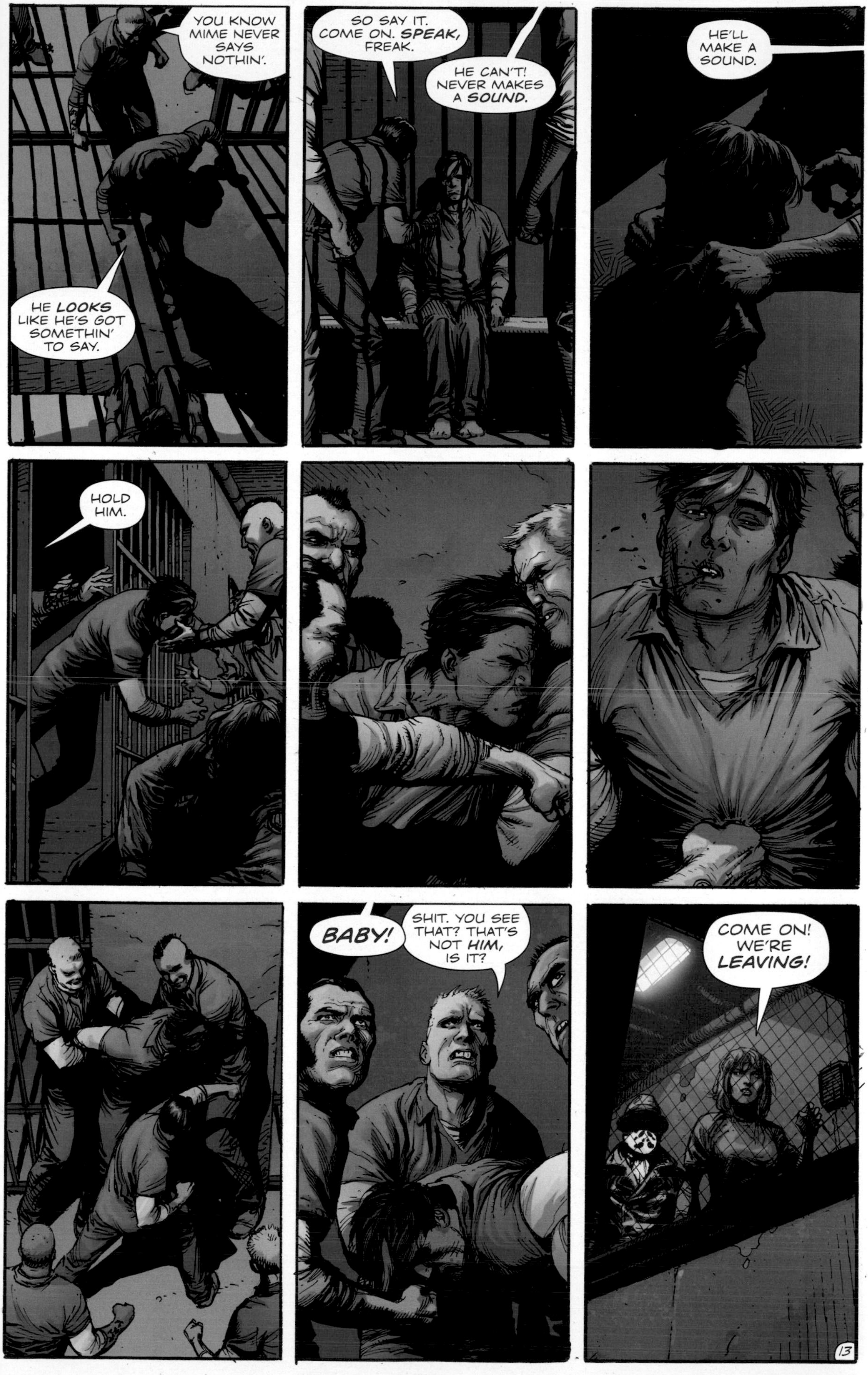
YOU KNOW MIME NEVER SAYS NOTHIN'.
HE LOOKS LIKE HE'S GOT SOMETHIN' TO SAY.
SO SAY IT. COME ON. SPEAK, FREAK.
HE CAN'T! NEVER MAKES A SOUND.
HE'LL MAKE A SOUND.
HOLD HIM.
BABY!
SHIT. YOU SEE THAT? THAT'S NOT HIM, IS IT?
COME ON! WE'RE LEAVING!
13

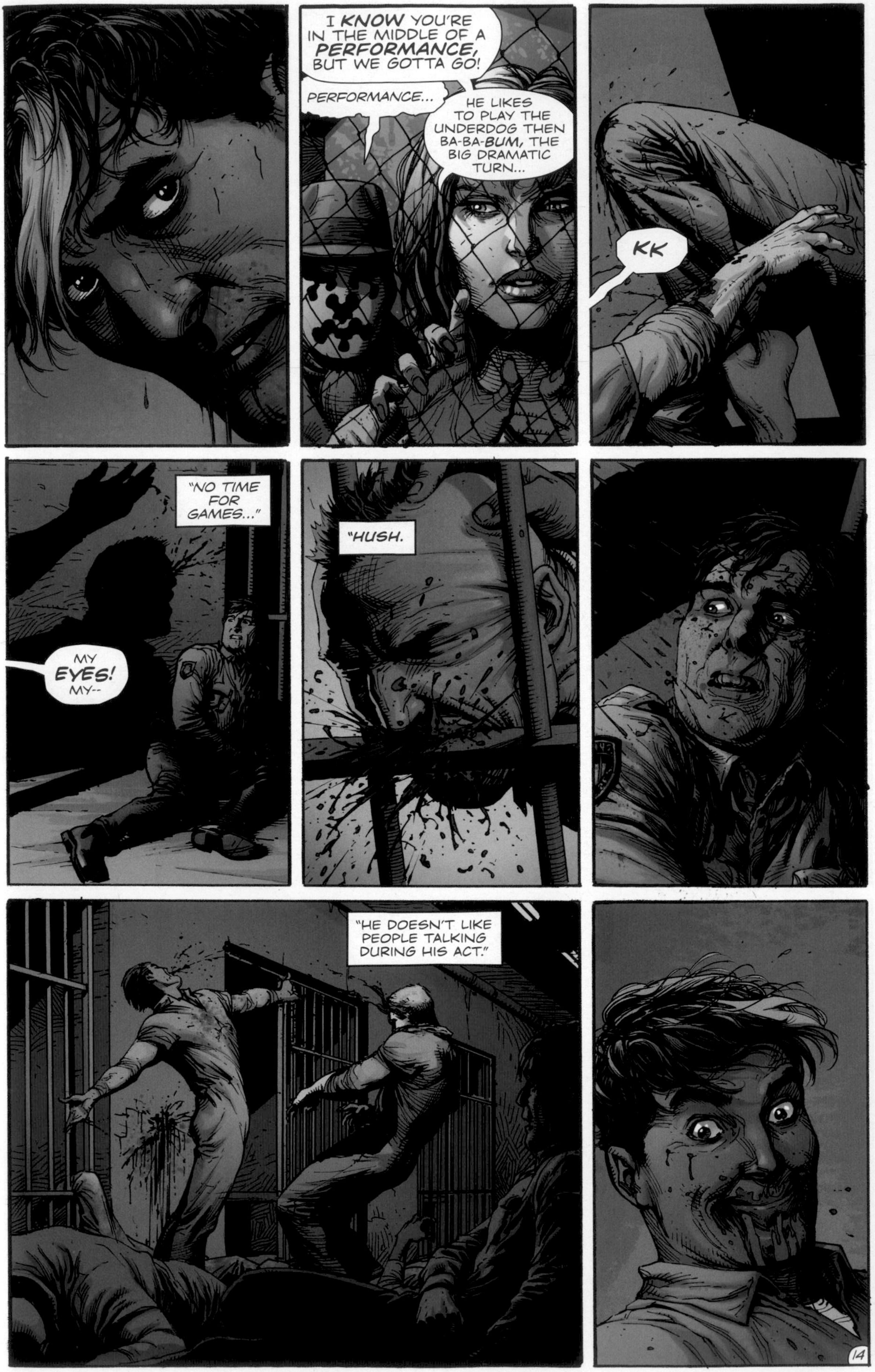
I KNOW YOU'RE IN THE MIDDLE OF A PERFORMANCE, BUT WE GOTTA GO!
PERFORMANCE...
HE LIKES TO PLAY THE UNDERDOG THEN BA-BA-BUM, THE BIG DRAMATIC TURN...
KK
"NO TIME FOR GAMES..."
MY EYES! MY--
"HUSH.
"HE DOESN'T LIKE PEOPLE TALKING DURING HIS ACT."

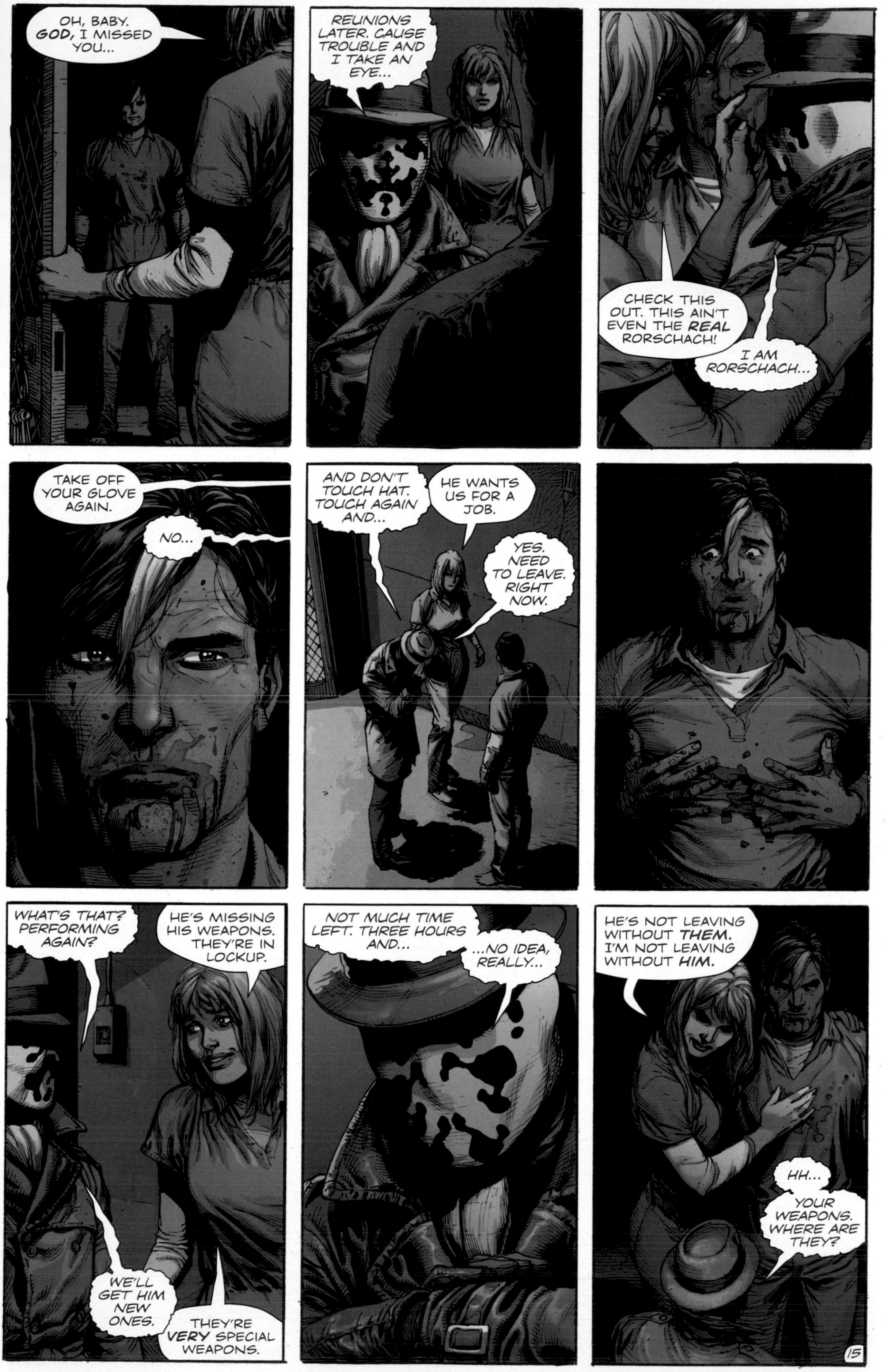
OH, BABY. GOD, I MISSED YOU...
REUNIONS LATER. CAUSE TROUBLE AND I TAKE AN EYE...
CHECK THIS OUT. THIS AIN'T EVEN THE REAL RORSCHACH!
I AM RORSCHACH...
TAKE OFF YOUR GLOVE AGAIN.
NO...
AND DON'T TOUCH HAT. TOUCH AGAIN AND...
HE WANTS US FOR A JOB.
YES. NEED TO LEAVE. RIGHT NOW.
WHAT'S THAT? PERFORMING AGAIN?
HE'S MISSING HIS WEAPONS. THEY'RE IN LOCKUP.
WE'LL GET HIM NEW ONES.
THEY'RE VERY SPECIAL WEAPONS.
NOT MUCH TIME LEFT. THREE HOURS AND...
...NO IDEA, REALLY...
HE'S NOT LEAVING WITHOUT THEM. I'M NOT LEAVING WITHOUT HIM.
HH...
YOUR WEAPONS. WHERE ARE THEY?
15

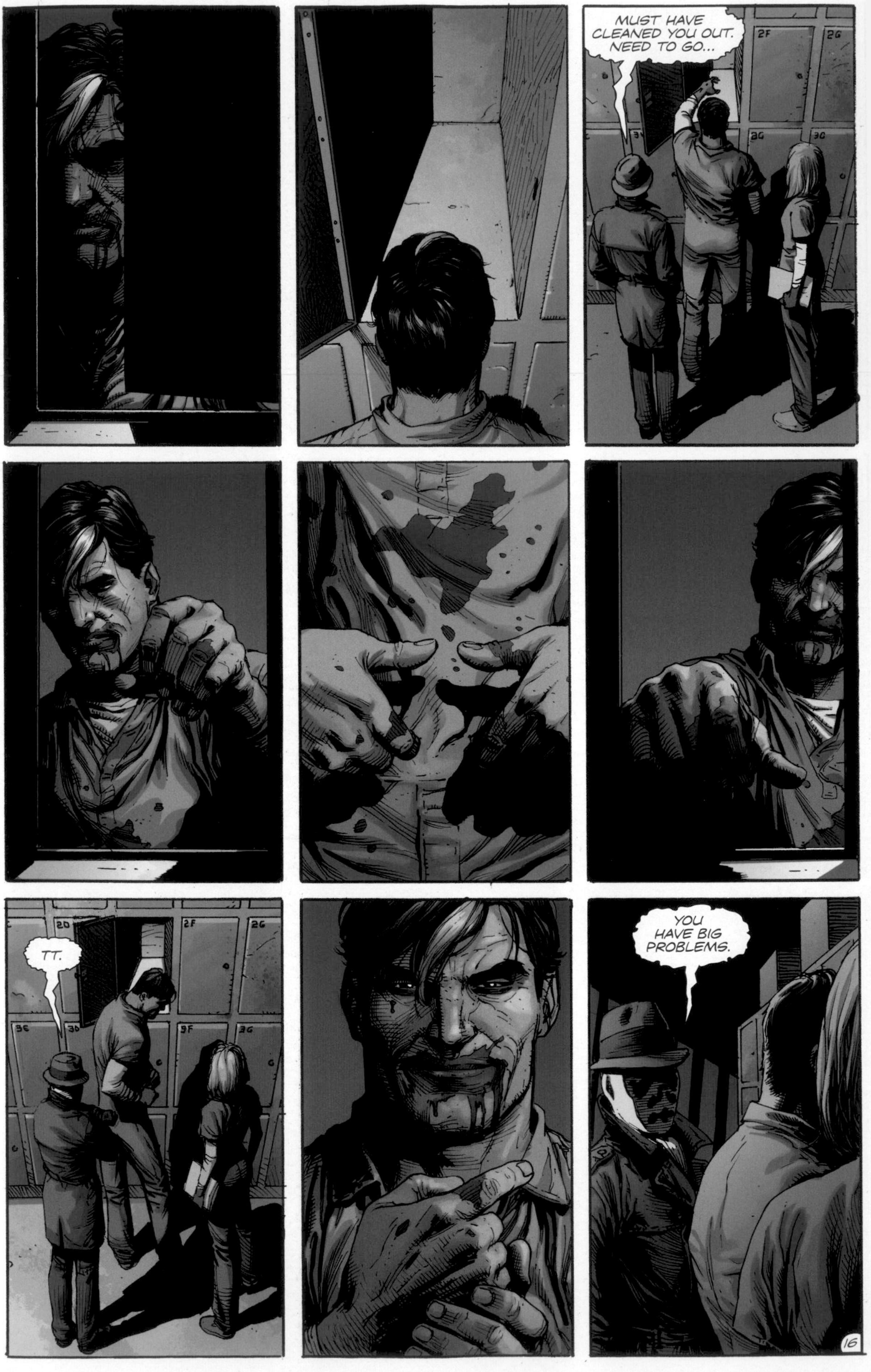
MUST HAVE CLEANED YOU OUT. NEED TO GO...
TT.
YOU HAVE BIG PROBLEMS.
16

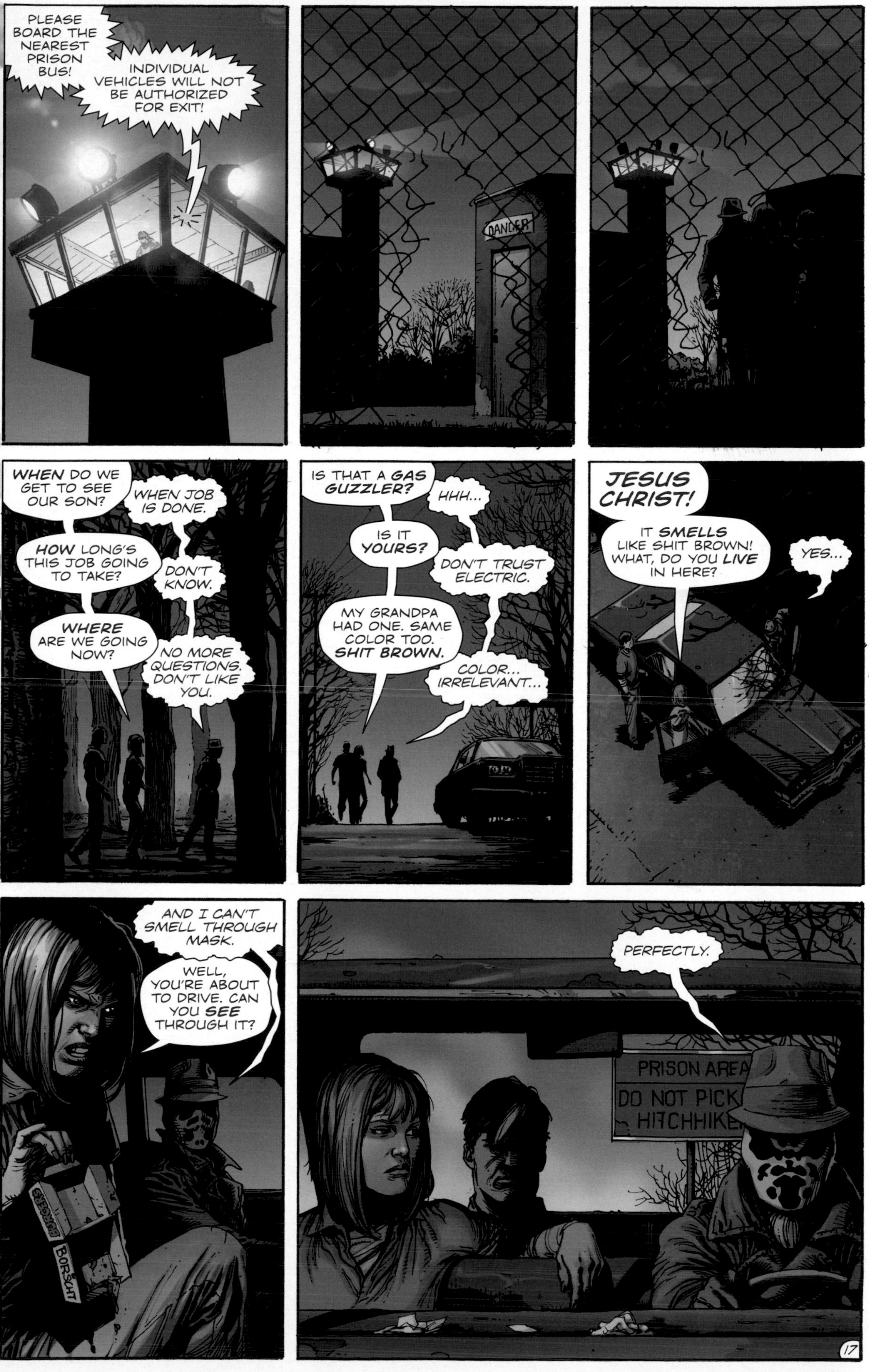
PLEASE BOARD THE NEAREST PRISON BUS!
INDIVIDUAL VEHICLES WILL NOT BE AUTHORIZED FOR EXIT!
DANGER
WHEN DO WE GET TO SEE OUR SON?
WHEN JOB IS DONE.
HOW LONG'S THIS JOB GOING TO TAKE?
DON'T KNOW.
WHERE ARE WE GOING NOW?
NO MORE QUESTIONS. DON'T LIKE YOU.
IS THAT A GAS GUZZLER?
HHH...
IS IT YOURS?
DON'T TRUST ELECTRIC.
MY GRANDPA HAD ONE. SAME COLOR TOO. SHIT BROWN.
COLOR... IRRELEVANT...
JESUS CHRIST!
IT SMELLS LIKE SHIT BROWN! WHAT, DO YOU LIVE IN HERE?
YES...
AND I CAN'T SMELL THROUGH MASK.
WELL, YOU'RE ABOUT TO DRIVE. CAN YOU SEE THROUGH IT?
BORSCHT
PERFECTLY.
PRISON AREA
DO NOT PICK
HITCHHIKE

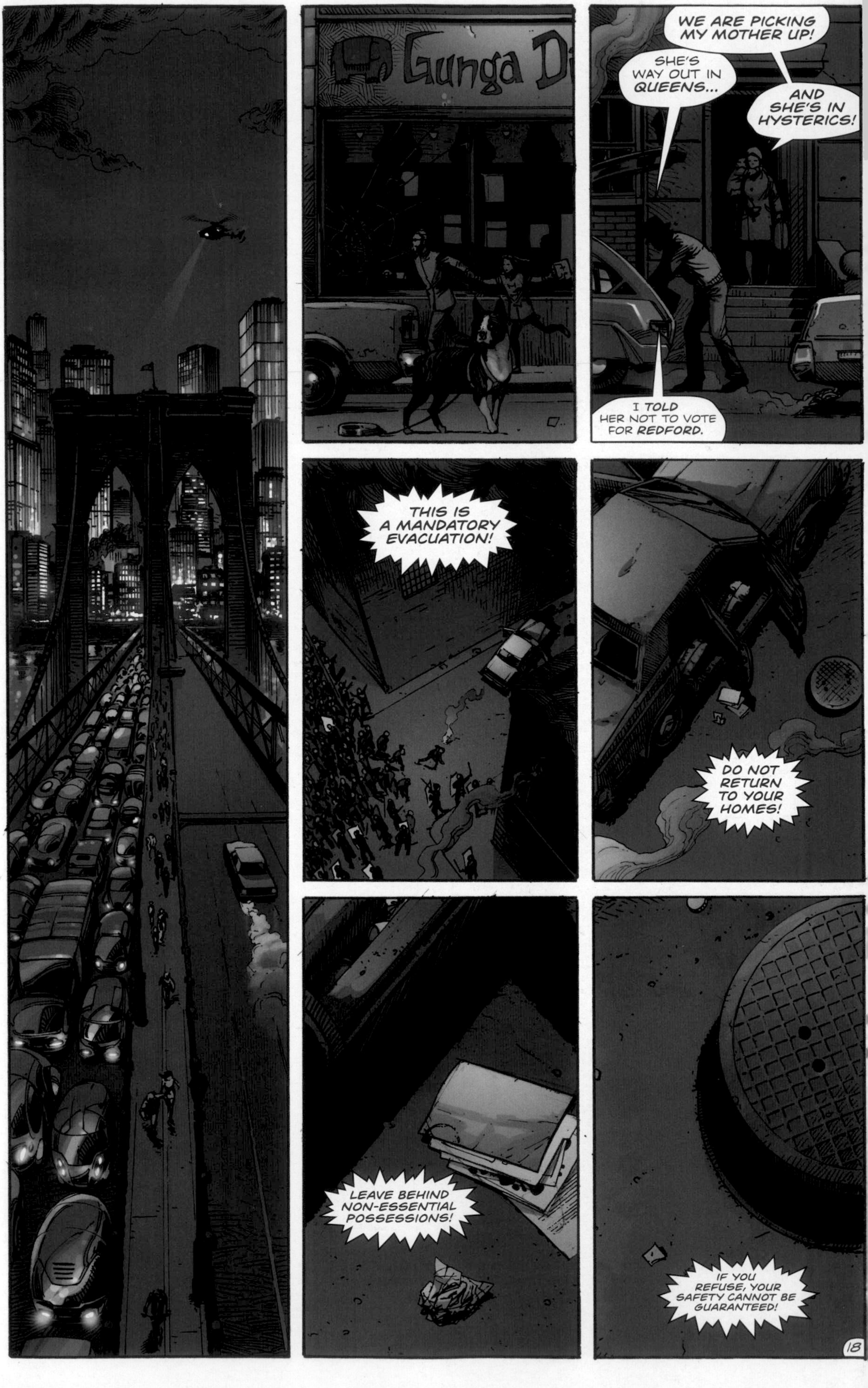
Gunga Di
WE ARE PICKING MY MOTHER UP!
SHE'S WAY OUT IN QUEENS...
AND SHE'S IN HYSTERICS!
I TOLD HER NOT TO VOTE FOR REDFORD.
THIS IS A MANDATORY EVACUATION!
DO NOT RETURN TO YOUR HOMES!
LEAVE BEHIND NON-ESSENTIAL POSSESSIONS!
IF YOU REFUSE, YOUR SAFETY CANNOT BE GUARANTEED!

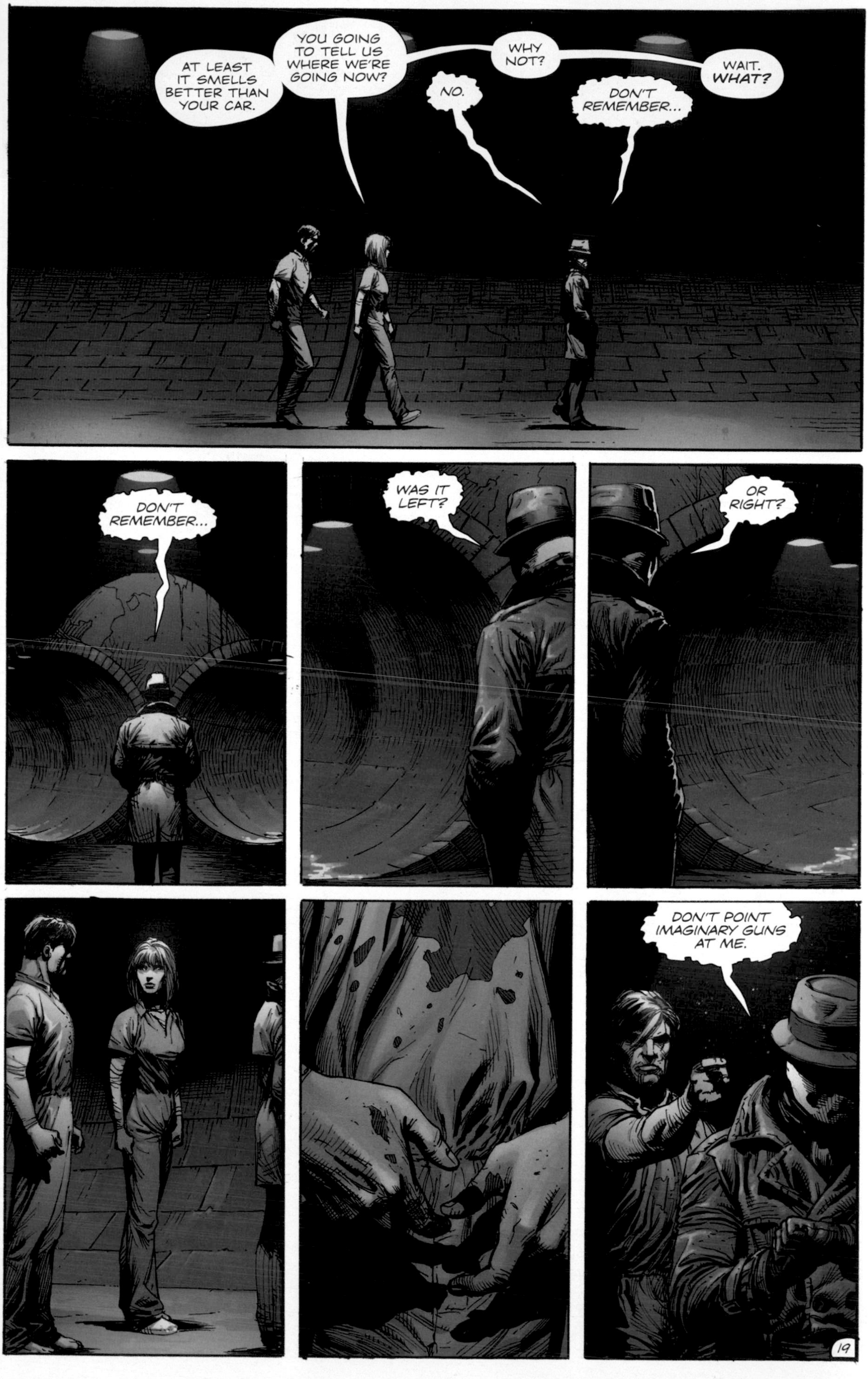
AT LEAST IT SMELLS BETTER THAN YOUR CAR.
YOU GOING TO TELL US WHERE WE'RE GOING NOW?
NO.
WHY NOT?
DON'T REMEMBER...
WAIT. WHAT?
DON'T REMEMBER...
WAS IT LEFT?
OR RIGHT?
DON'T POINT IMAGINARY GUNS AT ME.

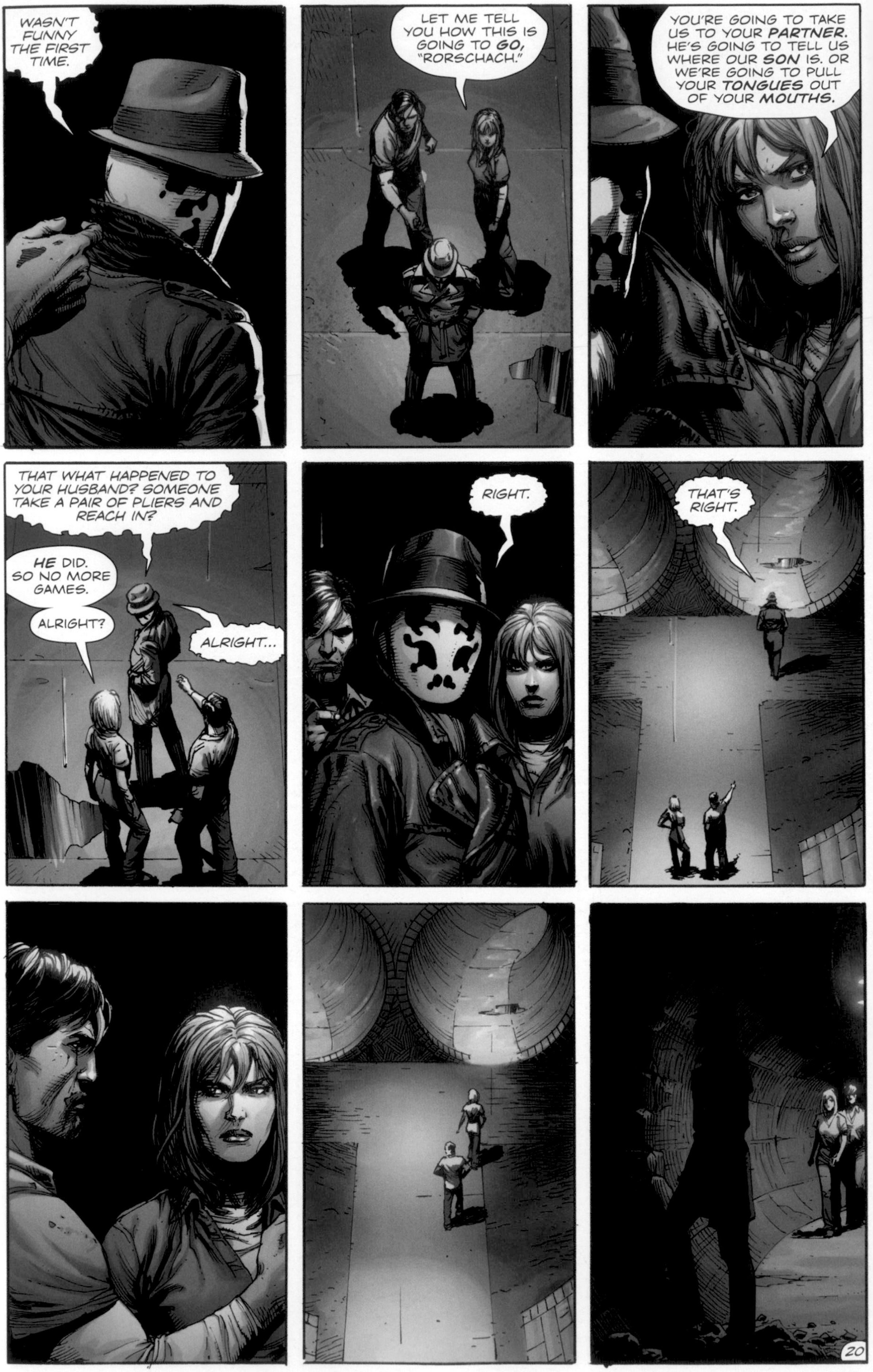

WASN'T FUNNY THE FIRST TIME.
LET ME TELL YOU HOW THIS IS GOING TO GO, "RORSCHACH."
YOU'RE GOING TO TAKE US TO YOUR PARTNER. HE'S GOING TO TELL US WHERE OUR SON IS. OR WE'RE GOING TO PULL YOUR TONGUES OUT OF YOUR MOUTHS.
THAT WHAT HAPPENED TO YOUR HUSBAND? SOMEONE TAKE A PAIR OF PLIERS AND REACH IN?
HE DID. SO NO MORE GAMES.
ALRIGHT?
ALRIGHT...
RIGHT.
THAT'S RIGHT.

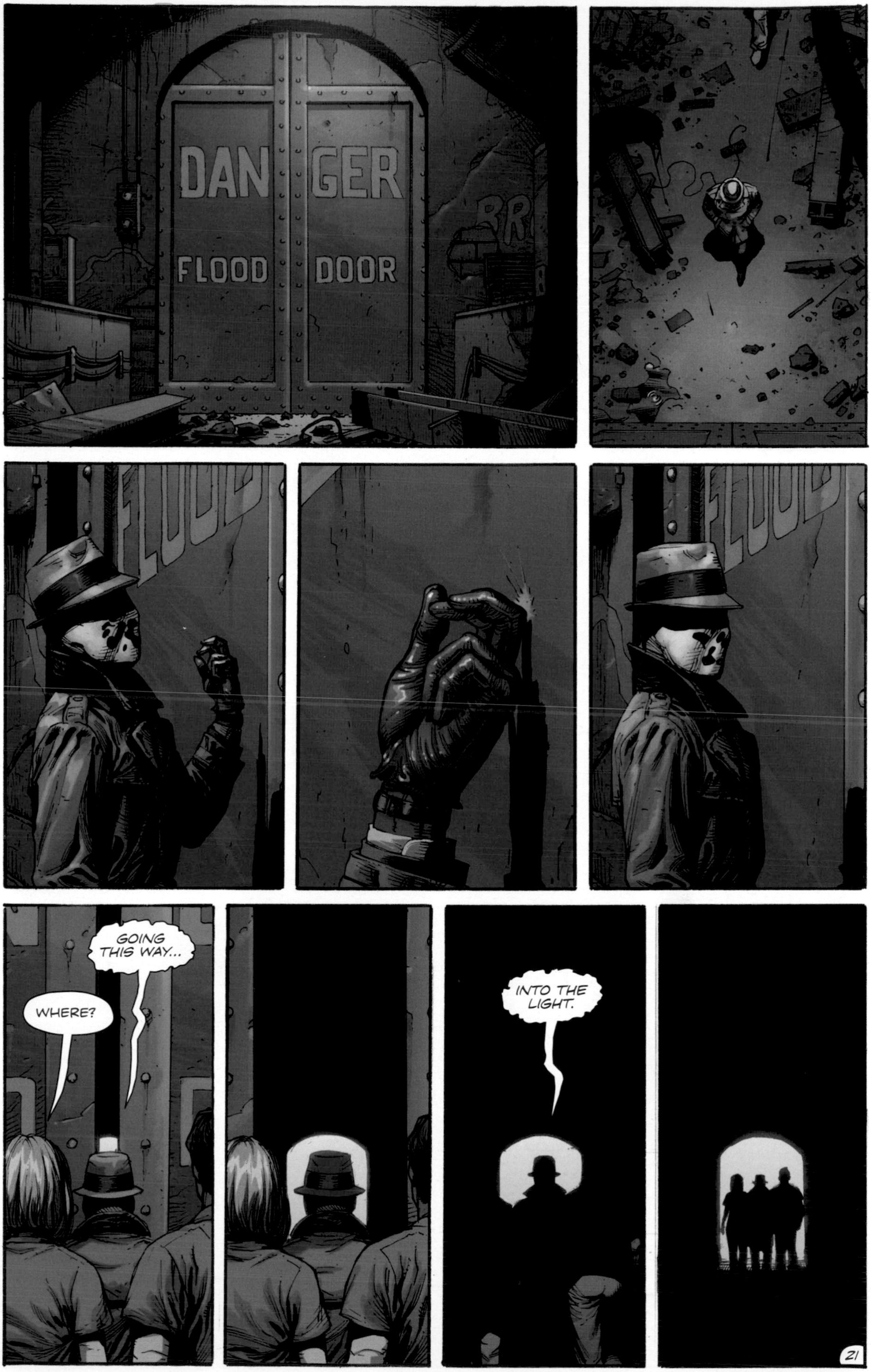
DANGER
FLOOD DOOR
GOING THIS WAY...
WHERE?
INTO THE LIGHT.

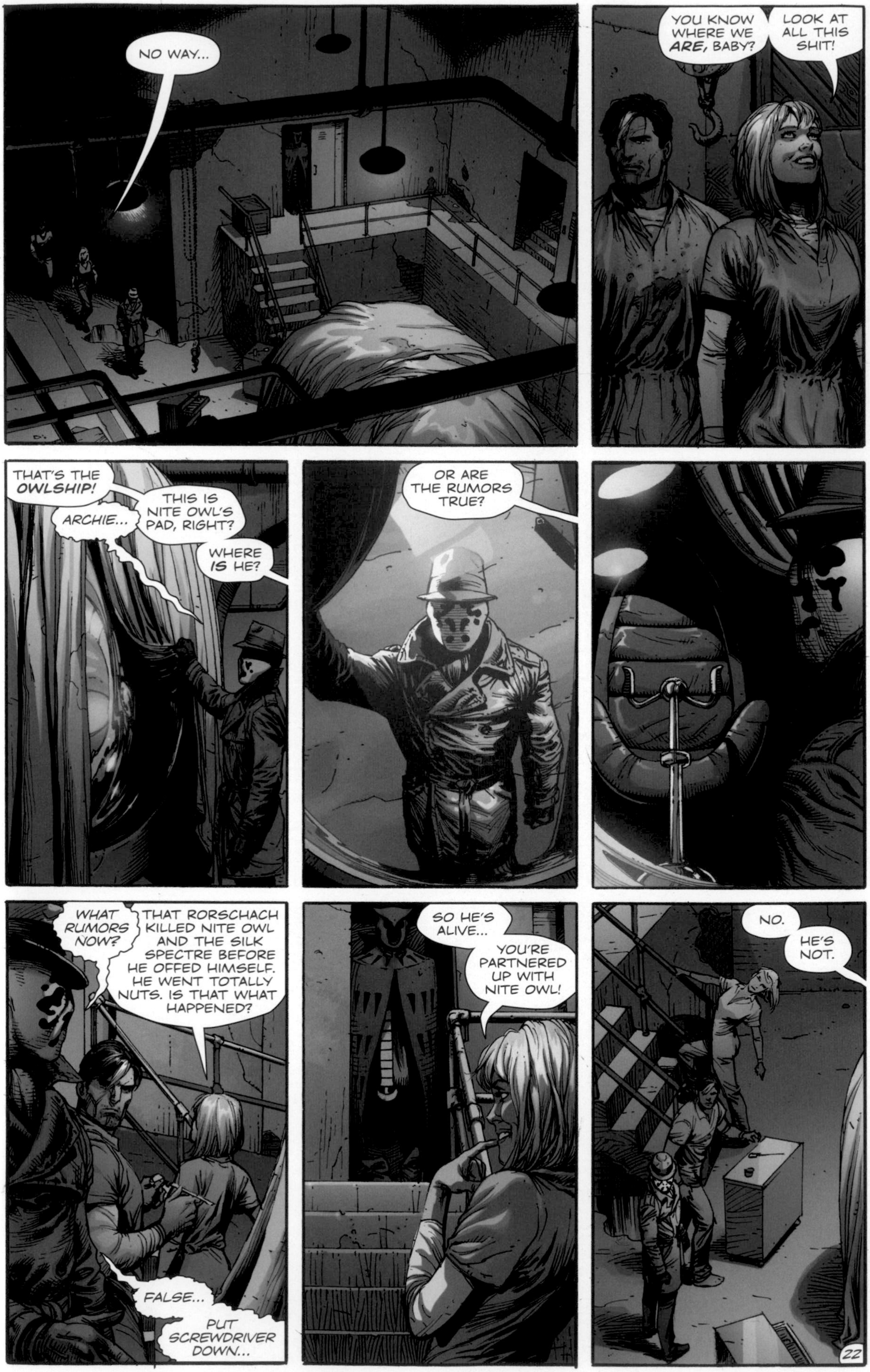
NO WAY...
YOU KNOW WHERE WE ARE, BABY?
LOOK AT ALL THIS SHIT!
THAT'S THE OWLSHIP!
ARCHIE...
THIS IS NITE OWL'S PAD, RIGHT?
WHERE IS HE?
OR ARE THE RUMORS TRUE?
WHAT RUMORS NOW?
THAT RORSCHACH KILLED NITE OWL AND THE SILK SPECTRE BEFORE HE OFFED HIMSELF. HE WENT TOTALLY NUTS. IS THAT WHAT HAPPENED?
FALSE...
PUT SCREWDRIVER DOWN...
SO HE'S ALIVE...
YOU'RE PARTNERED UP WITH NITE OWL!
NO.
HE'S NOT.

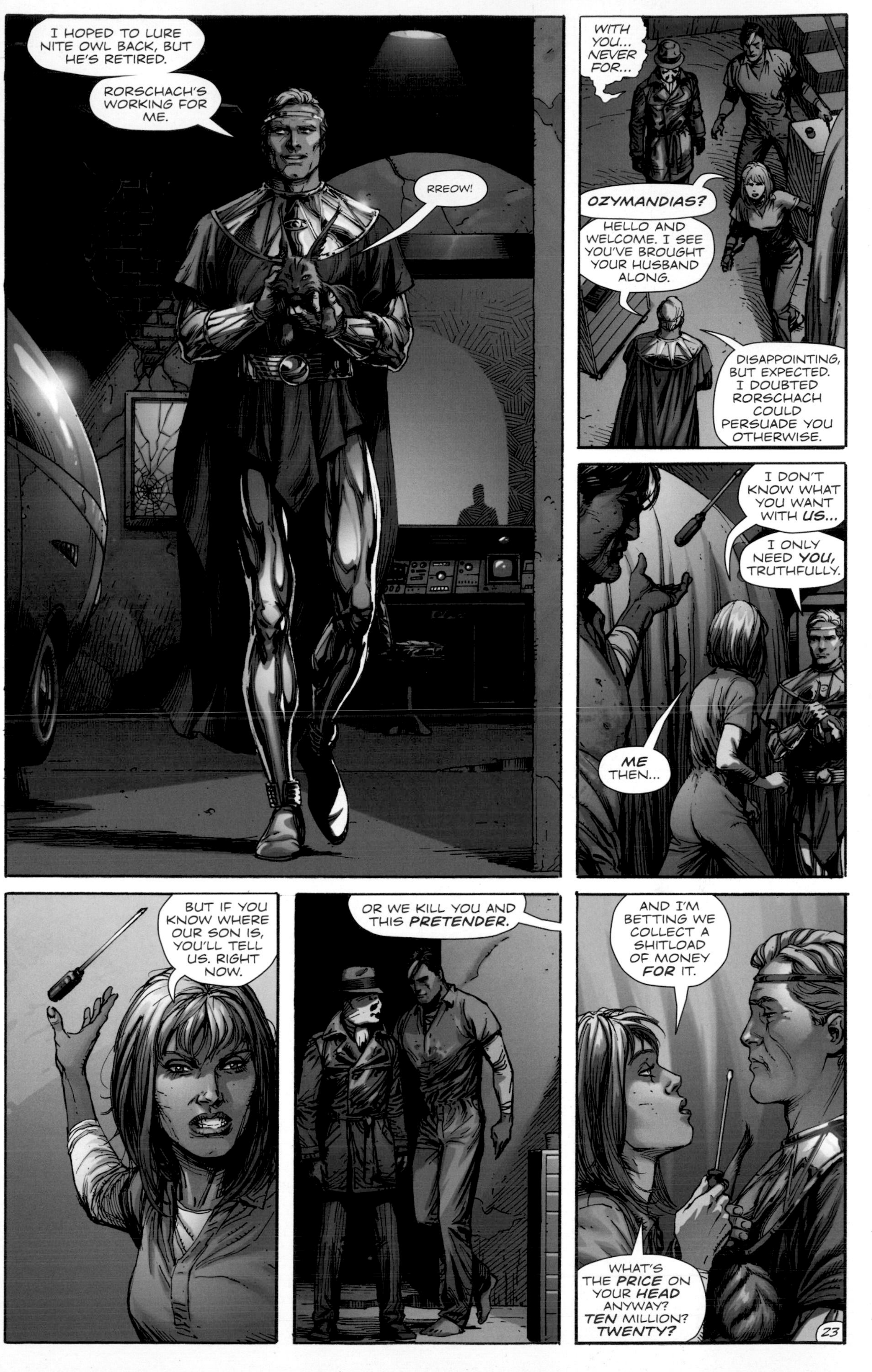
I HOPED TO LURE NITE OWL BACK, BUT HE'S RETIRED.
RORSCHACH'S WORKING FOR ME.
RREOW!
WITH YOU... NEVER FOR...
OZYMANDIAS?
HELLO AND WELCOME. I SEE YOU'VE BROUGHT YOUR HUSBAND ALONG.
DISAPPOINTING, BUT EXPECTED. I DOUBTED RORSCHACH COULD PERSUADE YOU OTHERWISE.
I DON'T KNOW WHAT YOU WANT WITH US...
I ONLY NEED YOU, TRUTHFULLY.
ME THEN...
BUT IF YOU KNOW WHERE OUR SON IS, YOU'LL TELL US. RIGHT NOW.
OR WE KILL YOU AND THIS PRETENDER.
AND I'M BETTING WE COLLECT A SHITLOAD OF MONEY FOR IT.
WHAT'S THE PRICE ON YOUR HEAD ANYWAY? TEN MILLION? TWENTY?

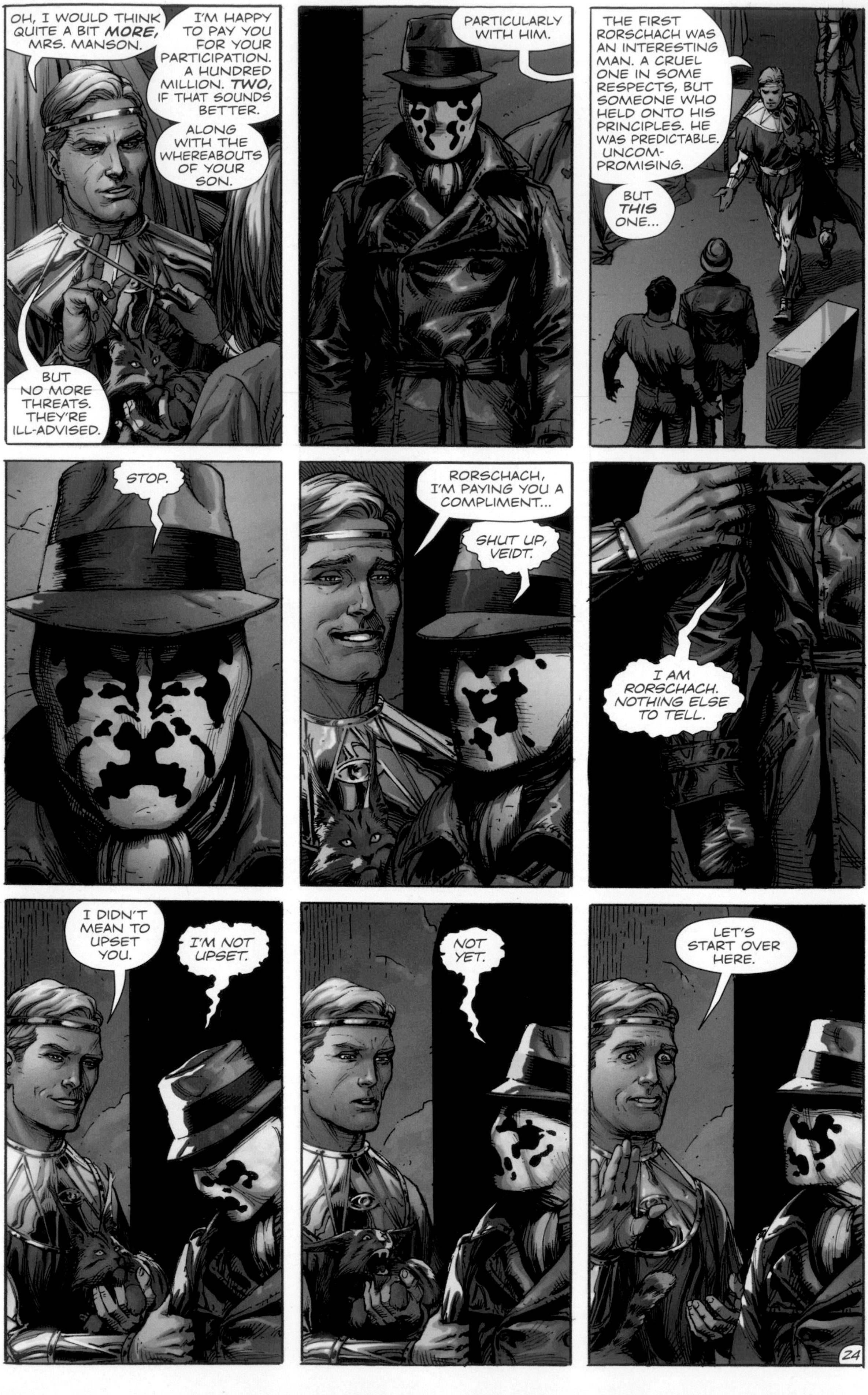

OH, I WOULD THINK QUITE A BIT MORE, MRS. MANSON.
I'M HAPPY TO PAY YOU FOR YOUR PARTICIPATION. A HUNDRED MILLION. TWO, IF THAT SOUNDS BETTER.
ALONG WITH THE WHEREABOUTS OF YOUR SON.
BUT NO MORE THREATS. THEY'RE ILL-ADVISED.
PARTICULARLY WITH HIM.
THE FIRST RORSCHACH WAS AN INTERESTING MAN. A CRUEL ONE IN SOME RESPECTS, BUT SOMEONE WHO HELD ONTO HIS PRINCIPLES. HE WAS PREDICTABLE. UNCOM-PROMISING.
BUT THIS ONE...
STOP.
RORSCHACH, I'M PAYING YOU A COMPLIMENT...
SHUT UP, VEIDT.
I AM RORSCHACH. NOTHING ELSE TO TELL.
I DIDN'T MEAN TO UPSET YOU.
I'M NOT UPSET.
NOT YET.
LET'S START OVER HERE.

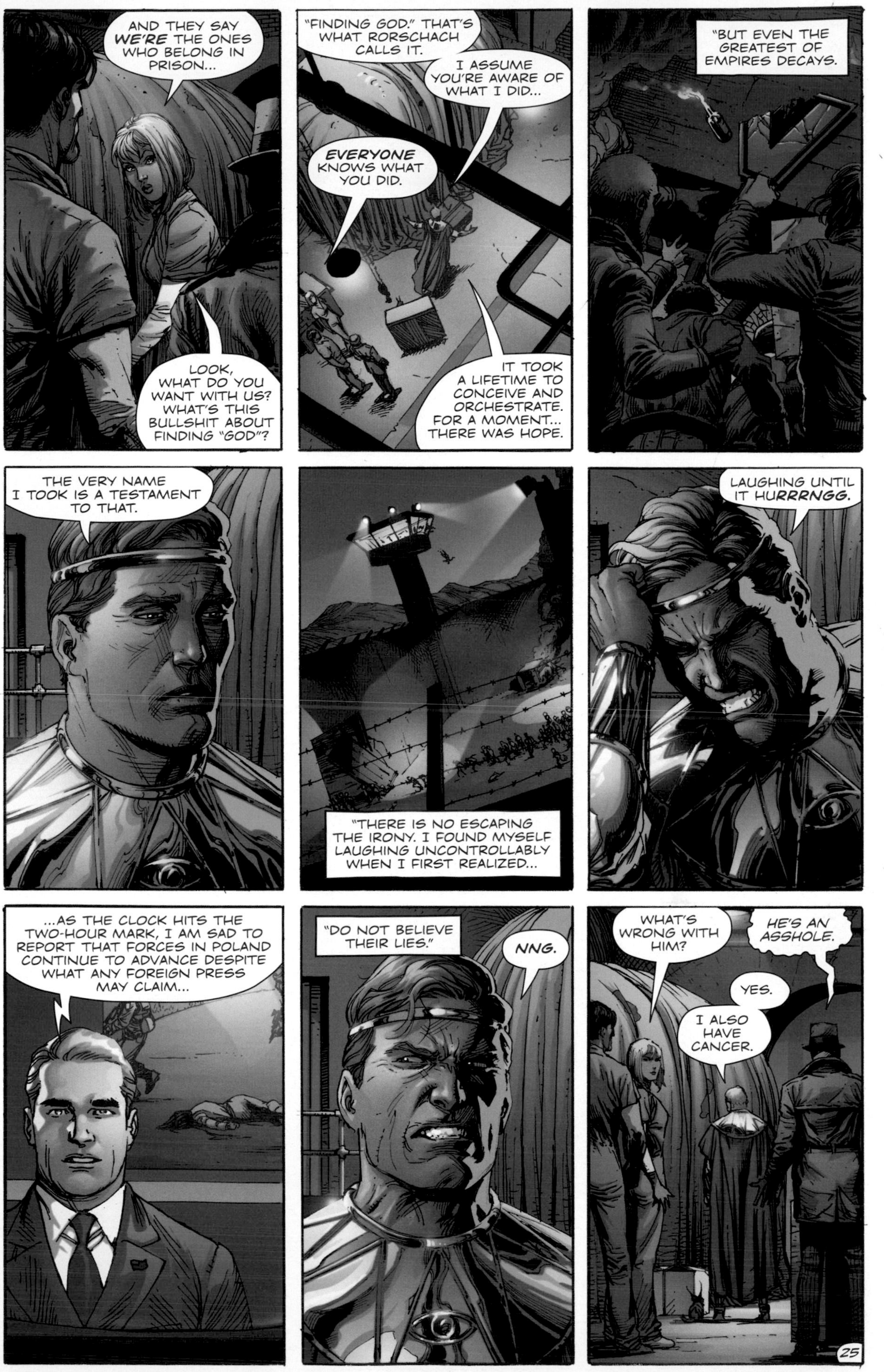
AND THEY SAY *WE'RE* THE ONES WHO BELONG IN PRISON...
LOOK, WHAT DO YOU WANT WITH US? WHAT'S THIS BULLSHIT ABOUT FINDING "GOD"?
"FINDING GOD." THAT'S WHAT RORSCHACH CALLS IT.
I ASSUME YOU'RE AWARE OF WHAT I DID...
EVERYONE KNOWS WHAT YOU DID.
IT TOOK A LIFETIME TO CONCEIVE AND ORCHESTRATE. FOR A MOMENT... THERE WAS HOPE.
"BUT EVEN THE GREATEST OF EMPIRES DECAYS.
THE VERY NAME I TOOK IS A TESTAMENT TO THAT.
"THERE IS NO ESCAPING THE IRONY. I FOUND MYSELF LAUGHING UNCONTROLLABLY WHEN I FIRST REALIZED...
LAUGHING UNTIL IT HU*RRRNGG.*
...AS THE CLOCK HITS THE TWO-HOUR MARK, I AM SAD TO REPORT THAT FORCES IN POLAND CONTINUE TO ADVANCE DESPITE WHAT ANY FOREIGN PRESS MAY CLAIM...
"DO NOT BELIEVE THEIR LIES."
NNG.
WHAT'S WRONG WITH HIM?
HE'S AN ASSHOLE.
YES.
I ALSO HAVE CANCER.

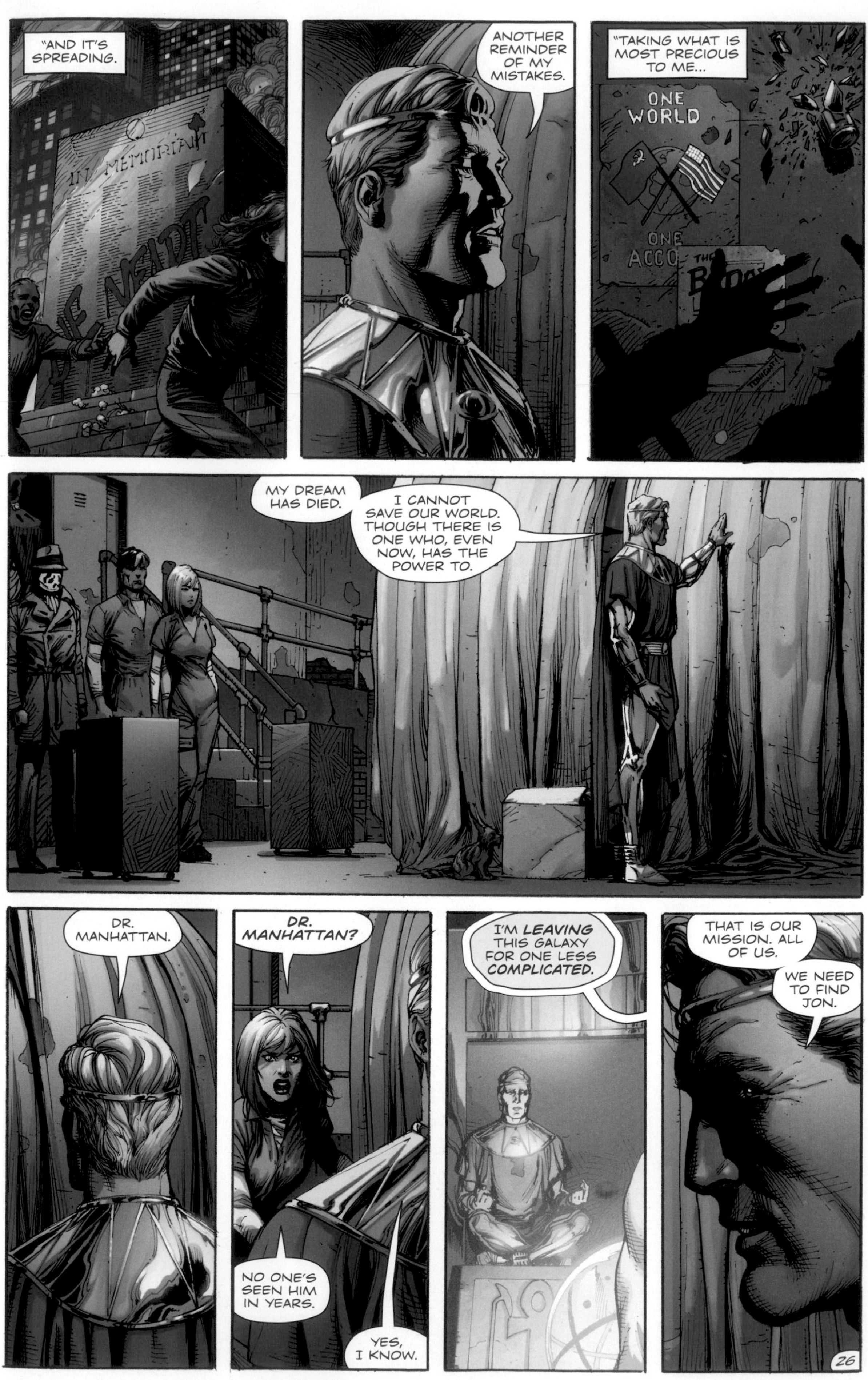

"AND IT'S SPREADING.
IN MEMORIAM
ANOTHER REMINDER OF MY MISTAKES.
"TAKING WHAT IS MOST PRECIOUS TO ME...
ONE WORLD
ONE ACCO
MY DREAM HAS DIED.
I CANNOT SAVE OUR WORLD. THOUGH THERE IS ONE WHO, EVEN NOW, HAS THE POWER TO.
DR. MANHATTAN.
DR. MANHATTAN?
NO ONE'S SEEN HIM IN YEARS.
YES, I KNOW.
I'M LEAVING THIS GALAXY FOR ONE LESS COMPLICATED.
THAT IS OUR MISSION. ALL OF US.
WE NEED TO FIND JON.

"WHEREVER HE'S RETREATED TO."

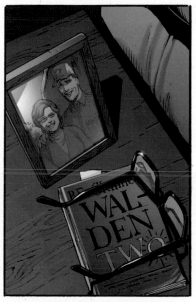

WAL
DEN
TWO

"THEY'VE NEVER SEEN ANYTHING LIKE YOU, CLARK."

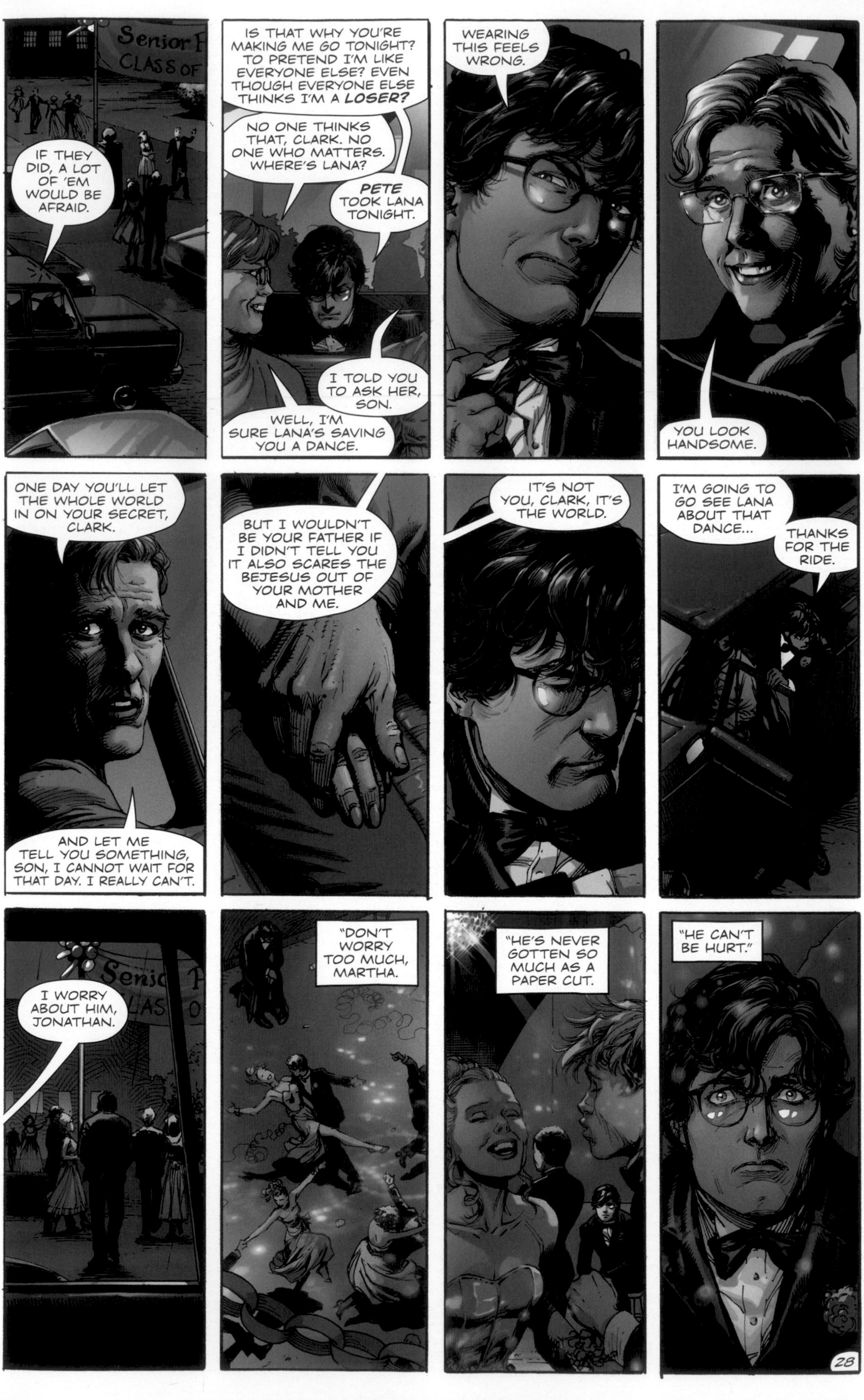
Senior
CLASS OF
IF THEY DID, A LOT OF 'EM WOULD BE AFRAID.
IS THAT WHY YOU'RE MAKING ME GO TONIGHT? TO PRETEND I'M LIKE EVERYONE ELSE? EVEN THOUGH EVERYONE ELSE THINKS I'M A **LOSER?**
NO ONE THINKS THAT, CLARK. NO ONE WHO MATTERS. WHERE'S LANA?
PETE TOOK LANA TONIGHT.
I TOLD YOU TO ASK HER, SON.
WELL, I'M SURE LANA'S SAVING YOU A DANCE.
WEARING THIS FEELS WRONG.
YOU LOOK HANDSOME.
ONE DAY YOU'LL LET THE WHOLE WORLD IN ON YOUR SECRET, CLARK.
AND LET ME TELL YOU SOMETHING, SON, I CANNOT WAIT FOR THAT DAY. I REALLY CAN'T.
BUT I WOULDN'T BE YOUR FATHER IF I DIDN'T TELL YOU IT ALSO SCARES THE BEJESUS OUT OF YOUR MOTHER AND ME.
IT'S NOT YOU, CLARK, IT'S THE WORLD.
I'M GOING TO GO SEE LANA ABOUT THAT DANCE...
THANKS FOR THE RIDE.
I WORRY ABOUT HIM, JONATHAN.
"DON'T WORRY TOO MUCH, MARTHA.
"HE'S NEVER GOTTEN SO MUCH AS A PAPER CUT.
"HE CAN'T BE HURT."

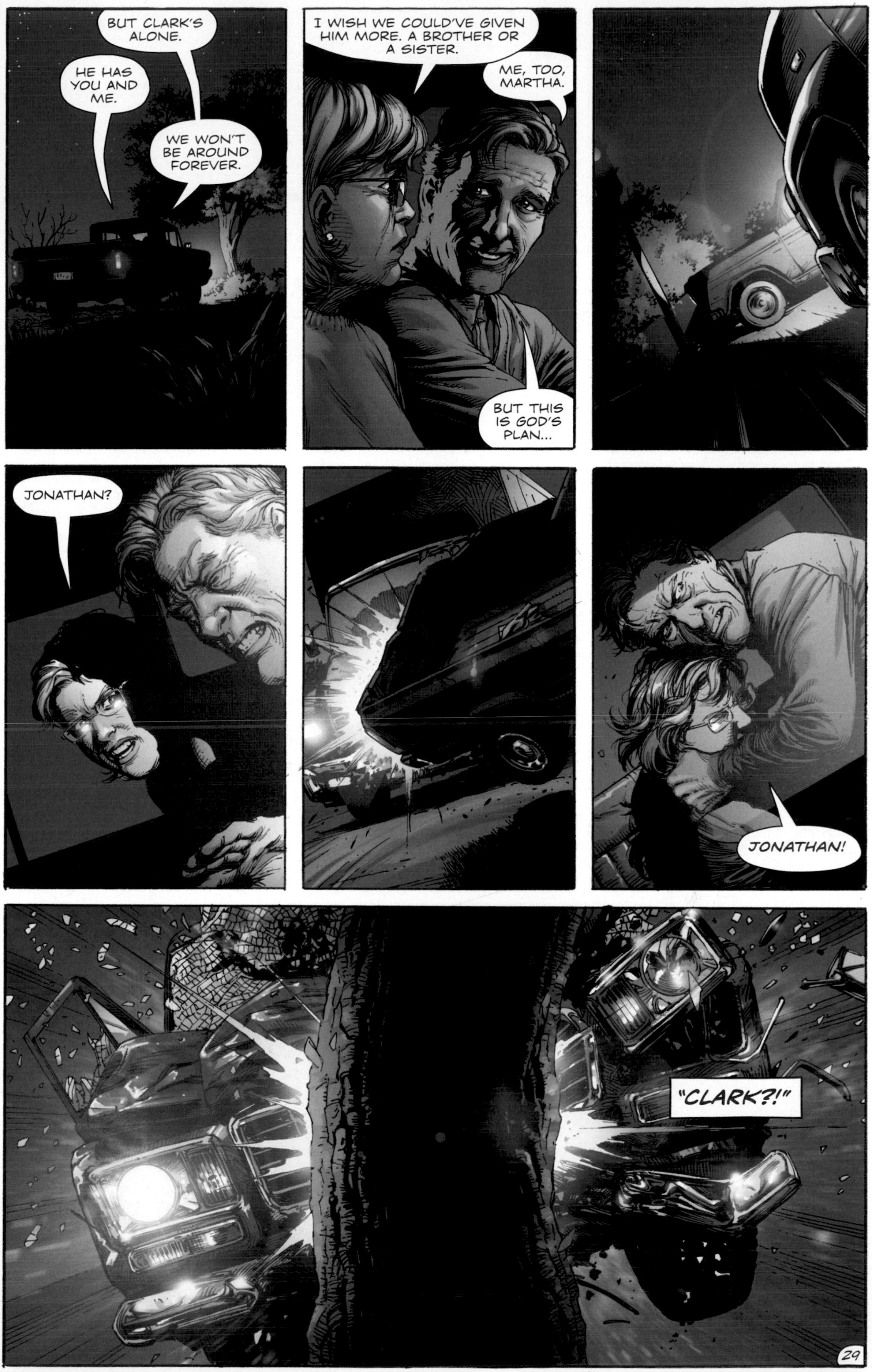
BUT CLARK'S ALONE.
HE HAS YOU AND ME.
WE WON'T BE AROUND FOREVER.
I WISH WE COULD'VE GIVEN HIM MORE. A BROTHER OR A SISTER.
ME, TOO, MARTHA.
BUT THIS IS GOD'S PLAN...
JONATHAN?
JONATHAN!
"CLARK?!"

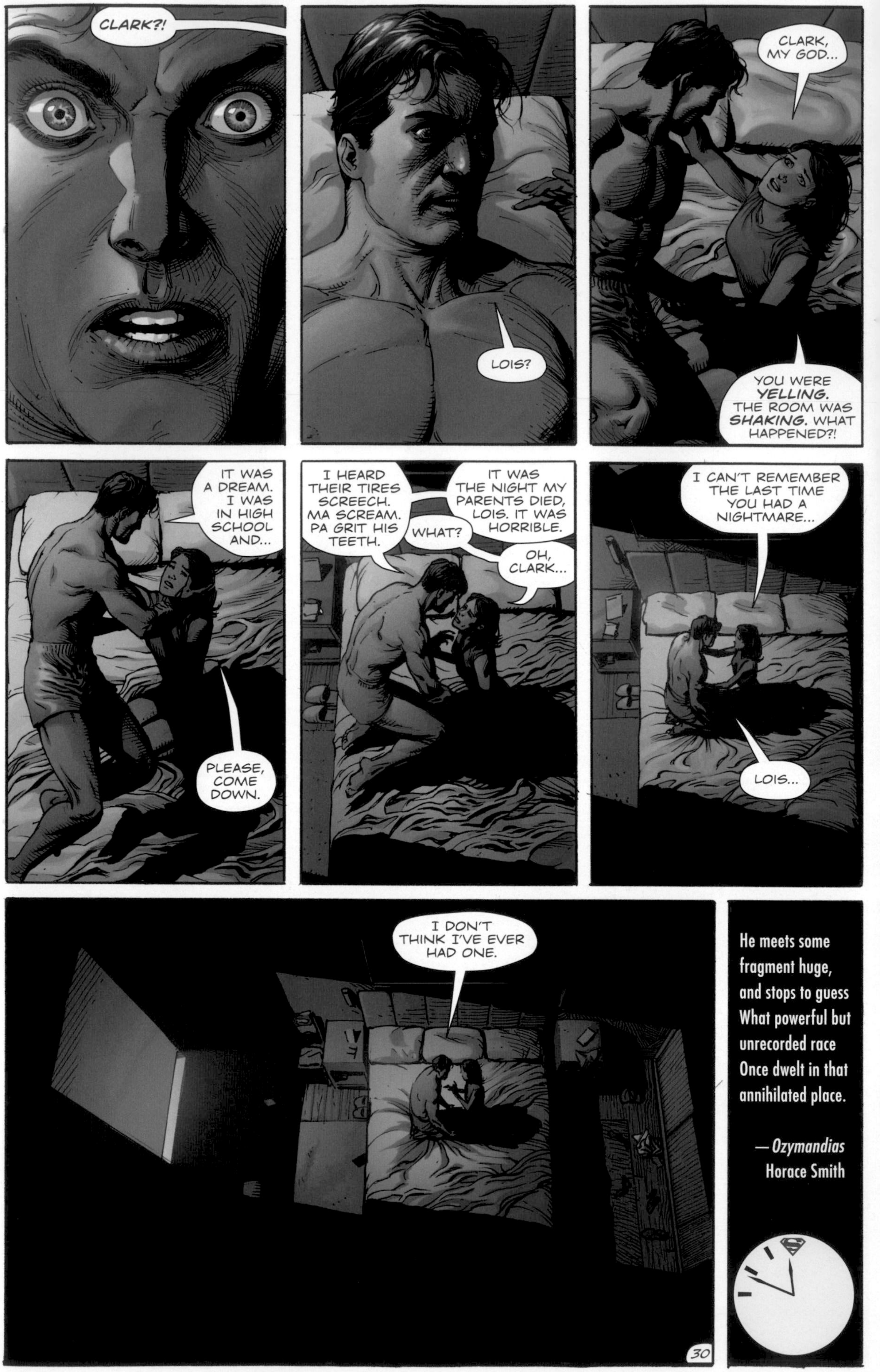
CLARK?!
LOIS?
CLARK, MY GOD...
YOU WERE **YELLING.** THE ROOM WAS **SHAKING.** WHAT HAPPENED?!
IT WAS A DREAM. I WAS IN HIGH SCHOOL AND...
PLEASE, COME DOWN.
IT WAS THE NIGHT MY PARENTS DIED, LOIS. IT WAS HORRIBLE.
I HEARD THEIR TIRES SCREECH. MA SCREAM. PA GRIT HIS TEETH.
WHAT?
OH, CLARK...
I CAN'T REMEMBER THE LAST TIME YOU HAD A NIGHTMARE...
LOIS...
I DON'T THINK I'VE EVER HAD ONE.
30
He meets some fragment huge, and stops to guess What powerful but unrecorded race Once dwelt in that annihilated place.
—*Ozymandias* Horace Smith

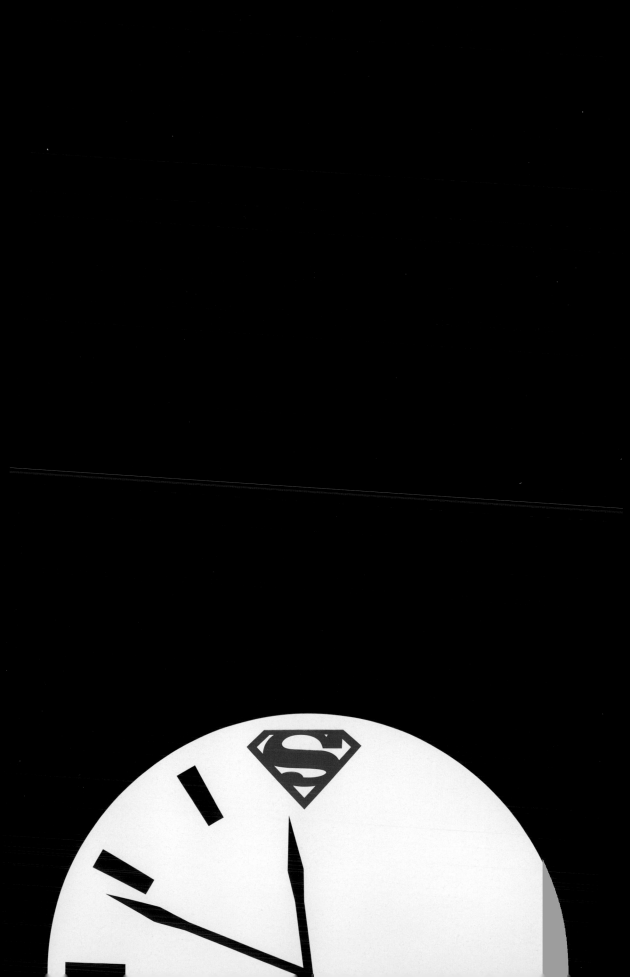

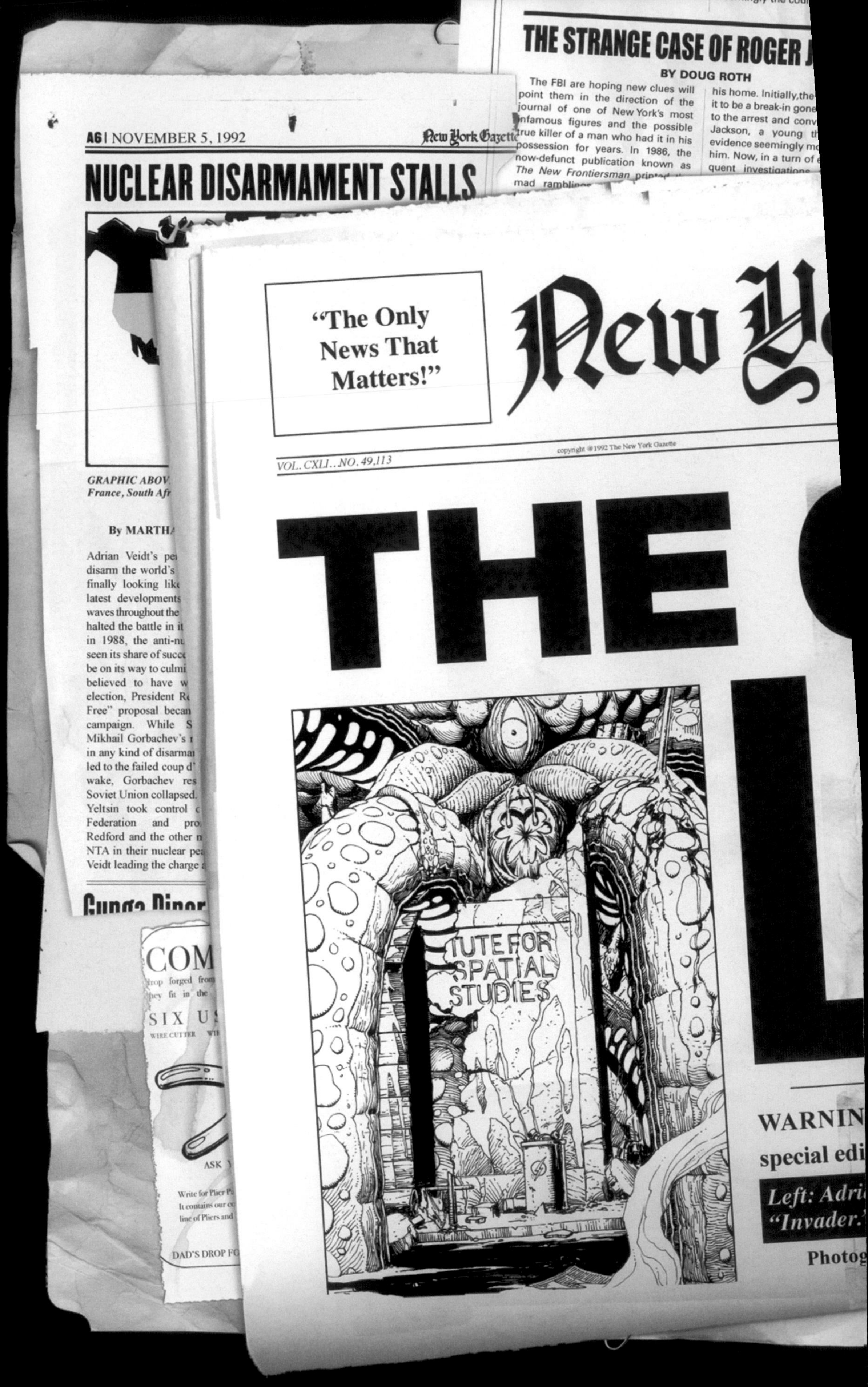
THE STRANGE CASE OF ROGER J
BY DOUG ROTH
The FBI are hoping new clues will point them in the direction of the journal of one of New York's most infamous figures and the possible true killer of a man who had it in his possession for years. In 1986, the now-defunct publication known as The New Frontiersman printed the mad ramblings
his home. Initially, the it to be a break-in gone to the arrest and conv Jackson, a young th evidence seemingly mo him. Now, in a turn of e quent investigations
A6 | NOVEMBER 5, 1992
New York Gazette
NUCLEAR DISARMAMENT STALLS
GRAPHIC ABOV France, South Afr
By MARTHA
Adrian Veidt's pe disarm the world's finally looking like latest developments waves throughout the halted the battle in it in 1988, the anti-nu seen its share of succe be on its way to culmi believed to have w election, President R Free" proposal becan campaign. While S Mikhail Gorbachev's in any kind of disarma led to the failed coup d' wake, Gorbachev res Soviet Union collapsed. Yeltsin took control Federation and pro Redford and the other n NTA in their nuclear pe Veidt leading the charge
COM
SIX U
WIRE CUTTER
ASK
DAD'S DROP FO
"The Only News That Matters!"
New Y
copyright ©1992 The New York Gazette
VOL. CXLI . . NO. 49,113
THE
TUTE FOR SPATIAL STUDIES
WARNIN
special edi
Left: Adri "Invader."
Photog

Late Edition

New York: **Today**, overcast.
High 52. **Tonight**, thunderstorms
possible. Low 38. **Tomorrow**,
limited sun, scattered thunderstorms. High 50. **Yesterday**,
high 75, low 55. Details, page B10.

50 CENTS

...ER 2, 1992

GREAT
...IE

By JACK N. ANDERSON
Special to The New York Gazette

MANHATTAN, New York, November 2 -- On the eve of
the election, while he trails behind in the polls, President
Redford will deliver a speech revealing the alien
monster that attacked New York was a hoax perpetrated
by "the world's smartest man" and "humanity's savior"
-- Adrian Veidt. At four o'clock today, the President will
unveil the details of a covert investigation dubbed
"Operation: Commodus" that was launched earlier this
year. "Operation: Commodus" was so secret, it was
run out of the White House and overseen by the
President directly.

The final report was turned into the President last night
and connects the mysterious and unsolved deaths of
writers, artists, engineers, physicists, journalists and
even Ozymandias' former costumed colleagues to
Adrian Veidt. In the wake of "The New York City
Massacre," wars ended, political enemies became allies
and Veidt stepped into the spotlight. For the last seven
years, he has influenced the world more than any other
man in history, creating new policies and brokering
alliances across the globe. Although never taking political
office, Veidt has been seen by the world as a ...

The images within this
... **of** *The New York Gazette*
...eidt's **are not suitable**
for children.
...h **by JAMES NACHTWEY**

NUCLEAR DISARMAMENT STALLS

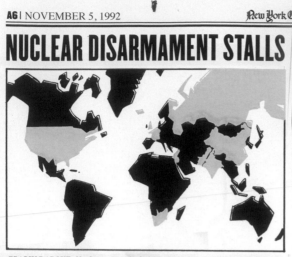

GRAPHIC ABOVE: *Nuclear powers include the United States, the United Kingdom, France, South Africa, Russia, Israel, Pakistan, India, China and North Korea.*

By MARTHA GELLHORN

Adrian Veidt's personal campaign to disarm the world's nuclear arsenal was finally looking like a reality, yet the latest developments have sent shockwaves throughout the world and seemingly halted the battle in its tracks. Launched in 1988, the anti-nuclear mission has seen its share of success and appeared to be on its way to culmination. Commonly believed to have won him the '88 election, President Redford's "Nuclear Free" proposal became central to his campaign. While Soviet President Mikhail Gorbachev's refusal to engage in any kind of disarmament discussions led to the failed *coup d'etat* of '89. In its wake, Gorbachev resigned and the Soviet Union collapsed. President Boris Yelstin took control of the Russian Federation and promptly joined Redford and the other members of the NTA in their nuclear peace talks. With Veidt leading the charge and the United

Nations embracing his Global Data Exchange Program, the NTA agreed to a disarming of all nuclear weapons over a 20-year period. But one world super-power was still standing in the way. Over the years, Israel has been steadfast in its refusal to confirm possession of nuclear weapons. That all changed with the Vela incident, long-rumored to be evidence of Israel's nuclear testing. Veidt's tenacity paid off when his investigation using global forensics to uncover the truth behind the mysterious event of 1979 forced Israel to admit the existence of its nuclear arsenal. The country reluctantly joined the NTA's disarmament plan. But just three years in, that plan has come to a grinding halt. As the world reels from the accusations against Adrian Veidt, President Redford has terminated his "Nuclear Free" program and withdrawn from the NTA. It's only a matter of time before the rest follow as everything Ozymandias has touched, crumbles.

THE STRANGE CASE OF ROGER JAC[...]

BY DOUG ROTH

The FBI is hoping new clues will point them in the direction of the journal of one of New York's most infamous figures and the possible true killer of a man who had it in his possession for years. In 1986, the now-defunct publication known as *The New Frontiersman* printed the mad ramblings of Walter Kovacs, today better known as the vigilante Rorschach. Pages from Rorschach's alleged journal were transcribed and squeezed between a Sunbursts candy ad and an interview with a man who Kovacs bit when they were children. It was ignored, as most things in *The New Frontiersman* were at the time. Shortly after the publication, the man who first found Rorschach's journal, Seymour David-- an employee at *The New Frontiersman*, was found brutally beaten to death in

his home. Initially, the police [...] it to be a break-in gone wron[...] to the arrest and conviction [...] Jackson, a young thief [...] evidence seemingly mounte[...] him. Now, in a turn of event[...] quent investigations are t[...] different story. New inform[...] pointing to Jackson's innoce[...] that this robbery was not ra[...] all. At the center of this [...] which could be the key to find[...] true killer, is what was missin[...] Seymour David's hands wh[...] body was found--Rorschach's j[...] Where is it and what add[...] information does it hold that [...] cause someone to kill for [...] FBI is tight-lipped, but Jac[...] attorneys have already fi[...] motion for the judge to ov[...] the jury's guilty verdict. ⊞

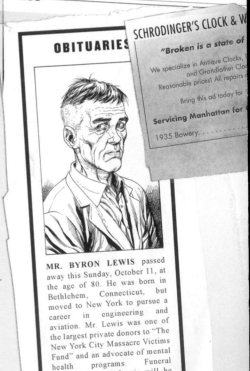

Mug shot of Walter Ko[...]

NOVA EXPRESS   *February 1987*

OBITUARIES

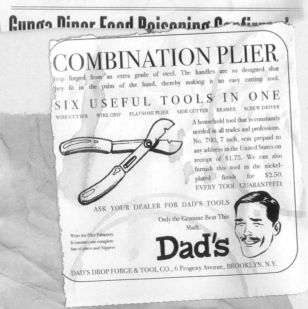

MR. BYRON LEWIS passed away this Sunday, October 11, at the age of 80. He was born in Bethlehem, Connecticut, but moved to New York to pursue a career in engineering and aviation. Mr. Lewis was one of the largest private donors to "The New York City Massacre Victims Fund" and an advocate of mental health programs. Funeral services for Mr. Lewis will be held at 9 o'clock Friday morning at the Fitzgerald Mental Home at 22 Second Street North, Waterville Maine where he spent the last years of his life. Burial will be in Pine Grove Cemetery. Donations in Mr. Lewis's name to the Fitzgerald Mental Home, which was damaged in a gas explosion last week, are encouraged.

Gunga Diner Food Poisoning Co[...]

MORNING JOE'S

WELCOME TO MORNING JOE'S!

Fruits and Juices

Orange Juice	$1.10
Grapefruit Juice	$1.25
Tomato Juice	$1.10
Apple Juice	$1.25
Pineapple Juice	$1.25
Half a Grapefruit	$1.25
Full Grapefruit	$2.00
Fresh Fruit (in season)	$1.25

Morning Joe's Famous Pancakes!

A small stack of Joe's Famous Pancakes	$2.00
A large stack of Joe's Famous Pancakes	$3.50
Joe's Famous Pancakes with Blueberries	add $1.00
Joe's Famous Pancakes with Strawberries	add $1.00
Joe's Famous Pancakes with Peaches & Cream	add $1.50
Joe's Cinnamon Swirl Pancakes	$3.75

JOE'S SPECIAL! ADD A SMALL STACK OF JOE'S FAMOUS PANCAKES TO ANY BREAKFAST FOR $1.50!

From The Grill!

Fresh Eggs (2) Fried, Boiled Poached or Scrambled	$2.50
Fresh Eggs with Ham, Bacon or Sausage Links	$3.75
Side Order of Ham, Bacon Or Sausage Links	$1.65
Plain Omelette (3 eggs) with Toast and Jelly	$3.75
Ham and Cheese Omelette	$3.60
Blini with Smoked Salmon	$3.25

Beverages

Cup of Joe's, Freshly Brewed	$0.60
Tea (Black or Mint)	$0.60
Milk (Skim or Whole)	$0.60
Hot Chocolate	$0.90

For The Kids!

Joe's Famous Silver Dollar Pancakes	$1.25
Sunny-side eggs and toast	$1.50
Sugar Frosted Flakes or Cornflakes and milk	$1.00

THE BEST BREAKFAST IN THE CITY!
SERVED FROM 5AM UNTIL 11AM!

PAIR

212-555-1985

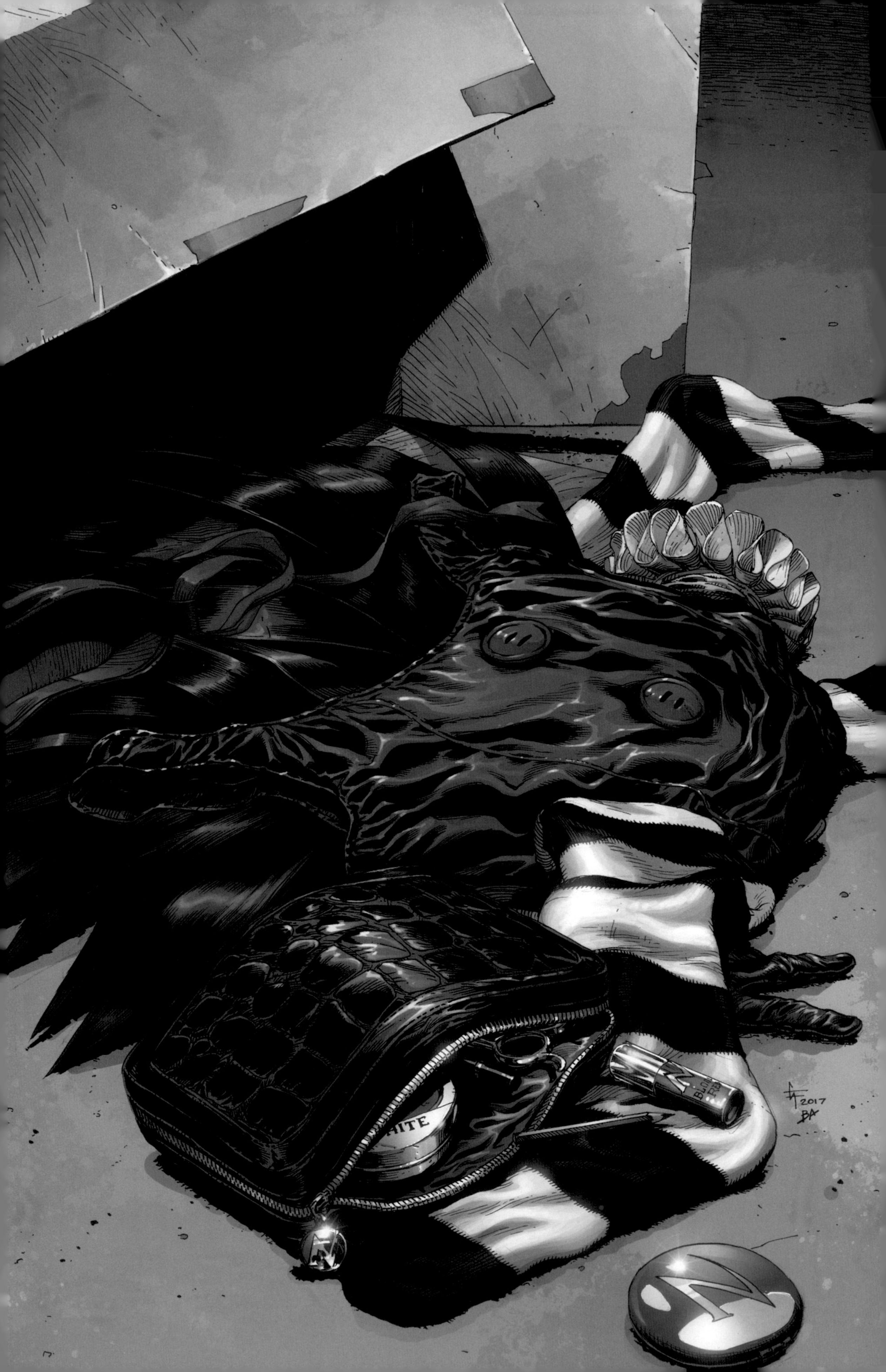

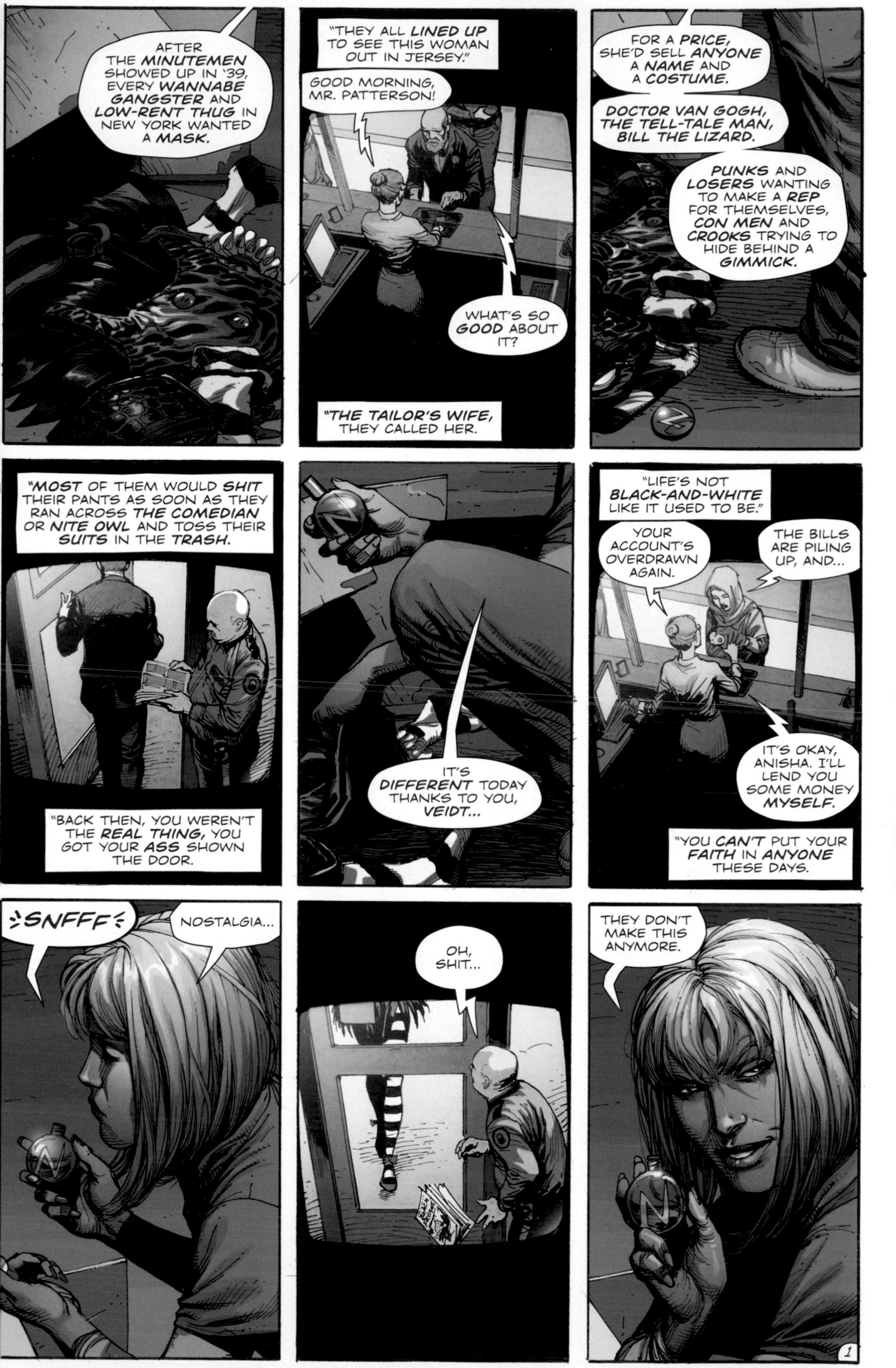
AFTER THE MINUTEMEN SHOWED UP IN '39, EVERY WANNABE GANGSTER AND LOW-RENT THUG IN NEW YORK WANTED A MASK.
"THEY ALL LINED UP TO SEE THIS WOMAN OUT IN JERSEY."
GOOD MORNING, MR. PATTERSON!
WHAT'S SO GOOD ABOUT IT?
"THE TAILOR'S WIFE, THEY CALLED HER.
FOR A PRICE, SHE'D SELL ANYONE A NAME AND A COSTUME.
DOCTOR VAN GOGH, THE TELL-TALE MAN, BILL THE LIZARD.
PUNKS AND LOSERS WANTING TO MAKE A REP FOR THEMSELVES, CON MEN AND CROOKS TRYING TO HIDE BEHIND A GIMMICK.
"MOST OF THEM WOULD SHIT THEIR PANTS AS SOON AS THEY RAN ACROSS THE COMEDIAN OR NITE OWL AND TOSS THEIR SUITS IN THE TRASH.
"BACK THEN, YOU WEREN'T THE REAL THING, YOU GOT YOUR ASS SHOWN THE DOOR.
IT'S DIFFERENT TODAY THANKS TO YOU, VEIDT...
"LIFE'S NOT BLACK-AND-WHITE LIKE IT USED TO BE."
YOUR ACCOUNT'S OVERDRAWN AGAIN.
THE BILLS ARE PILING UP, AND...
IT'S OKAY, ANISHA. I'LL LEND YOU SOME MONEY MYSELF.
"YOU CAN'T PUT YOUR FAITH IN ANYONE THESE DAYS.
SNFFF
NOSTALGIA...
OH, SHIT...
THEY DON'T MAKE THIS ANYMORE.

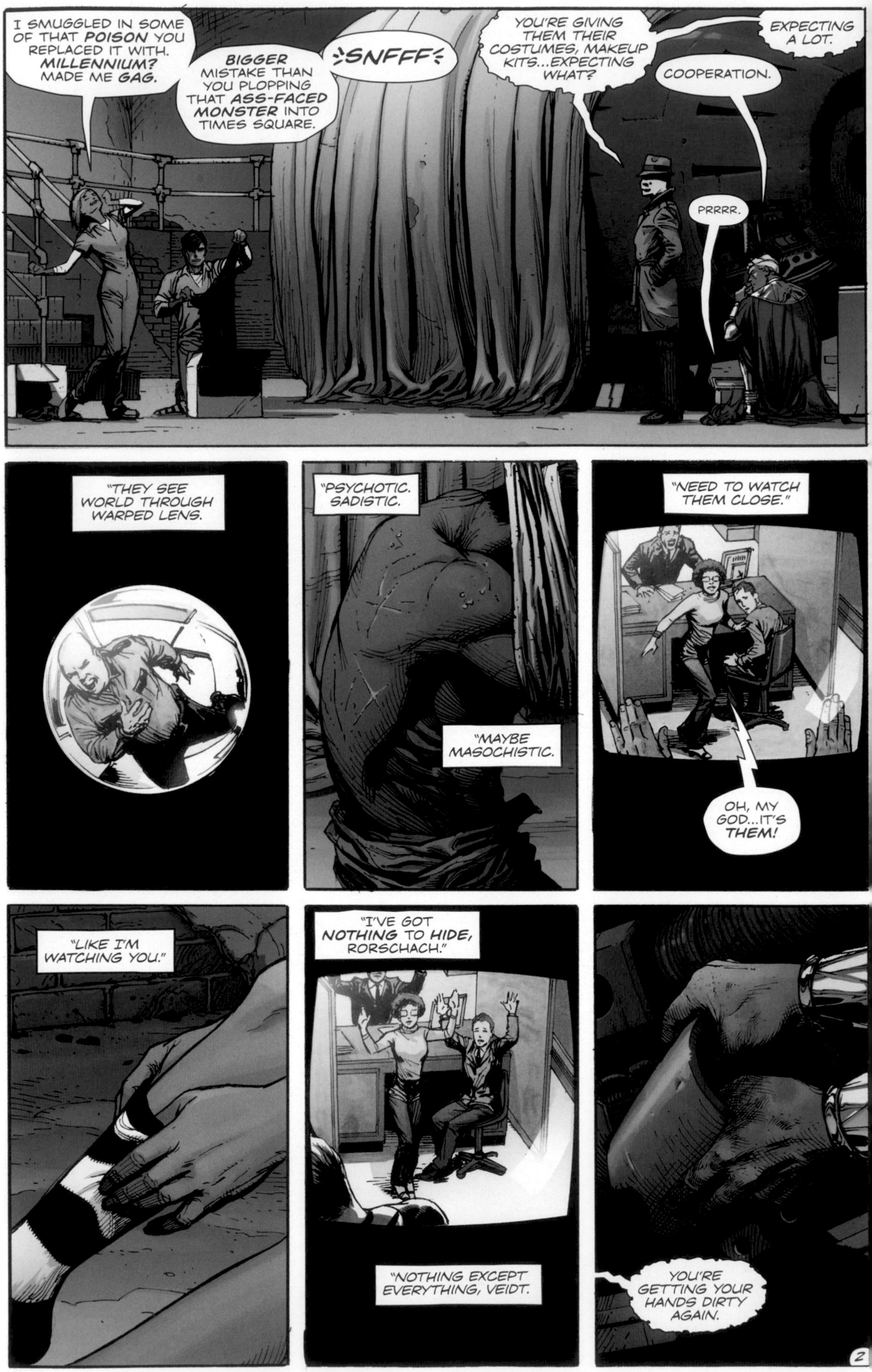
I SMUGGLED IN SOME OF THAT POISON YOU REPLACED IT WITH. MILLENNIUM? MADE ME GAG.
BIGGER MISTAKE THAN YOU PLOPPING THAT ASS-FACED MONSTER INTO TIMES SQUARE.
SNFFF
YOU'RE GIVING THEM THEIR COSTUMES, MAKEUP KITS...EXPECTING WHAT?
EXPECTING A LOT.
COOPERATION.
PRRRR.
"THEY SEE WORLD THROUGH WARPED LENS.
"PSYCHOTIC. SADISTIC.
"MAYBE MASOCHISTIC.
"NEED TO WATCH THEM CLOSE."
OH, MY GOD...IT'S THEM!
"LIKE I'M WATCHING YOU."
"I'VE GOT NOTHING TO HIDE, RORSCHACH."
"NOTHING EXCEPT EVERYTHING, VEIDT.
YOU'RE GETTING YOUR HANDS DIRTY AGAIN.

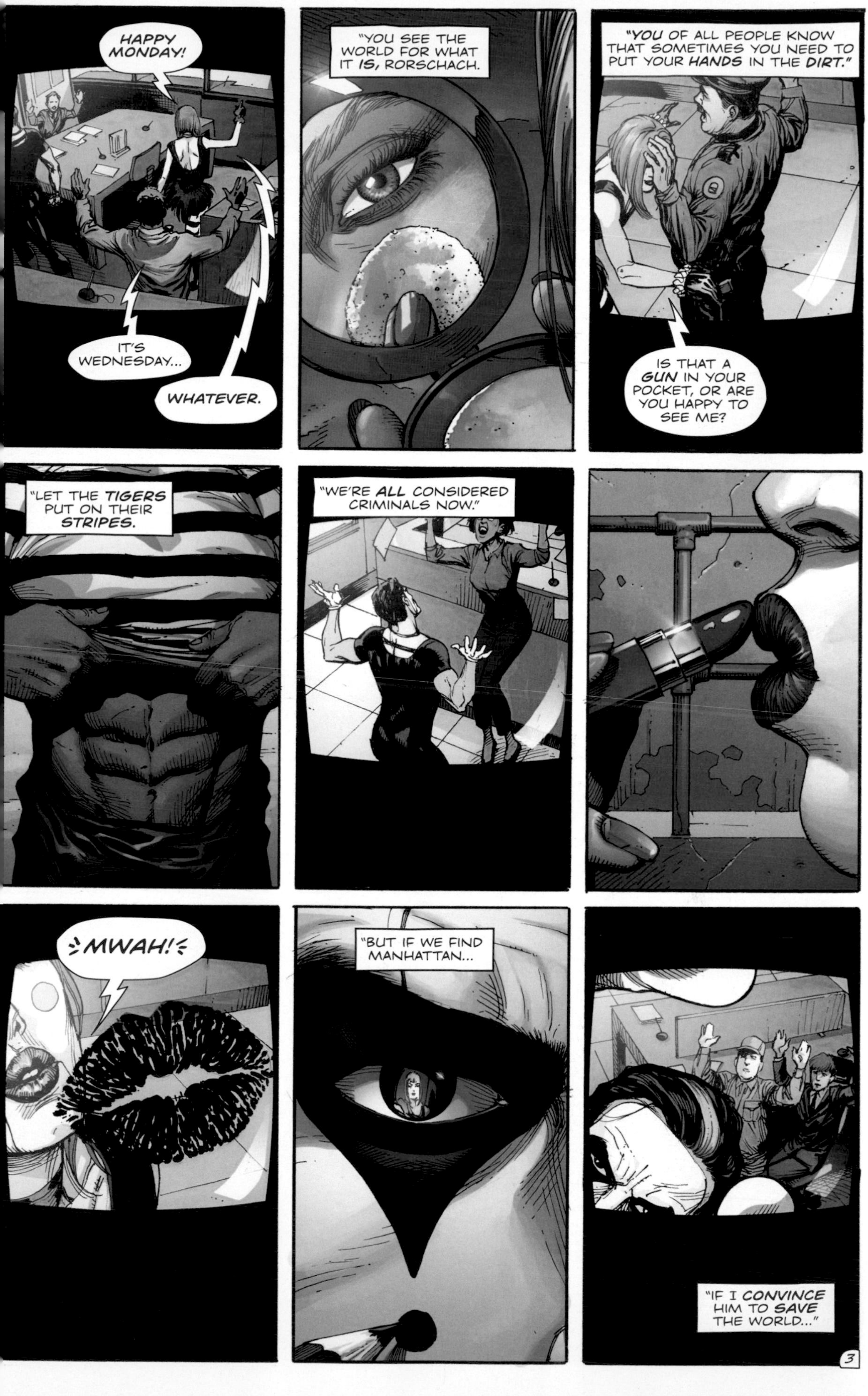
HAPPY MONDAY!
IT'S WEDNESDAY...
WHATEVER.
"YOU SEE THE WORLD FOR WHAT IT IS, RORSCHACH.
"YOU OF ALL PEOPLE KNOW THAT SOMETIMES YOU NEED TO PUT YOUR HANDS IN THE DIRT."
IS THAT A GUN IN YOUR POCKET, OR ARE YOU HAPPY TO SEE ME?
"LET THE TIGERS PUT ON THEIR STRIPES.
"WE'RE ALL CONSIDERED CRIMINALS NOW."
MWAH!
"BUT IF WE FIND MANHATTAN...
"IF I CONVINCE HIM TO SAVE THE WORLD..."

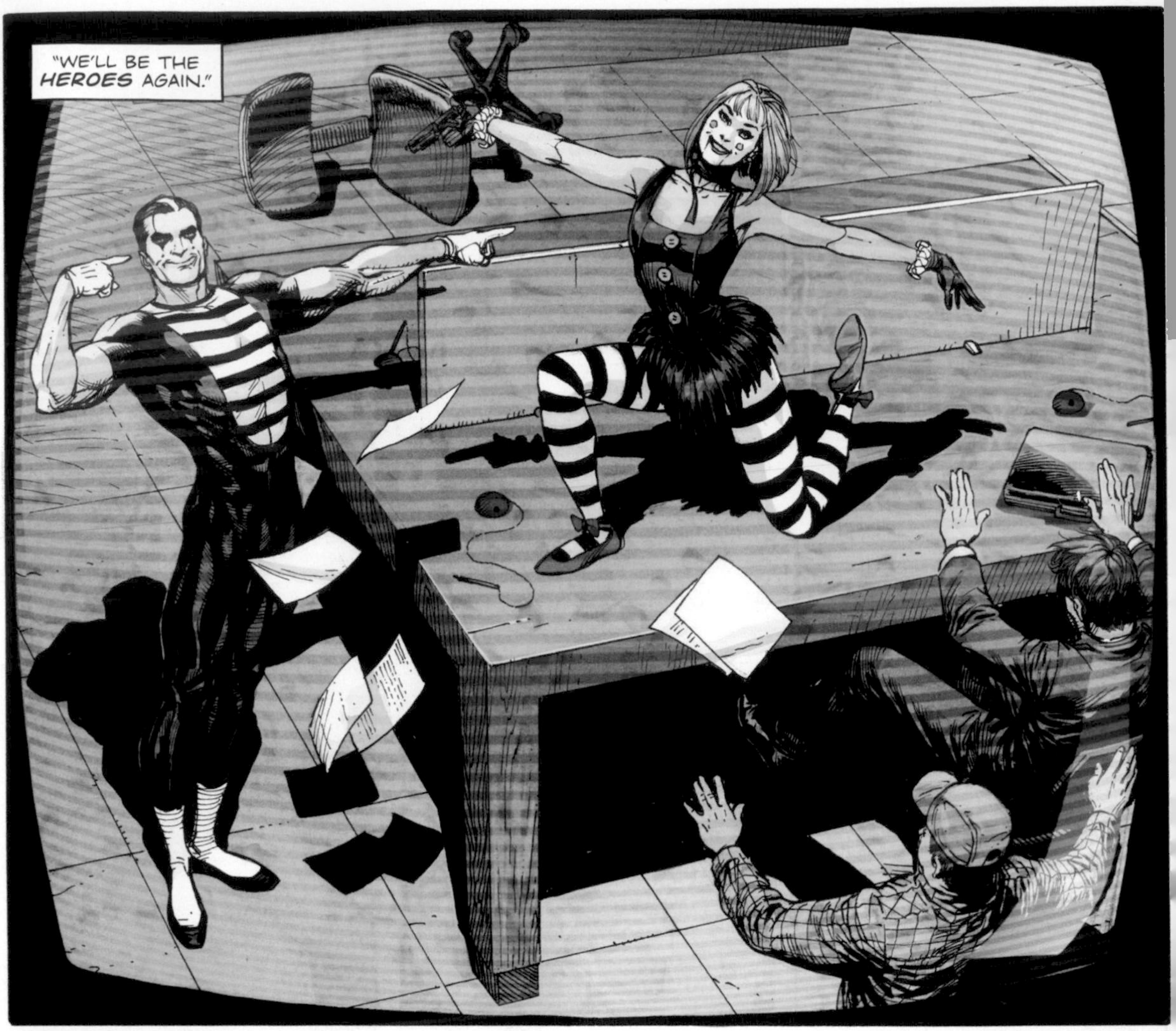
"WE'LL BE THE HEROES AGAIN."

PLACES WE HAVE NEVER KNOWN

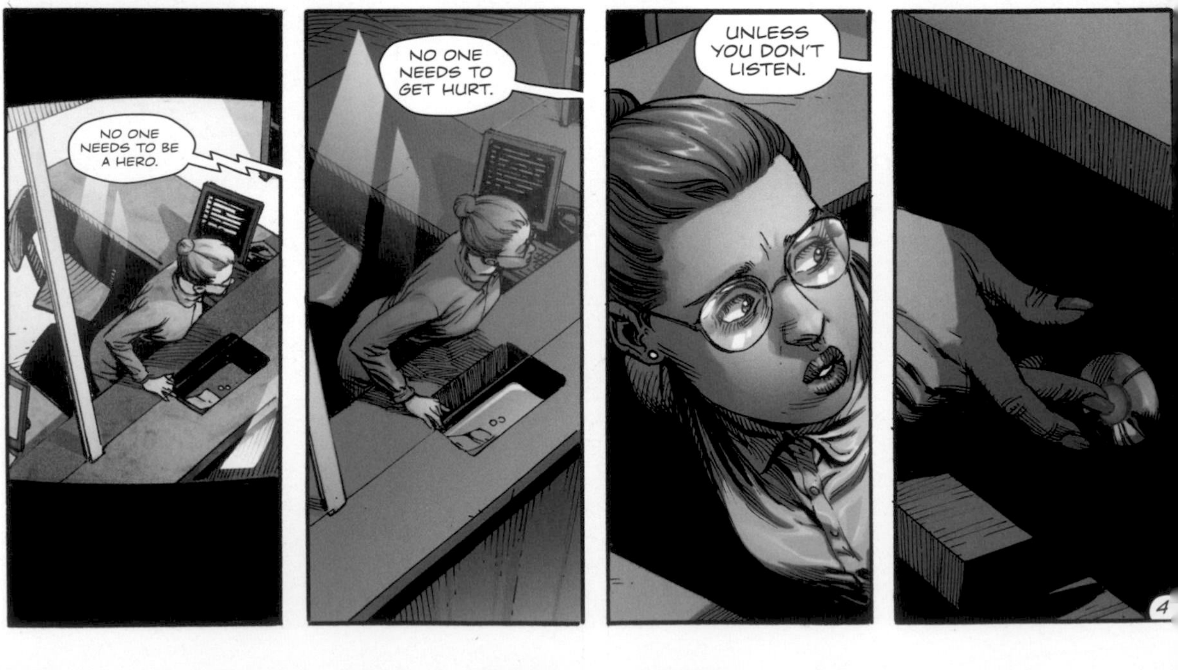
NO ONE NEEDS TO BE A HERO.
NO ONE NEEDS TO GET HURT.
UNLESS YOU DON'T LISTEN.

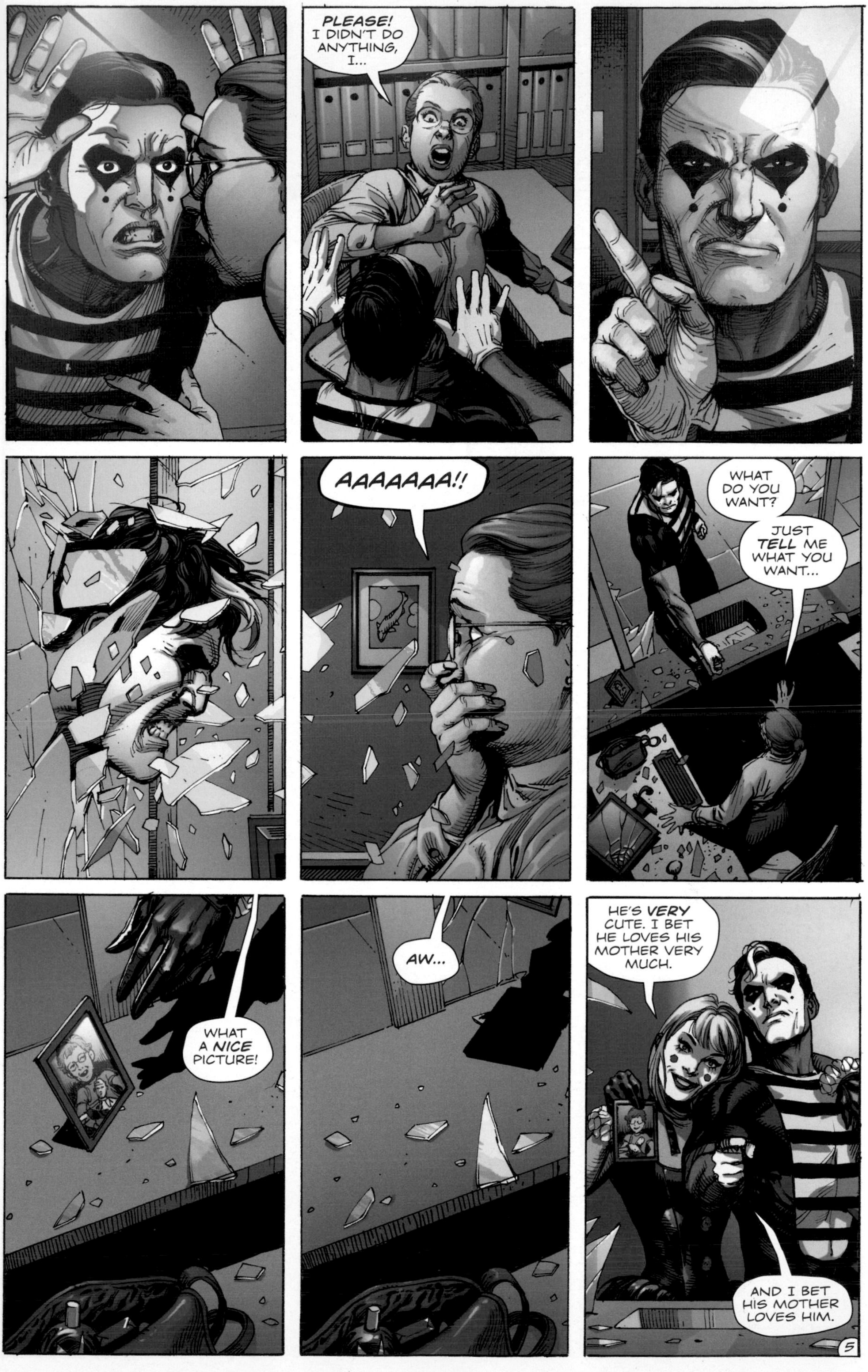

PLEASE! I DIDN'T DO ANYTHING, I...
AAAAAAA!!
WHAT DO YOU WANT?
JUST TELL ME WHAT YOU WANT...
WHAT A NICE PICTURE!
AW...
HE'S VERY CUTE. I BET HE LOVES HIS MOTHER VERY MUCH.
AND I BET HIS MOTHER LOVES HIM.

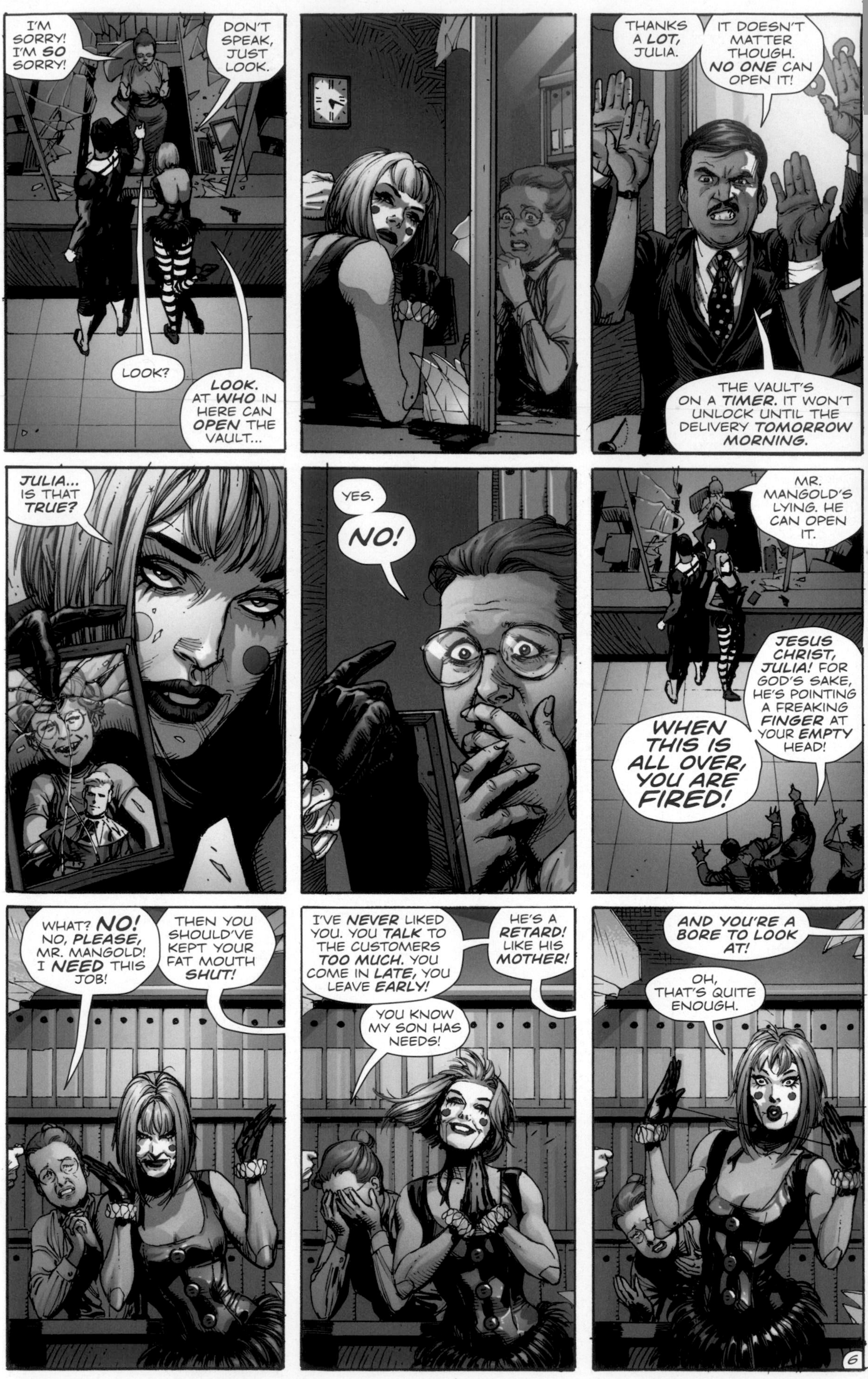
I'M SORRY! I'M SO SORRY!
DON'T SPEAK, JUST LOOK.
LOOK?
LOOK. AT WHO IN HERE CAN OPEN THE VAULT...
THANKS A LOT, JULIA.
IT DOESN'T MATTER THOUGH. NO ONE CAN OPEN IT!
THE VAULT'S ON A TIMER. IT WON'T UNLOCK UNTIL THE DELIVERY TOMORROW MORNING.
JULIA... IS THAT TRUE?
YES.
NO!
MR. MANGOLD'S LYING. HE CAN OPEN IT.
JESUS CHRIST, JULIA! FOR GOD'S SAKE, HE'S POINTING A FREAKING FINGER AT YOUR EMPTY HEAD!
WHEN THIS IS ALL OVER, YOU ARE FIRED!
WHAT? NO! NO, PLEASE, MR. MANGOLD! I NEED THIS JOB!
THEN YOU SHOULD'VE KEPT YOUR FAT MOUTH SHUT!
I'VE NEVER LIKED YOU. YOU TALK TO THE CUSTOMERS TOO MUCH. YOU COME IN LATE, YOU LEAVE EARLY!
HE'S A RETARD! LIKE HIS MOTHER!
YOU KNOW MY SON HAS NEEDS!
AND YOU'RE A BORE TO LOOK AT!
OH, THAT'S QUITE ENOUGH.

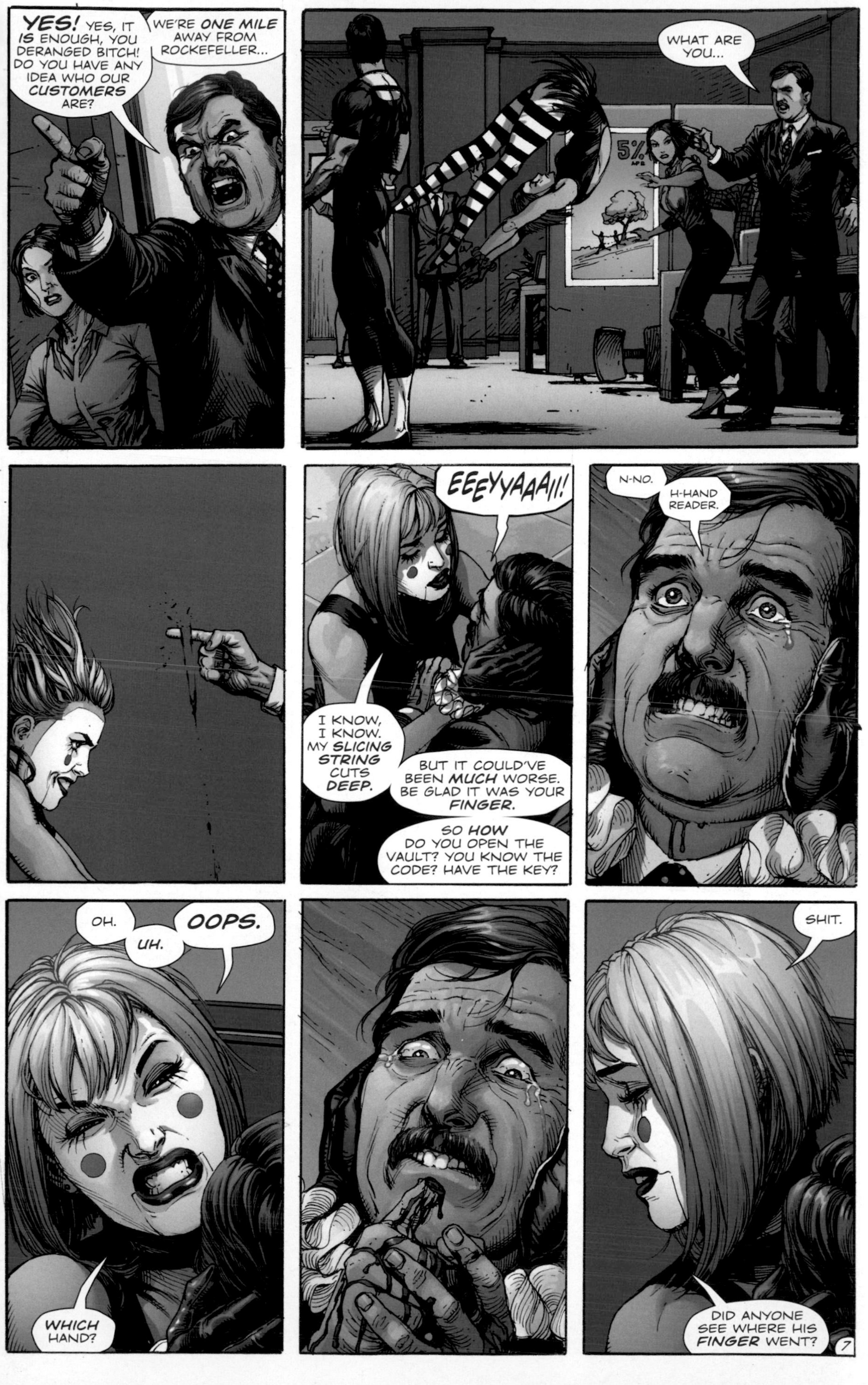
YES! YES, IT IS ENOUGH, YOU DERANGED BITCH! DO YOU HAVE ANY IDEA WHO OUR CUSTOMERS ARE?
WE'RE ONE MILE AWAY FROM ROCKEFELLER...
WHAT ARE YOU...
5%
EEEYYAAAII!
I KNOW, I KNOW. MY SLICING STRING CUTS DEEP.
BUT IT COULD'VE BEEN MUCH WORSE. BE GLAD IT WAS YOUR FINGER.
SO HOW DO YOU OPEN THE VAULT? YOU KNOW THE CODE? HAVE THE KEY?
N-NO.
H-HAND READER.
OH.
UH.
OOPS.
WHICH HAND?
SHIT.
DID ANYONE SEE WHERE HIS FINGER WENT?

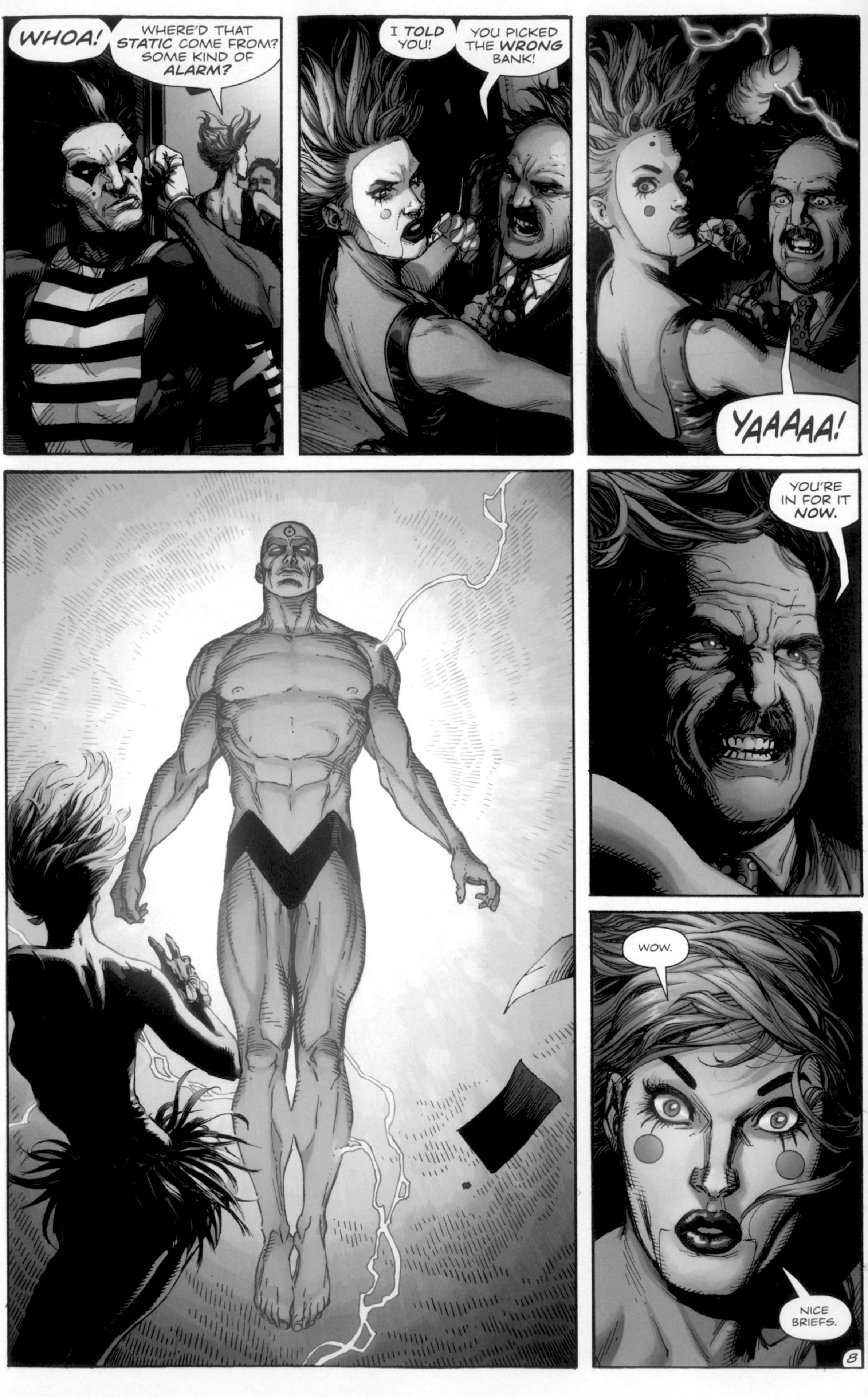

WHOA!
WHERE'D THAT STATIC COME FROM? SOME KIND OF ALARM?
I TOLD YOU!
YOU PICKED THE WRONG BANK!
YAAAAA!
YOU'RE IN FOR IT NOW.
WOW.
NICE BRIEFS.

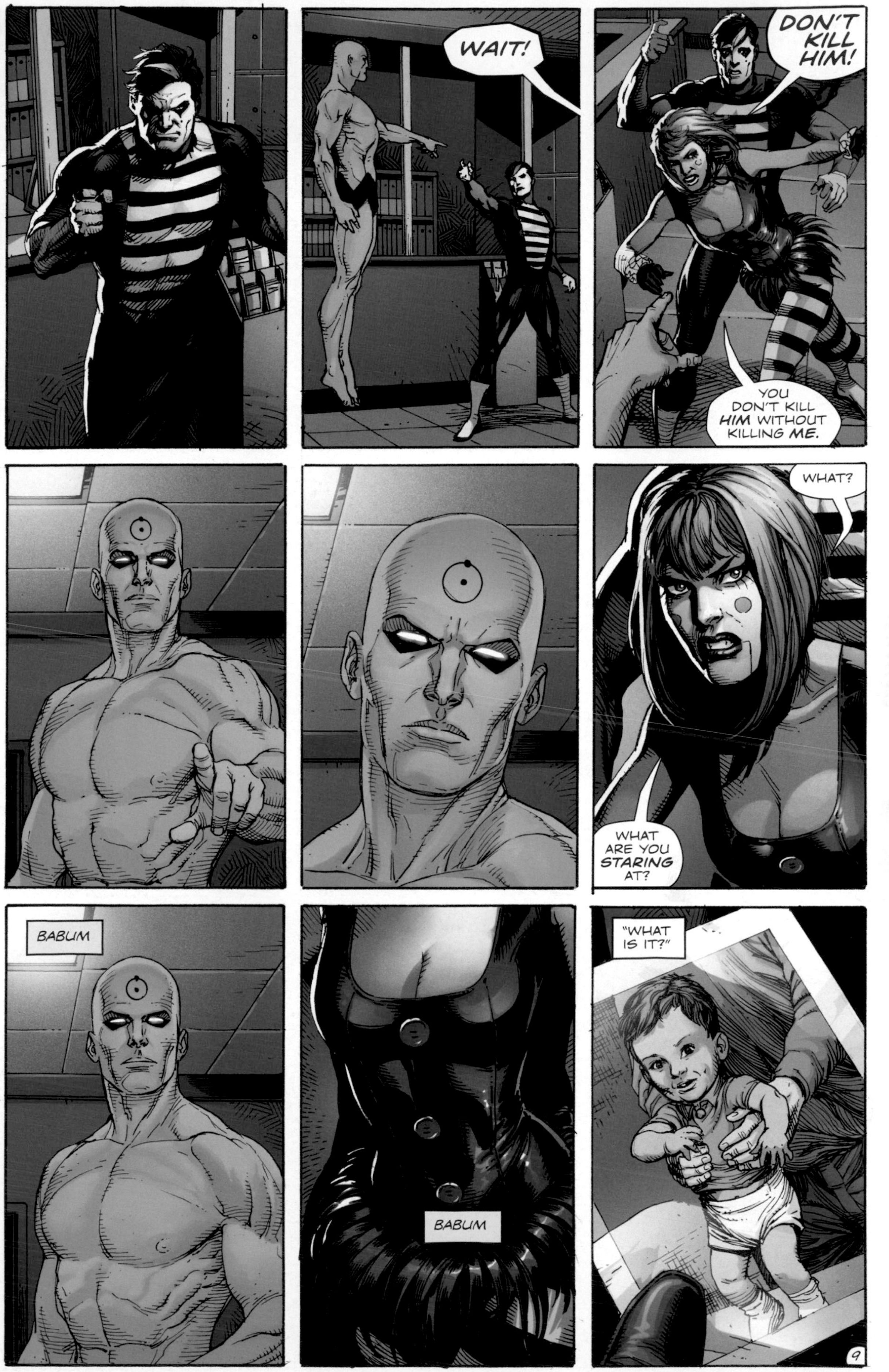
WAIT!
DON'T KILL HIM!
YOU DON'T KILL HIM WITHOUT KILLING ME.
WHAT?
WHAT ARE YOU STARING AT?
BABUM
BABUM
"WHAT IS IT?"

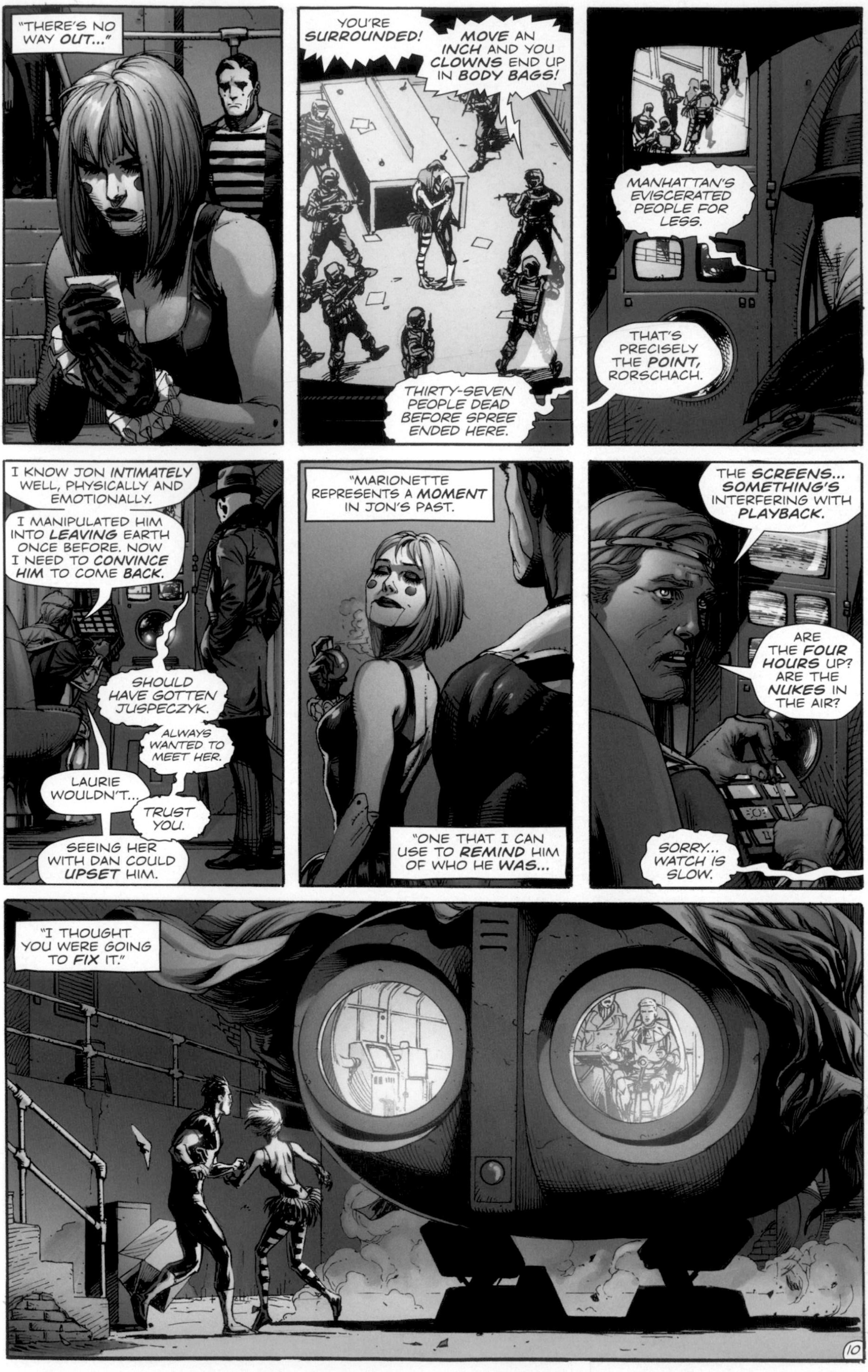
"THERE'S NO WAY OUT..."
YOU'RE SURROUNDED!
MOVE AN INCH AND YOU CLOWNS END UP IN BODY BAGS!
THIRTY-SEVEN PEOPLE DEAD BEFORE SPREE ENDED HERE.
MANHATTAN'S EVISCERATED PEOPLE FOR LESS.
THAT'S PRECISELY THE POINT, RORSCHACH.
I KNOW JON INTIMATELY WELL, PHYSICALLY AND EMOTIONALLY.
I MANIPULATED HIM INTO LEAVING EARTH ONCE BEFORE. NOW I NEED TO CONVINCE HIM TO COME BACK.
SHOULD HAVE GOTTEN JUSPECZYK.
ALWAYS WANTED TO MEET HER.
LAURIE WOULDN'T...
TRUST YOU.
SEEING HER WITH DAN COULD UPSET HIM.
"MARIONETTE REPRESENTS A MOMENT IN JON'S PAST.
"ONE THAT I CAN USE TO REMIND HIM OF WHO HE WAS...
THE SCREENS... SOMETHING'S INTERFERING WITH PLAYBACK.
ARE THE FOUR HOURS UP? ARE THE NUKES IN THE AIR?
SORRY... WATCH IS SLOW.
"I THOUGHT YOU WERE GOING TO FIX IT."
10

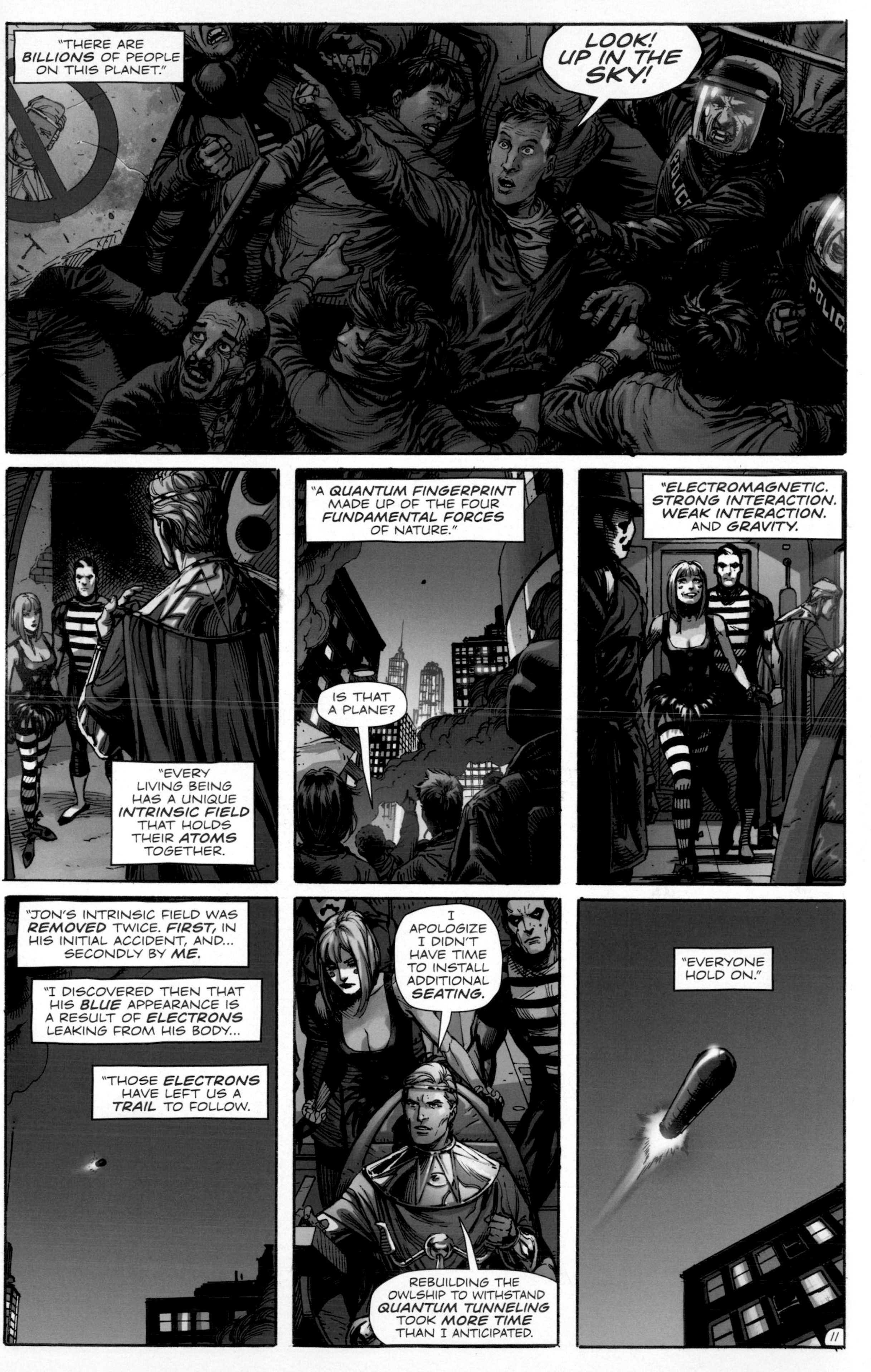
"THERE ARE BILLIONS OF PEOPLE ON THIS PLANET."
LOOK! UP IN THE SKY!
POLICE
"EVERY LIVING BEING HAS A UNIQUE INTRINSIC FIELD THAT HOLDS THEIR ATOMS TOGETHER.
"A QUANTUM FINGERPRINT MADE UP OF THE FOUR FUNDAMENTAL FORCES OF NATURE."
IS THAT A PLANE?
"ELECTROMAGNETIC. STRONG INTERACTION. WEAK INTERACTION. AND GRAVITY.
"JON'S INTRINSIC FIELD WAS REMOVED TWICE. FIRST, IN HIS INITIAL ACCIDENT, AND... SECONDLY BY ME.
"I DISCOVERED THEN THAT HIS BLUE APPEARANCE IS A RESULT OF ELECTRONS LEAKING FROM HIS BODY...
"THOSE ELECTRONS HAVE LEFT US A TRAIL TO FOLLOW.
I APOLOGIZE I DIDN'T HAVE TIME TO INSTALL ADDITIONAL SEATING.
REBUILDING THE OWLSHIP TO WITHSTAND QUANTUM TUNNELING TOOK MORE TIME THAN I ANTICIPATED.
"EVERYONE HOLD ON."

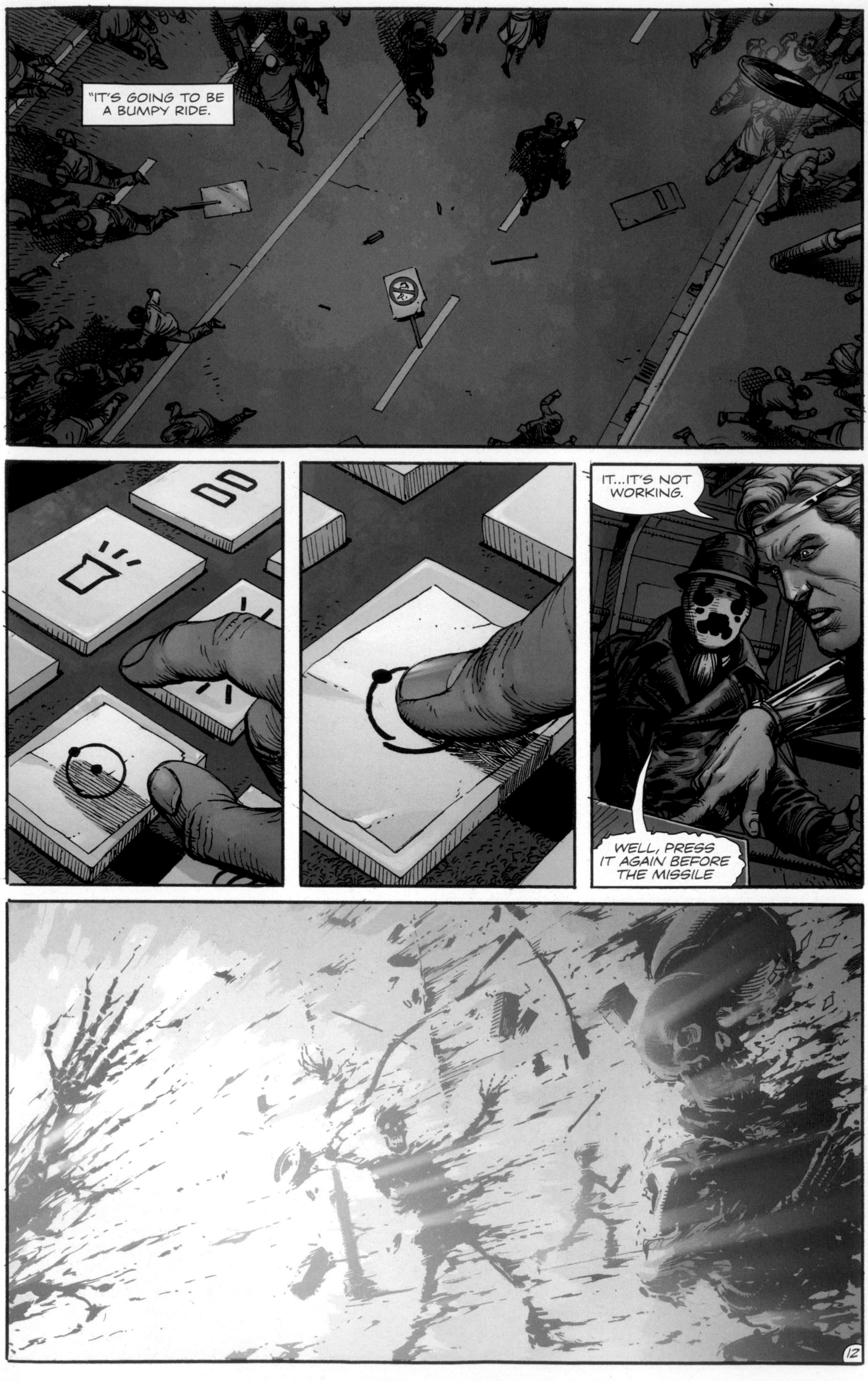
"IT'S GOING TO BE A BUMPY RIDE.
IT...IT'S NOT WORKING.
WELL, PRESS IT AGAIN BEFORE THE MISSILE
12

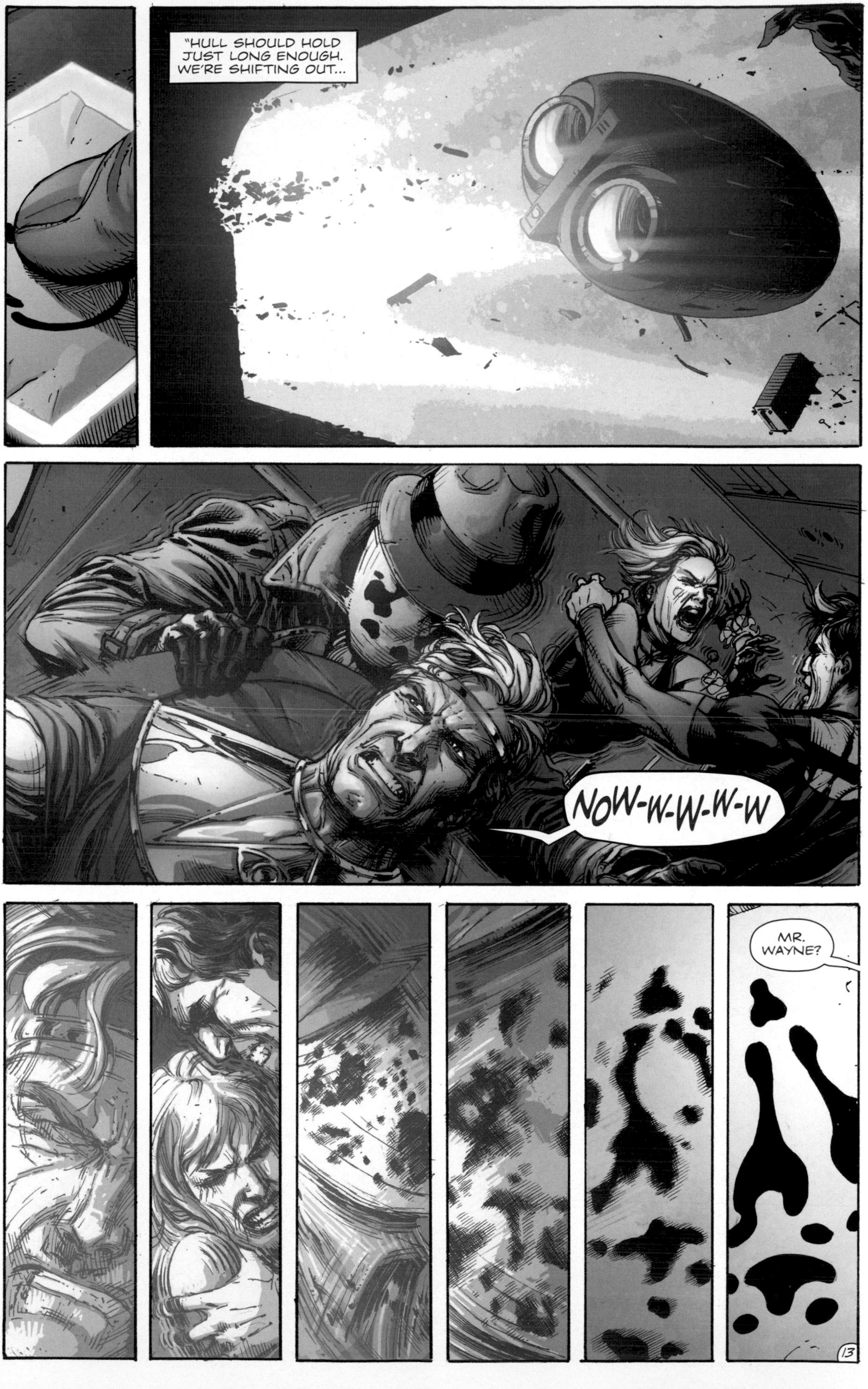
"HULL SHOULD HOLD JUST LONG ENOUGH. WE'RE SHIFTING OUT...
NOW-W-W-W-W
MR. WAYNE?

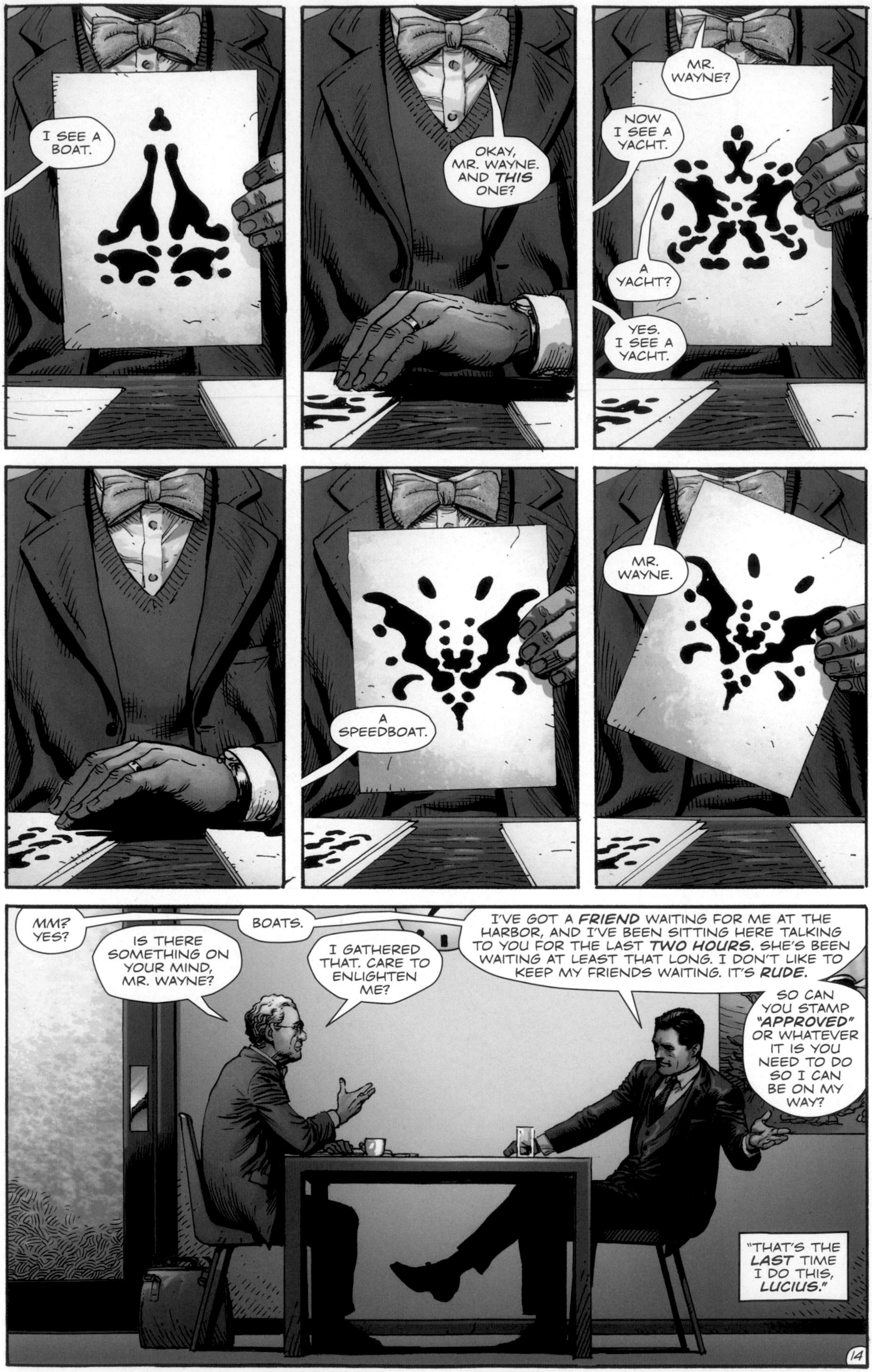
I SEE A BOAT.
OKAY, MR. WAYNE. AND THIS ONE?
MR. WAYNE?
NOW I SEE A YACHT.
A YACHT?
YES. I SEE A YACHT.
A SPEEDBOAT.
MR. WAYNE.
MM? YES?
BOATS.
IS THERE SOMETHING ON YOUR MIND, MR. WAYNE?
I GATHERED THAT. CARE TO ENLIGHTEN ME?
I'VE GOT A FRIEND WAITING FOR ME AT THE HARBOR, AND I'VE BEEN SITTING HERE TALKING TO YOU FOR THE LAST TWO HOURS. SHE'S BEEN WAITING AT LEAST THAT LONG. I DON'T LIKE TO KEEP MY FRIENDS WAITING. IT'S RUDE.
SO CAN YOU STAMP "APPROVED" OR WHATEVER IT IS YOU NEED TO DO SO I CAN BE ON MY WAY?
"THAT'S THE LAST TIME I DO THIS, LUCIUS."
14

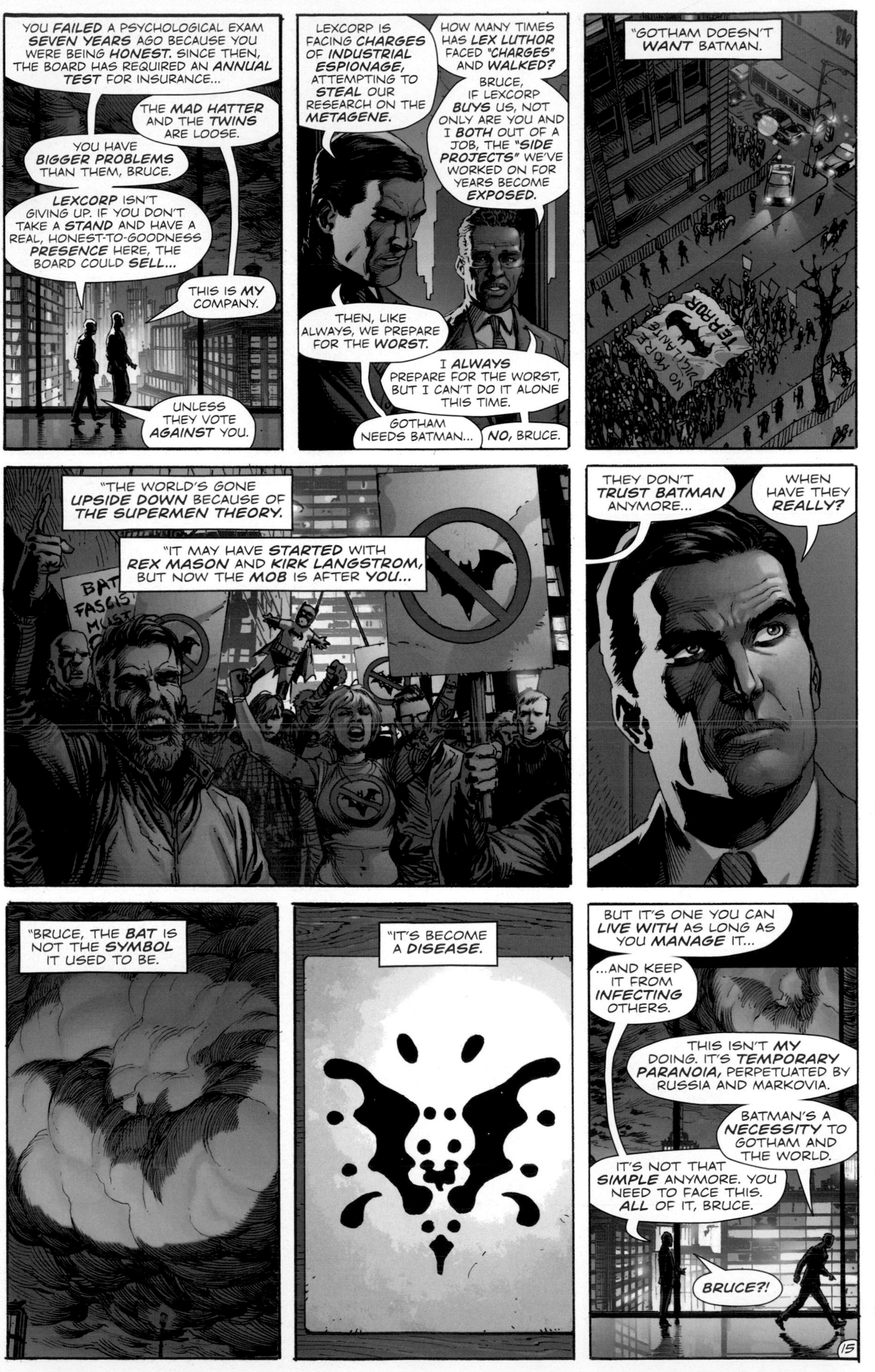

YOU FAILED A PSYCHOLOGICAL EXAM SEVEN YEARS AGO BECAUSE YOU WERE BEING HONEST. SINCE THEN, THE BOARD HAS REQUIRED AN ANNUAL TEST FOR INSURANCE...
THE MAD HATTER AND THE TWINS ARE LOOSE.
YOU HAVE BIGGER PROBLEMS THAN THEM, BRUCE.
LEXCORP ISN'T GIVING UP. IF YOU DON'T TAKE A STAND AND HAVE A REAL, HONEST-TO-GOODNESS PRESENCE HERE, THE BOARD COULD SELL...
THIS IS MY COMPANY.
UNLESS THEY VOTE AGAINST YOU.
LEXCORP IS FACING CHARGES OF INDUSTRIAL ESPIONAGE, ATTEMPTING TO STEAL OUR RESEARCH ON THE METAGENE.
HOW MANY TIMES HAS LEX LUTHOR FACED "CHARGES" AND WALKED?
BRUCE, IF LEXCORP BUYS US, NOT ONLY ARE YOU AND I BOTH OUT OF A JOB, THE "SIDE PROJECTS" WE'VE WORKED ON FOR YEARS BECOME EXPOSED.
THEN, LIKE ALWAYS, WE PREPARE FOR THE WORST.
I ALWAYS PREPARE FOR THE WORST, BUT I CAN'T DO IT ALONE THIS TIME.
GOTHAM NEEDS BATMAN...
NO, BRUCE.
"GOTHAM DOESN'T WANT BATMAN.
NO MORE VIGILANTE TERROR
"THE WORLD'S GONE UPSIDE DOWN BECAUSE OF THE SUPERMEN THEORY.
"IT MAY HAVE STARTED WITH REX MASON AND KIRK LANGSTROM, BUT NOW THE MOB IS AFTER YOU...
BAT FASCIST MUST
THEY DON'T TRUST BATMAN ANYMORE...
WHEN HAVE THEY REALLY?
"BRUCE, THE BAT IS NOT THE SYMBOL IT USED TO BE.
"IT'S BECOME A DISEASE.
BUT IT'S ONE YOU CAN LIVE WITH AS LONG AS YOU MANAGE IT...
...AND KEEP IT FROM INFECTING OTHERS.
THIS ISN'T MY DOING. IT'S TEMPORARY PARANOIA, PERPETUATED BY RUSSIA AND MARKOVIA.
BATMAN'S A NECESSITY TO GOTHAM AND THE WORLD.
IT'S NOT THAT SIMPLE ANYMORE. YOU NEED TO FACE THIS. ALL OF IT, BRUCE.
BRUCE?!

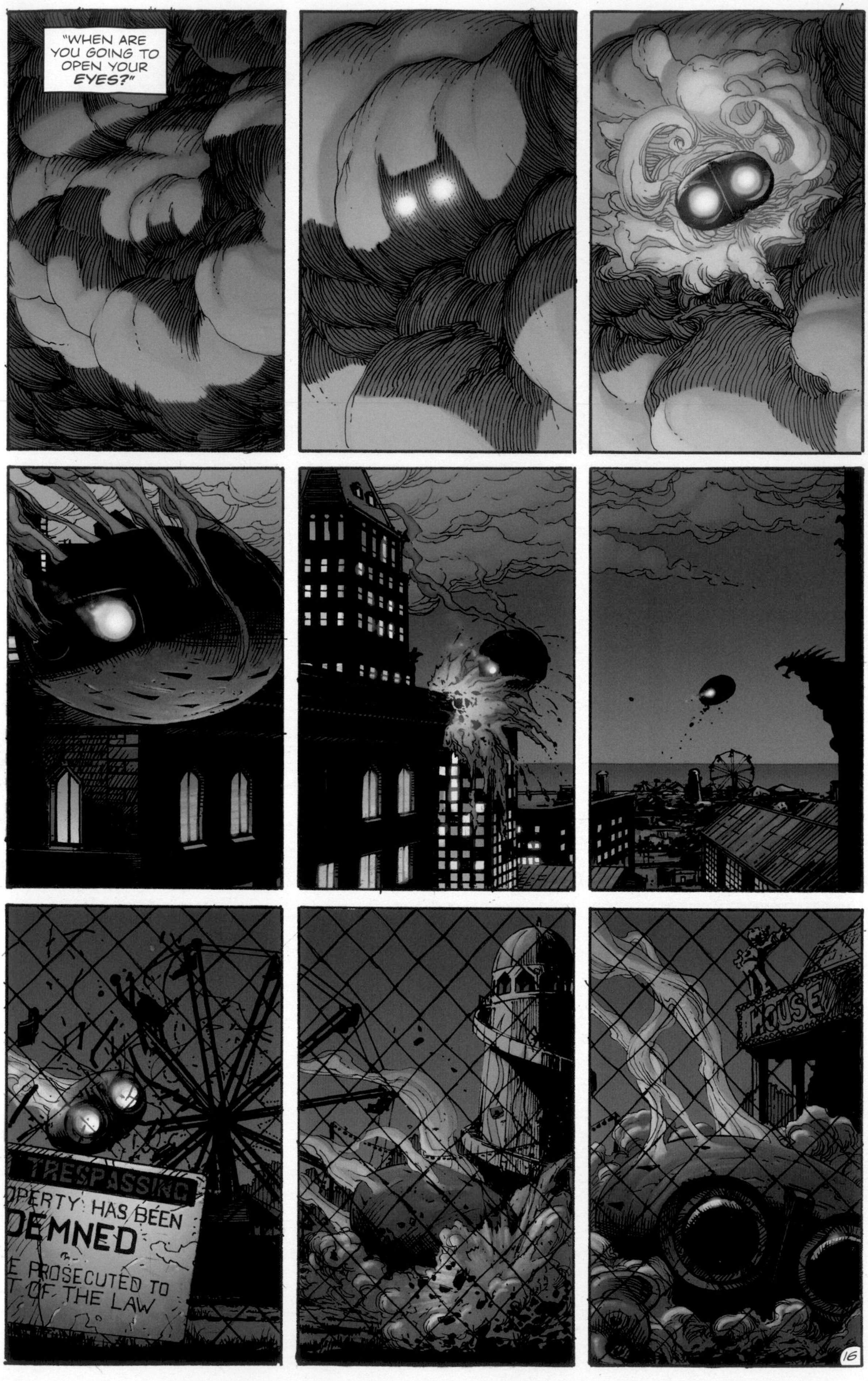
"WHEN ARE YOU GOING TO OPEN YOUR *EYES?*"
TRESPASSING
OPERTY HAS BEEN
DEMNED
E PROSECUTED TO
T OF THE LAW
HOUSE

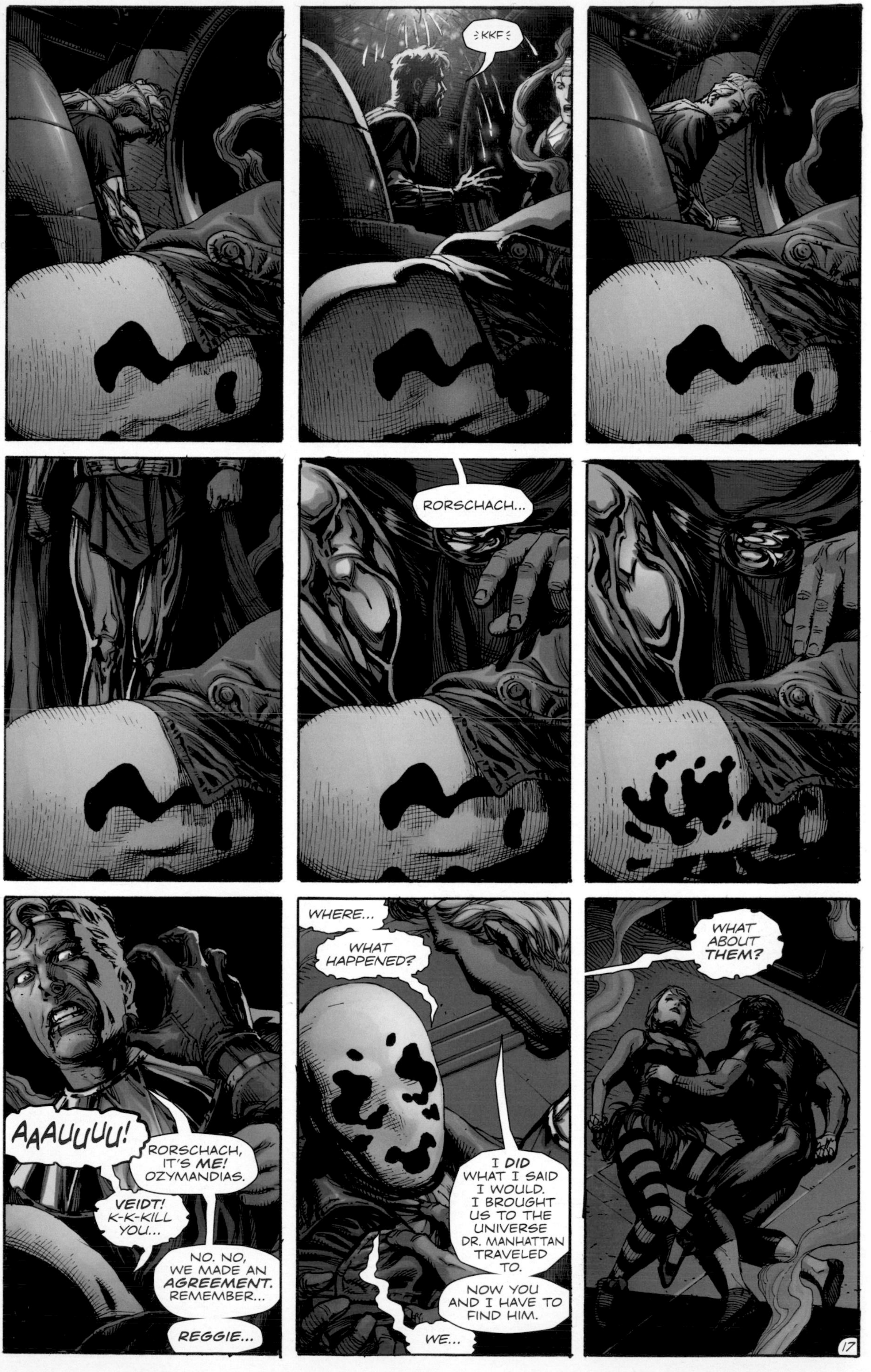
KKF
RORSCHACH...
AAAUUUU!
RORSCHACH, IT'S ME! OZYMANDIAS.
VEIDT! K-K-KILL YOU...
NO. NO, WE MADE AN AGREEMENT. REMEMBER...
REGGIE...
WHERE...
WHAT HAPPENED?
I DID WHAT I SAID I WOULD. I BROUGHT US TO THE UNIVERSE DR. MANHATTAN TRAVELED TO.
NOW YOU AND I HAVE TO FIND HIM.
WE...
WHAT ABOUT THEM?

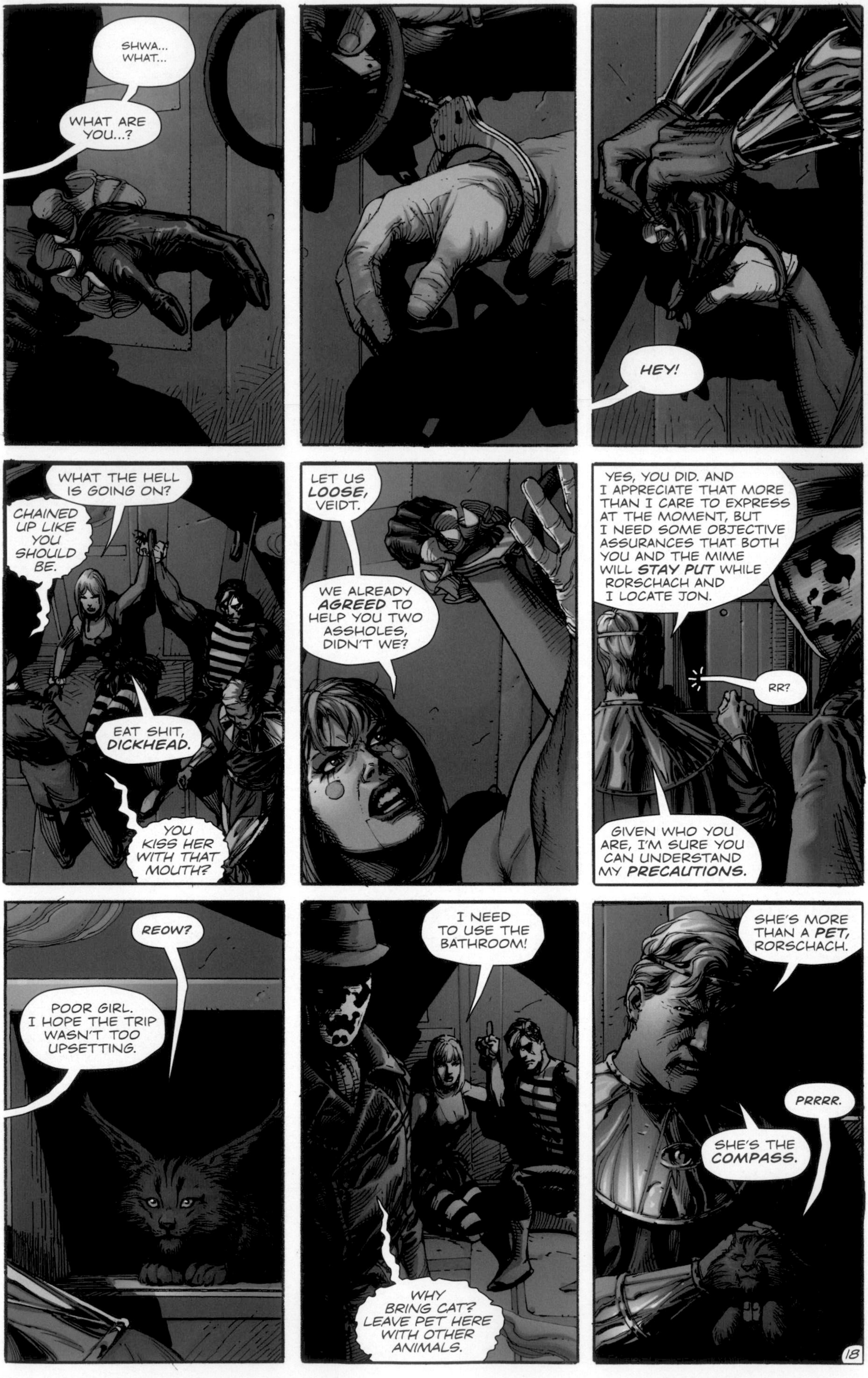
SHWA... WHAT...
WHAT ARE YOU...?
HEY!
WHAT THE HELL IS GOING ON?
CHAINED UP LIKE YOU SHOULD BE.
EAT SHIT, DICKHEAD.
YOU KISS HER WITH THAT MOUTH?
LET US LOOSE, VEIDT.
WE ALREADY AGREED TO HELP YOU TWO ASSHOLES, DIDN'T WE?
YES, YOU DID. AND I APPRECIATE THAT MORE THAN I CARE TO EXPRESS AT THE MOMENT, BUT I NEED SOME OBJECTIVE ASSURANCES THAT BOTH YOU AND THE MIME WILL STAY PUT WHILE RORSCHACH AND I LOCATE JON.
RR?
GIVEN WHO YOU ARE, I'M SURE YOU CAN UNDERSTAND MY PRECAUTIONS.
REOW?
POOR GIRL. I HOPE THE TRIP WASN'T TOO UPSETTING.
I NEED TO USE THE BATHROOM!
WHY BRING CAT? LEAVE PET HERE WITH OTHER ANIMALS.
SHE'S MORE THAN A PET, RORSCHACH.
PRRRR.
SHE'S THE COMPASS.

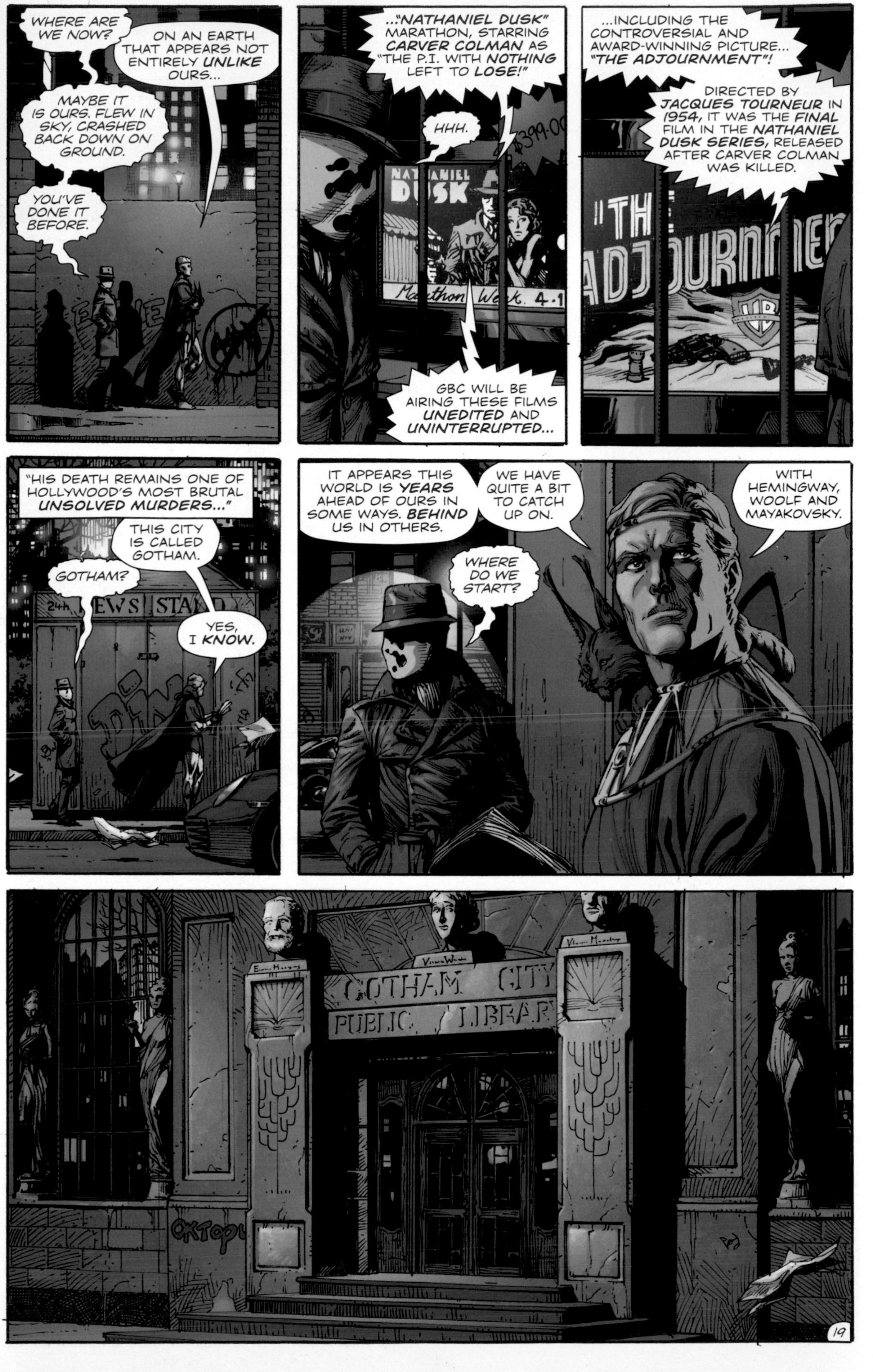

WHERE ARE WE NOW?
ON AN EARTH THAT APPEARS NOT ENTIRELY UNLIKE OURS...
MAYBE IT IS OURS. FLEW IN SKY, CRASHED BACK DOWN ON GROUND.
YOU'VE DONE IT BEFORE.
...“NATHANIEL DUSK” MARATHON, STARRING CARVER COLMAN AS “THE P.I. WITH NOTHING LEFT TO LOSE!”
HHH.
NATHANIEL DUSK
Marathon Week 4-1
GBC WILL BE AIRING THESE FILMS UNEDITED AND UNINTERRUPTED...
...INCLUDING THE CONTROVERSIAL AND AWARD-WINNING PICTURE... “THE ADJOURNMENT”!
DIRECTED BY JACQUES TOURNEUR IN 1954, IT WAS THE FINAL FILM IN THE NATHANIEL DUSK SERIES, RELEASED AFTER CARVER COLMAN WAS KILLED.
“HIS DEATH REMAINS ONE OF HOLLYWOOD'S MOST BRUTAL UNSOLVED MURDERS...”
THIS CITY IS CALLED GOTHAM.
GOTHAM?
YES, I KNOW.
24h
IT APPEARS THIS WORLD IS YEARS AHEAD OF OURS IN SOME WAYS. BEHIND US IN OTHERS.
WE HAVE QUITE A BIT TO CATCH UP ON.
WHERE DO WE START?
WITH HEMINGWAY, WOOLF AND MAYAKOVSKY.
GOTHAM CITY PUBLIC LIBRARY

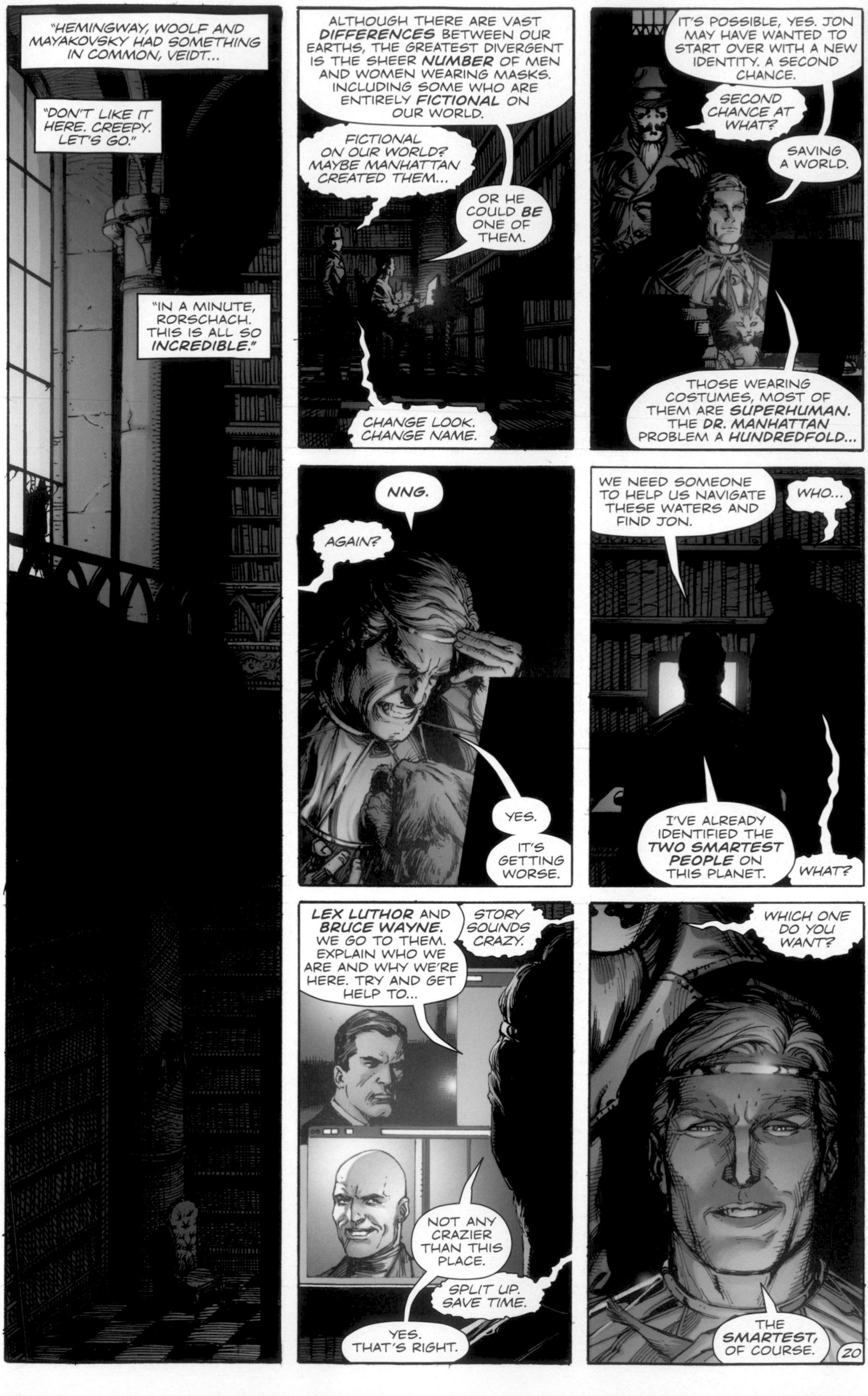
"HEMINGWAY, WOOLF AND MAYAKOVSKY HAD SOMETHING IN COMMON, VEIDT...
"DON'T LIKE IT HERE. CREEPY. LET'S GO."
"IN A MINUTE, RORSCHACH. THIS IS ALL SO INCREDIBLE."
ALTHOUGH THERE ARE VAST DIFFERENCES BETWEEN OUR EARTHS, THE GREATEST DIVERGENT IS THE SHEER NUMBER OF MEN AND WOMEN WEARING MASKS. INCLUDING SOME WHO ARE ENTIRELY FICTIONAL ON OUR WORLD.
FICTIONAL ON OUR WORLD? MAYBE MANHATTAN CREATED THEM...
OR HE COULD BE ONE OF THEM.
CHANGE LOOK. CHANGE NAME.
IT'S POSSIBLE, YES. JON MAY HAVE WANTED TO START OVER WITH A NEW IDENTITY. A SECOND CHANCE.
SECOND CHANCE AT WHAT?
SAVING A WORLD.
THOSE WEARING COSTUMES, MOST OF THEM ARE SUPERHUMAN. THE DR. MANHATTAN PROBLEM A HUNDREDFOLD...
NNG.
AGAIN?
YES.
IT'S GETTING WORSE.
WE NEED SOMEONE TO HELP US NAVIGATE THESE WATERS AND FIND JON.
WHO...
I'VE ALREADY IDENTIFIED THE TWO SMARTEST PEOPLE ON THIS PLANET.
WHAT?
LEX LUTHOR AND BRUCE WAYNE. WE GO TO THEM. EXPLAIN WHO WE ARE AND WHY WE'RE HERE. TRY AND GET HELP TO...
STORY SOUNDS CRAZY.
NOT ANY CRAZIER THAN THIS PLACE.
SPLIT UP. SAVE TIME.
YES. THAT'S RIGHT.
WHICH ONE DO YOU WANT?
THE SMARTEST, OF COURSE.
20

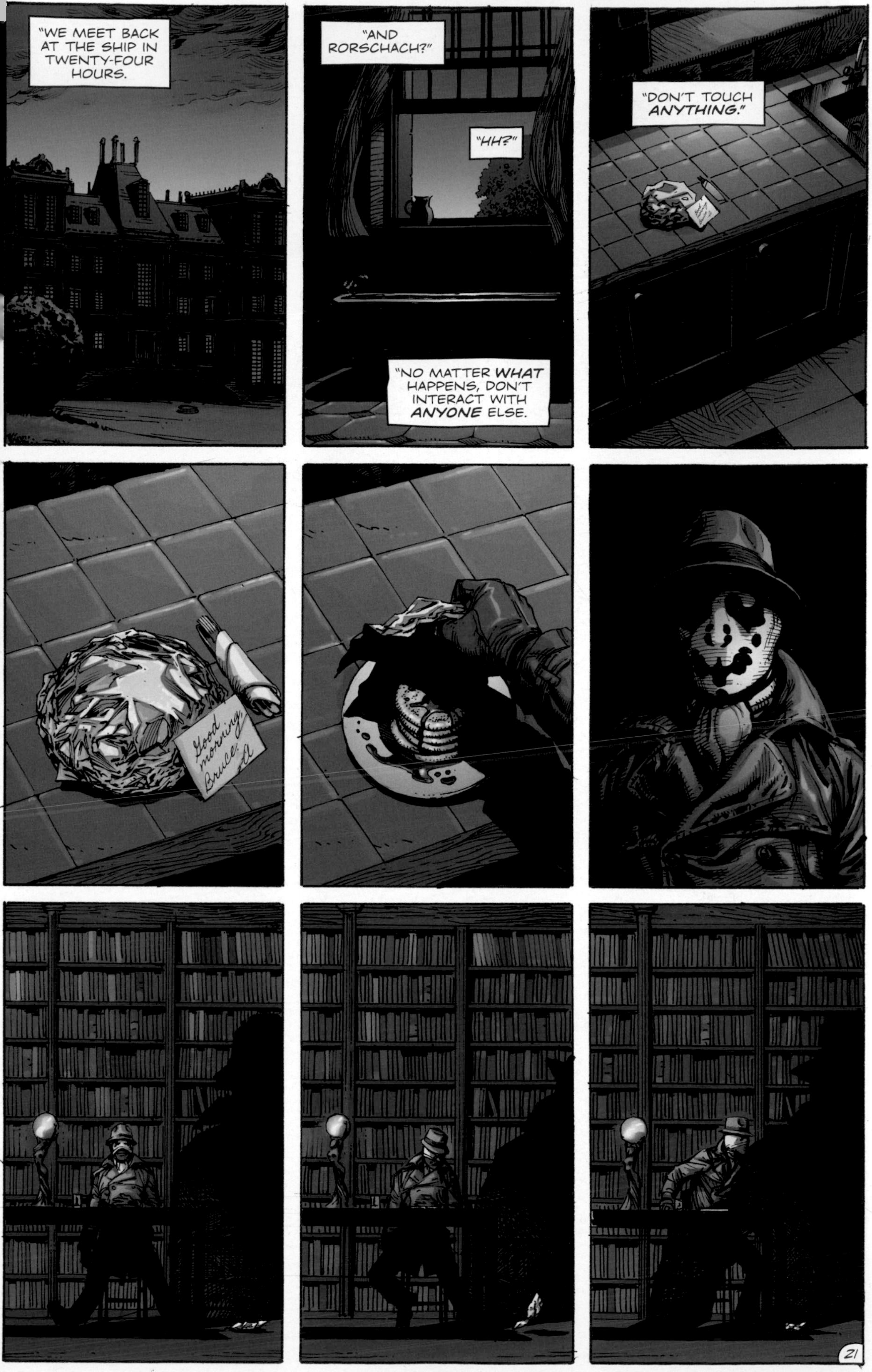
"WE MEET BACK AT THE SHIP IN TWENTY-FOUR HOURS.
"AND RORSCHACH?"
"HH?"
"NO MATTER WHAT HAPPENS, DON'T INTERACT WITH ANYONE ELSE.
"DON'T TOUCH ANYTHING."
Good morning, Bruce. -A

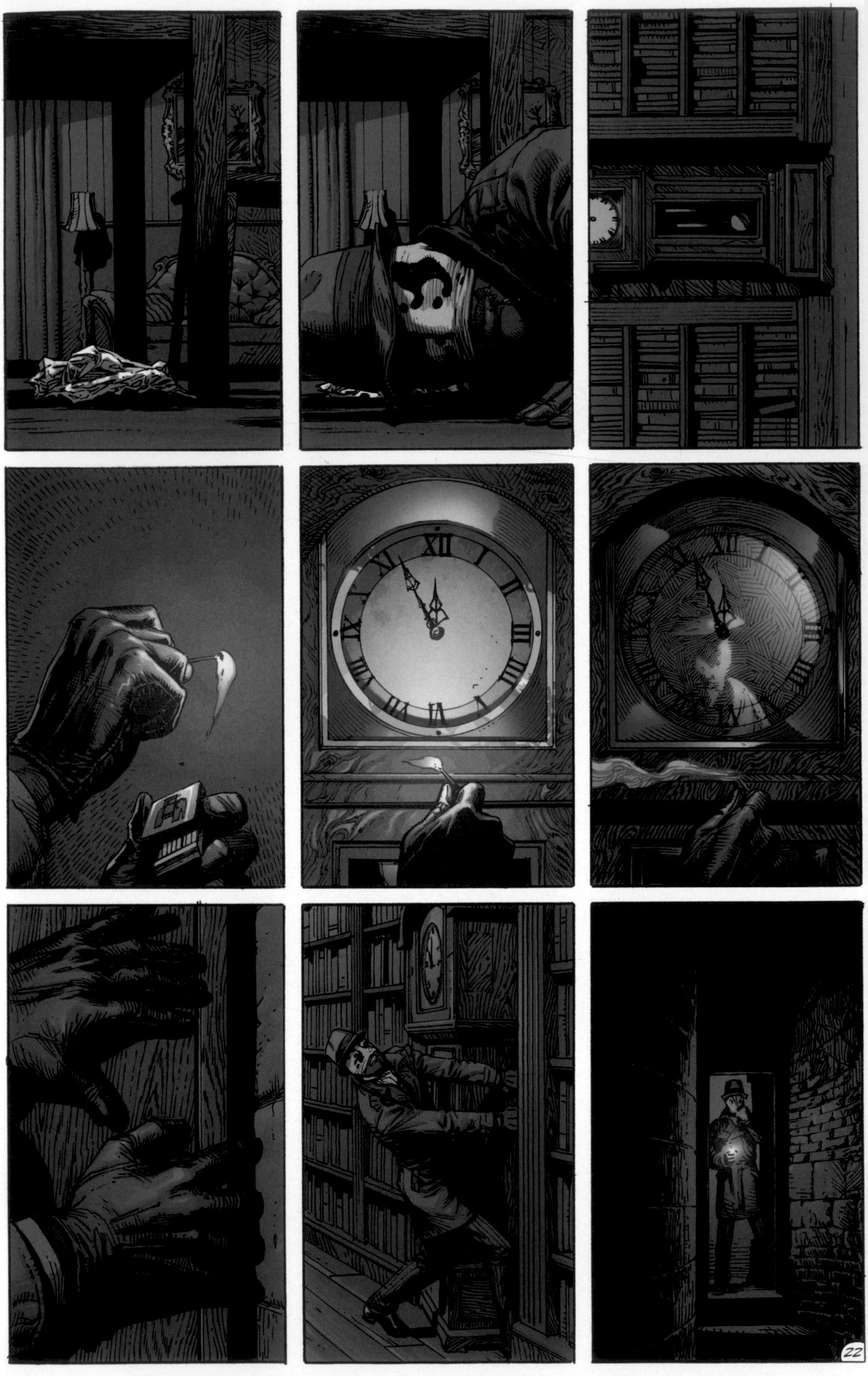

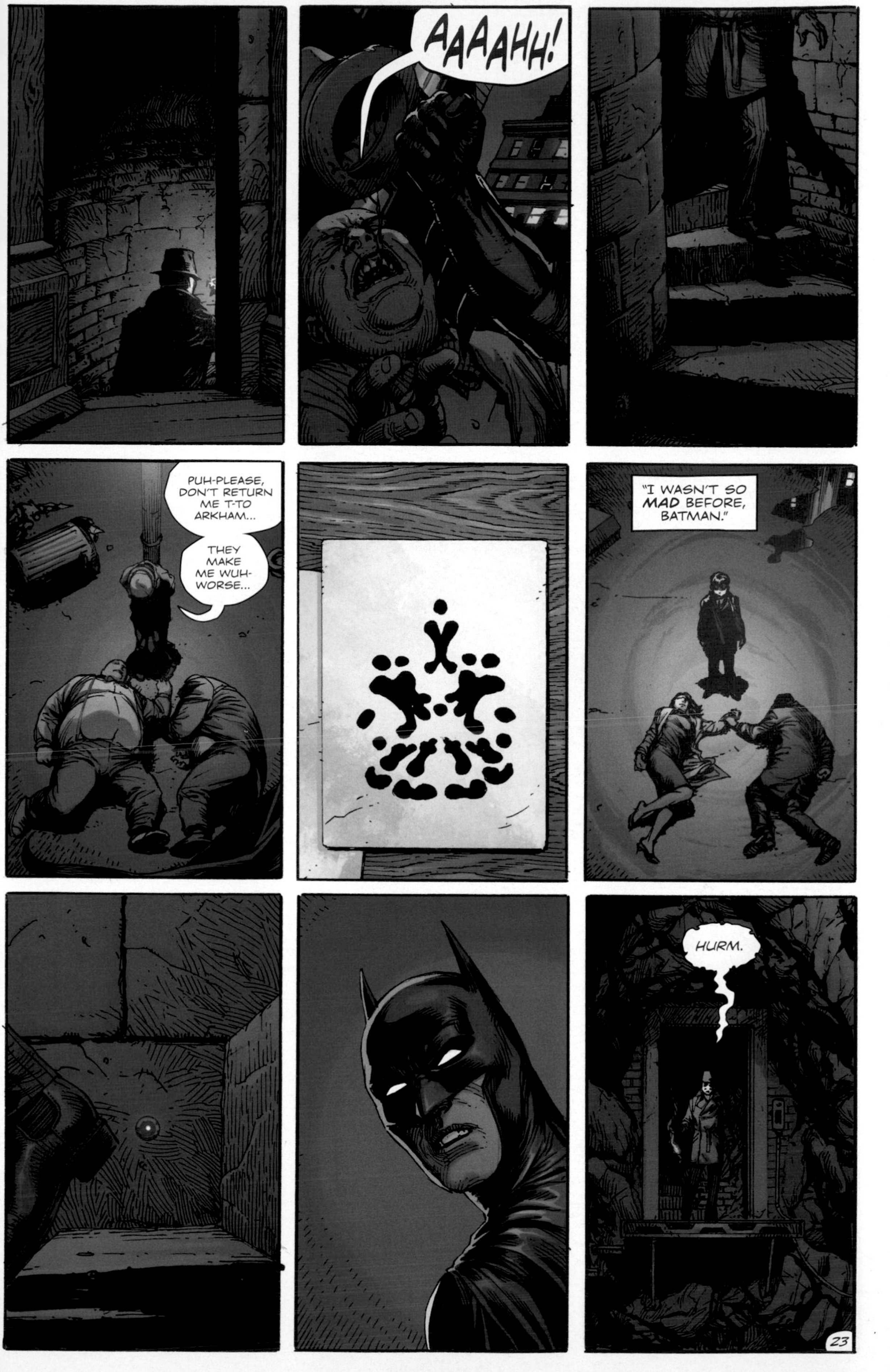
AAAAHH!
PUH-PLEASE, DON'T RETURN ME T-TO ARKHAM...
THEY MAKE ME WUH-WORSE...
"I WASN'T SO MAD BEFORE, BATMAN."
HURM.

YOU'RE ALL FIRED.

EXCORP LABS
...RIZED PERSONNEL ONLY
...LL BE PROSECUTED

GO PISSING

I WILL *END* THIS WORLD BEFORE I LET WAYNE *WIN.*

EXCUSE ME...

HOW DID YOU GET IN HERE?

I LET MYSELF IN.

I ADMIRE YOUR TASTE, MR. LUTHOR.

AND YOUR ASPIRATIONS.

WHO ARE YOU?

I'M THE *SMARTEST MAN* ON MY EARTH.

AND YOU'RE THE *SMARTEST MAN* ON YOURS.

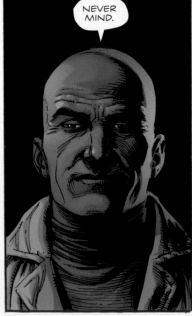

NEVER MIND.

SECURITY WILL SHOW YOU OUT BEFORE I *TERMINATE* THEM FOR ALLOWING YOU IN.

IF I COULD GET A MOMENT OF YOUR TIME...

OH, YOU *HAVE* IT. FEEL FREE TO APPEASE MY CURIOSITY UNTIL THEY GET HERE, "SMARTEST MAN."

24

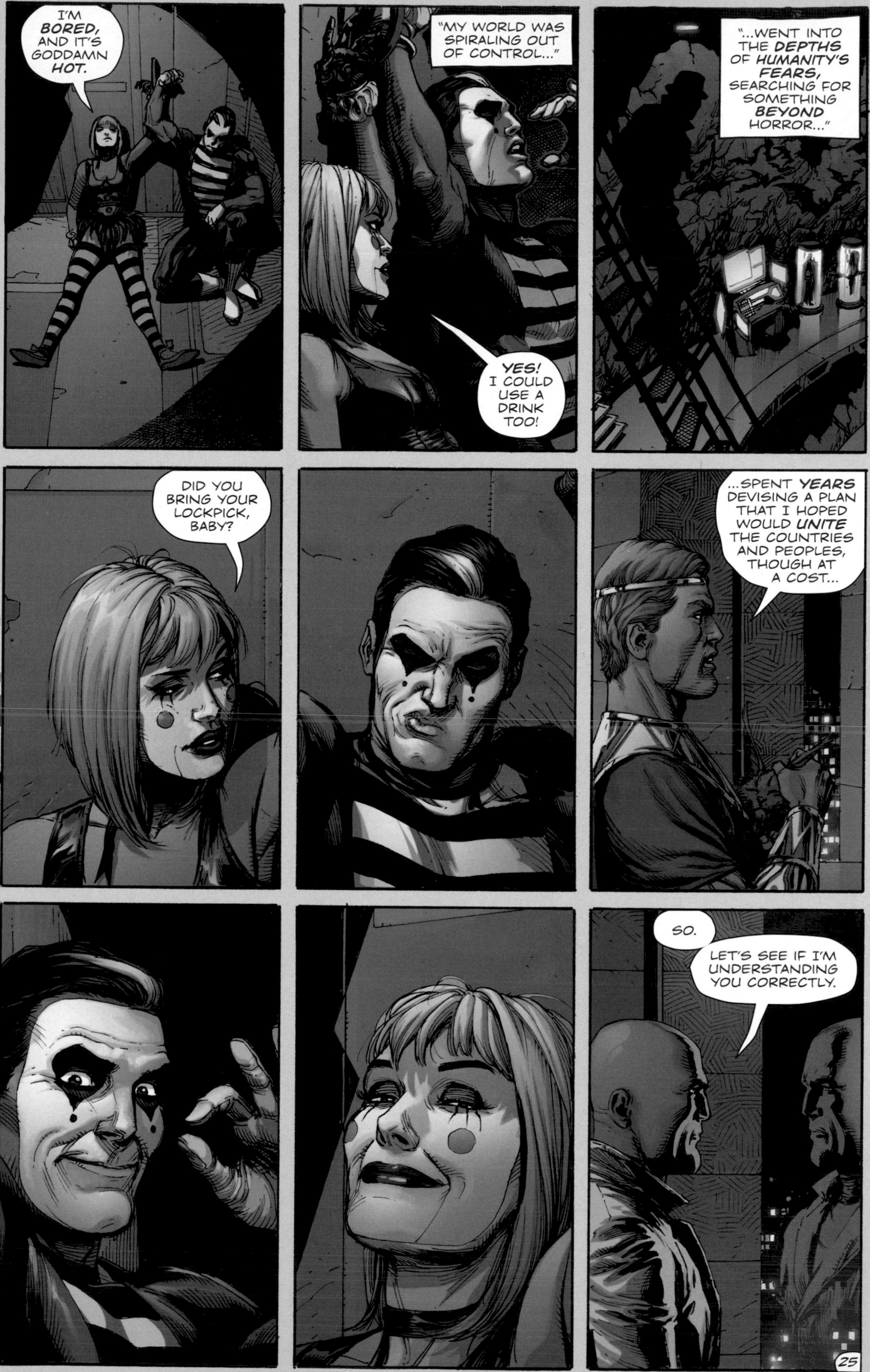
I'M **BORED,** AND IT'S GODDAMN **HOT.**
"MY WORLD WAS SPIRALING OUT OF CONTROL..."
YES! I COULD USE A DRINK TOO!
"...WENT INTO THE **DEPTHS** OF **HUMANITY'S FEARS,** SEARCHING FOR SOMETHING **BEYOND** HORROR..."
DID YOU BRING YOUR LOCKPICK, BABY?
...SPENT **YEARS** DEVISING A PLAN THAT I HOPED WOULD **UNITE** THE COUNTRIES AND PEOPLES, THOUGH AT A COST...
SO.
LET'S SEE IF I'M UNDERSTANDING YOU CORRECTLY.

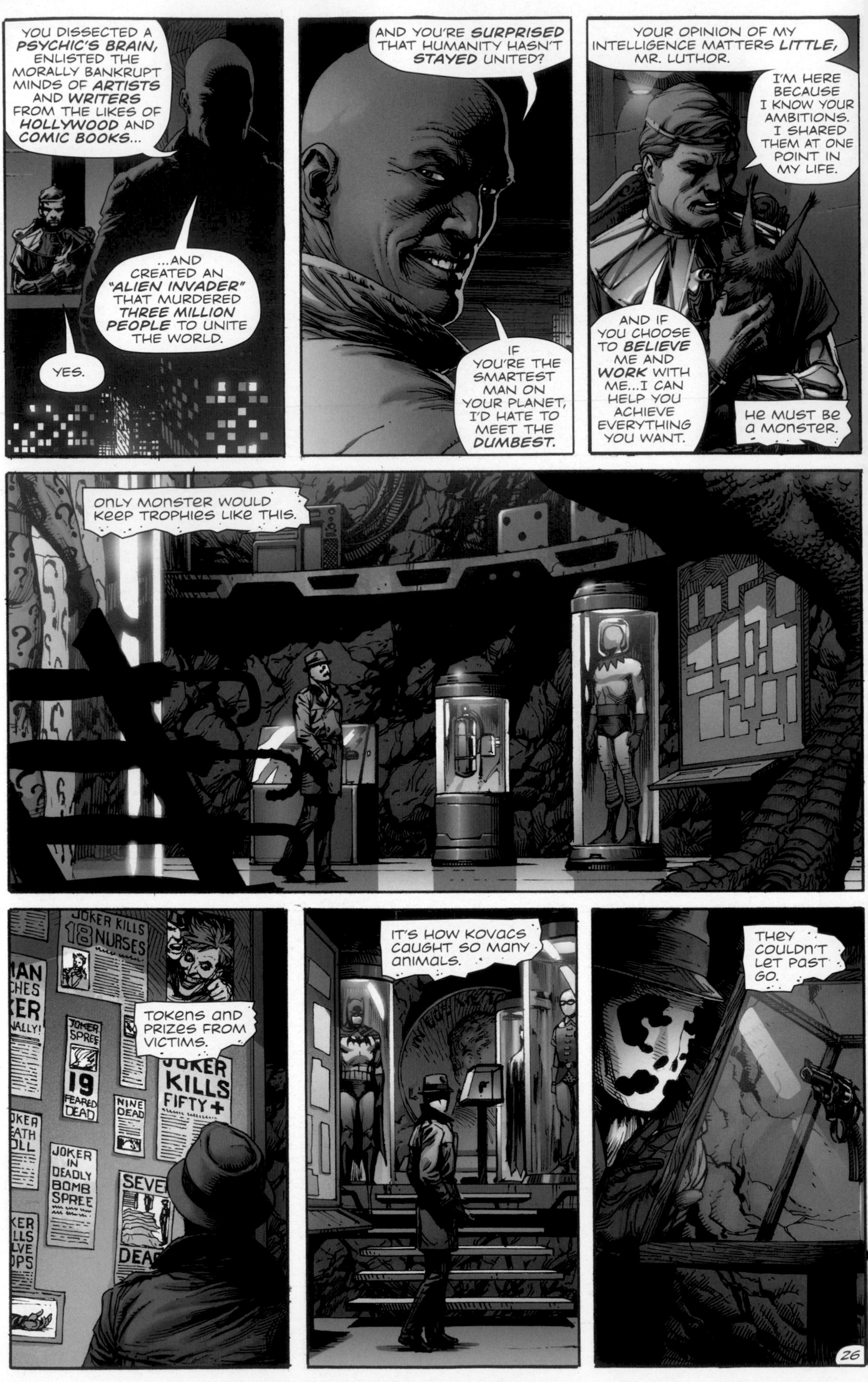

YOU DISSECTED A PSYCHIC'S BRAIN, ENLISTED THE MORALLY BANKRUPT MINDS OF ARTISTS AND WRITERS FROM THE LIKES OF HOLLYWOOD AND COMIC BOOKS...
...AND CREATED AN "ALIEN INVADER" THAT MURDERED THREE MILLION PEOPLE TO UNITE THE WORLD.
YES.
AND YOU'RE SURPRISED THAT HUMANITY HASN'T STAYED UNITED?
IF YOU'RE THE SMARTEST MAN ON YOUR PLANET, I'D HATE TO MEET THE DUMBEST.
YOUR OPINION OF MY INTELLIGENCE MATTERS LITTLE, MR. LUTHOR.
I'M HERE BECAUSE I KNOW YOUR AMBITIONS. I SHARED THEM AT ONE POINT IN MY LIFE.
AND IF YOU CHOOSE TO BELIEVE ME AND WORK WITH ME...I CAN HELP YOU ACHIEVE EVERYTHING YOU WANT.
He must be a monster.
Only monster would keep trophies like this.
JOKER KILLS 18 NURSES
JOKER SPREE
19 FEARED DEAD
NINE DEAD
JOKER KILLS FIFTY+
JOKER IN DEADLY BOMB SPREE
Tokens and prizes from victims.
It's how Kovacs caught so many animals.
They couldn't let past go.

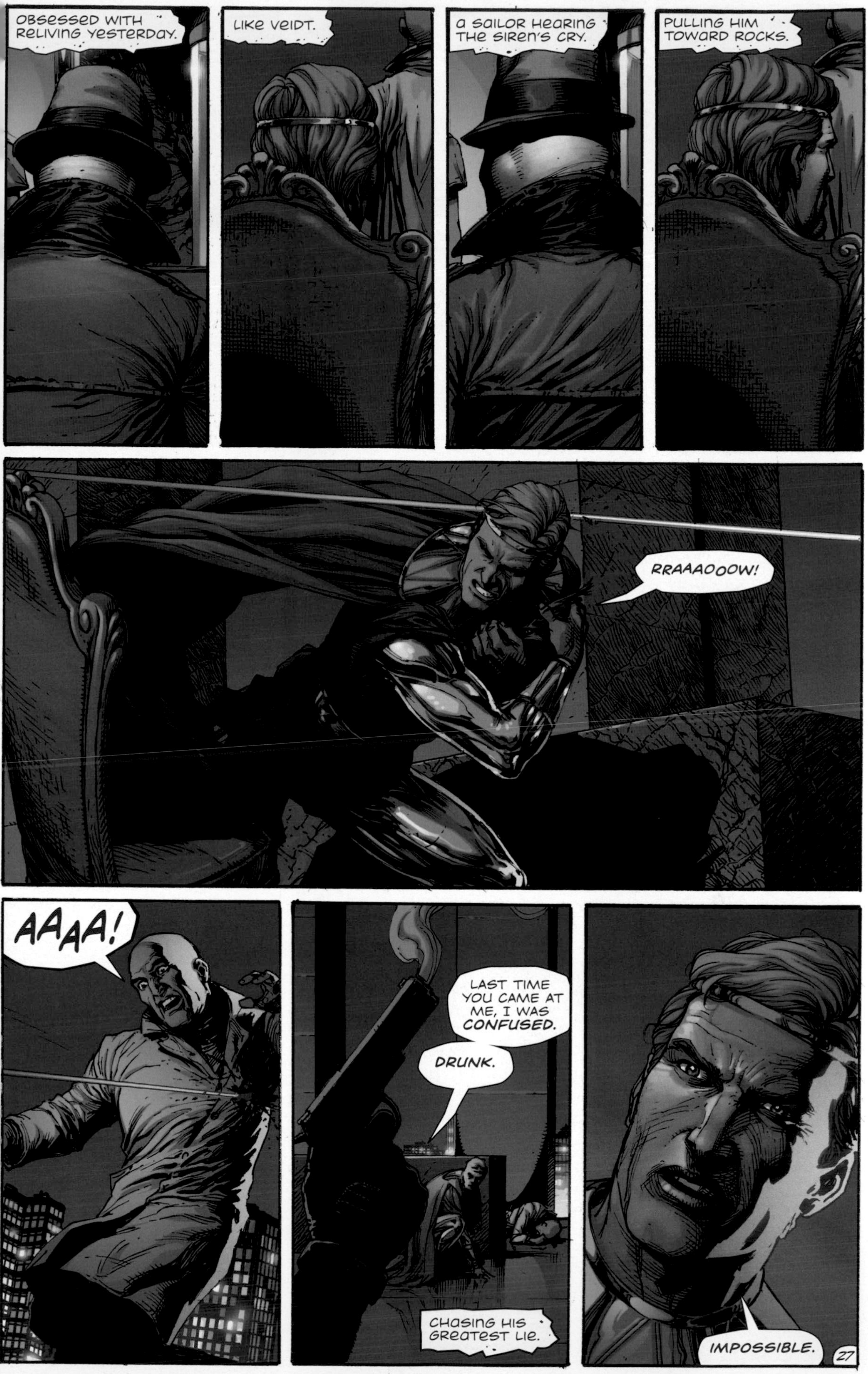
OBSESSED WITH RELIVING YESTERDAY.
LIKE VEIDT.
A SAILOR HEARING THE SIREN'S CRY.
PULLING HIM TOWARD ROCKS.
RRAAAOOOW!
AAAA!
LAST TIME YOU CAME AT ME, I WAS CONFUSED.
DRUNK.
CHASING HIS GREATEST LIE.
IMPOSSIBLE.
27

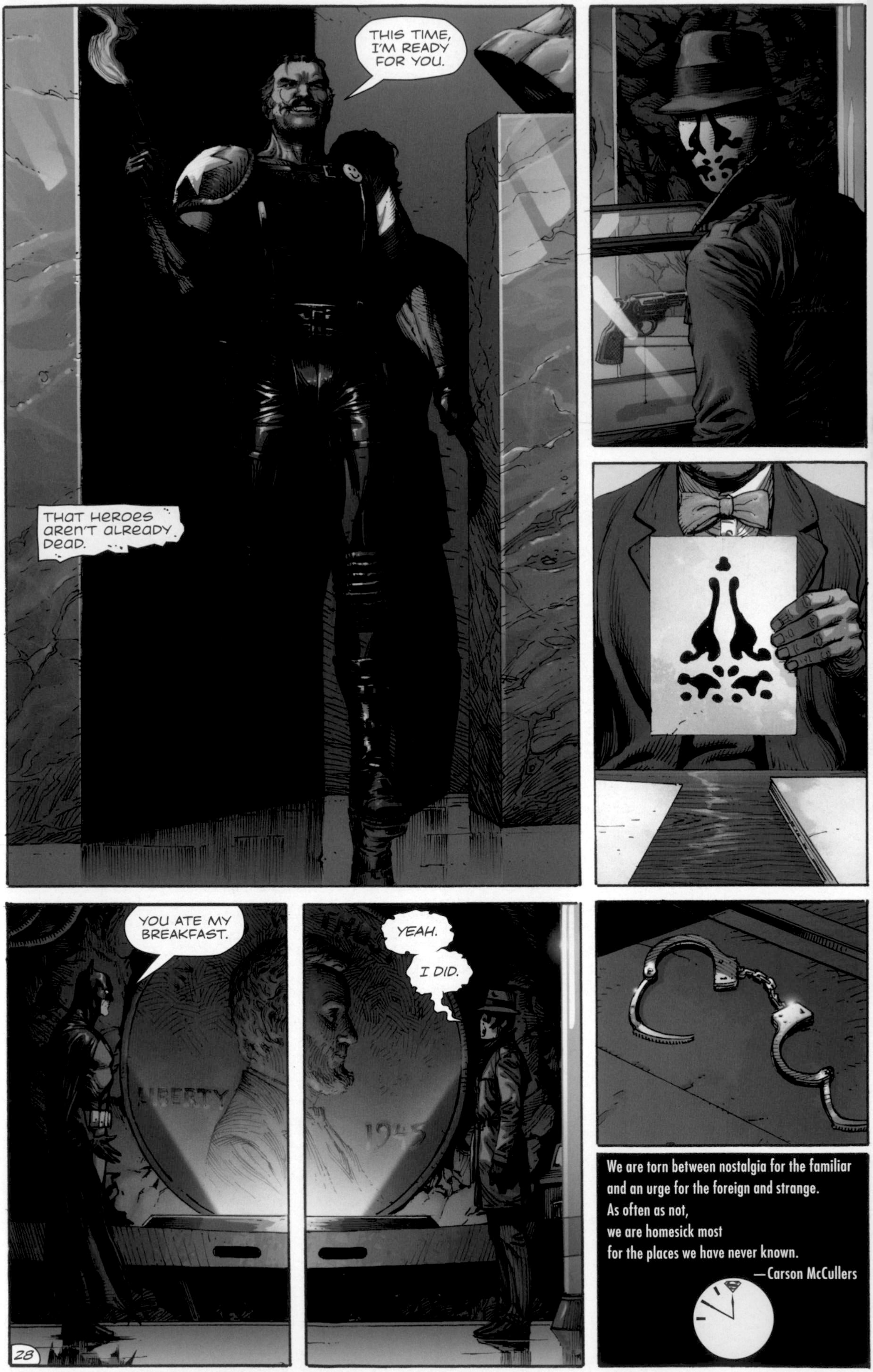
THIS TIME, I'M READY FOR YOU.
THAT HEROES AREN'T ALREADY DEAD.
YOU ATE MY BREAKFAST.
YEAH.
I DID.
LIBERTY
1945
We are torn between nostalgia for the familiar
and an urge for the foreign and strange.
As often as not,
we are homesick most
for the places we have never known.
—Carson McCullers

LexNet File Edit View History Window Help

www.thebulletin.press/2017/12/7/metahumannews/new-theory-on-concentration-of-metahumans/index

GCPL

theBulletin | Sign In | News | Sports | Weather | Shop | Earth | Travel | More | Search

NEWS

Home | Video | World | US & Canada | Business | Tech | Science | Stories | Entertainment & Arts | Health | More

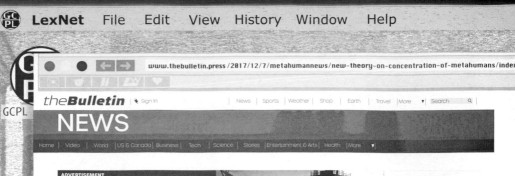

METAHUMAN NEWS

New Theory on Concentration of Metahumans in United States Raises Questions About Secret Origins

By Lowell Jeffries
Metahuman News Correspondent

December 7, 2017 – Metahuman News

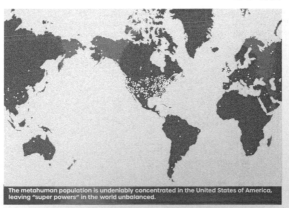

The metahuman population is undeniably concentrated in the United States of America, leaving "super powers" in the world unbalanced.

"The Supermen Theory" continues to be hotly debated as second metahuman's secret origin is tied to U.S. government.

The President continues to deny any government involvement in the secret origins of America's metahumans, calling "The Supermen Theory" and its implied accusations "outright lies" and "completely fictitious." Today these denials are once again under fire as another metahuman is revealed to have ties to the U.S. government, giving more credence to "The Supermen Theory."

"The Supermen Theory" began making the rounds six months ago when a Markovian geneticist, Dr. Helga Jace, led an international coalition of scientists looking to answer a question that has long confounded the world:

Why are the vast majority of the planet's metahumans American?

Most often referred to as "super-heroes" and "super-villains" by the general public who watch their exploits with both awe and fear, metahumans began appearing after Superman revealed himself to the world. Men, women and even children wielding a diverse range of superhuman abilities have since emerged across America at a rapid rate.

Superman's history has been well documented and generally accepted; the Man of Steel comes from another planet, the long-dead Krypton. However, the metahumans who followed Superman remain a mystery. The vast majority of them hide their true identities, a fact that has become more and more unsettling across the planet. "The Supermen Theory" suggests that the metahumans of America are, in truth, government sponsored

Top Stories

Multiple Arrests at LexCorp Following Accusations of Industrial Espionage
1 hour ago

Russia/Markovia military alliance expands in wake of "The Supermen Theory"
December 11, 2017

Sapphire Stagg speaks out against Stagg Industries and Rex Mason
1 day ago

Features

In pictures: Gotham Police join protests against the Batman

NO MOR

LexNet File Edit View History Window Help

www.thebulletin.com/2017/12/7/metahumannews/new-theory-on-concentration-of-metahumans/index.html

GCPL

theBulletin.com Sign in | News | Sports | Weather | Shop | Earth | Travel | More | Search

NEWS

Home | Video | World | US & Canada | Business | Tech | Science | Stories | Entertainment & Arts | Health | More

"The Supermen Theory" began making the rounds six months ago when a Markovian geneticist, Dr. Helga Jace, led an international coalition of scientists looking to answer a question that has long confounded the world:

Why are the vast majority of the planet's metahumans American?

Most often referred to as "super-heroes" and "super-villains" by the general public who watch their exploits with both awe and fear, metahumans began appearing after Superman revealed himself to the world. Men, women and even children wielding a diverse range of superhuman abilities have since emerged across America at a rapid rate.

Superman's history has been well documented and generally accepted; the Man of Steel comes from another planet, the long-dead Krypton. However, the metahumans who followed Superman remain a mystery. The vast majority of them hide their true identities, a fact that has become more and more unsettling across the planet. "The Supermen Theory" suggests that the metahumans of America are, in truth, government sponsored and controlled. Dr. Jace claims that the "theatrics of super-heroes and super-villains" are a calculated and designed cover for the continued experimentation on and creation of America's living weapons of mass destruction. Dr. Jace continues to suggest, "These super-heroes and super-villains are nukes hidden in plain sight."

To combat the initial skepticism toward "The Supermen Theory," Dr. Jace pointed to leaked documents from the U.S. Department of Metahuman Affairs detailing the secret origin of Rex Mason, better known as Metamorpho and sometime ally to the Batman. Although initial reports suggested the former soldier-for-hire was accidentally transformed into the shape-shifting metahuman, the leaked documents paint a very different picture. The documents reveal Simon Stagg and Stagg Industries were under government contract, along with Rex Mason. Under Stagg's supervision, Mason voluntarily exposed himself to an ancient energy source, ultimately triggering his metagene and transforming him into Metamorpho.

As Metamorpho, Mason was often seen in public blaming Simon Stagg for the accident. But new allegations suggest Mason and Stagg, along with many others, were coached to create a "super-hero narrative" designed to cover Metamorpho's covert activities as a government agent. In recent weeks, three former "enemies" of Metamorpho, "Doc Dread," "Stingaree" and "the Prosecutor," have come forward with claims they were paid by the U.S. government to undergo their own transformations and take on the role of "super-villain" to Metamorpho.

Today a second metahuman's ties to the U.S. government have been revealed. Kirk Langstrom, sometimes known as the creature called Man-Bat, has admitted that the research that led to his own transformation was sponsored by the U.S. Department of Metahuman Affairs. Since Langstrom's declaration, he has been unavailable for further comment, though the White House has issued a response.

CLICK HERE TO READ MORE

Features

In pictures: Gotham Police join protests against The Batman

NO MOR
BAT

Science: Doomsday Clock moves to three minutes 'til midnight

Unexplained: Bizarre "green" fire destroys All-American Steel factory

LexNet File Edit View History Window Help

GCPL #

www.thebulletin.press/2017/12/20/multiple-arrest-at-lexcorp-following-accusations-of-industrial-espionage/in

theBulletin | Sign In | News | Sports | Weather | Shop | Earth | Travel | More | Search

NEWS

Home | Video | World | US & Canada | Business | Tech | Science | Stories | Entertainment & Arts | Health | More

December 20, 2017 – Local News

JETTY IMAGES

Bruce Wayne at the Martha Wayne Mental Health Fundraiser

Multiple Arrests at LexCorp Following Accusations of Industrial Espionage

In what is arguably the greatest rivalry in American business today, the competition between LexCorp and Wayne Enterprises has reached new heights, leading to the arrests of four Wayne Enterprises employees -- each accused of helping LexCorp access highly confidential and experimental research. A genetic scientist, two managers and a security guard have all been charged after a breach in Wayne Enterprises systems was detected. Bruce Wayne claims the competition over the "metagene" is what motivated Lex Luthor to pay off employees within Wayne's company.

As "The Supermen Theory" has gained acceptance, if not outright validation, over the last several weeks, the competition between the two giants has entered a new and dangerous arena: metahuman biology. Technology that would control the metagene, or even eliminate it, could become the most valuable commodity in the world. The metagene, a genetic anomaly found in up to 12% of the human population, was discovered during the Dominator Invasion. This anomaly seems to be a step further from the human fight-or-flight response; when a traumatic or potentially lethal incident occurs, it can trigger the metagene, altering a person's genetic disposition and causing the development of superhuman abilities. Although many "super-heroes" and "super-villains" claim to derive their abilities from sources outside of the metagene, the truth behind their origins has come into question following the rise of "The Supermen Theory."

Since the theory was first presented, both LexCorp and Wayne Enterprises have been gobbling up every company that has done any kind of research on the metagene. LexCorp's stock soared after purchasing Kord Industries, Genetech and the Sunderland Corporation, while Wayne Enterprises has struggled to find the same kind of success through its acquisitions. The controversial decision to buy Dayton Labs, a troubled genetic research facility, sent Wayne stocks tumbling. Not helping matters, today Wayne Enterprises announced it is in the process of picking up the pieces of Stagg Industries in the wake of the Metamorpho scandal.

Although all four of the accused Wayne Enterprises employees claim to have had direct communication with Lex Luthor himself, he denies any involvement.

Top Stories

New Theory on Concentration of Metahumans in United States Raises Questions About Secret Origins
December 7, 2017

Russia/Markovia military alliance expands in wake of "The Supermen Theory"
December 11, 2017

Sapphire Stagg speaks out against Stagg Industries and Rex Mason
1 day ago

LexNet File Edit View History Window Help

www.thebulletin.press/2017/12/20/multiple-arrest-at-lexcorp-following-accusations-of-industrial-espionage/inde

theBulletin | Sign In | News | Sports | Weather | Shop | Earth | Travel | More | Search

NEWS

Home | Video | World | US & Canada | Business | Tech | Science | Stories | Entertainment & Arts | Health | More

December 20, 2017 - Local News

Bruce Wayne at

Multiple Arrests

In what is argu
competition be
heights, leading
accused of hel
research. A ger
been charged
Bruce Wayne cl
Lex Luthor to p

As "The Superm
over the last se
entered a new
would control t
valuable comm
in up to 12% of
Invasion. This a
fight-or-flight re
occurs, it can t
and causing th
"super-heroes"
outside of the
question follow

Since the theor
have been gob
on the metage
Genetech and
struggled to fin
controversial d
facility, sent W
Enterprises anr
Industries in th

Although all fou
have had direc
involvement.

Top Stories

New Theory on Concentration of Metahumans in United States Raises Questions About Secret Origins

December 7, 2017

Russia/Markovia military alliance expands in wake of "The Supermen Theory"

www.dailyplanet.com/2017/12/20/superman-takes-a-stand-against-metahuman-outrage/index.html

Sections | DAILY PLANET | Sign In

POLITICS

Superman Takes a Stand against Metahuman Outrage as the World Reacts to Conspiracy Theories on Their Origins

By Lois Lane
December 20, 2017

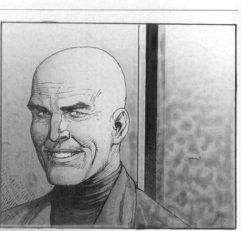

Lex Luthor receiving the Copley Medal for his work in metahuman biology

After Lex Luthor's unleashing of an all-out anti-metahuman campaign yesterday, Superman has called for calm in this time of chaos. In a statement given to the Daily Planet, Superman said, "We cannot allow paranoia, fear and distrust to be our driving motives in our actions at this difficult time. Although I applaud the men and women who have done so many amazing things at LexCorp that have helped the world, I find the words and ideas of its leader misguided and, quite frankly, dangerous."

While the United Nations is debating whether to force the United States to open up its metahuman prisons and medical institutions for inspection, other world leaders are tempering their reactions to "The Supermen Theory" in a wait-and-see approach. But the more strident Lex Luthor made his stance clear with his tirade yesterday about the supposed dangers of metahumans and their impact on society at large. The outspoken and controversial head of LexCorp has never shied away from denouncing the super-heroes of the world, including Superman, but his recent comments have taken a decidedly darker and more threatening turn. Luthor encouraged all business leaders to denounce metahumans until they unmask and reveal their origins to the world. Until that time, Luthor has stated he will dedicate all of the necessary resources within LexCorp to uncovering the truth behind metahumans, promising to expose "as many of them as humanly possible."

As of this publication, Lex Luthor did not return inquiries.

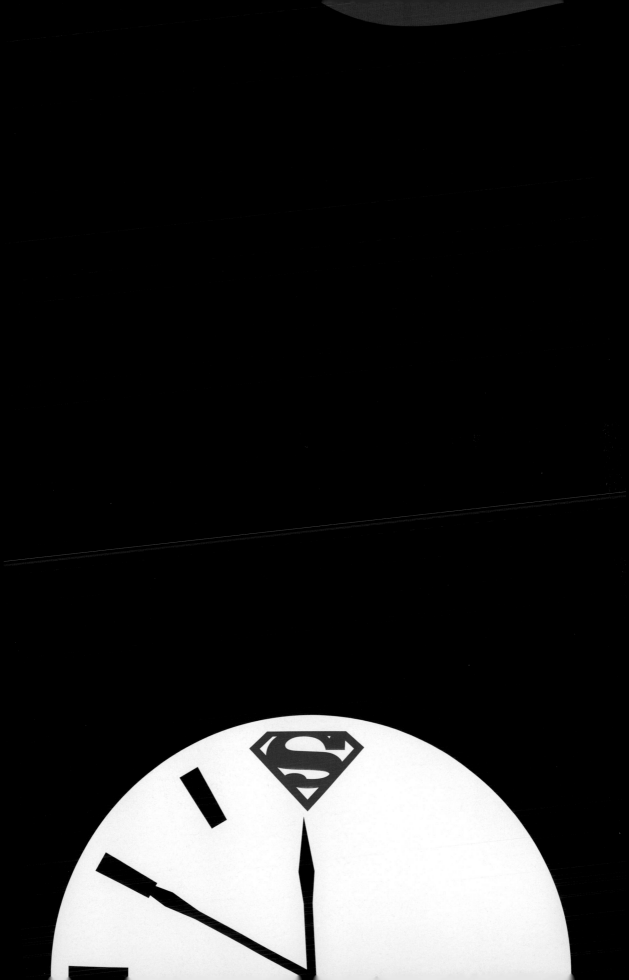

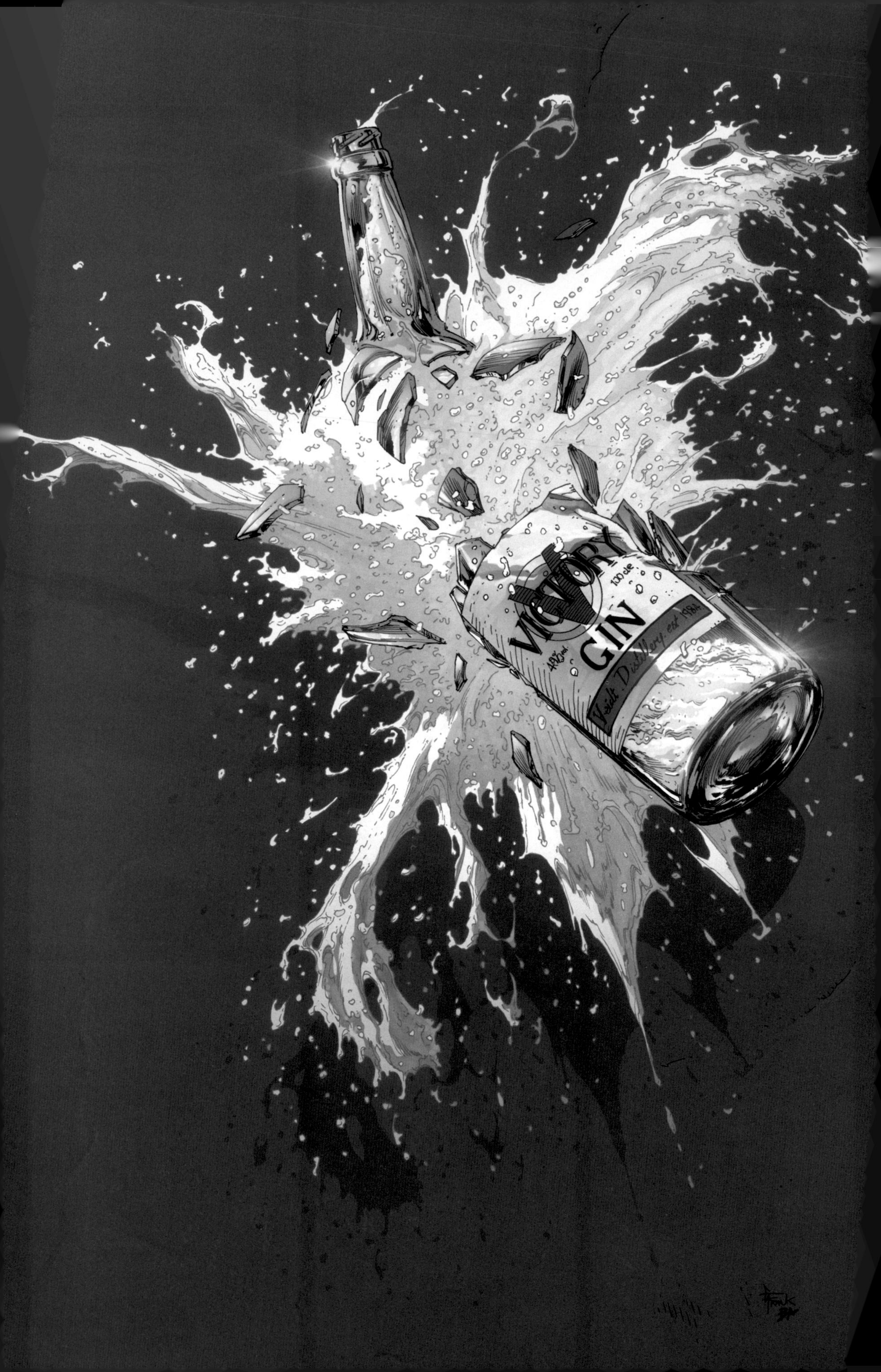
VICTORY
GIN
100 cle
Distillery est 1984

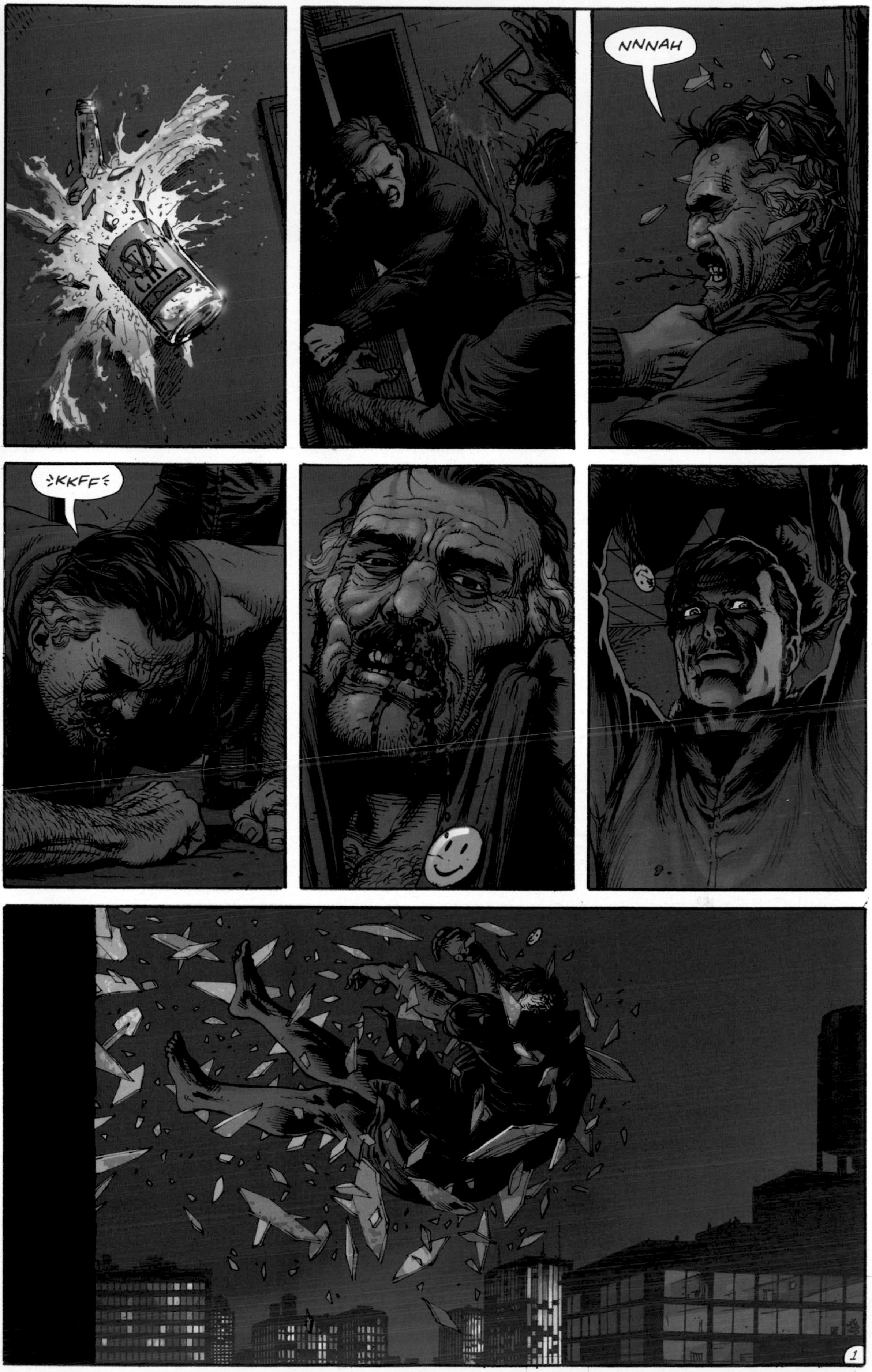
NNNAH
KKFF
1

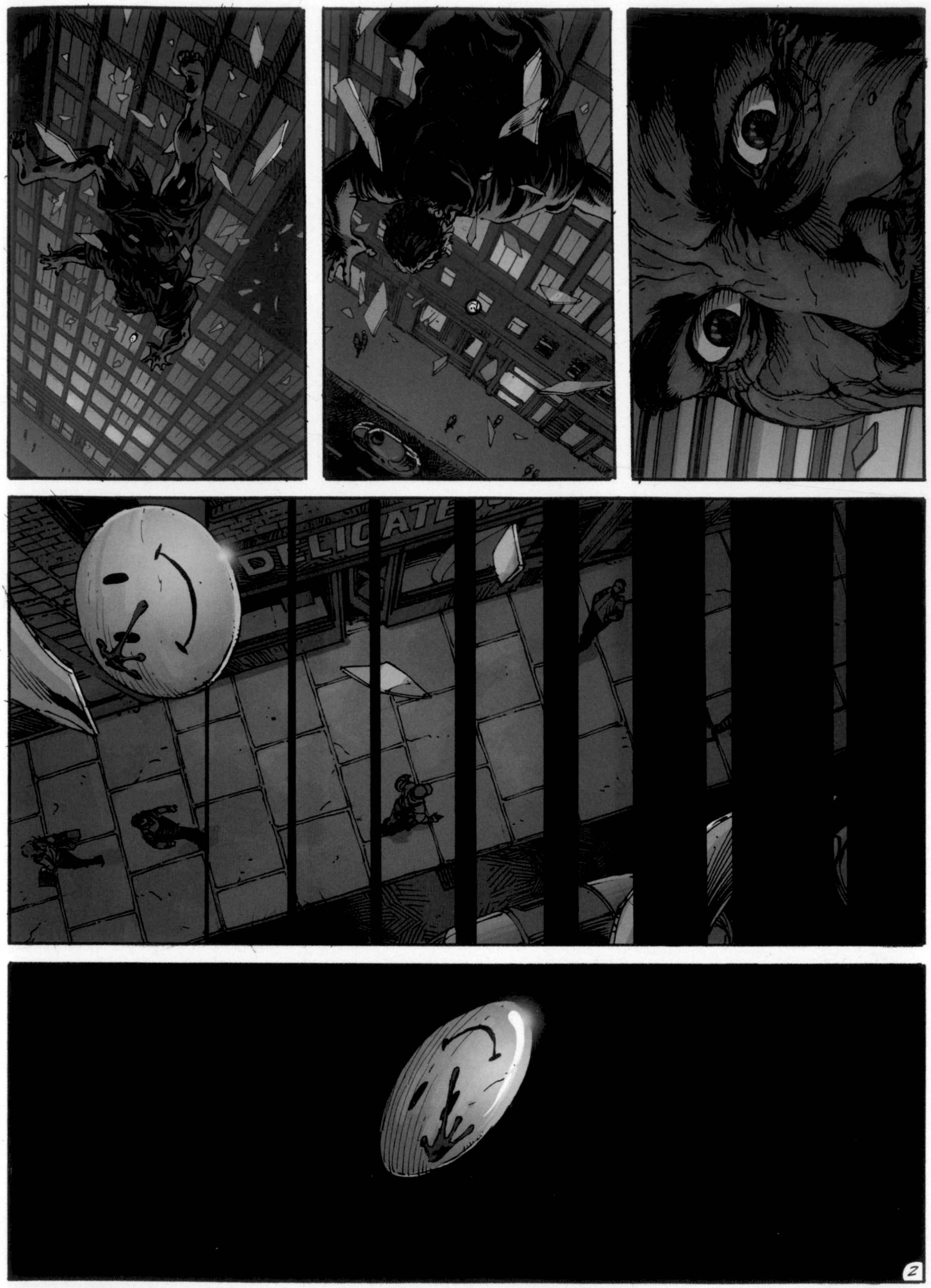

NOT VICTORY NOR DEFEAT

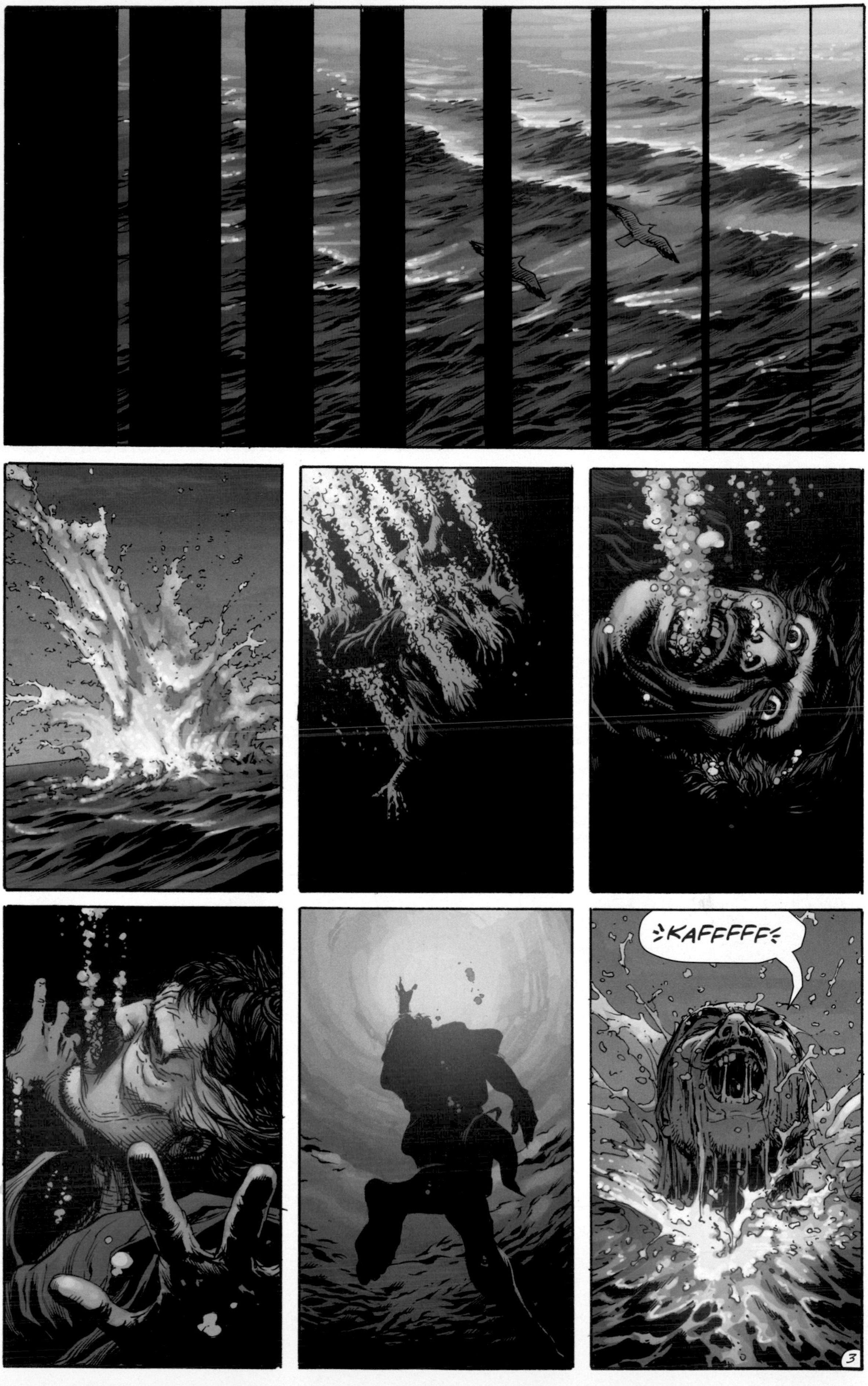
KAFFFFF
3

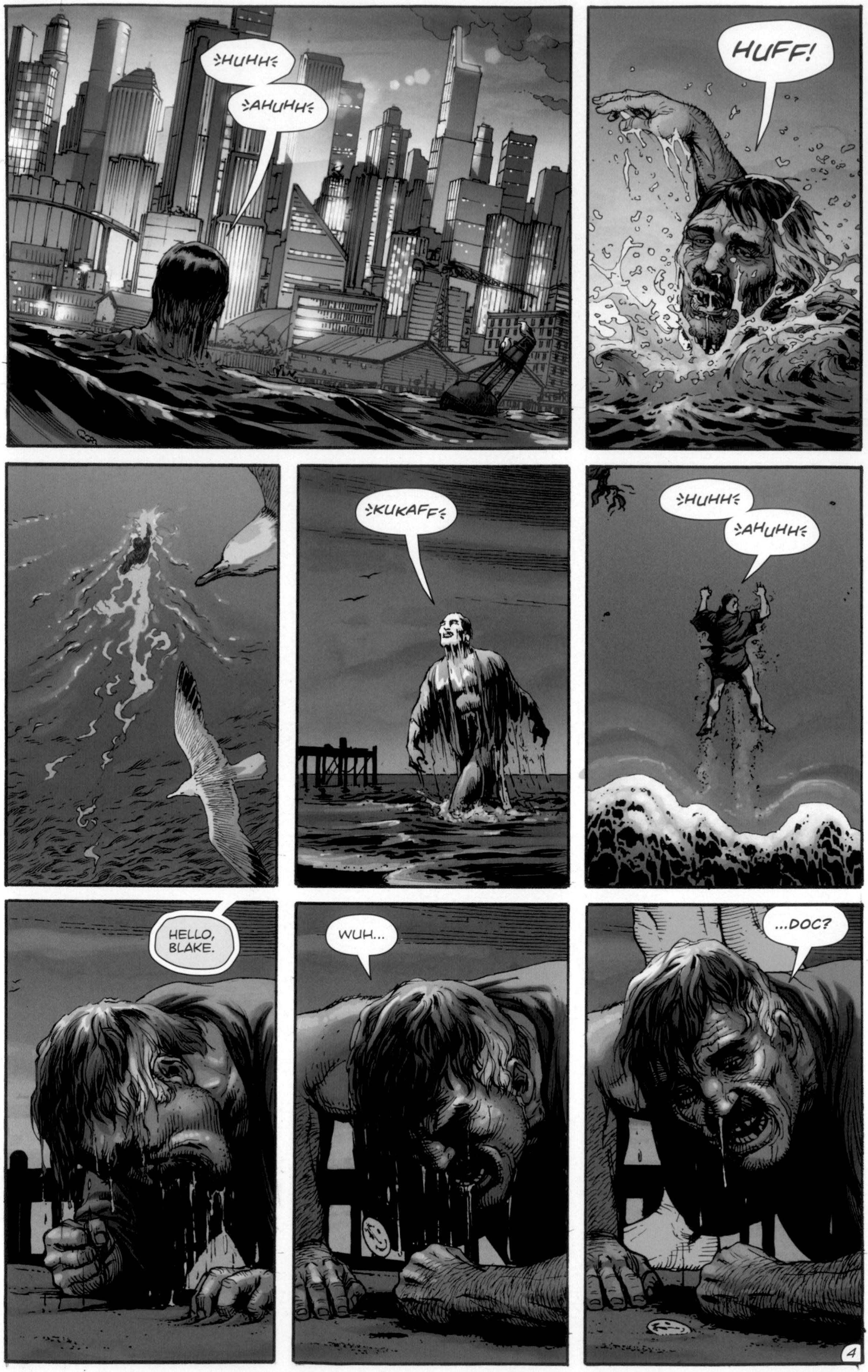
HUHH
AHUHH
HUFF!
KUKAFF
HUHH
AHUHH
HELLO, BLAKE.
WUH...
...DOC?

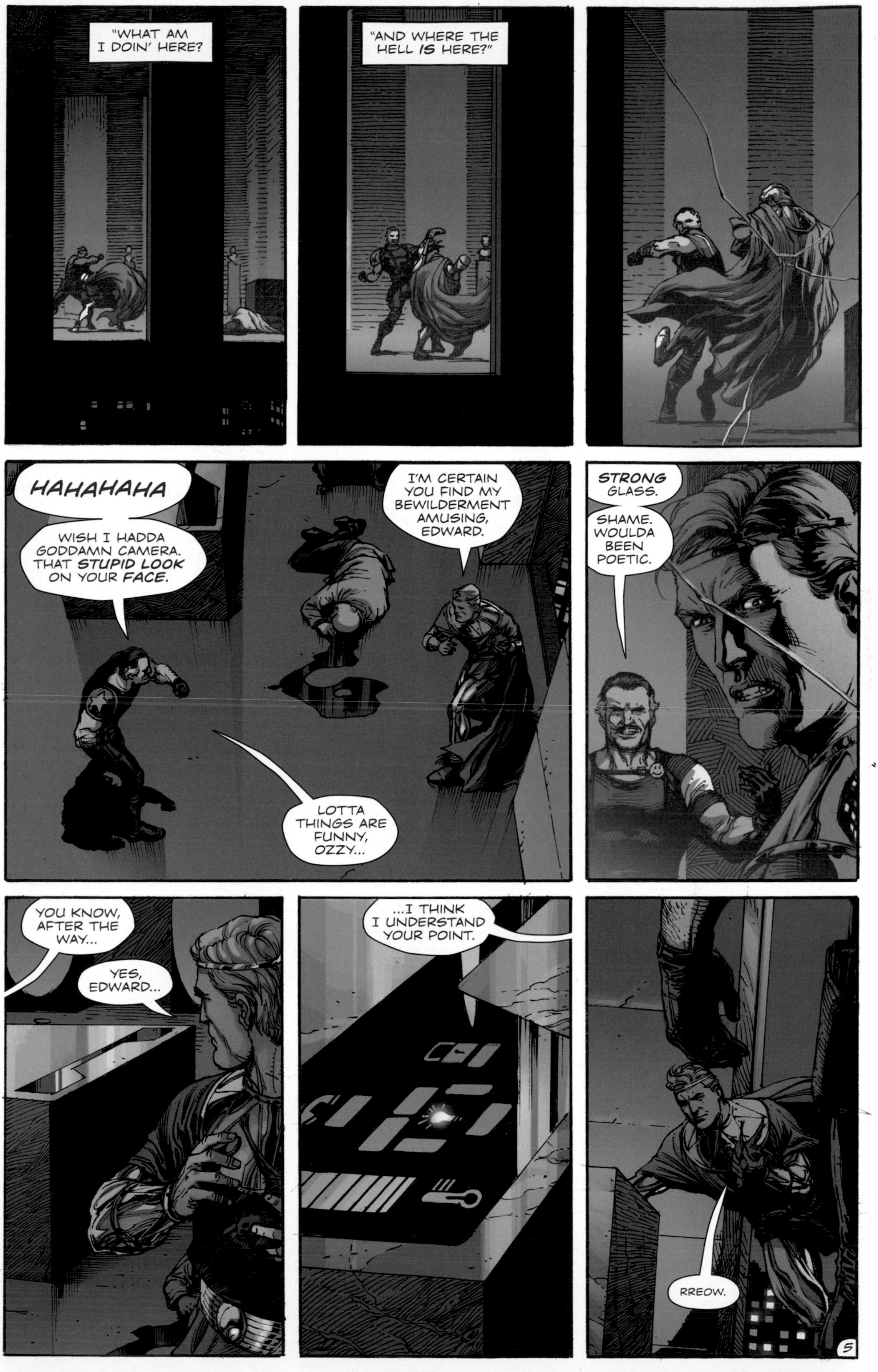
"WHAT AM I DOIN' HERE?
"AND WHERE THE HELL IS HERE?"
HAHAHAHA
WISH I HADDA GODDAMN CAMERA. THAT STUPID LOOK ON YOUR FACE.
I'M CERTAIN YOU FIND MY BEWILDERMENT AMUSING, EDWARD.
LOTTA THINGS ARE FUNNY, OZZY...
STRONG GLASS.
SHAME. WOULDA BEEN POETIC.
YOU KNOW, AFTER THE WAY...
YES, EDWARD...
...I THINK I UNDERSTAND YOUR POINT.
RREOW.
5

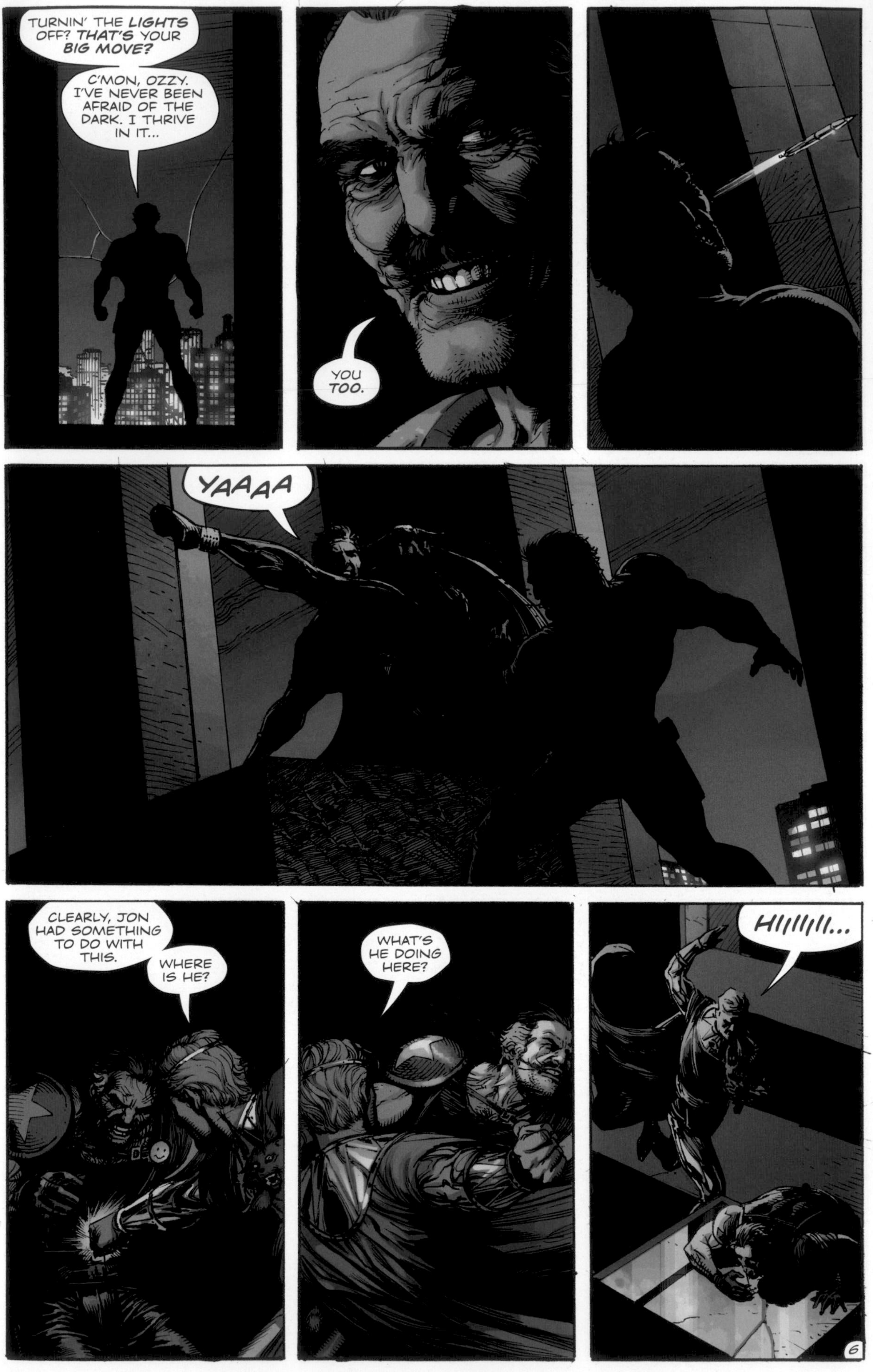
TURNIN' THE LIGHTS OFF? THAT'S YOUR BIG MOVE?
C'MON, OZZY. I'VE NEVER BEEN AFRAID OF THE DARK. I THRIVE IN IT...
YOU TOO.
YAAAA
CLEARLY, JON HAD SOMETHING TO DO WITH THIS.
WHERE IS HE?
WHAT'S HE DOING HERE?
HIIIIII...

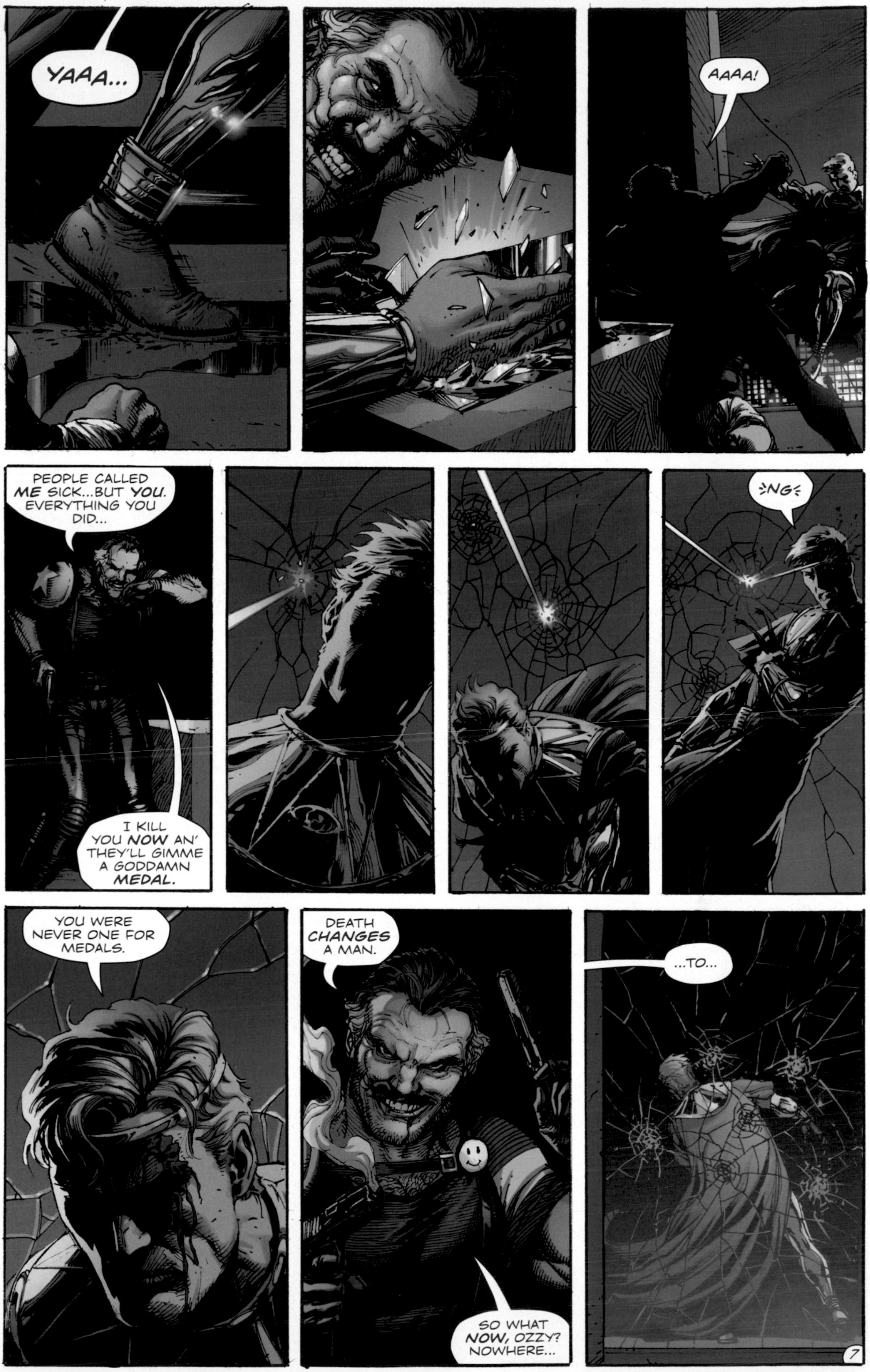
YAAA...
AAAA!
PEOPLE CALLED ME SICK...BUT YOU. EVERYTHING YOU DID...
I KILL YOU NOW AN' THEY'LL GIMME A GODDAMN MEDAL.
NG
YOU WERE NEVER ONE FOR MEDALS.
DEATH CHANGES A MAN.
SO WHAT NOW, OZZY? NOWHERE...
...TO...

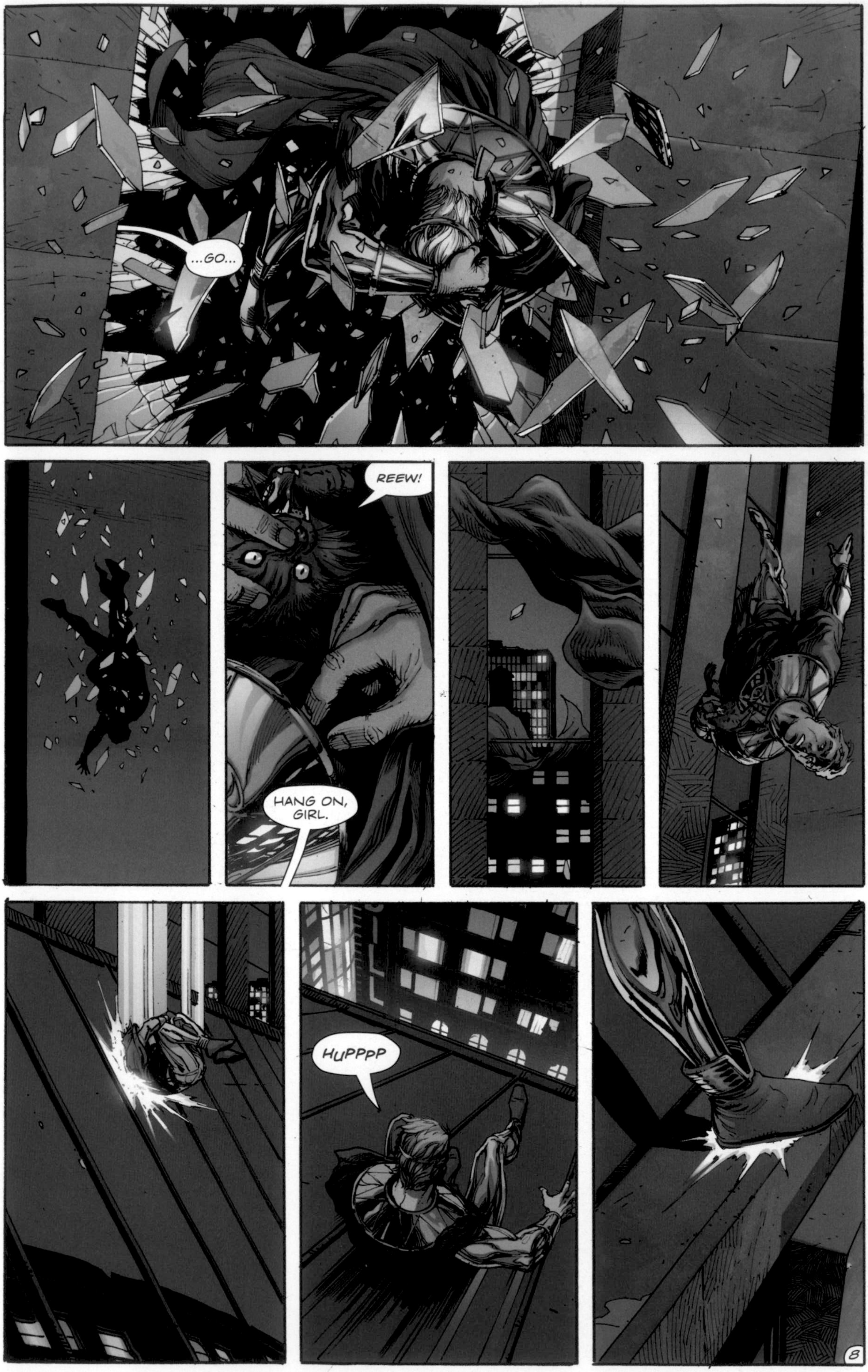
...GO...
REEW!
HANG ON, GIRL.
HUPPPP
8

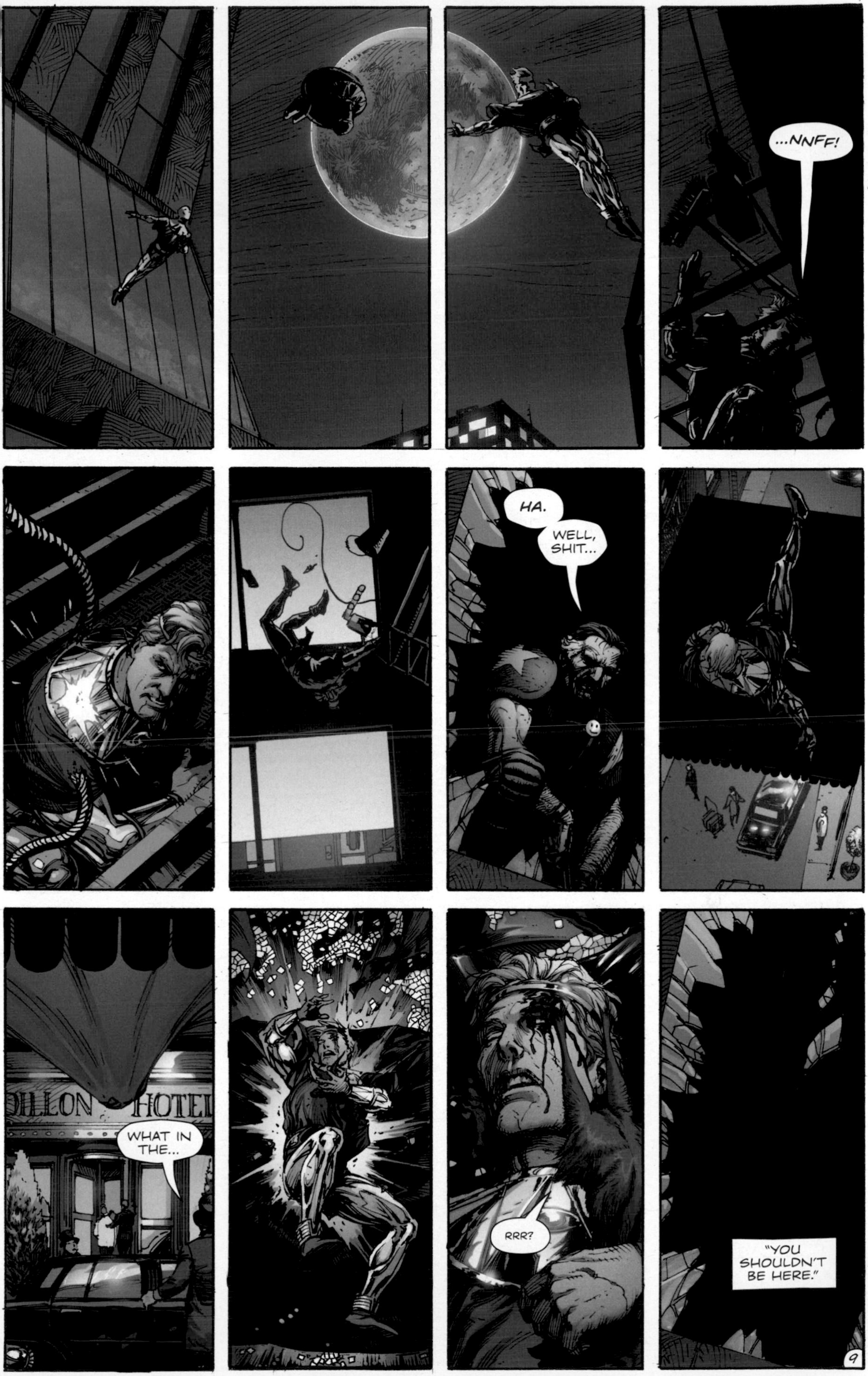
...NNFF!
HA.
WELL, SHIT...
DILLON HOTEL
WHAT IN THE...
RRR?
"YOU SHOULDN'T BE HERE."

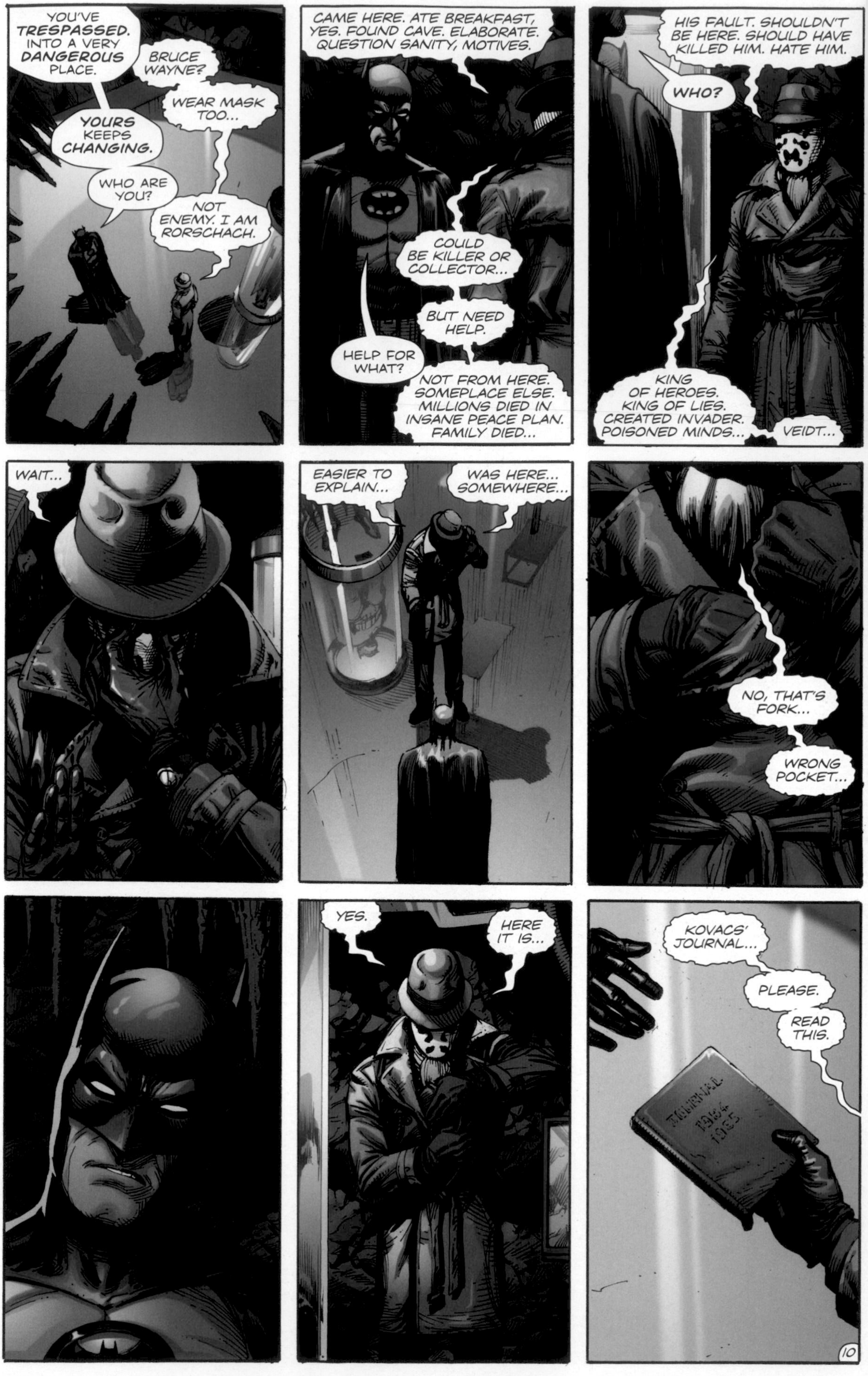
YOU'VE TRESPASSED. INTO A VERY DANGEROUS PLACE.
BRUCE WAYNE?
WEAR MASK TOO...
YOURS KEEPS CHANGING.
WHO ARE YOU?
NOT ENEMY. I AM RORSCHACH.
CAME HERE. ATE BREAKFAST, YES. FOUND CAVE. ELABORATE. QUESTION SANITY, MOTIVES.
COULD BE KILLER OR COLLECTOR...
BUT NEED HELP.
HELP FOR WHAT?
NOT FROM HERE. SOMEPLACE ELSE. MILLIONS DIED IN INSANE PEACE PLAN. FAMILY DIED...
HIS FAULT. SHOULDN'T BE HERE. SHOULD HAVE KILLED HIM. HATE HIM.
WHO?
KING OF HEROES. KING OF LIES. CREATED INVADER. POISONED MINDS...
VEIDT...
WAIT...
EASIER TO EXPLAIN...
WAS HERE... SOMEWHERE...
NO, THAT'S FORK...
WRONG POCKET...
YES.
HERE IT IS...
KOVACS' JOURNAL...
PLEASE.
READ THIS.

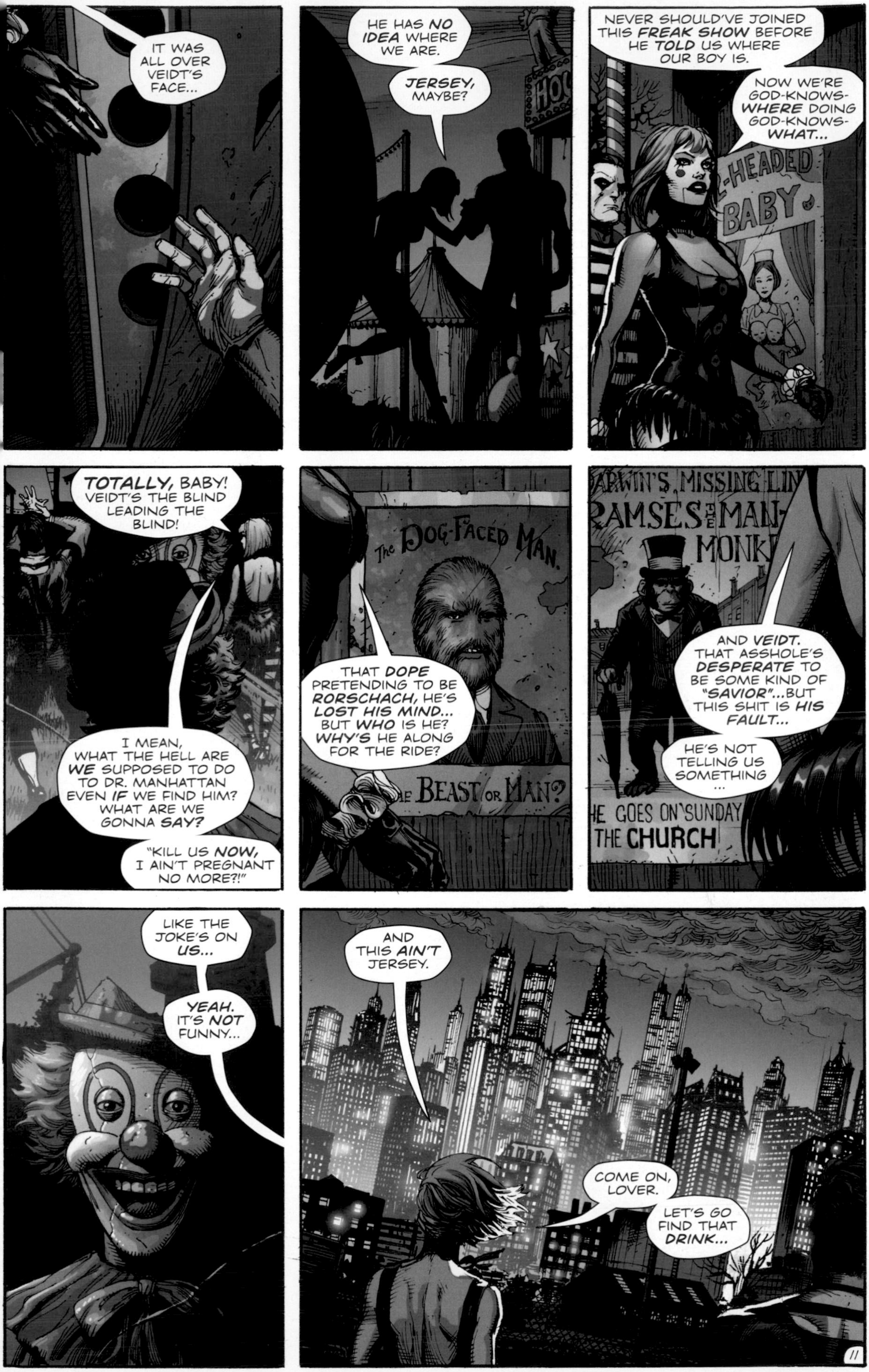
IT WAS ALL OVER VEIDT'S FACE...
HE HAS NO IDEA WHERE WE ARE.
JERSEY, MAYBE?
HO
NEVER SHOULD'VE JOINED THIS FREAK SHOW BEFORE HE TOLD US WHERE OUR BOY IS.
NOW WE'RE GOD-KNOWS-WHERE DOING GOD-KNOWS-WHAT...
-HEADED BABY
TOTALLY, BABY! VEIDT'S THE BLIND LEADING THE BLIND!
I MEAN, WHAT THE HELL ARE WE SUPPOSED TO DO TO DR. MANHATTAN EVEN IF WE FIND HIM? WHAT ARE WE GONNA SAY?
"KILL US NOW, I AIN'T PREGNANT NO MORE?!"
The DOG-FACED MAN.
THAT DOPE PRETENDING TO BE RORSCHACH, HE'S LOST HIS MIND... BUT WHO IS HE? WHY'S HE ALONG FOR THE RIDE?
BEAST OR MAN?
DARWIN'S MISSING LIN
RAMSES THE MAN-MONK
AND VEIDT. THAT ASSHOLE'S DESPERATE TO BE SOME KIND OF "SAVIOR"...BUT THIS SHIT IS HIS FAULT...
HE'S NOT TELLING US SOMETHING ...
HE GOES ON SUNDAY THE CHURCH
LIKE THE JOKE'S ON US...
YEAH. IT'S NOT FUNNY...
AND THIS AIN'T JERSEY.
COME ON, LOVER.
LET'S GO FIND THAT DRINK...

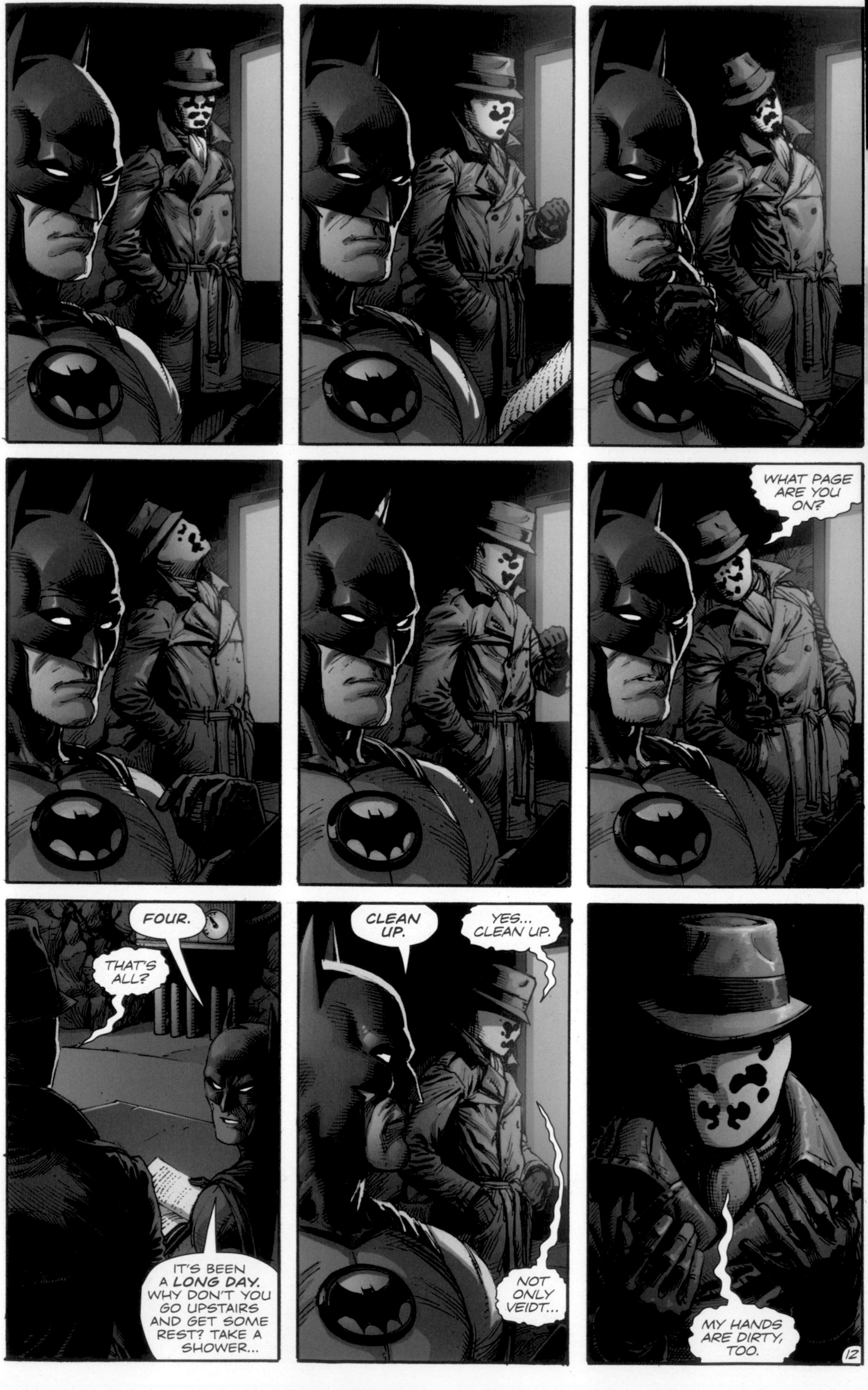
WHAT PAGE ARE YOU ON?
FOUR.
THAT'S ALL?
IT'S BEEN A **LONG DAY.** WHY DON'T YOU GO UPSTAIRS AND GET SOME REST? TAKE A SHOWER...
CLEAN UP.
YES... CLEAN UP.
NOT ONLY VEIDT...
MY HANDS ARE DIRTY, TOO.

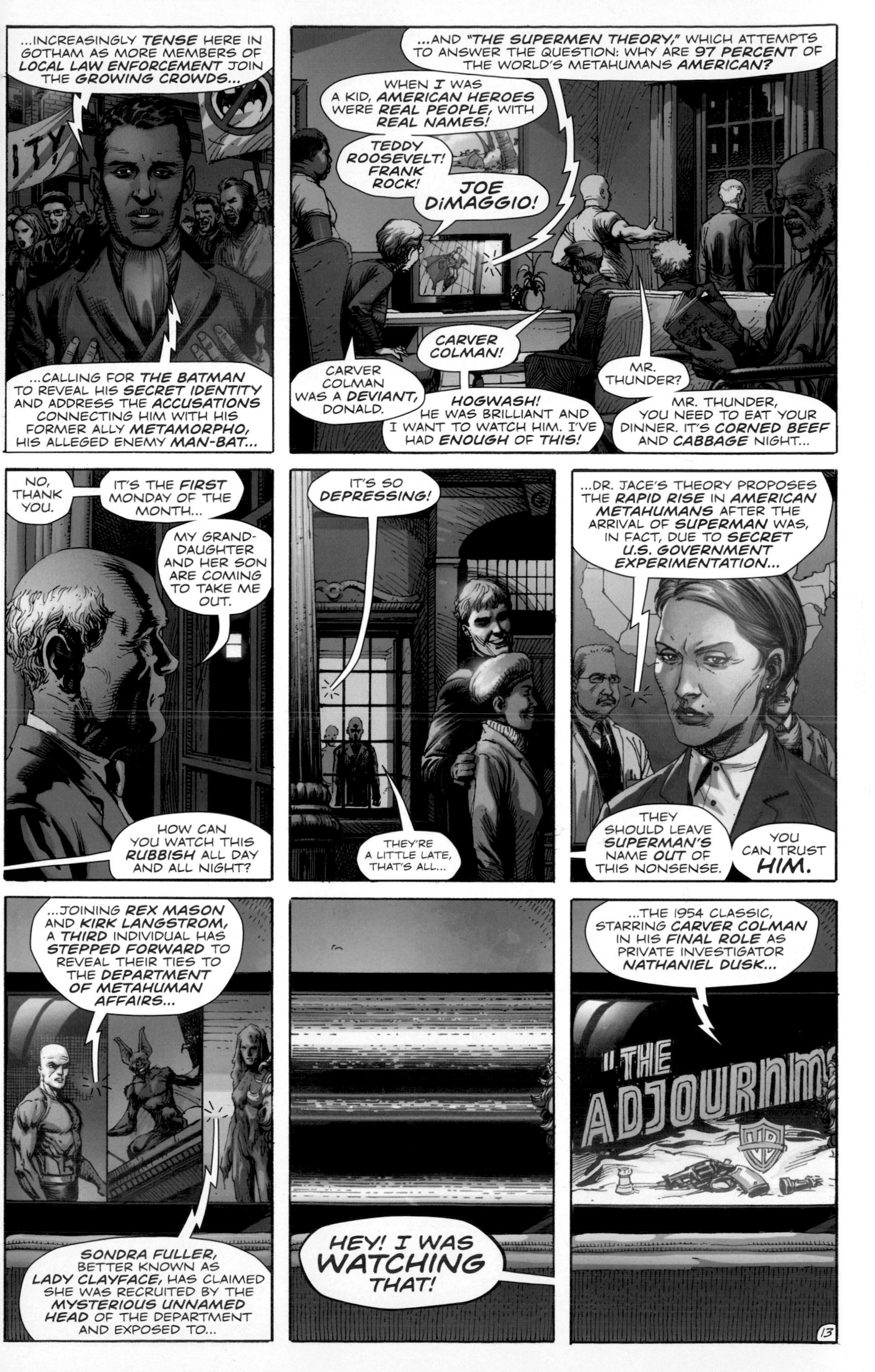

...INCREASINGLY TENSE HERE IN GOTHAM AS MORE MEMBERS OF LOCAL LAW ENFORCEMENT JOIN THE GROWING CROWDS...
...CALLING FOR THE BATMAN TO REVEAL HIS SECRET IDENTITY AND ADDRESS THE ACCUSATIONS CONNECTING HIM WITH HIS FORMER ALLY METAMORPHO, HIS ALLEGED ENEMY MAN-BAT...
...AND "THE SUPERMEN THEORY," WHICH ATTEMPTS TO ANSWER THE QUESTION: WHY ARE 97 PERCENT OF THE WORLD'S METAHUMANS AMERICAN?
WHEN I WAS A KID, AMERICAN HEROES WERE REAL PEOPLE, WITH REAL NAMES!
TEDDY ROOSEVELT! FRANK ROCK!
JOE DiMAGGIO!
CARVER COLMAN!
CARVER COLMAN WAS A DEVIANT, DONALD.
HOGWASH! HE WAS BRILLIANT AND I WANT TO WATCH HIM. I'VE HAD ENOUGH OF THIS!
MR. THUNDER?
MR. THUNDER, YOU NEED TO EAT YOUR DINNER. IT'S CORNED BEEF AND CABBAGE NIGHT...
NO, THANK YOU.
IT'S THE FIRST MONDAY OF THE MONTH...
MY GRAND-DAUGHTER AND HER SON ARE COMING TO TAKE ME OUT.
HOW CAN YOU WATCH THIS RUBBISH ALL DAY AND ALL NIGHT?
IT'S SO DEPRESSING!
THEY'RE A LITTLE LATE, THAT'S ALL...
...DR. JACE'S THEORY PROPOSES THE RAPID RISE IN AMERICAN METAHUMANS AFTER THE ARRIVAL OF SUPERMAN WAS, IN FACT, DUE TO SECRET U.S. GOVERNMENT EXPERIMENTATION...
THEY SHOULD LEAVE SUPERMAN'S NAME OUT OF THIS NONSENSE.
YOU CAN TRUST HIM.
...JOINING REX MASON AND KIRK LANGSTROM, A THIRD INDIVIDUAL HAS STEPPED FORWARD TO REVEAL THEIR TIES TO THE DEPARTMENT OF METAHUMAN AFFAIRS...
SONDRA FULLER, BETTER KNOWN AS LADY CLAYFACE, HAS CLAIMED SHE WAS RECRUITED BY THE MYSTERIOUS UNNAMED HEAD OF THE DEPARTMENT AND EXPOSED TO...
HEY! I WAS WATCHING THAT!
...THE 1954 CLASSIC, STARRING CARVER COLMAN IN HIS FINAL ROLE AS PRIVATE INVESTIGATOR NATHANIEL DUSK...
"THE ADJOURNM

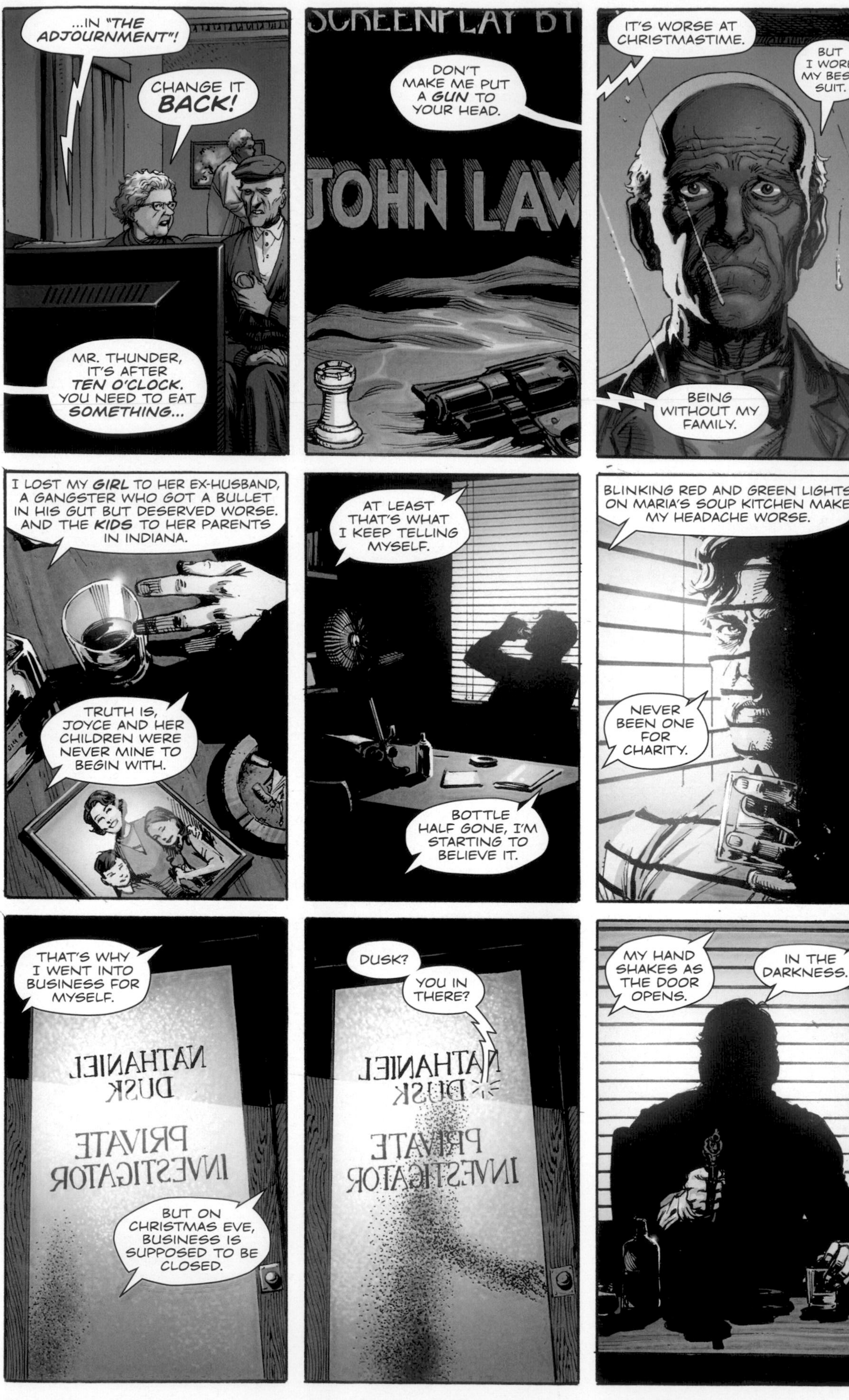
...IN "THE ADJOURNMENT"!
CHANGE IT BACK!
MR. THUNDER, IT'S AFTER TEN O'CLOCK. YOU NEED TO EAT SOMETHING...
SCREENPLAY BY
DON'T MAKE ME PUT A GUN TO YOUR HEAD.
JOHN LAW
IT'S WORSE AT CHRISTMASTIME.
BUT I WORE MY BEST SUIT.
BEING WITHOUT MY FAMILY.
I LOST MY GIRL TO HER EX-HUSBAND, A GANGSTER WHO GOT A BULLET IN HIS GUT BUT DESERVED WORSE. AND THE KIDS TO HER PARENTS IN INDIANA.
TRUTH IS, JOYCE AND HER CHILDREN WERE NEVER MINE TO BEGIN WITH.
AT LEAST THAT'S WHAT I KEEP TELLING MYSELF.
BOTTLE HALF GONE, I'M STARTING TO BELIEVE IT.
BLINKING RED AND GREEN LIGHTS ON MARIA'S SOUP KITCHEN MAKE MY HEADACHE WORSE.
NEVER BEEN ONE FOR CHARITY.
THAT'S WHY I WENT INTO BUSINESS FOR MYSELF.
NATHANIEL DUSK PRIVATE INVESTIGATOR
BUT ON CHRISTMAS EVE, BUSINESS IS SUPPOSED TO BE CLOSED.
DUSK?
YOU IN THERE?
NATHANIEL DUSK PRIVATE INVESTIGATOR
MY HAND SHAKES AS THE DOOR OPENS.
IN THE DARKNESS...

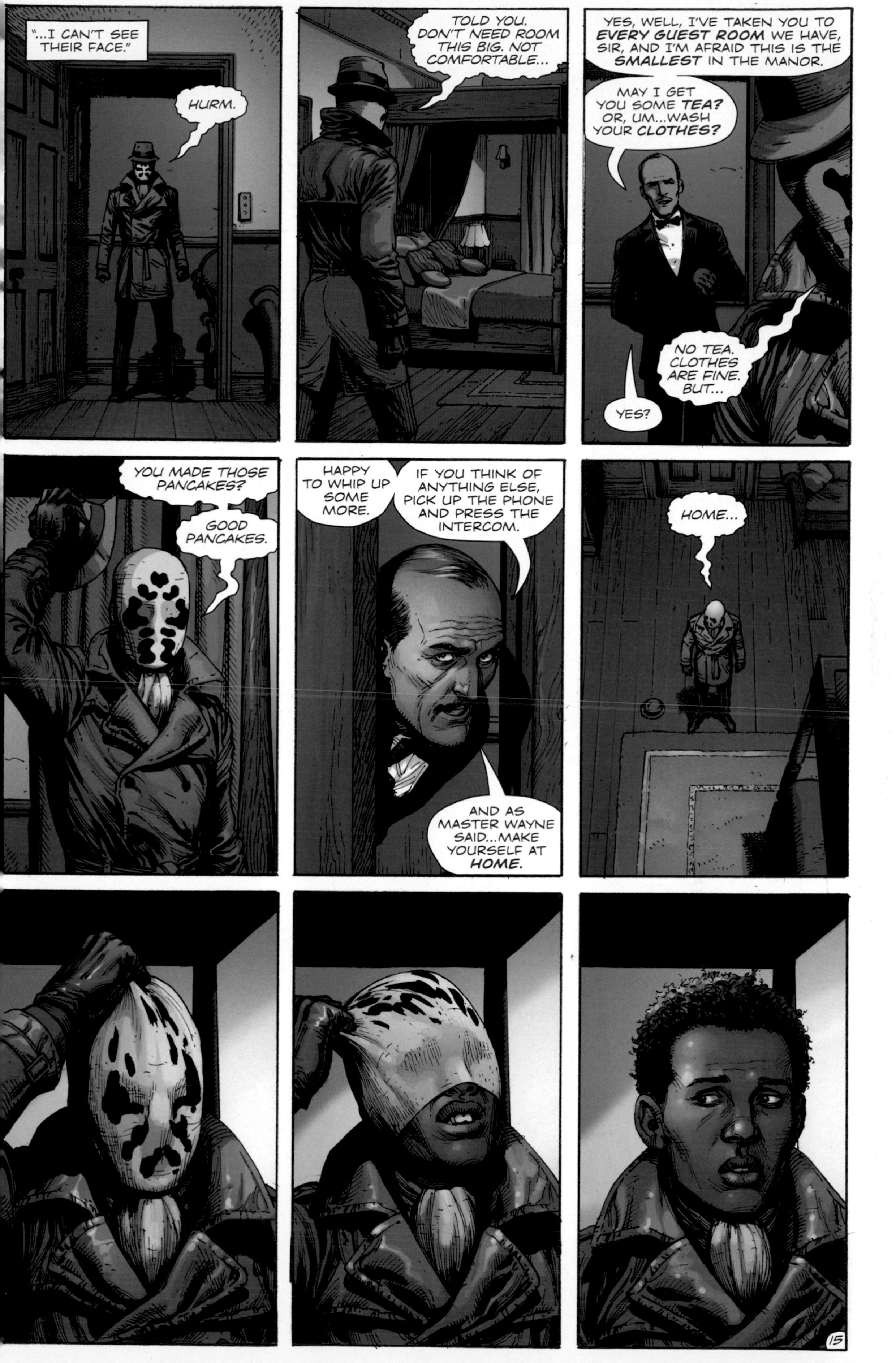
"...I CAN'T SEE THEIR FACE."
HURM.
TOLD YOU. DON'T NEED ROOM THIS BIG. NOT COMFORTABLE...
YES, WELL, I'VE TAKEN YOU TO EVERY GUEST ROOM WE HAVE, SIR, AND I'M AFRAID THIS IS THE SMALLEST IN THE MANOR.
MAY I GET YOU SOME TEA? OR, UM...WASH YOUR CLOTHES?
NO TEA. CLOTHES ARE FINE. BUT...
YES?
YOU MADE THOSE PANCAKES?
GOOD PANCAKES.
HAPPY TO WHIP UP SOME MORE.
IF YOU THINK OF ANYTHING ELSE, PICK UP THE PHONE AND PRESS THE INTERCOM.
AND AS MASTER WAYNE SAID...MAKE YOURSELF AT HOME.
HOME...
15

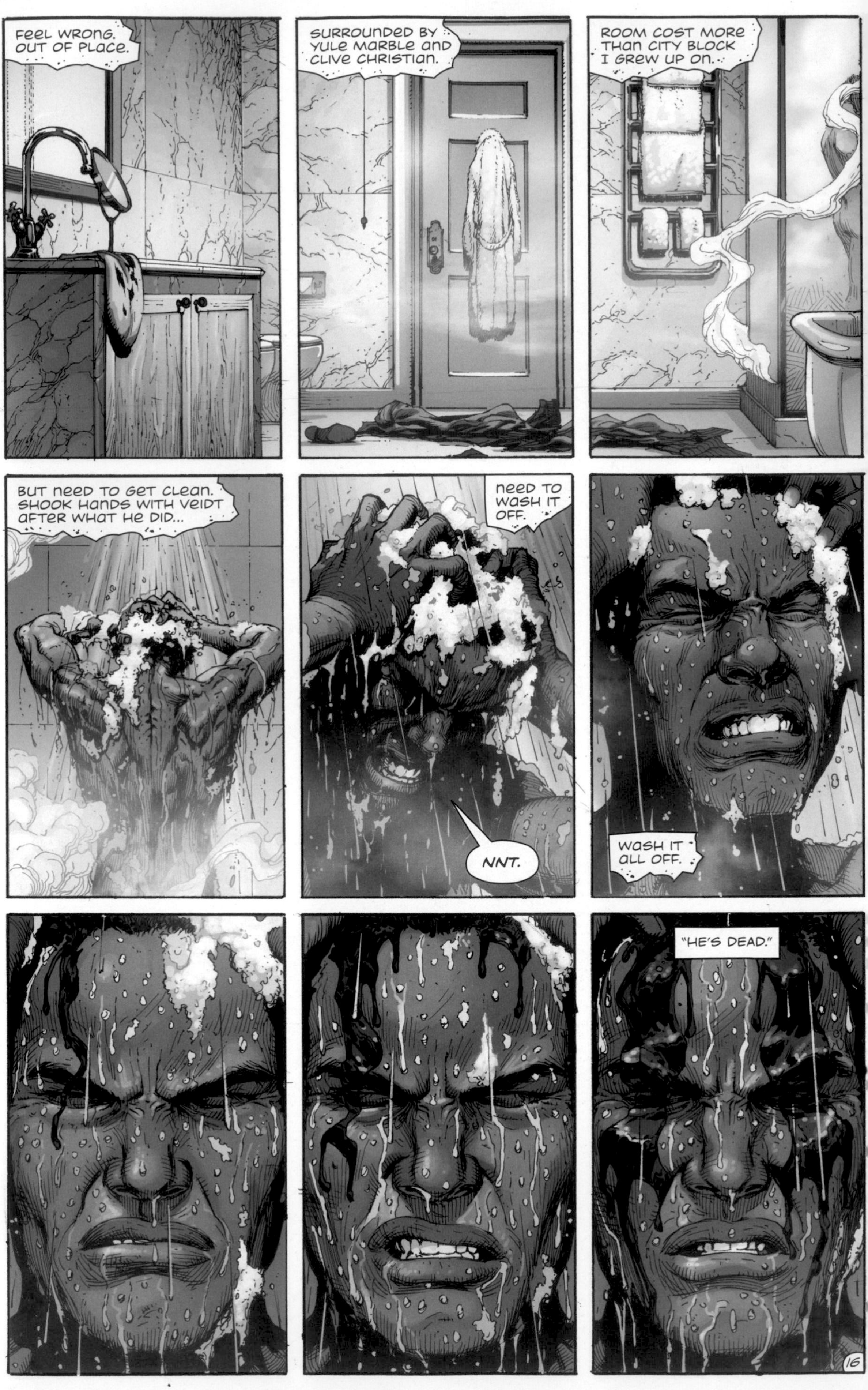
FEEL WRONG. OUT OF PLACE.
SURROUNDED BY YULE MARBLE AND CLIVE CHRISTIAN.
ROOM COST MORE THAN CITY BLOCK I GREW UP ON.
BUT NEED TO GET CLEAN. SHOOK HANDS WITH VEIDT AFTER WHAT HE DID...
NEED TO WASH IT OFF.
NNT.
WASH IT ALL OFF.
"HE'S DEAD."

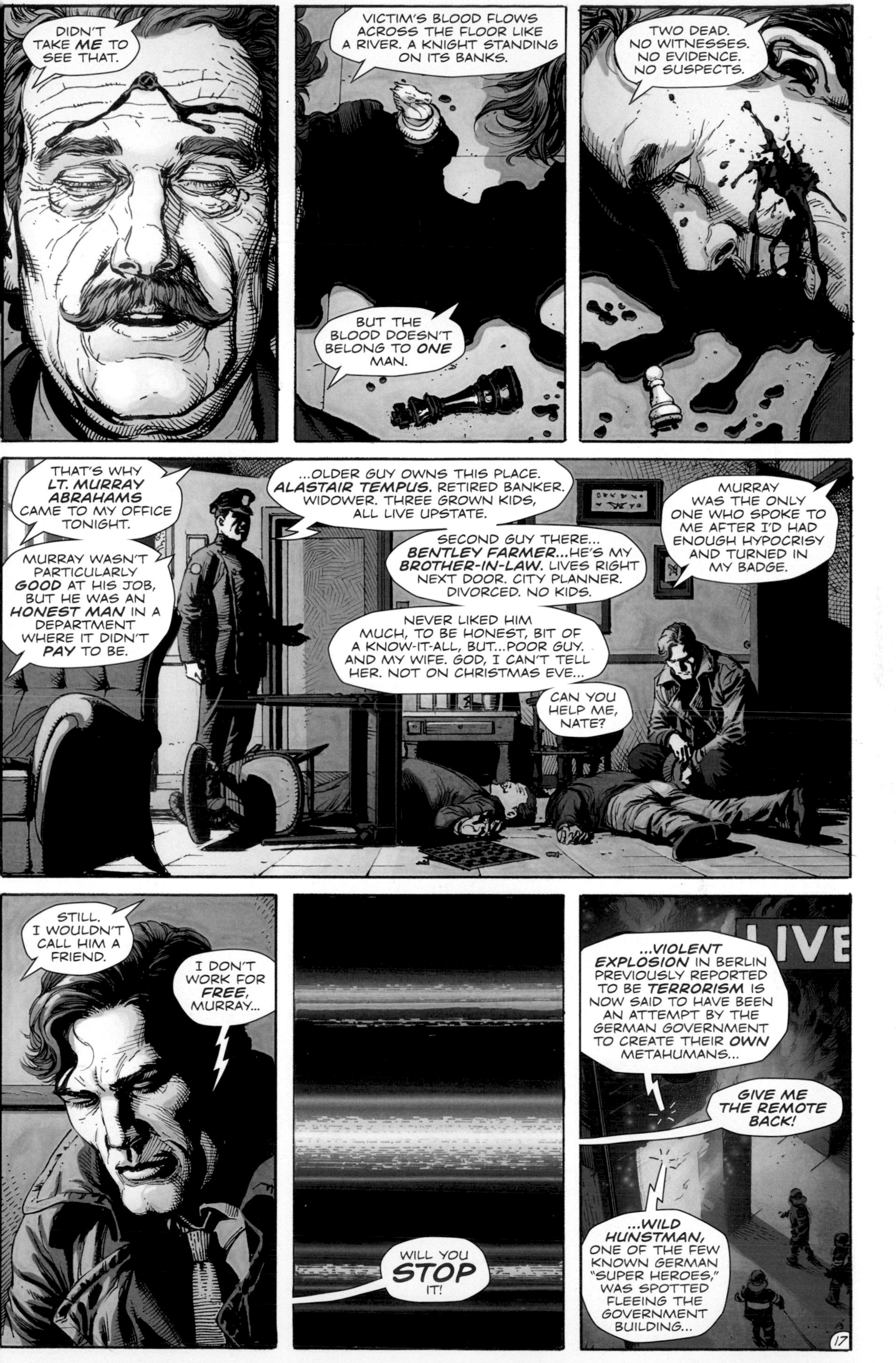
DIDN'T TAKE ME TO SEE THAT.
VICTIM'S BLOOD FLOWS ACROSS THE FLOOR LIKE A RIVER. A KNIGHT STANDING ON ITS BANKS.
BUT THE BLOOD DOESN'T BELONG TO ONE MAN.
TWO DEAD. NO WITNESSES. NO EVIDENCE. NO SUSPECTS.
THAT'S WHY LT. MURRAY ABRAHAMS CAME TO MY OFFICE TONIGHT.
MURRAY WASN'T PARTICULARLY GOOD AT HIS JOB, BUT HE WAS AN HONEST MAN IN A DEPARTMENT WHERE IT DIDN'T PAY TO BE.
...OLDER GUY OWNS THIS PLACE. ALASTAIR TEMPUS. RETIRED BANKER. WIDOWER. THREE GROWN KIDS, ALL LIVE UPSTATE.
SECOND GUY THERE... BENTLEY FARMER...HE'S MY BROTHER-IN-LAW. LIVES RIGHT NEXT DOOR. CITY PLANNER. DIVORCED. NO KIDS.
NEVER LIKED HIM MUCH, TO BE HONEST, BIT OF A KNOW-IT-ALL, BUT...POOR GUY. AND MY WIFE. GOD, I CAN'T TELL HER. NOT ON CHRISTMAS EVE...
CAN YOU HELP ME, NATE?
MURRAY WAS THE ONLY ONE WHO SPOKE TO ME AFTER I'D HAD ENOUGH HYPOCRISY AND TURNED IN MY BADGE.
STILL. I WOULDN'T CALL HIM A FRIEND.
I DON'T WORK FOR FREE, MURRAY...
WILL YOU STOP IT!
LIVE
...VIOLENT EXPLOSION IN BERLIN PREVIOUSLY REPORTED TO BE TERRORISM IS NOW SAID TO HAVE BEEN AN ATTEMPT BY THE GERMAN GOVERNMENT TO CREATE THEIR OWN METAHUMANS...
GIVE ME THE REMOTE BACK!
...WILD HUNSTMAN, ONE OF THE FEW KNOWN GERMAN "SUPER HEROES," WAS SPOTTED FLEEING THE GOVERNMENT BUILDING...
17

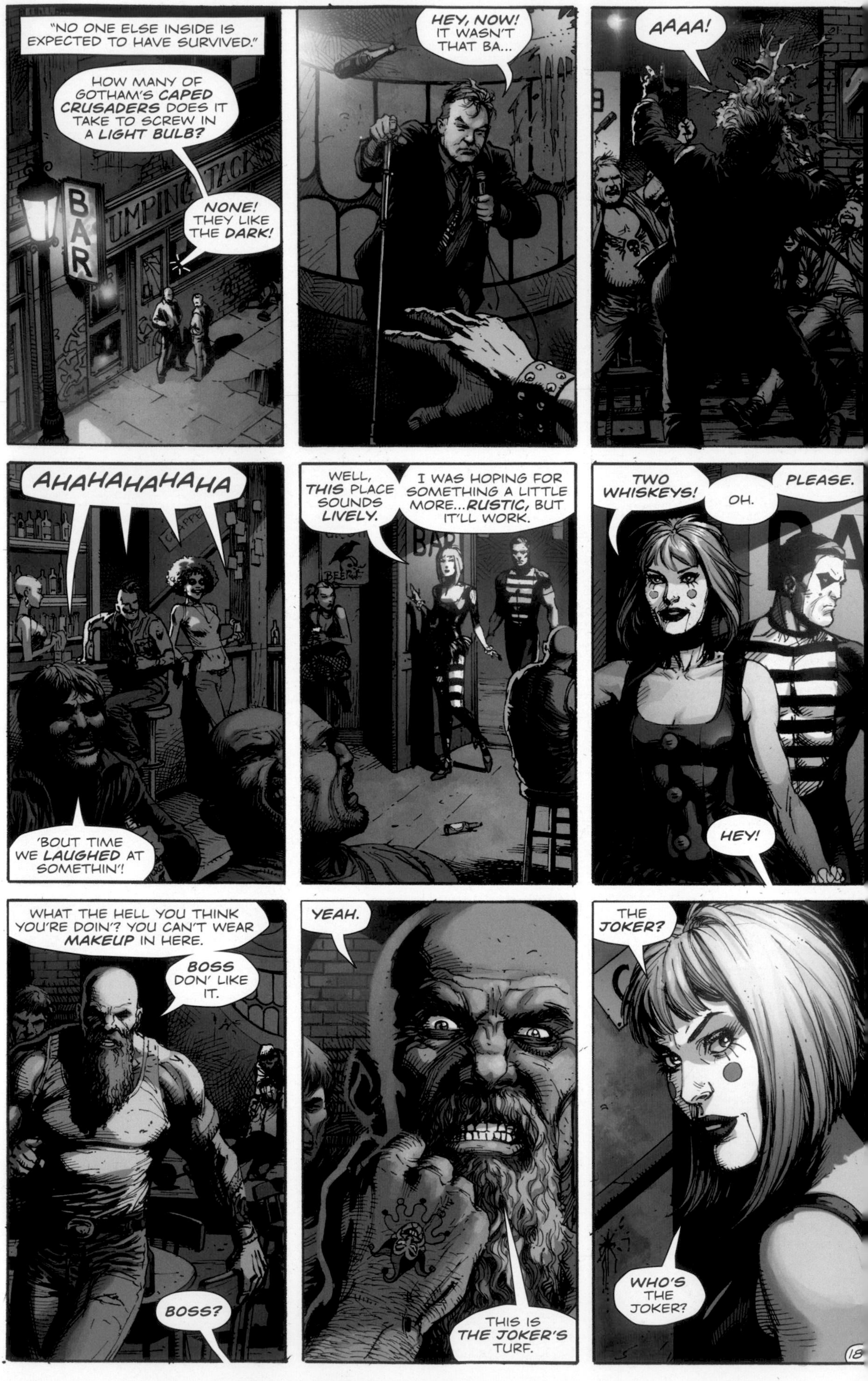
"NO ONE ELSE INSIDE IS EXPECTED TO HAVE SURVIVED."
HOW MANY OF GOTHAM'S CAPED CRUSADERS DOES IT TAKE TO SCREW IN A LIGHT BULB?
NONE! THEY LIKE THE DARK!
BAR
JUMPING JACKS
HEY, NOW! IT WASN'T THAT BA...
AAAA!
AHAHAHAHAHAHA
'BOUT TIME WE LAUGHED AT SOMETHIN'!
WELL, THIS PLACE SOUNDS LIVELY.
I WAS HOPING FOR SOMETHING A LITTLE MORE...RUSTIC, BUT IT'LL WORK.
TWO WHISKEYS!
OH.
PLEASE.
HEY!
WHAT THE HELL YOU THINK YOU'RE DOIN'? YOU CAN'T WEAR MAKEUP IN HERE.
BOSS DON' LIKE IT.
BOSS?
YEAH.
THIS IS THE JOKER'S TURF.
THE JOKER?
WHO'S THE JOKER?

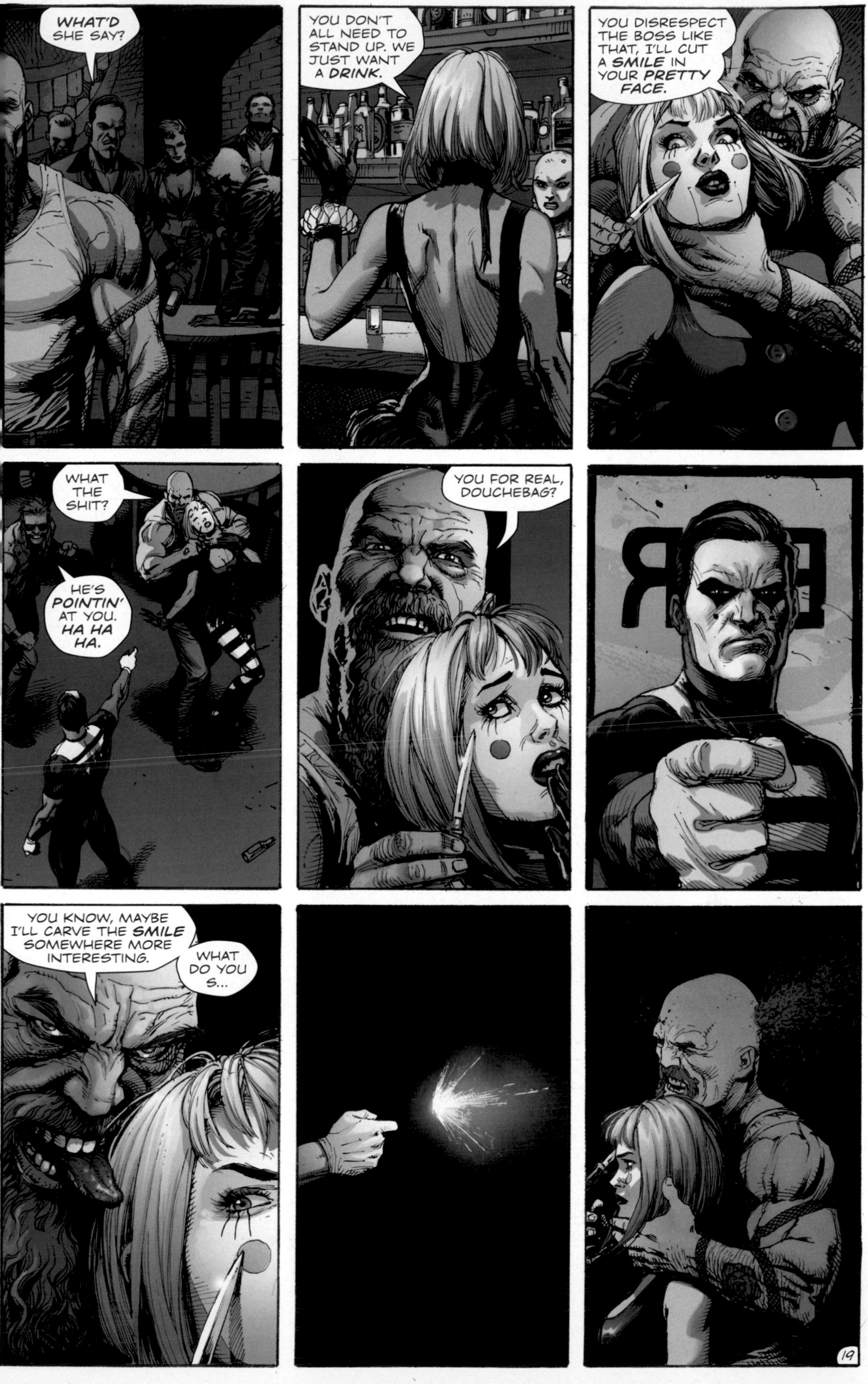
WHAT'D SHE SAY?
YOU DON'T ALL NEED TO STAND UP. WE JUST WANT A DRINK.
YOU DISRESPECT THE BOSS LIKE THAT, I'LL CUT A SMILE IN YOUR PRETTY FACE.
WHAT THE SHIT?
HE'S POINTIN' AT YOU. HA HA HA.
YOU FOR REAL, DOUCHEBAG?
YOU KNOW, MAYBE I'LL CARVE THE SMILE SOMEWHERE MORE INTERESTING.
WHAT DO YOU S...

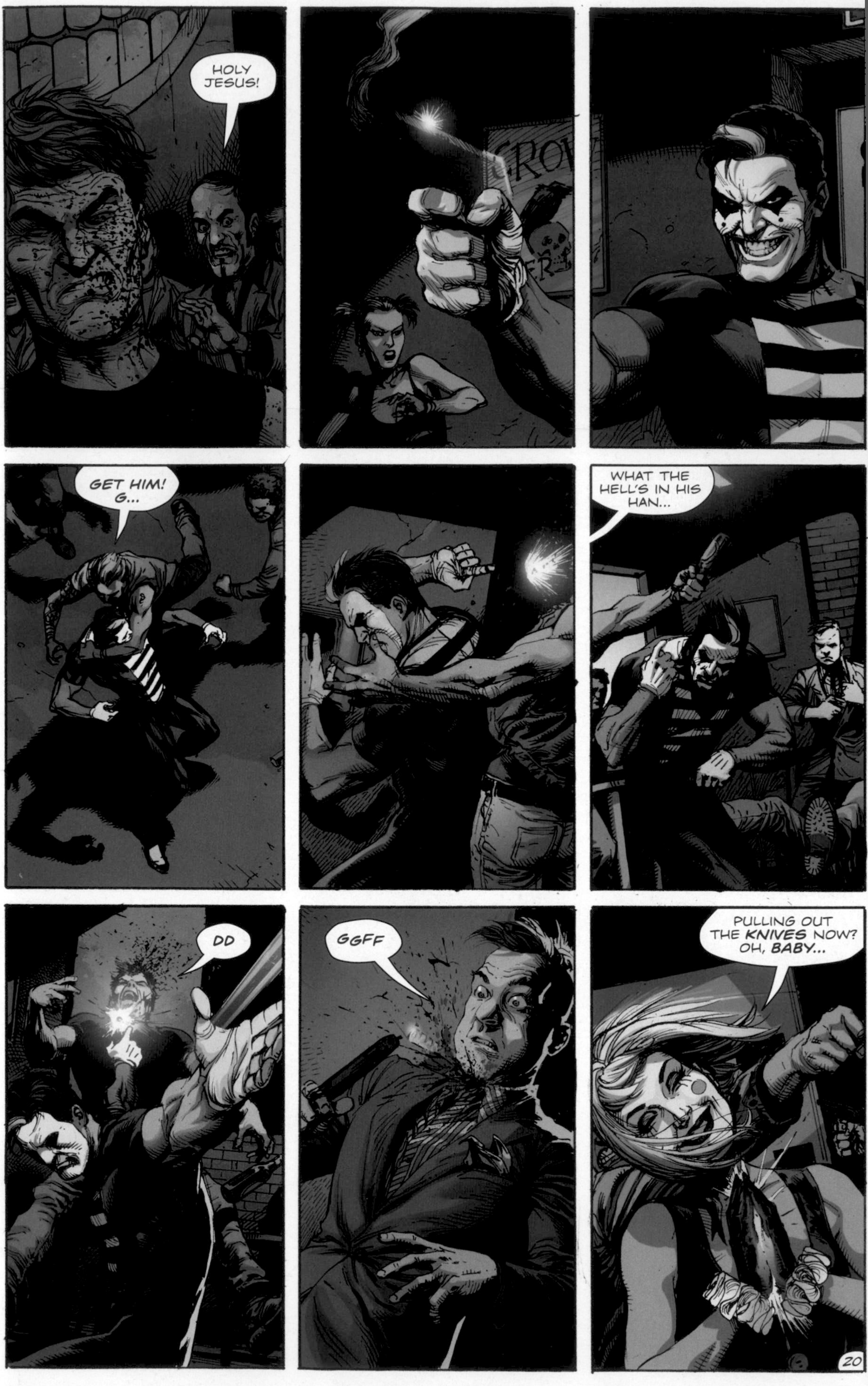
HOLY JESUS!
GET HIM! G...
WHAT THE HELL'S IN HIS HAN...
DD
GGFF
PULLING OUT THE **KNIVES** NOW? OH, **BABY**...

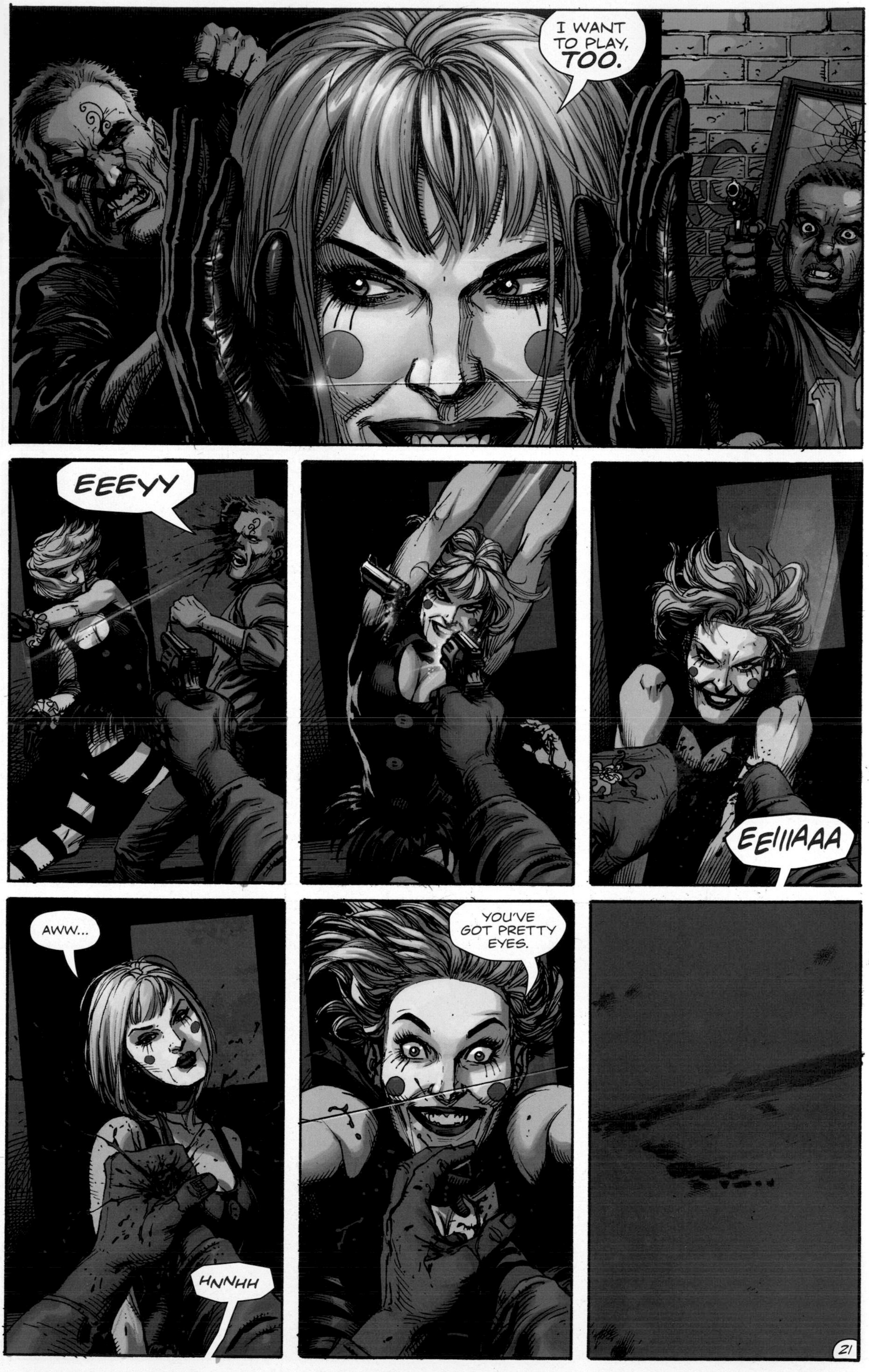

I WANT TO PLAY, TOO.
EEEYY
EEIIIAAA
AWW...
HNNHH
YOU'VE GOT PRETTY EYES.

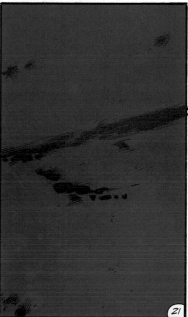

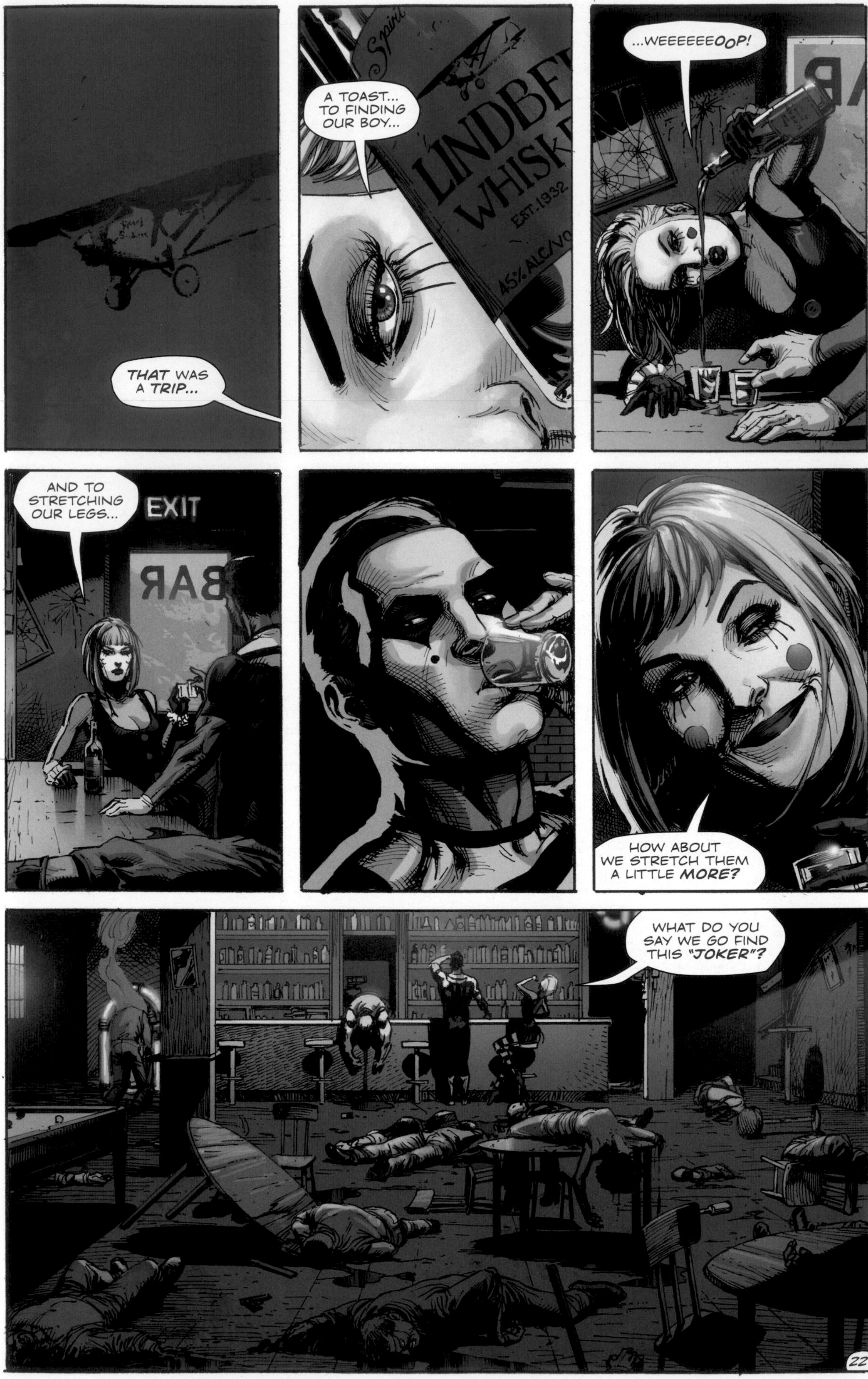
THAT WAS A TRIP...
A TOAST... TO FINDING OUR BOY...
LINDBE
WHISK
EST. 1932
45% ALC/VO
...WEEEEEEOOP!
AND TO STRETCHING OUR LEGS...
EXIT
BAR
HOW ABOUT WE STRETCH THEM A LITTLE MORE?
WHAT DO YOU SAY WE GO FIND THIS "JOKER"?

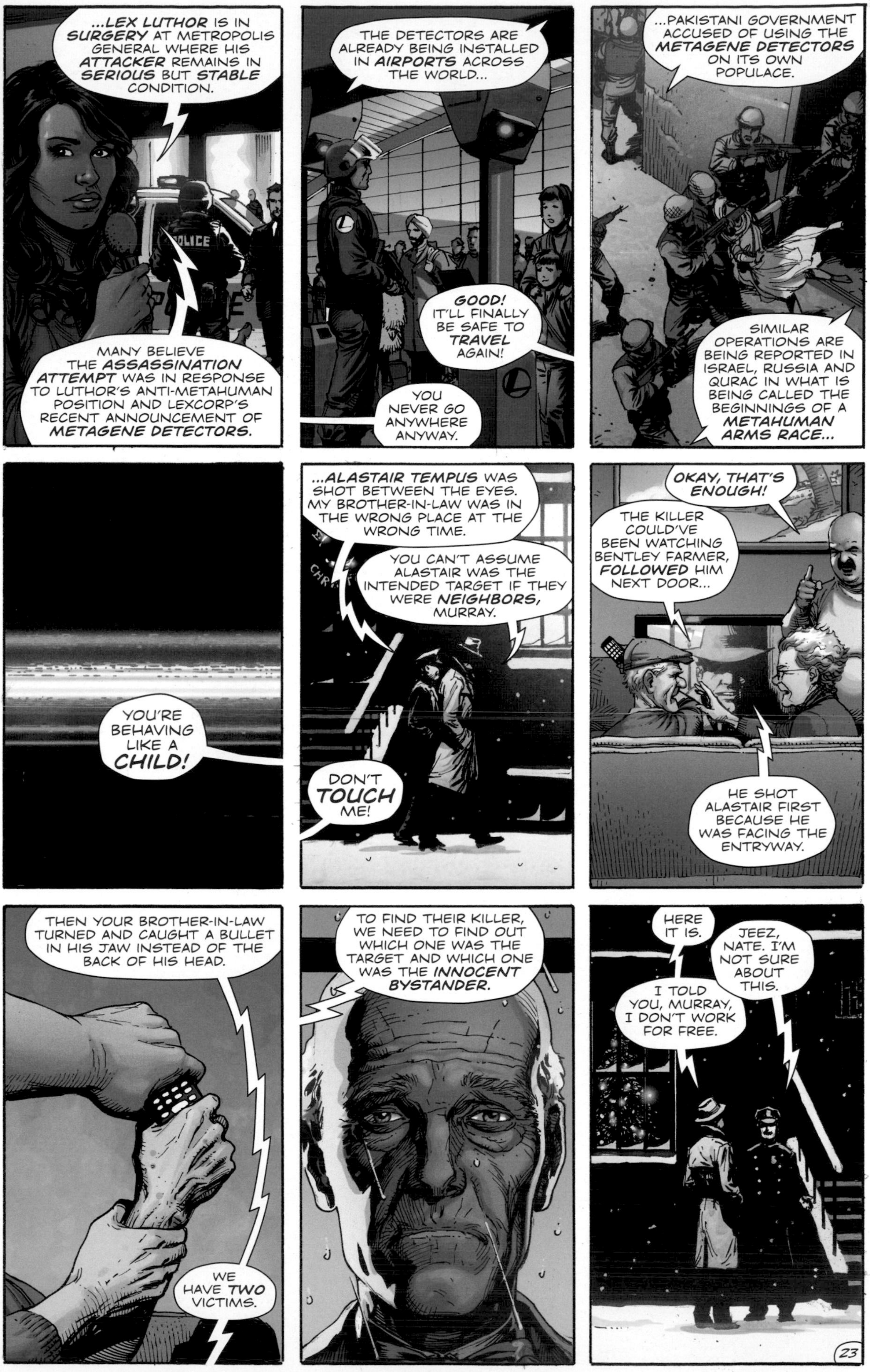
...LEX LUTHOR IS IN SURGERY AT METROPOLIS GENERAL WHERE HIS ATTACKER REMAINS IN SERIOUS BUT STABLE CONDITION.
POLICE
MANY BELIEVE THE ASSASSINATION ATTEMPT WAS IN RESPONSE TO LUTHOR'S ANTI-METAHUMAN POSITION AND LEXCORP'S RECENT ANNOUNCEMENT OF METAGENE DETECTORS.
THE DETECTORS ARE ALREADY BEING INSTALLED IN AIRPORTS ACROSS THE WORLD...
GOOD! IT'LL FINALLY BE SAFE TO TRAVEL AGAIN!
YOU NEVER GO ANYWHERE ANYWAY.
...PAKISTANI GOVERNMENT ACCUSED OF USING THE METAGENE DETECTORS ON ITS OWN POPULACE.
SIMILAR OPERATIONS ARE BEING REPORTED IN ISRAEL, RUSSIA AND QURAC IN WHAT IS BEING CALLED THE BEGINNINGS OF A METAHUMAN ARMS RACE...
YOU'RE BEHAVING LIKE A CHILD!
...ALASTAIR TEMPUS WAS SHOT BETWEEN THE EYES. MY BROTHER-IN-LAW WAS IN THE WRONG PLACE AT THE WRONG TIME.
YOU CAN'T ASSUME ALASTAIR WAS THE INTENDED TARGET IF THEY WERE NEIGHBORS, MURRAY.
DON'T TOUCH ME!
OKAY, THAT'S ENOUGH!
THE KILLER COULD'VE BEEN WATCHING BENTLEY FARMER, FOLLOWED HIM NEXT DOOR...
HE SHOT ALASTAIR FIRST BECAUSE HE WAS FACING THE ENTRYWAY.
THEN YOUR BROTHER-IN-LAW TURNED AND CAUGHT A BULLET IN HIS JAW INSTEAD OF THE BACK OF HIS HEAD.
WE HAVE TWO VICTIMS.
TO FIND THEIR KILLER, WE NEED TO FIND OUT WHICH ONE WAS THE TARGET AND WHICH ONE WAS THE INNOCENT BYSTANDER.
HERE IT IS.
JEEZ, NATE. I'M NOT SURE ABOUT THIS.
I TOLD YOU, MURRAY, I DON'T WORK FOR FREE.

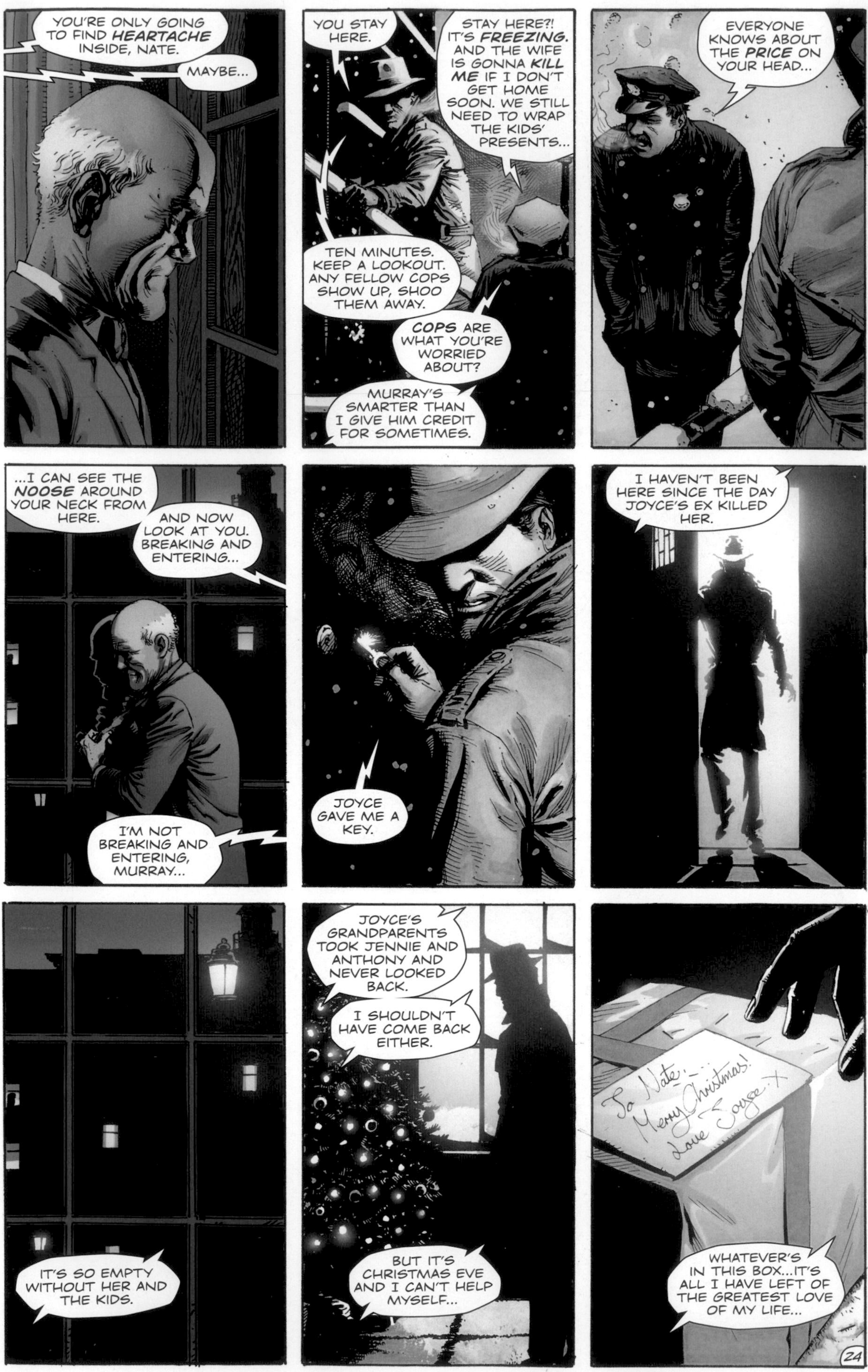
YOU'RE ONLY GOING TO FIND HEARTACHE INSIDE, NATE.
MAYBE...
YOU STAY HERE.
STAY HERE?! IT'S FREEZING. AND THE WIFE IS GONNA KILL ME IF I DON'T GET HOME SOON. WE STILL NEED TO WRAP THE KIDS' PRESENTS...
TEN MINUTES. KEEP A LOOKOUT. ANY FELLOW COPS SHOW UP, SHOO THEM AWAY.
COPS ARE WHAT YOU'RE WORRIED ABOUT?
MURRAY'S SMARTER THAN I GIVE HIM CREDIT FOR SOMETIMES.
EVERYONE KNOWS ABOUT THE PRICE ON YOUR HEAD...
...I CAN SEE THE NOOSE AROUND YOUR NECK FROM HERE.
AND NOW LOOK AT YOU. BREAKING AND ENTERING...
I'M NOT BREAKING AND ENTERING, MURRAY...
JOYCE GAVE ME A KEY.
I HAVEN'T BEEN HERE SINCE THE DAY JOYCE'S EX KILLED HER.
IT'S SO EMPTY WITHOUT HER AND THE KIDS.
JOYCE'S GRANDPARENTS TOOK JENNIE AND ANTHONY AND NEVER LOOKED BACK.
I SHOULDN'T HAVE COME BACK EITHER.
BUT IT'S CHRISTMAS EVE AND I CAN'T HELP MYSELF...
To Nate, Merry Christmas! Love Joyce x
WHATEVER'S IN THIS BOX...IT'S ALL I HAVE LEFT OF THE GREATEST LOVE OF MY LIFE...

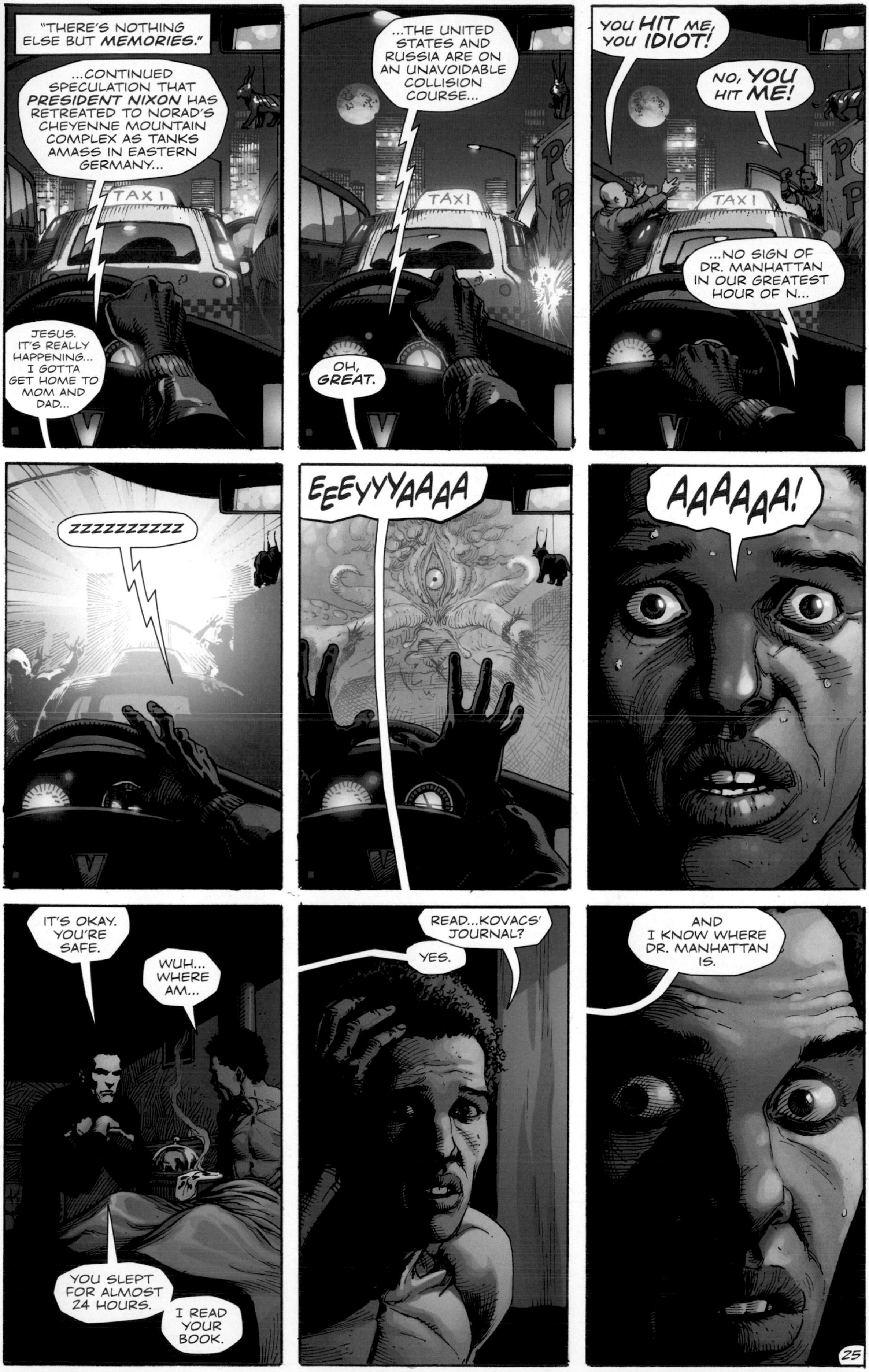
"THERE'S NOTHING ELSE BUT MEMORIES."
...CONTINUED SPECULATION THAT PRESIDENT NIXON HAS RETREATED TO NORAD'S CHEYENNE MOUNTAIN COMPLEX AS TANKS AMASS IN EASTERN GERMANY...
TAXI
JESUS. IT'S REALLY HAPPENING... I GOTTA GET HOME TO MOM AND DAD...
...THE UNITED STATES AND RUSSIA ARE ON AN UNAVOIDABLE COLLISION COURSE...
TAXI
OH, GREAT.
YOU HIT ME, YOU IDIOT!
NO, YOU HIT ME!
TAXI
...NO SIGN OF DR. MANHATTAN IN OUR GREATEST HOUR OF N...
ZZZZZZZZZZ
EEEYYYAAAA
AAAAAA!
IT'S OKAY. YOU'RE SAFE.
WUH... WHERE AM...
YOU SLEPT FOR ALMOST 24 HOURS.
I READ YOUR BOOK.
READ...KOVACS' JOURNAL?
YES.
AND I KNOW WHERE DR. MANHATTAN IS.

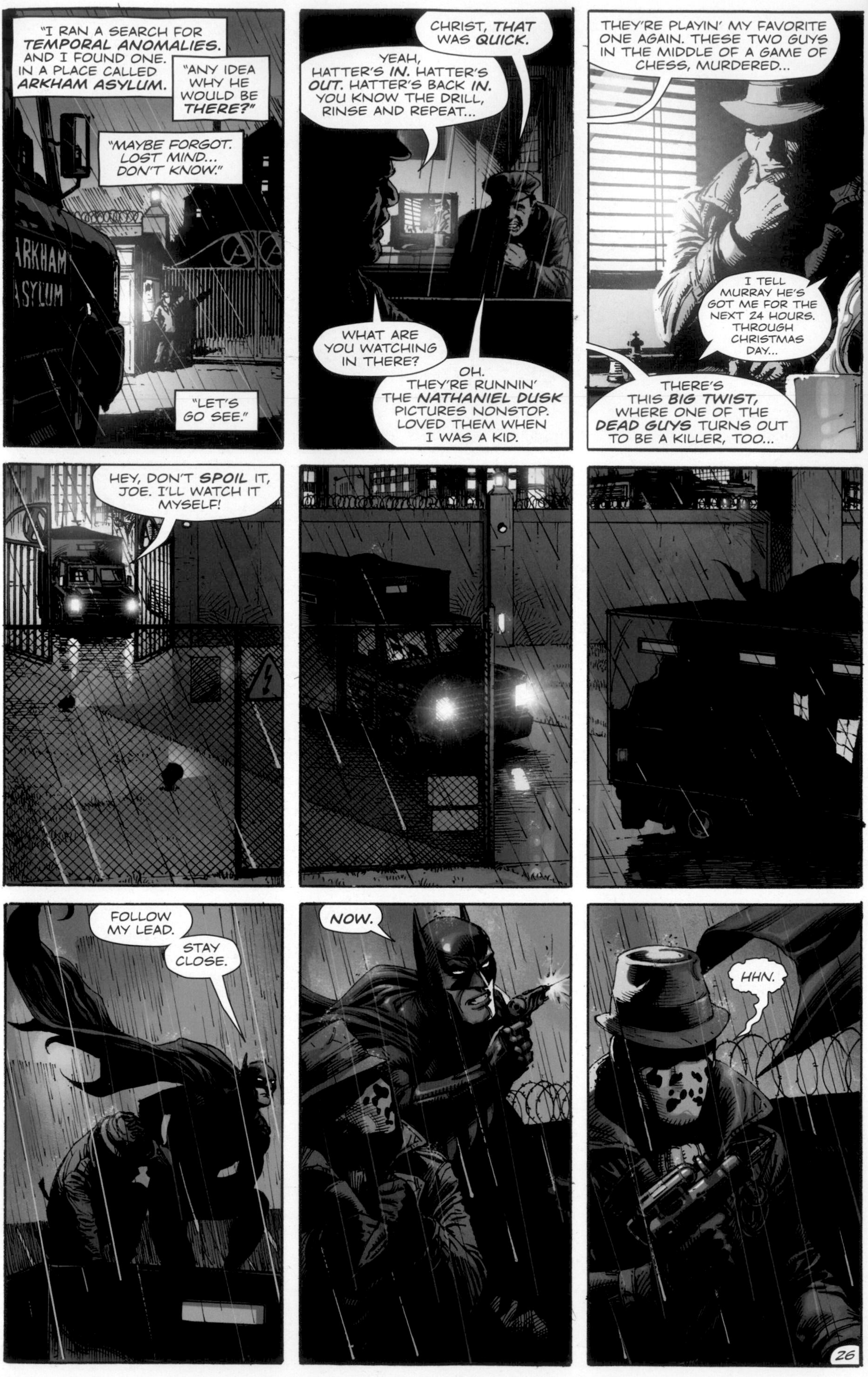

"I RAN A SEARCH FOR TEMPORAL ANOMALIES. AND I FOUND ONE. IN A PLACE CALLED ARKHAM ASYLUM.
"ANY IDEA WHY HE WOULD BE THERE?"
"MAYBE FORGOT. LOST MIND... DON'T KNOW."
ARKHAM ASYLUM
"LET'S GO SEE."
CHRIST, THAT WAS QUICK.
YEAH, HATTER'S IN. HATTER'S OUT. HATTER'S BACK IN. YOU KNOW THE DRILL, RINSE AND REPEAT...
WHAT ARE YOU WATCHING IN THERE?
OH. THEY'RE RUNNIN' THE NATHANIEL DUSK PICTURES NONSTOP. LOVED THEM WHEN I WAS A KID.
THEY'RE PLAYIN' MY FAVORITE ONE AGAIN. THESE TWO GUYS IN THE MIDDLE OF A GAME OF CHESS, MURDERED...
I TELL MURRAY HE'S GOT ME FOR THE NEXT 24 HOURS. THROUGH CHRISTMAS DAY...
THERE'S THIS BIG TWIST, WHERE ONE OF THE DEAD GUYS TURNS OUT TO BE A KILLER, TOO...
HEY, DON'T SPOIL IT, JOE. I'LL WATCH IT MYSELF!
FOLLOW MY LEAD.
STAY CLOSE.
NOW.
HHN.

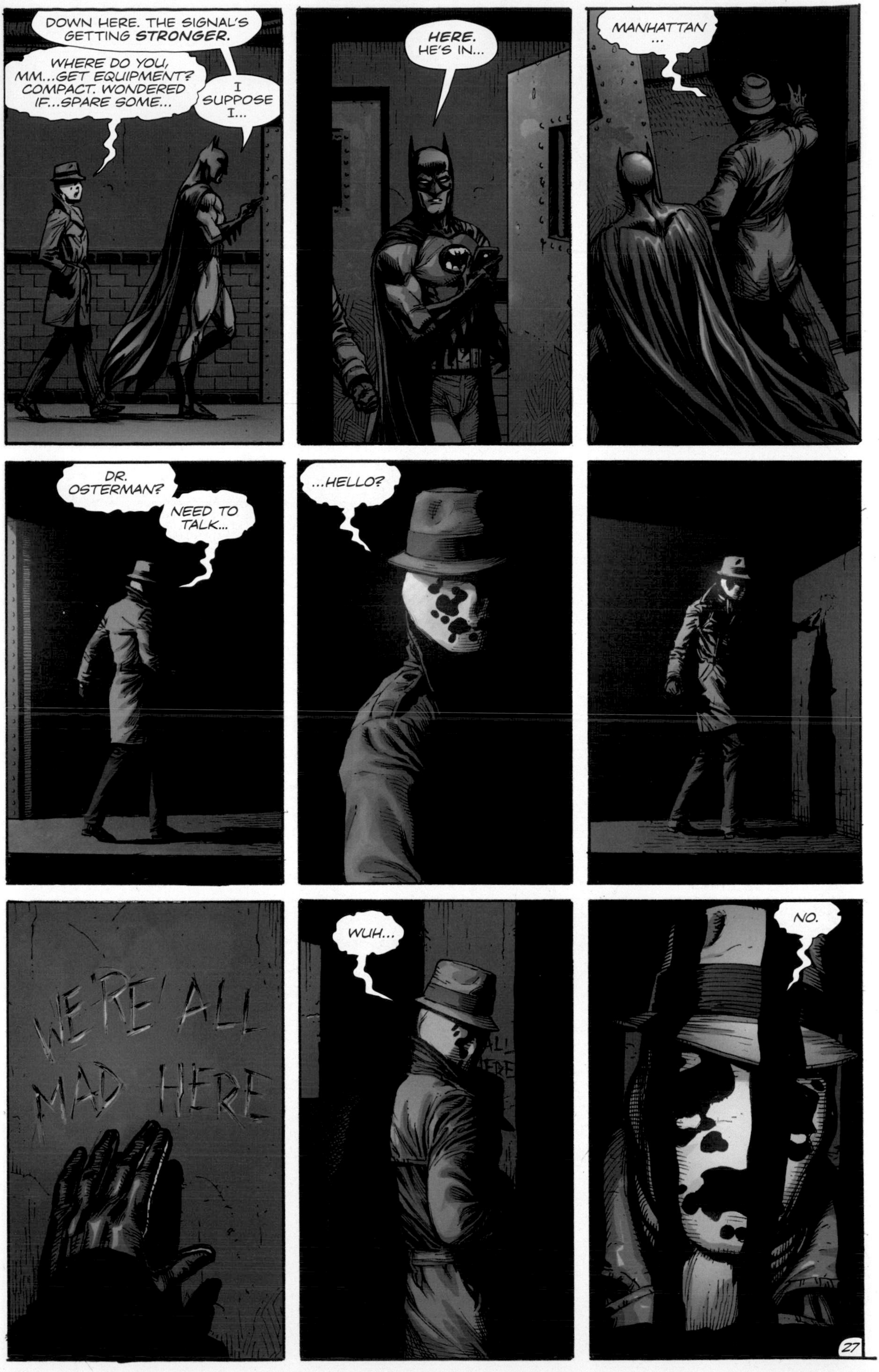
DOWN HERE. THE SIGNAL'S GETTING **STRONGER.**
WHERE DO YOU, MM...GET EQUIPMENT? COMPACT. WONDERED IF...SPARE SOME...
I SUPPOSE I...
HERE. HE'S IN...
MANHATTAN ...
DR. OSTERMAN?
NEED TO TALK...
...HELLO?
WE'RE ALL MAD HERE
WUH...
NO.

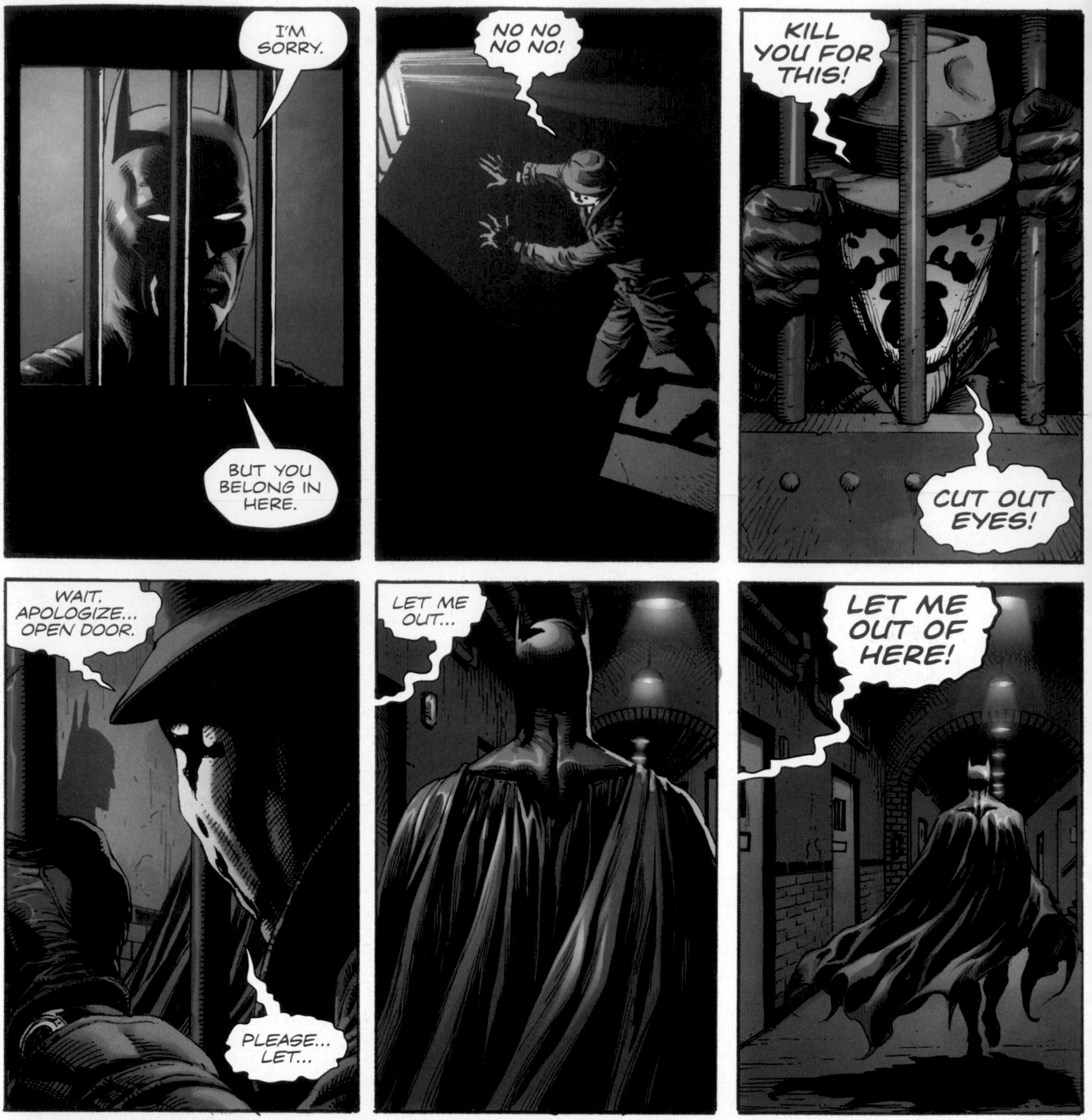
I'M SORRY.
BUT YOU BELONG IN HERE.
NO NO NO NO!
KILL YOU FOR THIS!
CUT OUT EYES!
WAIT. APOLOGIZE... OPEN DOOR.
PLEASE... LET...
LET ME OUT...
LET ME OUT OF HERE!

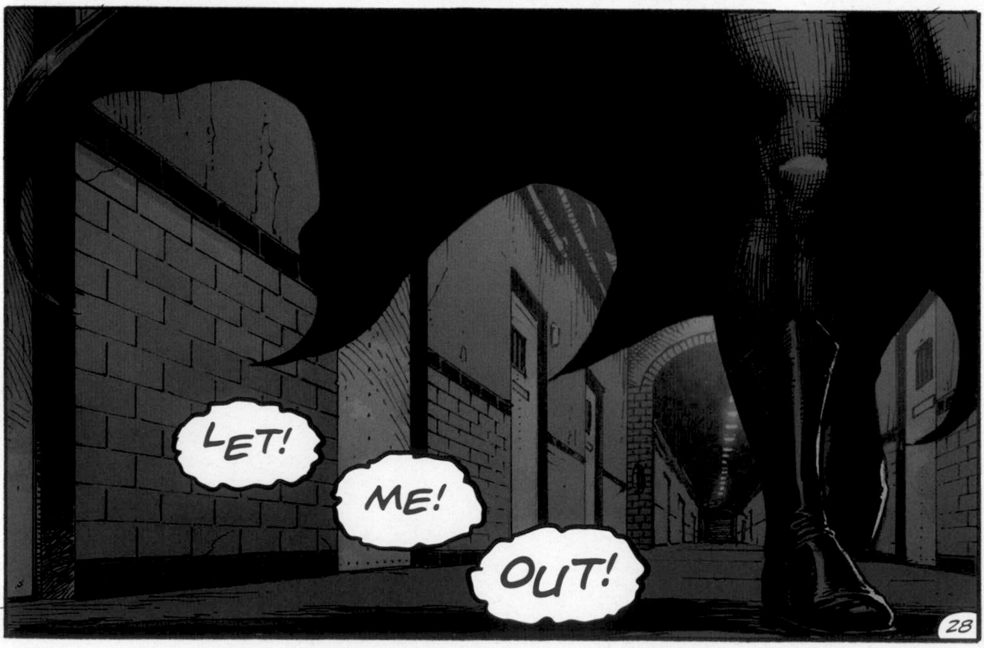
LET!
ME!
OUT!

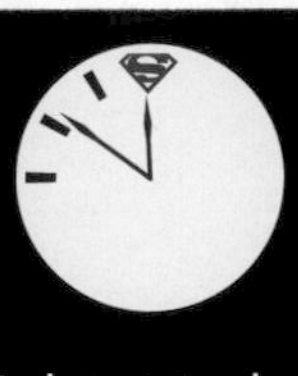

Far better is it to dare mighty things, to win glorious triumphs, even though checkered by failure...than to rank with those poor spirits who neither enjoy nor suffer much, because they live in a gray twilight that knows not victory nor defeat.

—Theodore Roosevelt

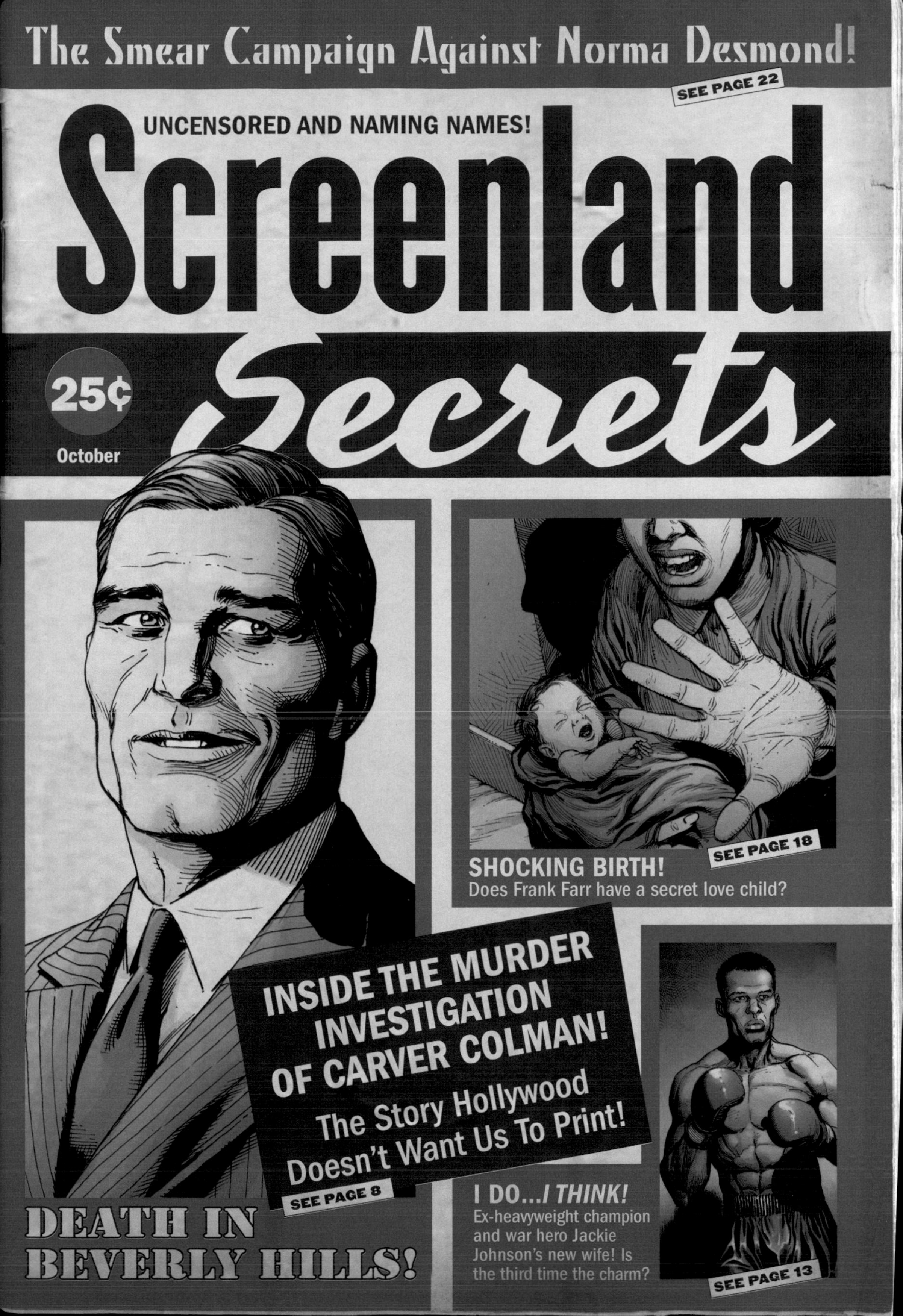
The Smear Campaign Against Norma Desmond!
SEE PAGE 22
UNCENSORED AND NAMING NAMES!
Screenland Secrets
25¢
October
SHOCKING BIRTH!
Does Frank Farr have a secret love child?
SEE PAGE 18
INSIDE THE MURDER INVESTIGATION OF CARVER COLMAN!
The Story Hollywood Doesn't Want Us To Print!
SEE PAGE 8
DEATH IN BEVERLY HILLS!
I DO...I THINK!
Ex-heavyweight champion and war hero Jackie Johnson's new wife! Is the third time the charm?
SEE PAGE 13

The Detective Becomes The Victim!

By Hedda Hopper

An actor at the height of his career, Carver Colman, the beloved star of the Nathaniel Dusk pictures, kept his private life secret for a reason.

In the early hours of June 9, Carver Colman's body was found on the floor of his living room by his housekeeper. He had been out at Tam O'Shanter's for dinner the night before, celebrating the completion of "The Adjournment" with friends, including director Jacques Tourneur and studio heads Albert and Karl Verner, only to be discovered hours later, brutally beaten to death. The murder weapon? The award Colman won for his work in "Lovers Die at

Won for his work in "Lovers Die at Dusk", Carver Colman's award was found near his body, covered in blood.

Dusk." The only thing missing from his body was a watch he always wore, given to him by his parents the day he left home. Other details surrounding the bloody crime were kept confidential by the Beverly Hills Police Department to "protect their investigation." But months later, Carver Colman's murder remains unsolved. His name seems destined to join the likes of William Desmond Taylor and Elizabeth Short…or does it?

"Screenland Secrets" has uncovered shocking evidence pointing to a secret in Carver Colman's past that you can believe his Studio would have been desperate to keep hidden at any cost! In fact, Verner Bros collected millions of dollars in insurance because of Carver Colman's death…

Carver Colman was the only son of Irish immigrants who settled in Merillville, Indiana. Colman told stories of working his family's farm while dreaming of starring in the pictures his father often took him to. Colman once said, "I saw 'In Old Arizona' on Christmas Day in '28 and I was mesmerized. I packed up some clothes and left Merillville the next morning." He arrived in Hollywood on New Year's Eve. Colman eventually landed a handful of small roles in various pictures, but it was his performance as a drifter alongside Gary Cooper in "The Westerner" in 1940 that led to him being cast as Nathaniel Dusk. Despite the controversy surrounding "Nothing Left to Lose," the first Nathaniel Dusk picture became a hit and

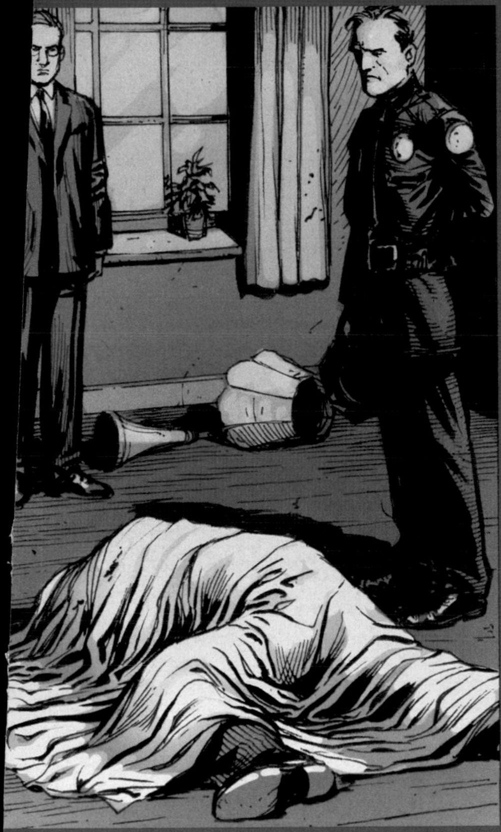

Carver Colman was murdered in his home, his face beaten until it was unrecognizable by even his closest friends.

transformed Carver Colman into a household name. However, Colman kept his personal life private. He claimed he enjoyed a quiet life outside of work, gardening and collecting watches. But Colman's "life" may have been as false as the sets he filmed on. We've learned that after Colman's death, the police were unable to locate his parents or the farm he claimed he grew up on. And then weeks into the investigation, police made a shocking discovery within Colman's home in Beverly Hills: a secret room in Colman's house! The walls were filled with clocks, his extensive watch collection on display. And in the center of this secret "ticktock room" was a desk overflowing with papers and documents. One in particular stood out to police. It was a letter from a woman claiming to be Carver Colman's actual mother--a retired dancer from Philadelphia named Charlotte Colman who had once been associated with the Sabella crime family. She was attempting to blackmail her "son" for money, but she disappeared shortly after. So was this woman really Colman's mother? Was Carver Colman tied to the Sabella crime family? Or was this all a blackmail scam gone wrong? Did he refuse to pay and pay the price? Detective Bruce Nelson, a specialist called down from the San Francisco Police Department to review the case, suspects Albert and Karl Verner know more than they've said…but they aren't spilling any more secrets. Yet!

NOT FOR THE CHILDREN!

Carver Colman's controversial Nathaniel Dusk pictures may have been some of the most successful films to have come from Verner Bros Studios, but many also call them an example of the morally destitute society of Hollywood!

Nothing Left To Lose (1943)
Directed by Robert Siodmak, the first Dusk picture earned notoriety for using words like virgin and abortion and featuring a Private Investigator suffering from battle fatigue and fighting police corruption.

A Killer Calls (1945)
Directed by Otto Preminger, the second film in the Dusk series was banned in seven States for its depiction of dope use. Something Hollywood knows a lot about!

Murder at Home (1947)
Director Jules Dassin helmed one of the more balanced pictures in the Dusk series which featured Frank Farr as Dusk's fellow army veteran who is suspected of killing their former officer. However, during its release screenwriter Ring Lardner Jr. was in prison for contempt of Congress for failing to answer any questions to the House Un-American Activities Committee. He was released in October the same year, but has since left the business. Good riddance!

A Killer's Kiss (1950)
Otto Preminger and the mysterious murderer from "A Killer Calls" both returned in a picture that was plagued with production problems, including the untimely death of Colman's would-be co-star, Jean Gillie. She died of pneumonia at the age of 33. Gillie was replaced by Hedy Lamarr.

Lovers Die at Dusk (1952)
This picture was nominated for four Academy Awards, winning two. Carver Colman took home the award for Best Actor and Don McGregor for Best Director. Colman's award would later be used to bludgeon him to death.

The Adjournment (1954)
Directed by Jacques Tourneur, "The Adjournment" will not be released until the winter of this year. Tragically marking the final picture for Carver Colman, the film tells the tale of Nathaniel Dusk as he struggles after the death of his fiancé, Joyce Gulino. Dusk is recruited on Christmas Eve by the police he once worked alongside to help solve a bizarre murder scene. But we're told he soon uncovers an even more chilling secret that puts him in the killer's sites.

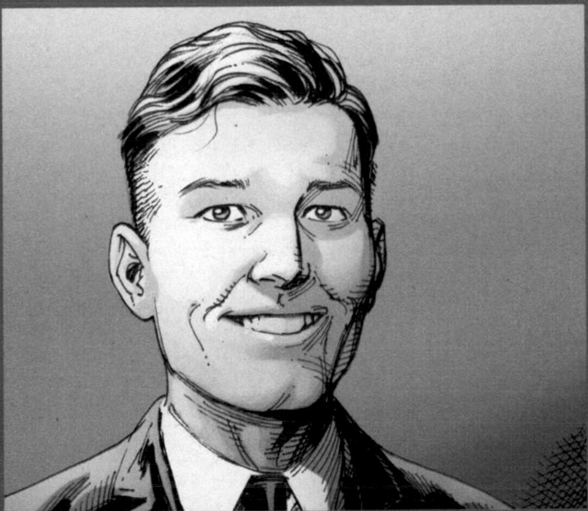

Carver Colman first arrived in Hollywood in 1928. At the age of 16, he delivered mail at Paramount Pictures before landing his first role as a young soldier in Frank Turtle's "Only the Brave" in 1930.

SUNSET BLVD. 6200

VINE ST. 1400

COAST TO COAST

BROADWAY

42ND STREET

Secrets

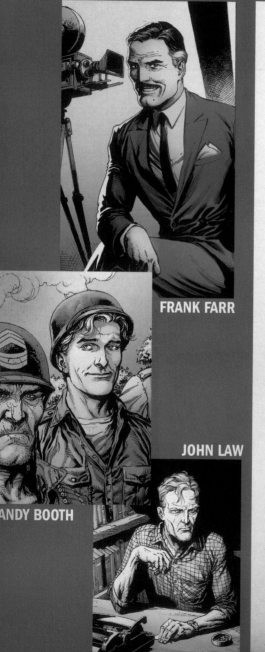

FRANK FARR

JOHN LAW

RANDY BOOTH

THE RUMOR: Frank Farr strayed from his marriage to Barbara Stanwyck and is now the new father of a secret love child!

THE FACT: Memo to maidens: *Beware!* It's definitely true! Frank Farr, the star of last year's smash hit "Another Holiday Affair," was seen nine months ago at the Golden Nugget in Las Vegas with actress Rachel Drake on his arm. Rumors swirled, but Frank insisted they were just friends. Then last week, Rachel gave birth to a new baby girl named Rita, telling close family and friends it was indeed Frank's daughter. Barbara Stanwyck filed for divorce the day Rita Farr was born.

* * *

THE RUMOR: Randy "Tin Soldier" Booth was thrown out of Jackie Johnson's wedding!

THE FACT: It's true…for the most part! Jackie's fellow war vets from Easy Company were all in attendance in Beverly Hills last Sunday to celebrate the ex-heavyweight champion's third marriage! Yes, third! But when Jackie requested a moment of silence to honor Easy Company's fallen leader and war hero, Sgt. Frank Rock, Randy "Tin Soldier" Booth – a moderately successful actor from several drama pictures in the 30's – interrupted the proceedings, arguing with Jackie about Frank Rock's death and a conspiracy tied to it. It took several of the attendees, including boxing champion Ted Grant, to restrain Booth so that the ceremony could proceed. Currently, Booth is undergoing treatment at Walter Reed General Hospital for Combat stress reaction.

* * *

THE RUMOR: Screenwriter John Law is the prime suspect in Carver Colman's murder!

THE FACT: It's true that John Law, the Academy Award nominated screenwriter, was questioned by police in the days after Carver Colman's murder, but he was never on the suspect list due to an airtight alibi: John was in the drunk tank the night of Colman's death! Following his break-up with his wife, former Olympian Libby Lawrence, John had been on a bender across Hollywood. The night Carver Colman was murdered, John was at the Formosa on Santa Monica Blvd. buying round after round. He was on his way home to Hancock Park when he crashed into a street lamp and was arrested.

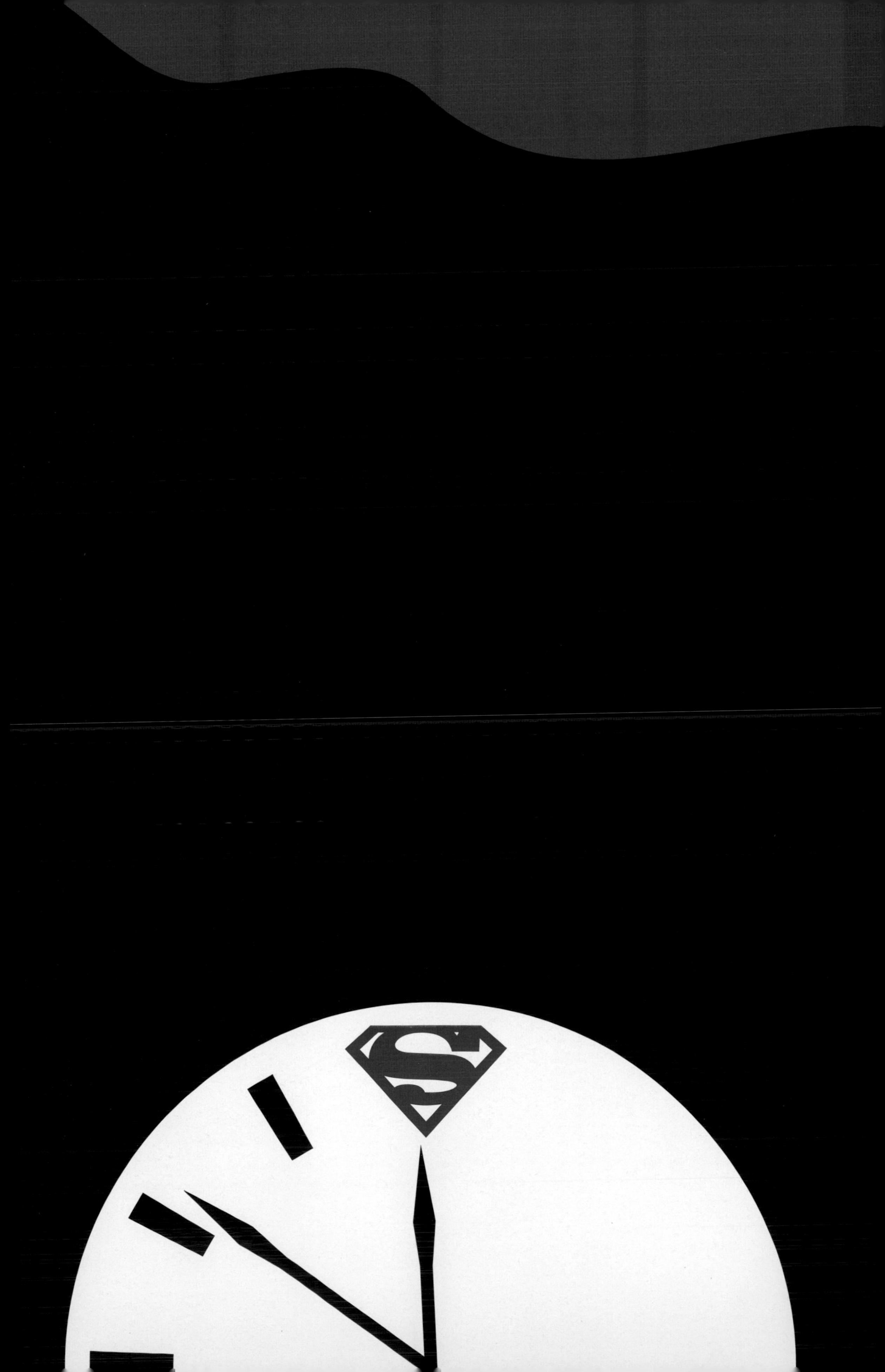

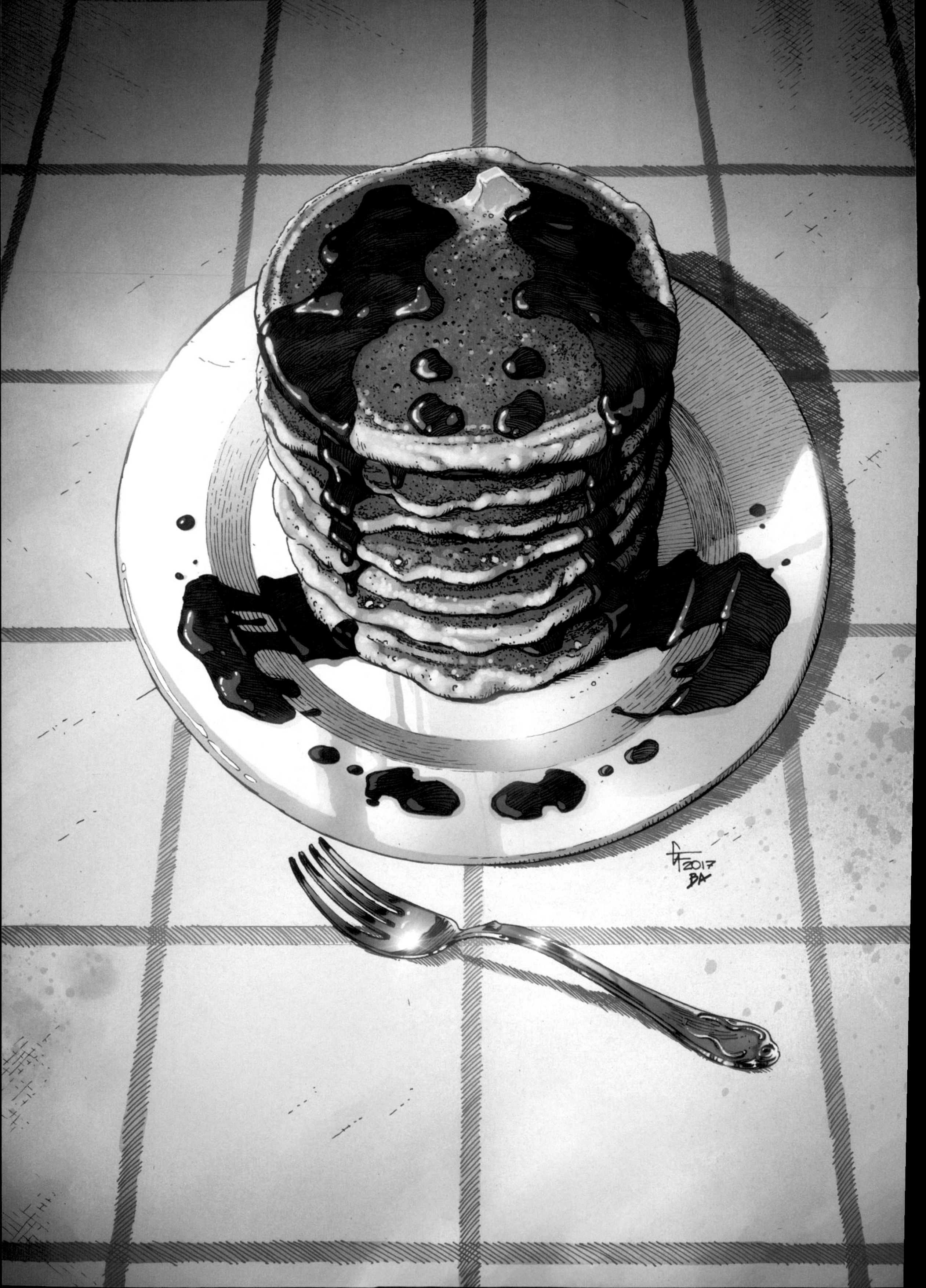

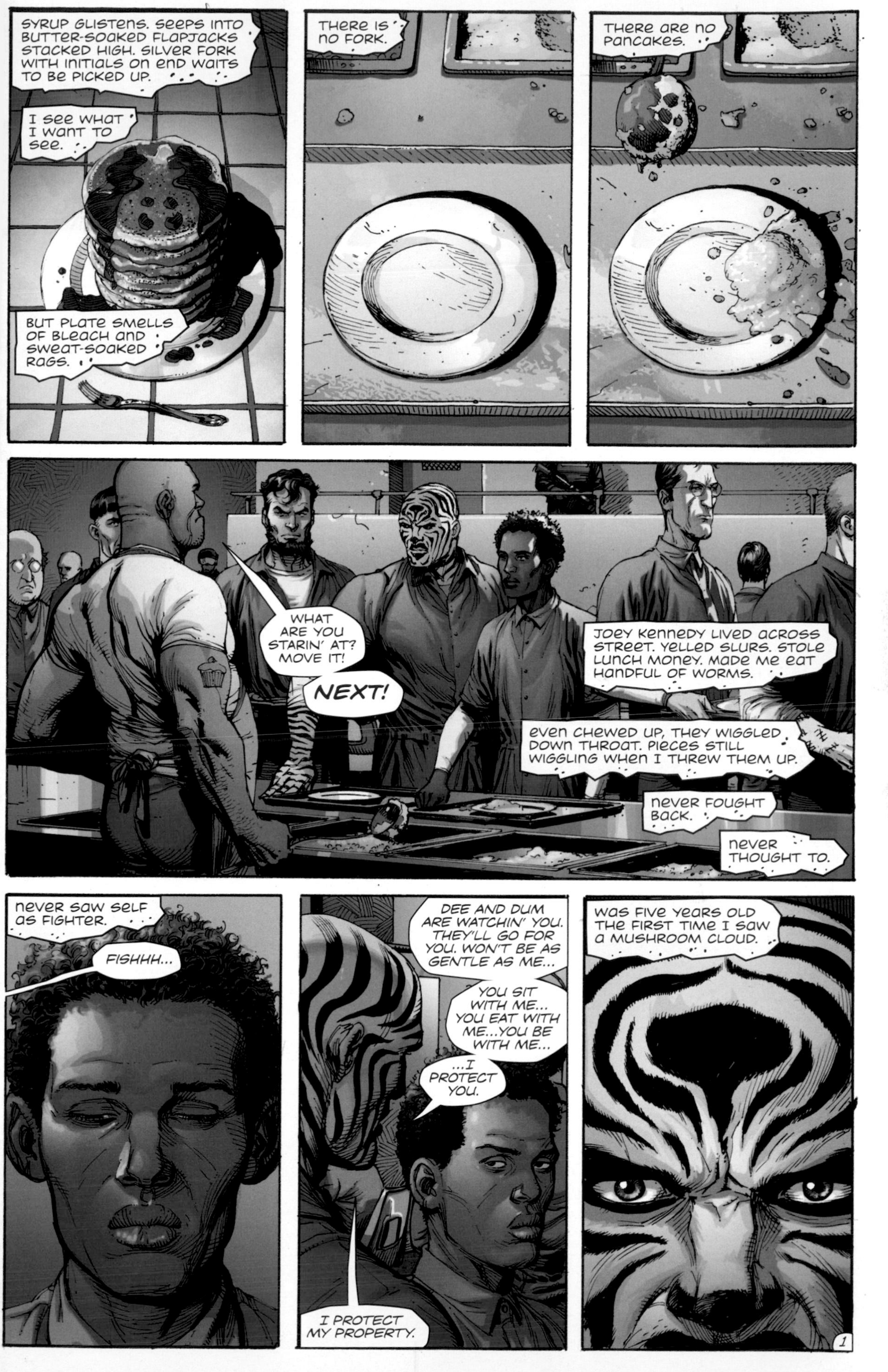
SYRUP GLISTENS. SEEPS INTO BUTTER-SOAKED FLAPJACKS STACKED HIGH. SILVER FORK WITH INITIALS ON END WAITS TO BE PICKED UP.
I SEE WHAT I WANT TO SEE.
BUT PLATE SMELLS OF BLEACH AND SWEAT-SOAKED RAGS.
THERE IS NO FORK.
THERE ARE NO PANCAKES.
WHAT ARE YOU STARIN' AT? MOVE IT!
NEXT!
JOEY KENNEDY LIVED ACROSS STREET. YELLED SLURS. STOLE LUNCH MONEY. MADE ME EAT HANDFUL OF WORMS.
EVEN CHEWED UP, THEY WIGGLED DOWN THROAT. PIECES STILL WIGGLING WHEN I THREW THEM UP.
NEVER FOUGHT BACK.
NEVER THOUGHT TO.
NEVER SAW SELF AS FIGHTER.
FISHHH...
DEE AND DUM ARE WATCHIN' YOU. THEY'LL GO FOR YOU. WON'T BE AS GENTLE AS ME...
YOU SIT WITH ME... YOU EAT WITH ME...YOU BE WITH ME...
...I PROTECT YOU.
I PROTECT MY PROPERTY.
WAS FIVE YEARS OLD THE FIRST TIME I SAW A MUSHROOM CLOUD.
1

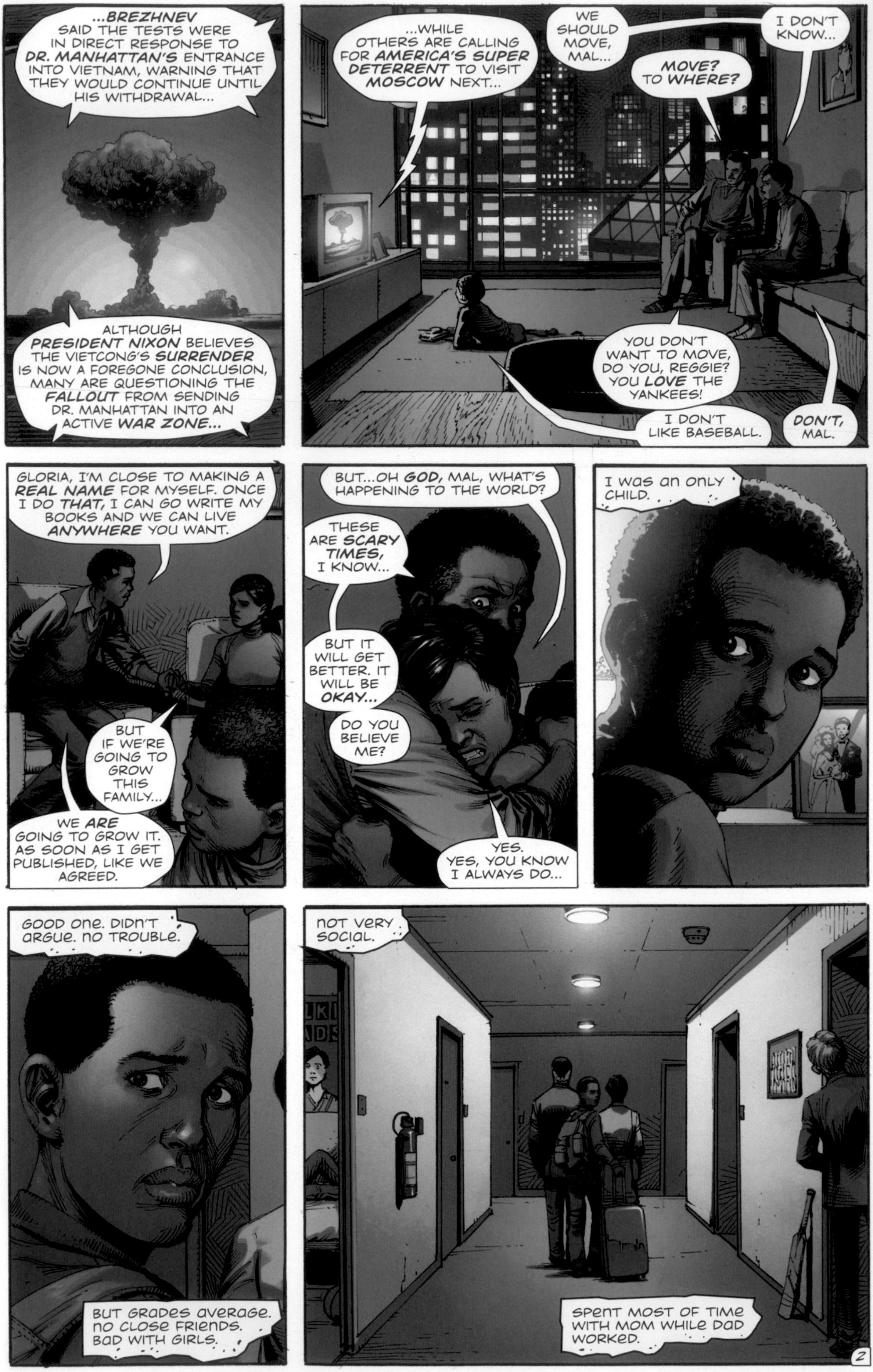
...BREZHNEV SAID THE TESTS WERE IN DIRECT RESPONSE TO DR. MANHATTAN'S ENTRANCE INTO VIETNAM, WARNING THAT THEY WOULD CONTINUE UNTIL HIS WITHDRAWAL...
ALTHOUGH PRESIDENT NIXON BELIEVES THE VIETCONG'S SURRENDER IS NOW A FOREGONE CONCLUSION, MANY ARE QUESTIONING THE FALLOUT FROM SENDING DR. MANHATTAN INTO AN ACTIVE WAR ZONE...
...WHILE OTHERS ARE CALLING FOR AMERICA'S SUPER DETERRENT TO VISIT MOSCOW NEXT...
WE SHOULD MOVE, MAL...
I DON'T KNOW...
MOVE? TO WHERE?
YOU DON'T WANT TO MOVE, DO YOU, REGGIE? YOU LOVE THE YANKEES!
I DON'T LIKE BASEBALL.
DON'T, MAL.
GLORIA, I'M CLOSE TO MAKING A REAL NAME FOR MYSELF. ONCE I DO THAT, I CAN GO WRITE MY BOOKS AND WE CAN LIVE ANYWHERE YOU WANT.
BUT IF WE'RE GOING TO GROW THIS FAMILY...
WE ARE GOING TO GROW IT. AS SOON AS I GET PUBLISHED, LIKE WE AGREED.
BUT...OH GOD, MAL, WHAT'S HAPPENING TO THE WORLD?
THESE ARE SCARY TIMES, I KNOW...
BUT IT WILL GET BETTER. IT WILL BE OKAY...
DO YOU BELIEVE ME?
YES. YES, YOU KNOW I ALWAYS DO...
I was an only child.
Good one. Didn't argue. no trouble.
But grades average. no close friends. Bad with girls.
not very social.
spent most of time with mom while dad worked.

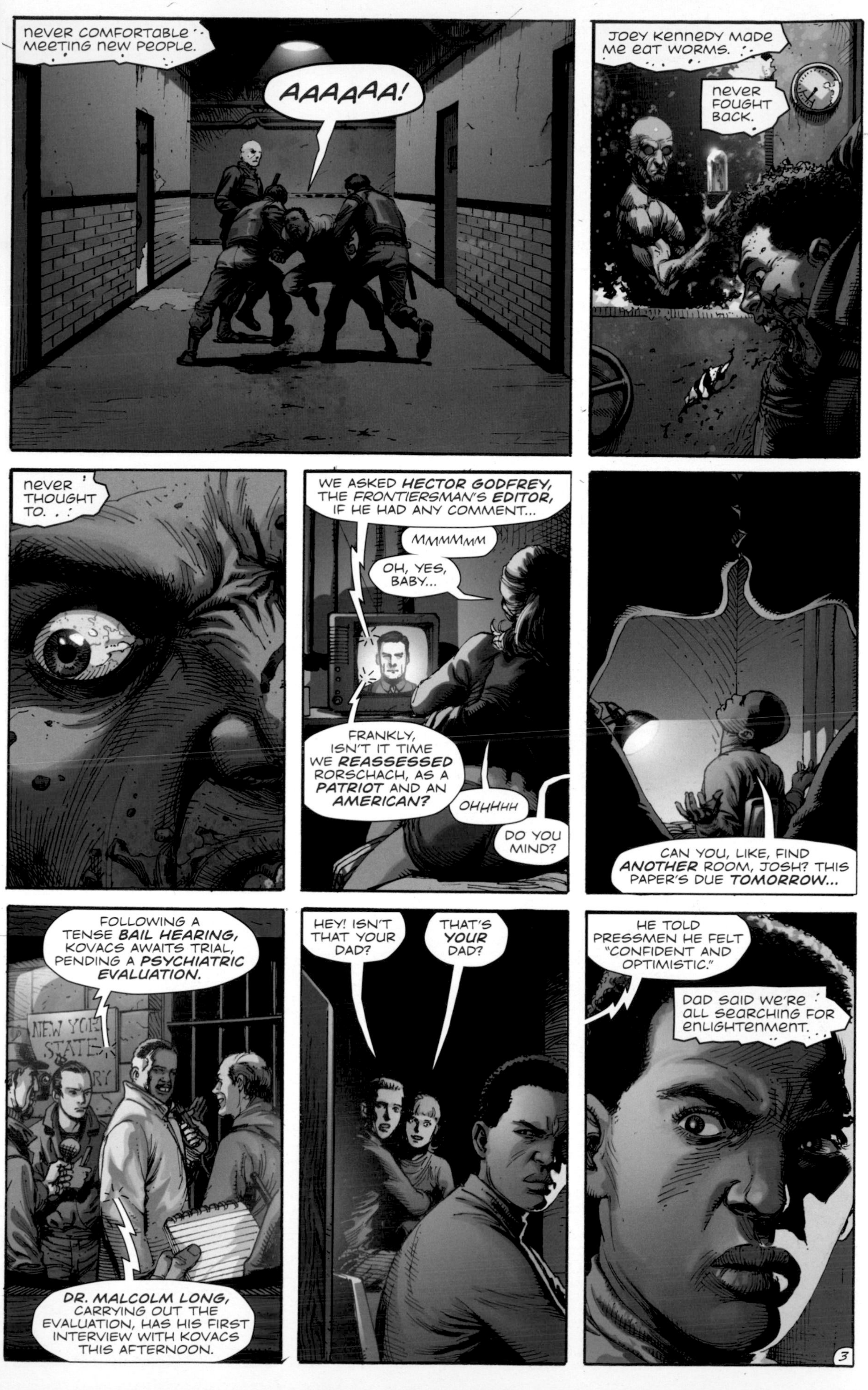
never comfortable meeting new people.
AAAAAA!
Joey Kennedy made me eat worms.
never fought back.
never thought to.
WE ASKED HECTOR GODFREY, THE FRONTIERSMAN'S EDITOR, IF HE HAD ANY COMMENT...
MMMMMM
OH, YES, BABY...
FRANKLY, ISN'T IT TIME WE REASSESSED RORSCHACH, AS A PATRIOT AND AN AMERICAN?
OHHHHH
DO YOU MIND?
CAN YOU, LIKE, FIND ANOTHER ROOM, JOSH? THIS PAPER'S DUE TOMORROW...
FOLLOWING A TENSE BAIL HEARING, KOVACS AWAITS TRIAL, PENDING A PSYCHIATRIC EVALUATION.
NEW YORK STATE ... RY
DR. MALCOLM LONG, CARRYING OUT THE EVALUATION, HAS HIS FIRST INTERVIEW WITH KOVACS THIS AFTERNOON.
HEY! ISN'T THAT YOUR DAD?
THAT'S YOUR DAD?
HE TOLD PRESSMEN HE FELT "CONFIDENT AND OPTIMISTIC."
Dad said we're all searching for enlightenment.
3

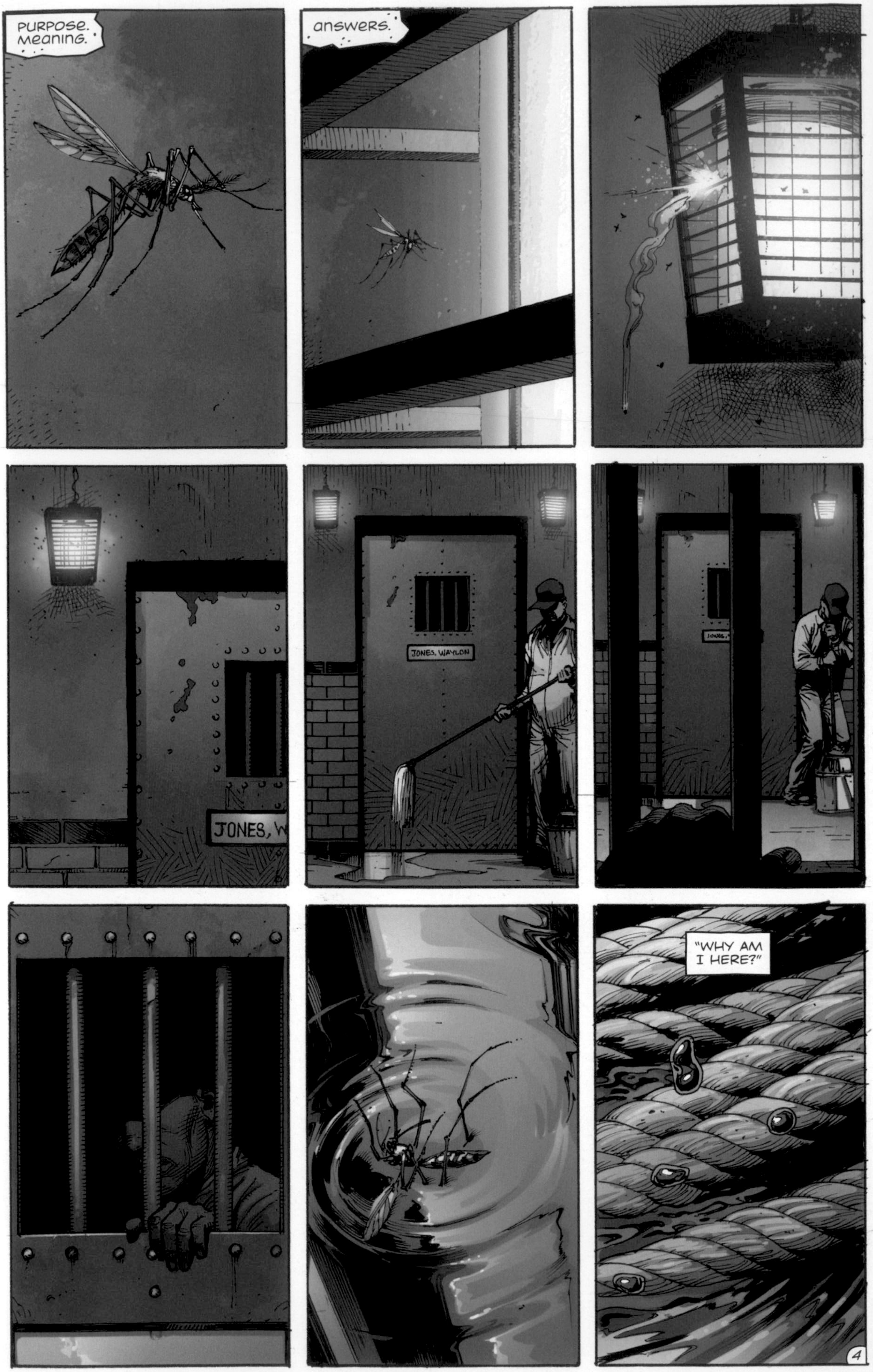
PURPOSE. MEANING.
answers.
JONES, W
JONES, WAYLON
"WHY AM I HERE?"

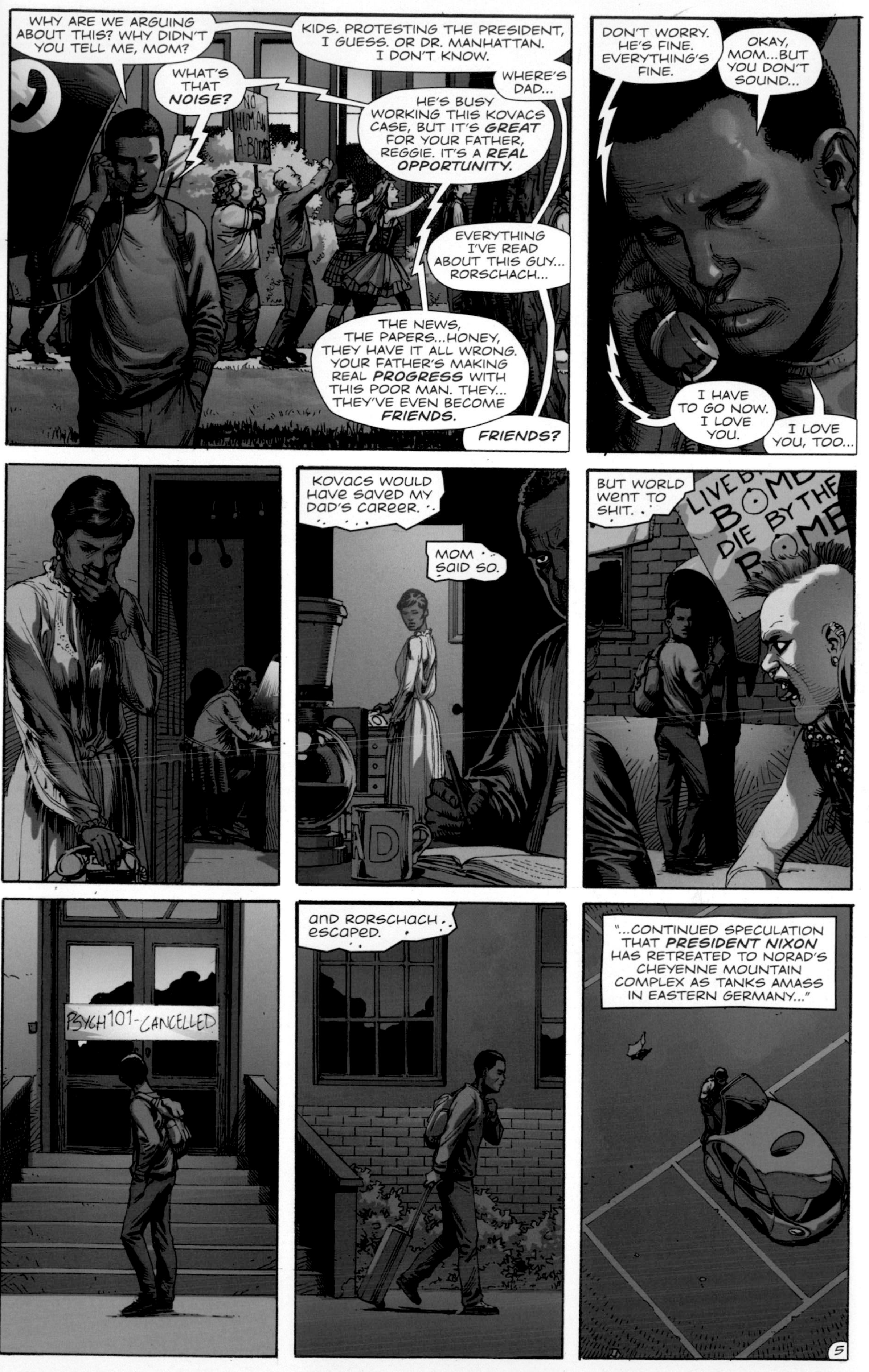

WHY ARE WE ARGUING ABOUT THIS? WHY DIDN'T YOU TELL ME, MOM?
KIDS. PROTESTING THE PRESIDENT, I GUESS. OR DR. MANHATTAN. I DON'T KNOW.
WHAT'S THAT NOISE?
NO HUMAN A-BOMB
WHERE'S DAD...
HE'S BUSY WORKING THIS KOVACS CASE, BUT IT'S GREAT FOR YOUR FATHER, REGGIE. IT'S A REAL OPPORTUNITY.
EVERYTHING I'VE READ ABOUT THIS GUY... RORSCHACH...
THE NEWS, THE PAPERS...HONEY, THEY HAVE IT ALL WRONG. YOUR FATHER'S MAKING REAL PROGRESS WITH THIS POOR MAN. THEY... THEY'VE EVEN BECOME FRIENDS.
FRIENDS?
DON'T WORRY. HE'S FINE. EVERYTHING'S FINE.
OKAY, MOM...BUT YOU DON'T SOUND...
I HAVE TO GO NOW. I LOVE YOU.
I LOVE YOU, TOO...
Kovacs would have saved my dad's career.
Mom said so.
But world went to shit.
LIVE B... BOMB DIE BY THE BOMB
PSYCH 101- CANCELLED
and Rorschach escaped.
"...CONTINUED SPECULATION THAT PRESIDENT NIXON HAS RETREATED TO NORAD'S CHEYENNE MOUNTAIN COMPLEX AS TANKS AMASS IN EASTERN GERMANY..."

...THE UNITED STATES AND RUSSIA ARE ON AN UNAVOIDABLE COLLISION COURSE...

NO, YOU HIT ME!

YOU HIT ME, YOU IDIOT!

TAXI

801

...NO SIGN OF DR. MANHATTAN IN OUR GREATEST HOUR OF N...

ZZZZZZZZZZ

EEEYYYAAAA

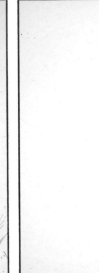

AAAAA!

LET ME OUT...

LET ME OUT OF HERE!

...NO, YOU DON'T NEED TO COME IN. I'LL BE FINE...

GOOD AFTERNOON. I'M DR. MATTHEW MASON. YOU CAN CALL ME DR. MASON OR MATTHEW, WHATEVER YOU PREFER.

I HEAR YOUR FIRST DAY IN ARKHAM HAS BEEN RATHER UNPLEASANT...

6

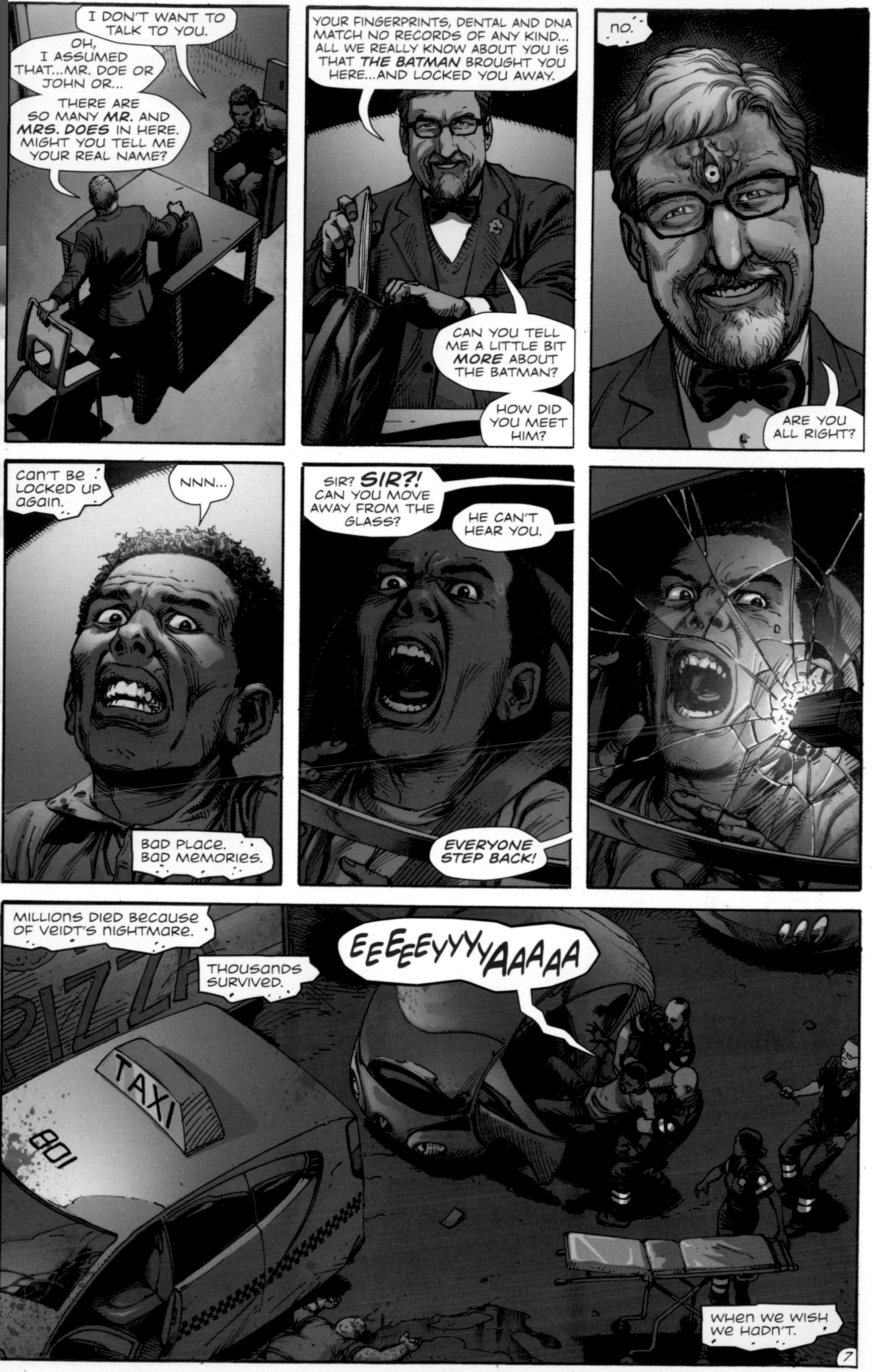
I DON'T WANT TO TALK TO YOU.
OH, I ASSUMED THAT...MR. DOE OR JOHN OR...
THERE ARE SO MANY MR. AND MRS. DOES IN HERE. MIGHT YOU TELL ME YOUR REAL NAME?
YOUR FINGERPRINTS, DENTAL AND DNA MATCH NO RECORDS OF ANY KIND... ALL WE REALLY KNOW ABOUT YOU IS THAT THE BATMAN BROUGHT YOU HERE...AND LOCKED YOU AWAY.
CAN YOU TELL ME A LITTLE BIT MORE ABOUT THE BATMAN?
HOW DID YOU MEET HIM?
no.
ARE YOU ALL RIGHT?
can't be locked up again.
NNN...
Bad place. Bad memories.
SIR? SIR?! CAN YOU MOVE AWAY FROM THE GLASS?
HE CAN'T HEAR YOU.
EVERYONE STEP BACK!
Millions died because of Veidt's nightmare.
Thousands survived.
EEEEEYYYYAAAAA
PIZZA
TAXI
801
when we wish we hadn't.
7

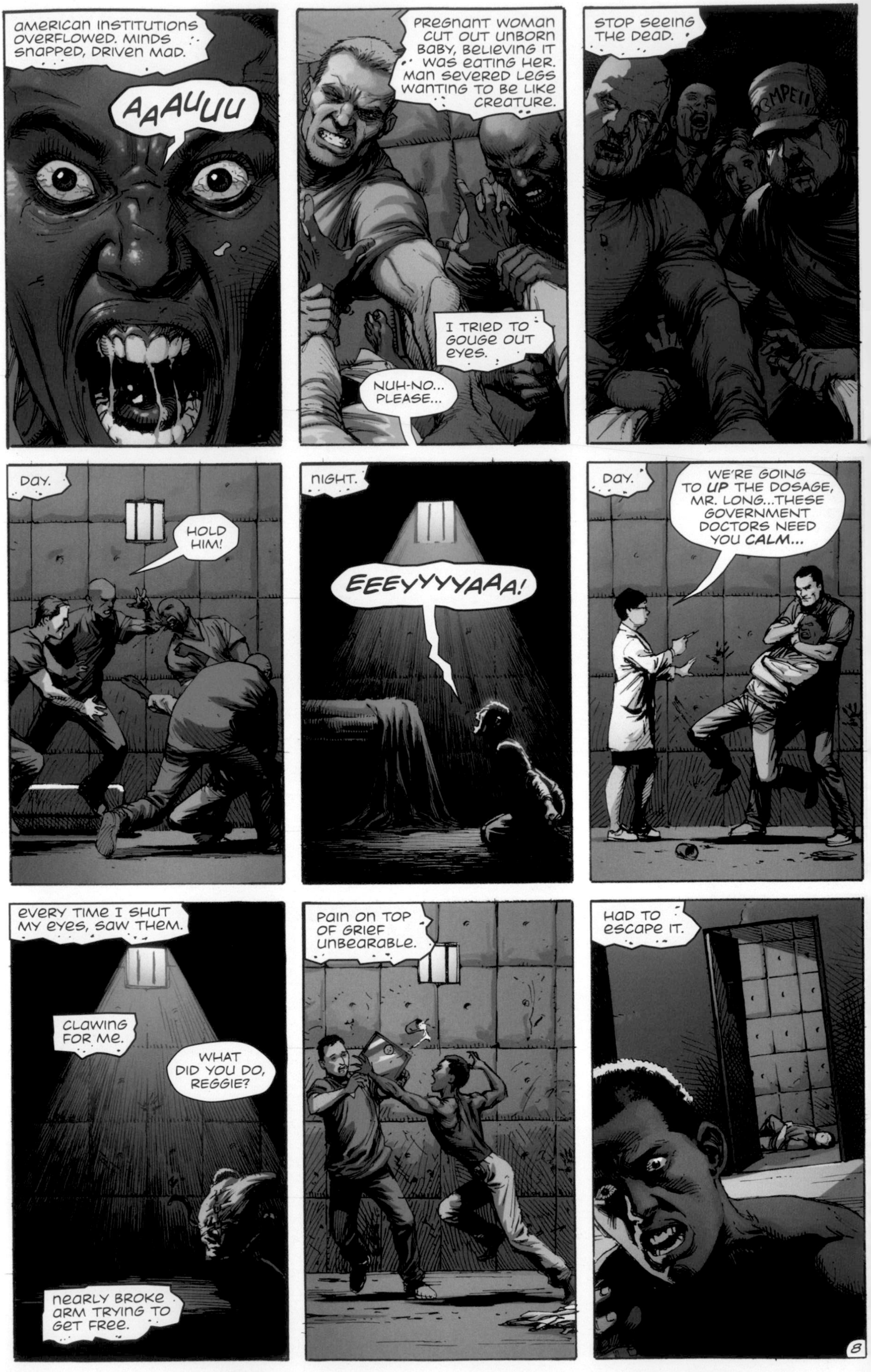
american institutions overflowed. minds snapped, driven mad.
AAAUUUU
pregnant woman cut out unborn baby, believing it was eating her. man severed legs wanting to be like creature.
I TRIED TO GOUGE OUT EYES.
NUH-NO... PLEASE...
stop seeing the dead.
day.
HOLD HIM!
night.
EEEYYYYAAA!
day.
WE'RE GOING TO UP THE DOSAGE, MR. LONG...THESE GOVERNMENT DOCTORS NEED YOU CALM...
every time I shut my eyes, saw them.
clawing for me.
WHAT DID YOU DO, REGGIE?
nearly broke arm trying to get free.
pain on top of grief unbearable.
had to escape it.
8

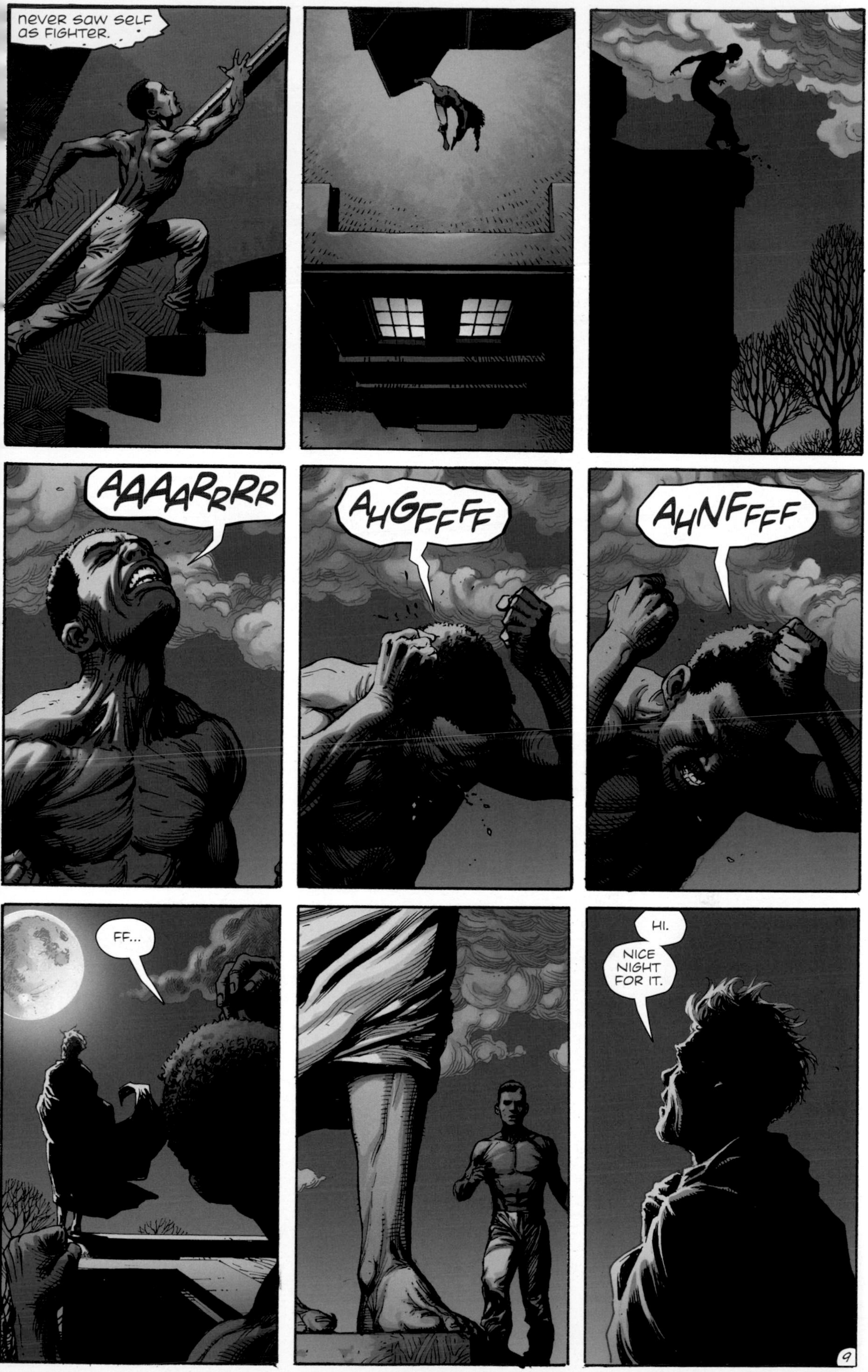
never saw self
as FIGHTER.
AAAARRRR
AHGFFFF
AHNFFFF
FF...
HI.
NICE
NIGHT
FOR IT.

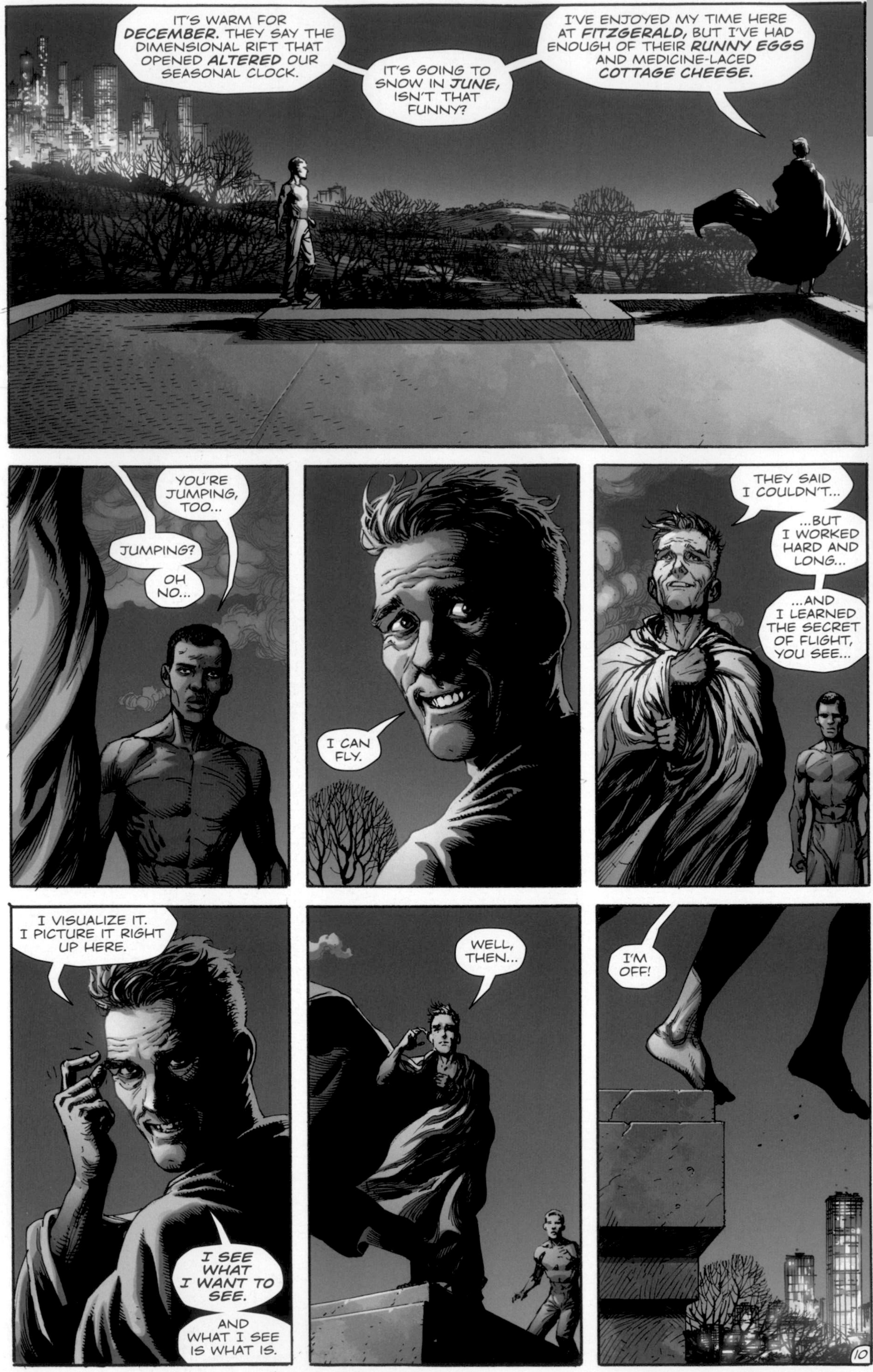
IT'S WARM FOR DECEMBER. THEY SAY THE DIMENSIONAL RIFT THAT OPENED ALTERED OUR SEASONAL CLOCK.
IT'S GOING TO SNOW IN JUNE, ISN'T THAT FUNNY?
I'VE ENJOYED MY TIME HERE AT FITZGERALD, BUT I'VE HAD ENOUGH OF THEIR RUNNY EGGS AND MEDICINE-LACED COTTAGE CHEESE.
YOU'RE JUMPING, TOO...
JUMPING?
OH NO...
I CAN FLY.
THEY SAID I COULDN'T...
...BUT I WORKED HARD AND LONG...
...AND I LEARNED THE SECRET OF FLIGHT, YOU SEE...
I VISUALIZE IT. I PICTURE IT RIGHT UP HERE.
I SEE WHAT I WANT TO SEE.
AND WHAT I SEE IS WHAT IS.
WELL, THEN...
I'M OFF!
10

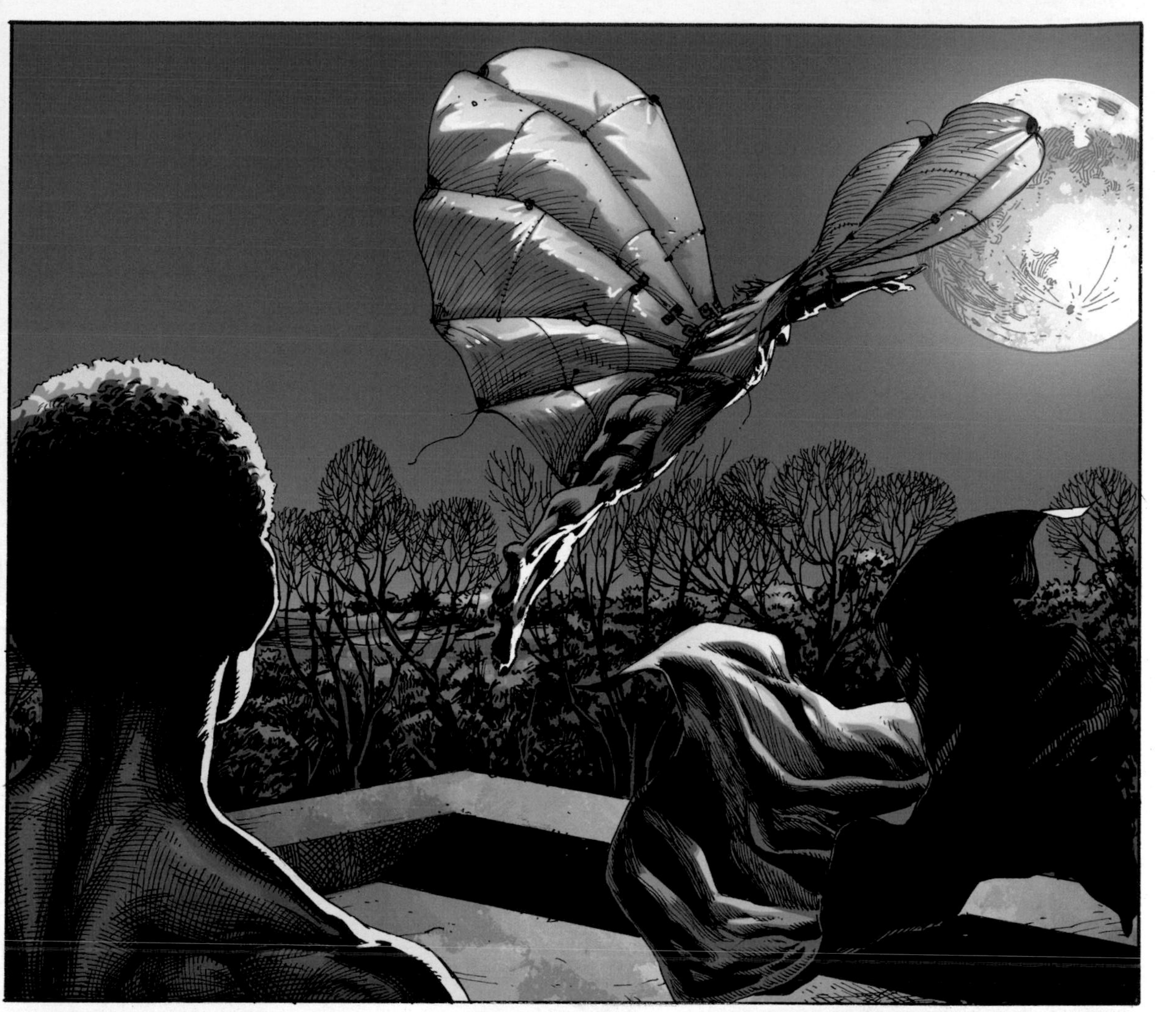

WALK ON WATER

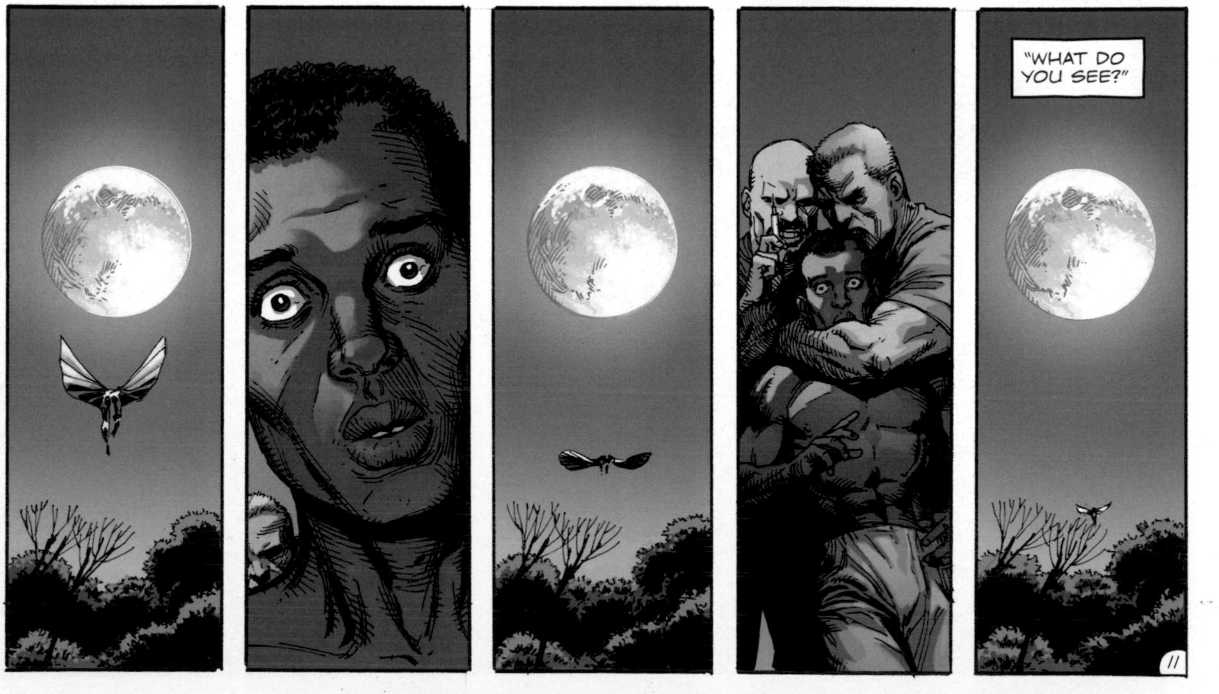
"WHAT DO YOU SEE?"

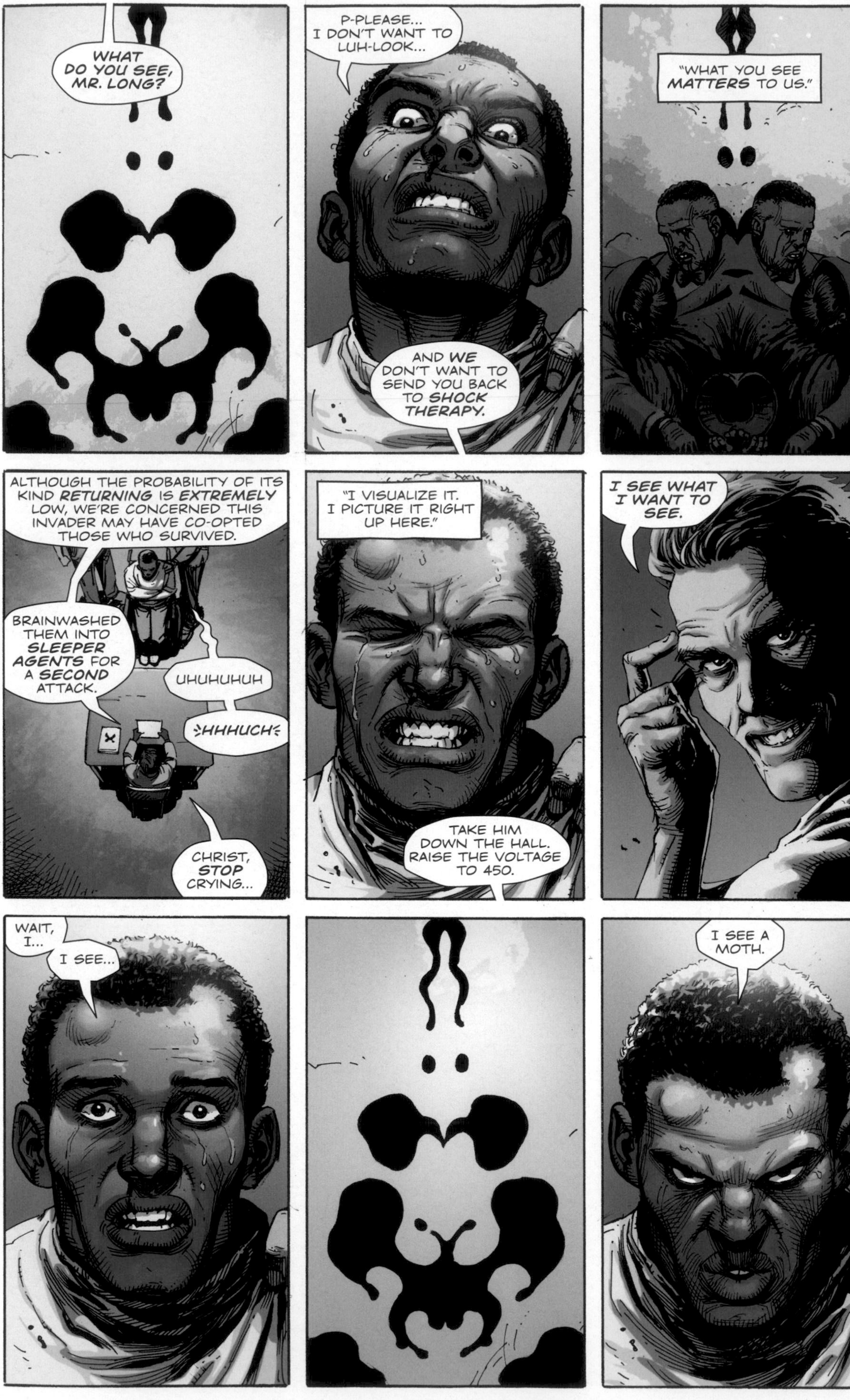
WHAT DO YOU SEE, MR. LONG?
P-PLEASE... I DON'T WANT TO LUH-LOOK...
AND WE DON'T WANT TO SEND YOU BACK TO SHOCK THERAPY.
"WHAT YOU SEE MATTERS TO US."
ALTHOUGH THE PROBABILITY OF ITS KIND RETURNING IS EXTREMELY LOW, WE'RE CONCERNED THIS INVADER MAY HAVE CO-OPTED THOSE WHO SURVIVED.
BRAINWASHED THEM INTO SLEEPER AGENTS FOR A SECOND ATTACK.
UHUHUHUH
HHHUCH
CHRIST, STOP CRYING...
"I VISUALIZE IT. I PICTURE IT RIGHT UP HERE."
TAKE HIM DOWN THE HALL. RAISE THE VOLTAGE TO 450.
I SEE WHAT I WANT TO SEE.
WAIT, I...
I SEE...
I SEE A MOTH.
12

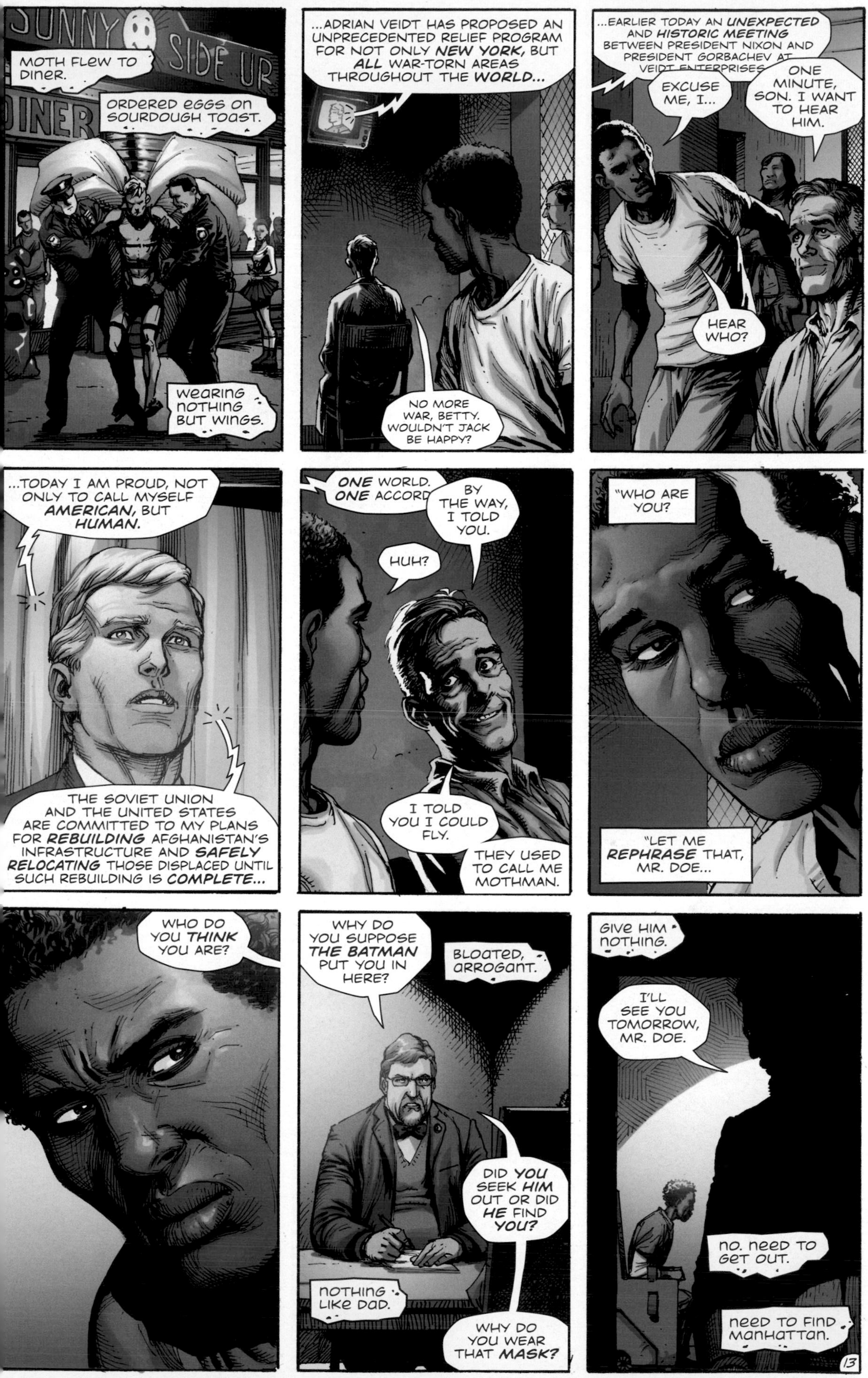
SUNNY SIDE UP DINER
MOTH FLEW TO DINER.
ORDERED EGGS ON SOURDOUGH TOAST.
WEARING NOTHING BUT WINGS.
...ADRIAN VEIDT HAS PROPOSED AN UNPRECEDENTED RELIEF PROGRAM FOR NOT ONLY NEW YORK, BUT ALL WAR-TORN AREAS THROUGHOUT THE WORLD...
NO MORE WAR, BETTY. WOULDN'T JACK BE HAPPY?
...EARLIER TODAY AN UNEXPECTED AND HISTORIC MEETING BETWEEN PRESIDENT NIXON AND PRESIDENT GORBACHEV AT VEIDT ENTERPRISES
EXCUSE ME, I...
ONE MINUTE, SON. I WANT TO HEAR HIM.
HEAR WHO?
...TODAY I AM PROUD, NOT ONLY TO CALL MYSELF AMERICAN, BUT HUMAN.
THE SOVIET UNION AND THE UNITED STATES ARE COMMITTED TO MY PLANS FOR REBUILDING AFGHANISTAN'S INFRASTRUCTURE AND SAFELY RELOCATING THOSE DISPLACED UNTIL SUCH REBUILDING IS COMPLETE...
ONE WORLD. ONE ACCORD
BY THE WAY, I TOLD YOU.
HUH?
I TOLD YOU I COULD FLY.
THEY USED TO CALL ME MOTHMAN.
"WHO ARE YOU?
"LET ME REPHRASE THAT, MR. DOE...
WHO DO YOU THINK YOU ARE?
WHY DO YOU SUPPOSE THE BATMAN PUT YOU IN HERE?
BLOATED, ARROGANT.
DID YOU SEEK HIM OUT OR DID HE FIND YOU?
NOTHING LIKE DAD.
WHY DO YOU WEAR THAT MASK?
GIVE HIM NOTHING.
I'LL SEE YOU TOMORROW, MR. DOE.
NO. NEED TO GET OUT.
NEED TO FIND MANHATTAN.

COULD BE ANYONE.

OR NO ONE.

PROBABLY WATCHING NOW.

LET'S GO, DOE.

DOE JANE

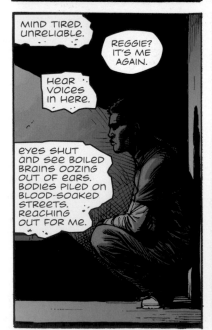

MIND TIRED. UNRELIABLE.

REGGIE? IT'S ME AGAIN.

HEAR VOICES IN HERE.

EYES SHUT AND SEE BOILED BRAINS OOZING OUT OF EARS. BODIES PILED ON BLOOD-SOAKED STREETS. REACHING OUT FOR ME.

USED TO BE A PROBLEM.

BUT LEARNED TO CHANGE IT...

...SEE WHAT I WANT TO SEE.

DAD AND MOM. HAPPY. ALIVE.

14

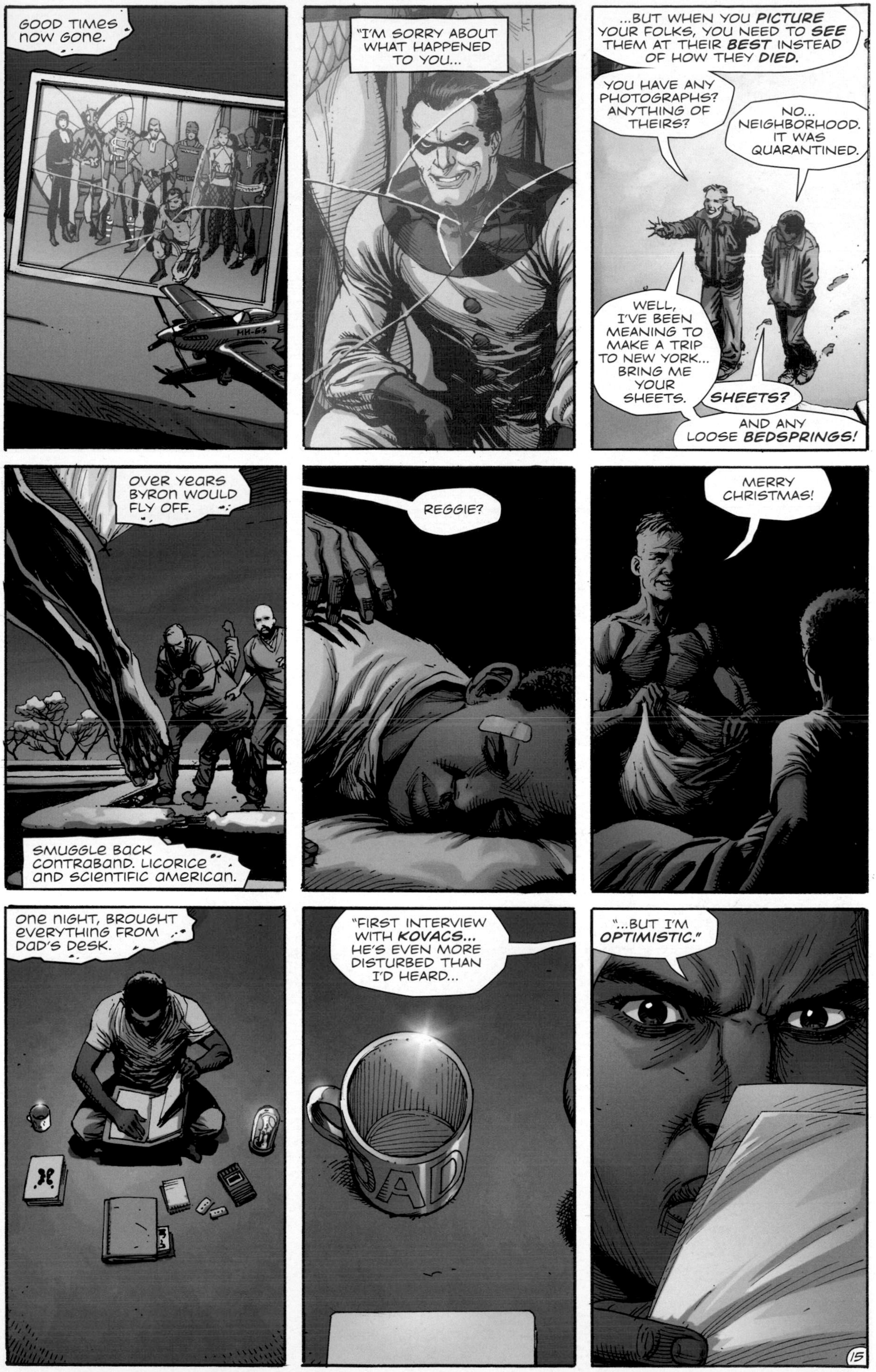
GOOD TIMES now gone.
"I'M SORRY ABOUT WHAT HAPPENED TO YOU...
...BUT WHEN YOU PICTURE YOUR FOLKS, YOU NEED TO SEE THEM AT THEIR BEST INSTEAD OF HOW THEY DIED.
YOU HAVE ANY PHOTOGRAPHS? ANYTHING OF THEIRS?
NO... NEIGHBORHOOD. IT WAS QUARANTINED.
WELL, I'VE BEEN MEANING TO MAKE A TRIP TO NEW YORK... BRING ME YOUR SHEETS.
SHEETS?
AND ANY LOOSE BEDSPRINGS!
OVER YEARS BYRON WOULD FLY OFF.
SMUGGLE BACK CONTRABAND. LICORICE AND SCIENTIFIC AMERICAN.
REGGIE?
MERRY CHRISTMAS!
ONE NIGHT, BROUGHT EVERYTHING FROM DAD'S DESK.
"FIRST INTERVIEW WITH KOVACS... HE'S EVEN MORE DISTURBED THAN I'D HEARD...
"...BUT I'M OPTIMISTIC."

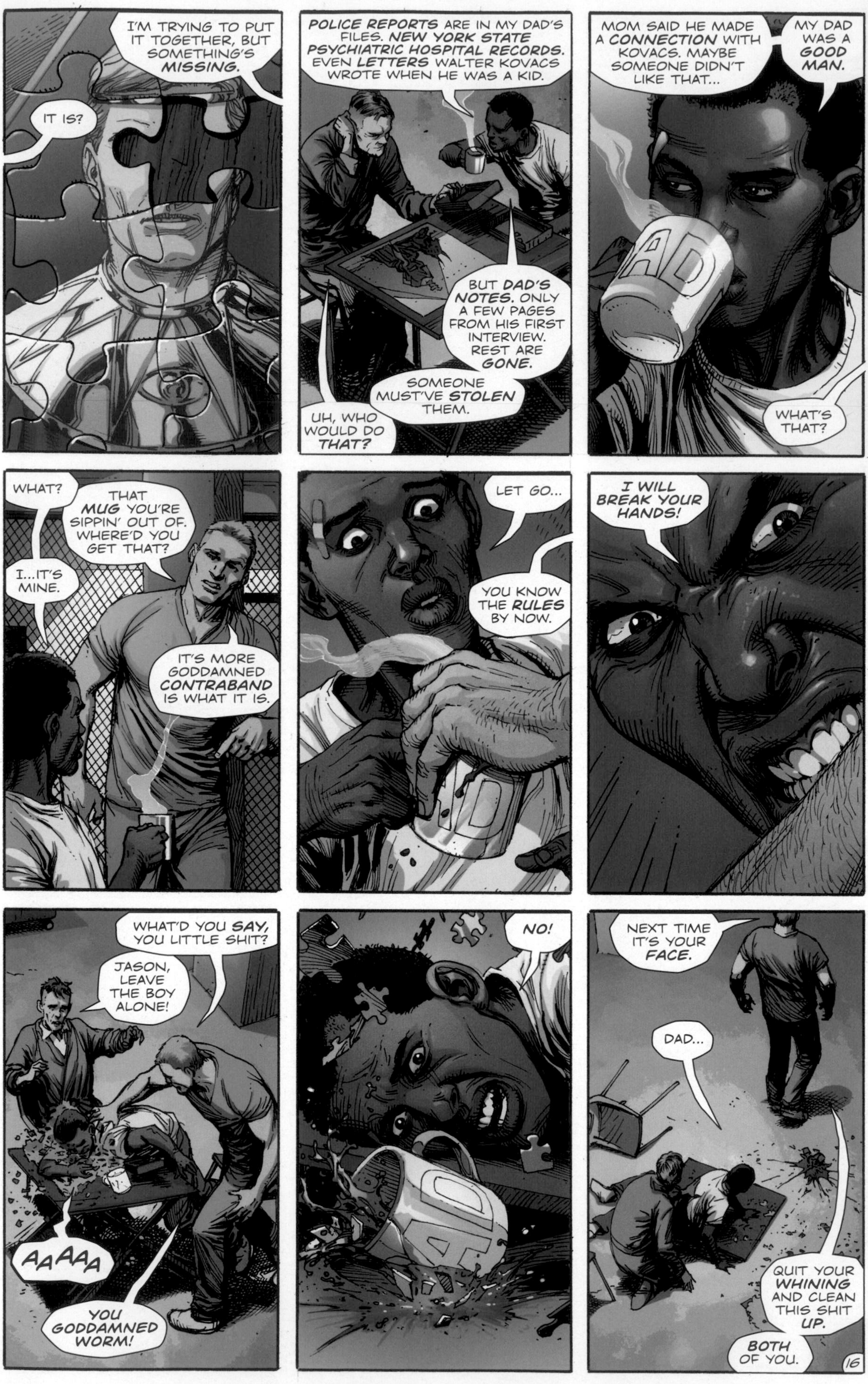

I'M TRYING TO PUT IT TOGETHER, BUT SOMETHING'S **MISSING.**
IT IS?
POLICE REPORTS ARE IN MY DAD'S FILES. **NEW YORK STATE PSYCHIATRIC HOSPITAL RECORDS.** EVEN **LETTERS** WALTER KOVACS WROTE WHEN HE WAS A KID.
BUT **DAD'S NOTES.** ONLY A FEW PAGES FROM HIS FIRST INTERVIEW. REST ARE **GONE.**
SOMEONE MUST'VE **STOLEN** THEM.
UH, WHO WOULD DO **THAT?**
MOM SAID HE MADE A **CONNECTION** WITH KOVACS. MAYBE SOMEONE DIDN'T LIKE THAT...
MY DAD WAS A **GOOD MAN.**
DAD
WHAT'S THAT?
WHAT?
THAT **MUG** YOU'RE SIPPIN' OUT OF. WHERE'D YOU GET THAT?
I...IT'S MINE.
IT'S MORE GODDAMNED **CONTRABAND** IS WHAT IT IS.
LET GO...
YOU KNOW THE **RULES** BY NOW.
I WILL BREAK YOUR HANDS!
WHAT'D YOU **SAY,** YOU LITTLE SHIT?
JASON, LEAVE THE BOY ALONE!
AAAAA
YOU GODDAMNED WORM!
NO!
NEXT TIME IT'S YOUR **FACE.**
DAD...
QUIT YOUR **WHINING** AND CLEAN THIS SHIT **UP.**
BOTH OF YOU.

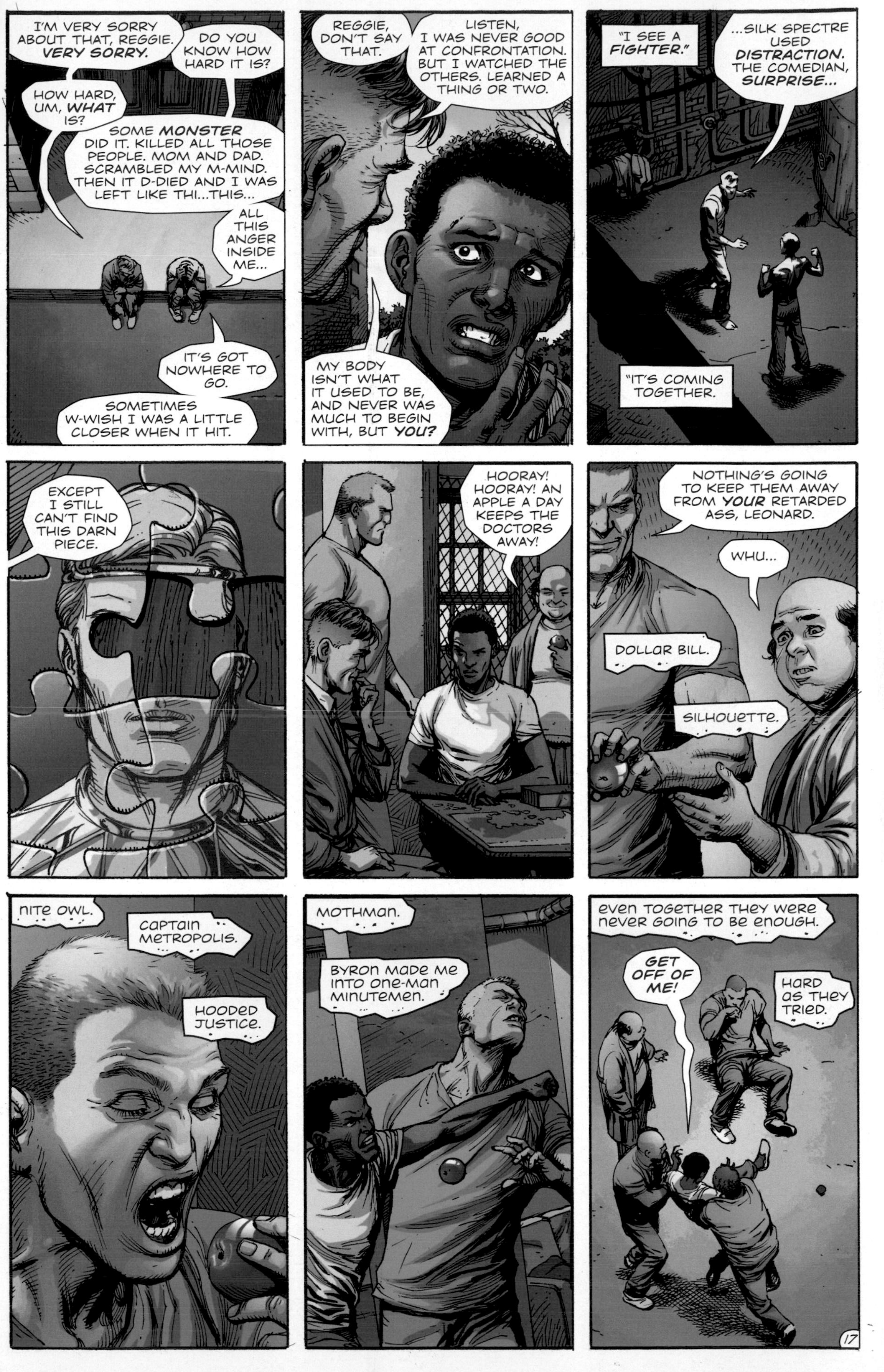
I'M VERY SORRY ABOUT THAT, REGGIE. VERY SORRY.
DO YOU KNOW HOW HARD IT IS?
HOW HARD, UM, WHAT IS?
SOME MONSTER DID IT. KILLED ALL THOSE PEOPLE. MOM AND DAD. SCRAMBLED MY M-MIND. THEN IT D-DIED AND I WAS LEFT LIKE THI...THIS...
ALL THIS ANGER INSIDE ME...
IT'S GOT NOWHERE TO GO.
SOMETIMES W-WISH I WAS A LITTLE CLOSER WHEN IT HIT.
REGGIE, DON'T SAY THAT.
LISTEN, I WAS NEVER GOOD AT CONFRONTATION. BUT I WATCHED THE OTHERS. LEARNED A THING OR TWO.
MY BODY ISN'T WHAT IT USED TO BE, AND NEVER WAS MUCH TO BEGIN WITH, BUT YOU?
"I SEE A FIGHTER."
...SILK SPECTRE USED DISTRACTION. THE COMEDIAN, SURPRISE...
"IT'S COMING TOGETHER.
EXCEPT I STILL CAN'T FIND THIS DARN PIECE.
HOORAY! HOORAY! AN APPLE A DAY KEEPS THE DOCTORS AWAY!
NOTHING'S GOING TO KEEP THEM AWAY FROM YOUR RETARDED ASS, LEONARD.
WHU...
DOLLAR BILL.
SILHOUETTE.
nite owl.
captain metropolis.
hooded justice.
mothman.
byron made me into one-man minutemen.
even together they were never going to be enough.
GET OFF OF ME!
hard as they tried.
17

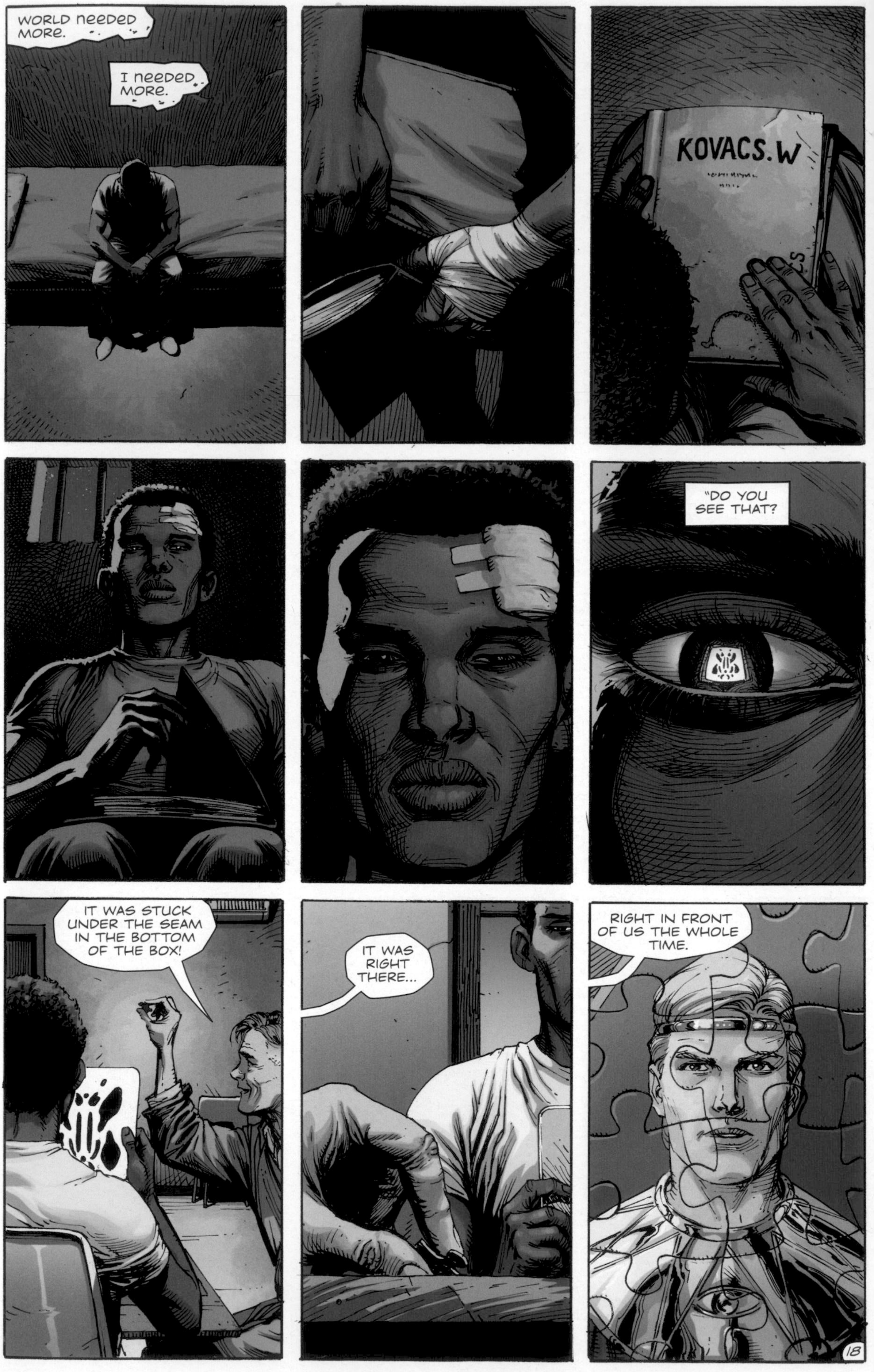
WORLD NEEDED MORE.
I NEEDED MORE.
KOVACS. W
"DO YOU SEE THAT?
IT WAS STUCK UNDER THE SEAM IN THE BOTTOM OF THE BOX!
IT WAS RIGHT THERE...
RIGHT IN FRONT OF US THE WHOLE TIME.

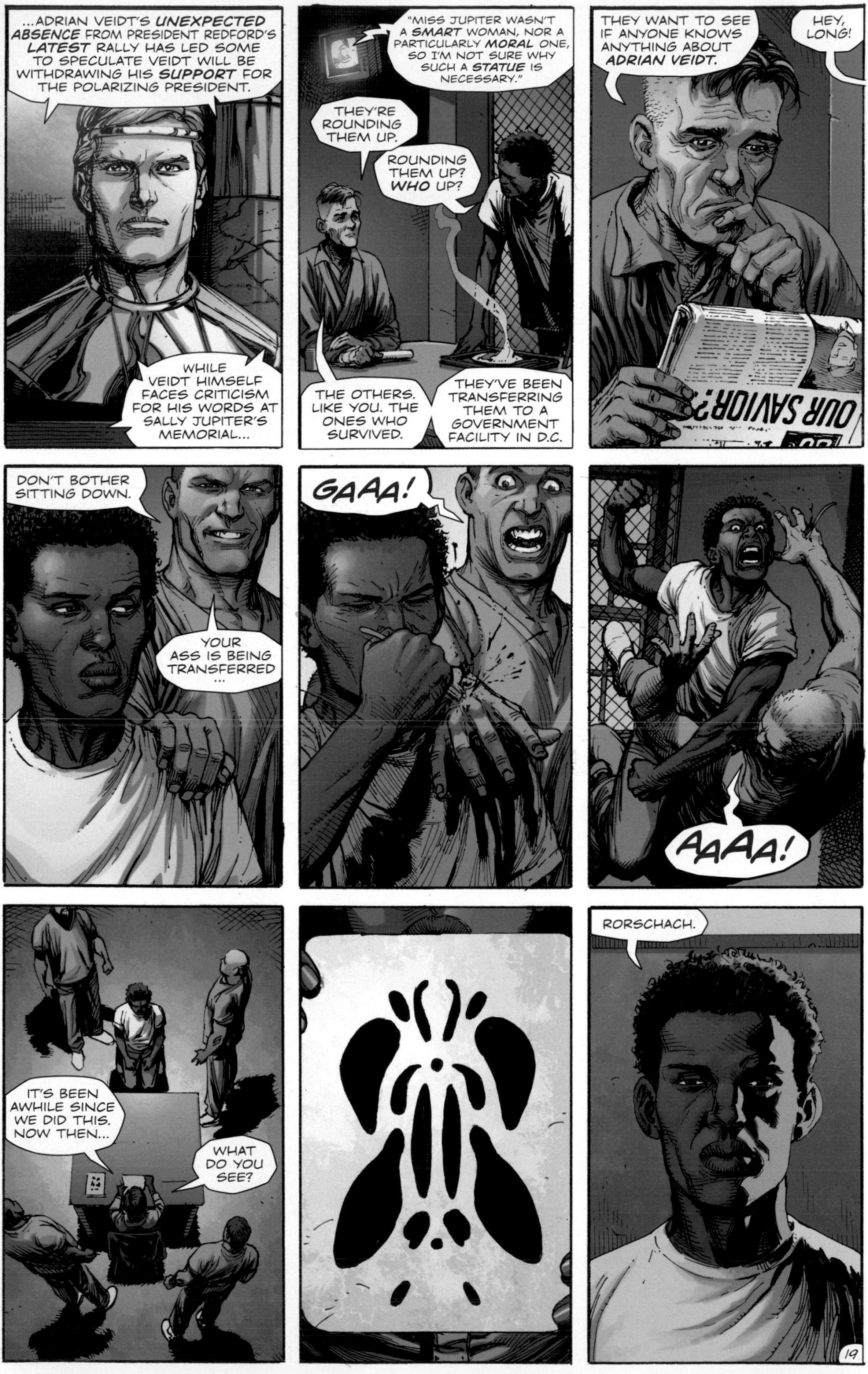
...ADRIAN VEIDT'S UNEXPECTED ABSENCE FROM PRESIDENT REDFORD'S LATEST RALLY HAS LED SOME TO SPECULATE VEIDT WILL BE WITHDRAWING HIS SUPPORT FOR THE POLARIZING PRESIDENT.
WHILE VEIDT HIMSELF FACES CRITICISM FOR HIS WORDS AT SALLY JUPITER'S MEMORIAL...
"MISS JUPITER WASN'T A SMART WOMAN, NOR A PARTICULARLY MORAL ONE, SO I'M NOT SURE WHY SUCH A STATUE IS NECESSARY."
THEY'RE ROUNDING THEM UP.
ROUNDING THEM UP? WHO UP?
THE OTHERS. LIKE YOU. THE ONES WHO SURVIVED.
THEY'VE BEEN TRANSFERRING THEM TO A GOVERNMENT FACILITY IN D.C.
THEY WANT TO SEE IF ANYONE KNOWS ANYTHING ABOUT ADRIAN VEIDT.
HEY, LONG!
OUR SAVIOR?
DON'T BOTHER SITTING DOWN.
YOUR ASS IS BEING TRANSFERRED ...
GAAA!
AAAA!
IT'S BEEN AWHILE SINCE WE DID THIS. NOW THEN...
WHAT DO YOU SEE?
RORSCHACH.

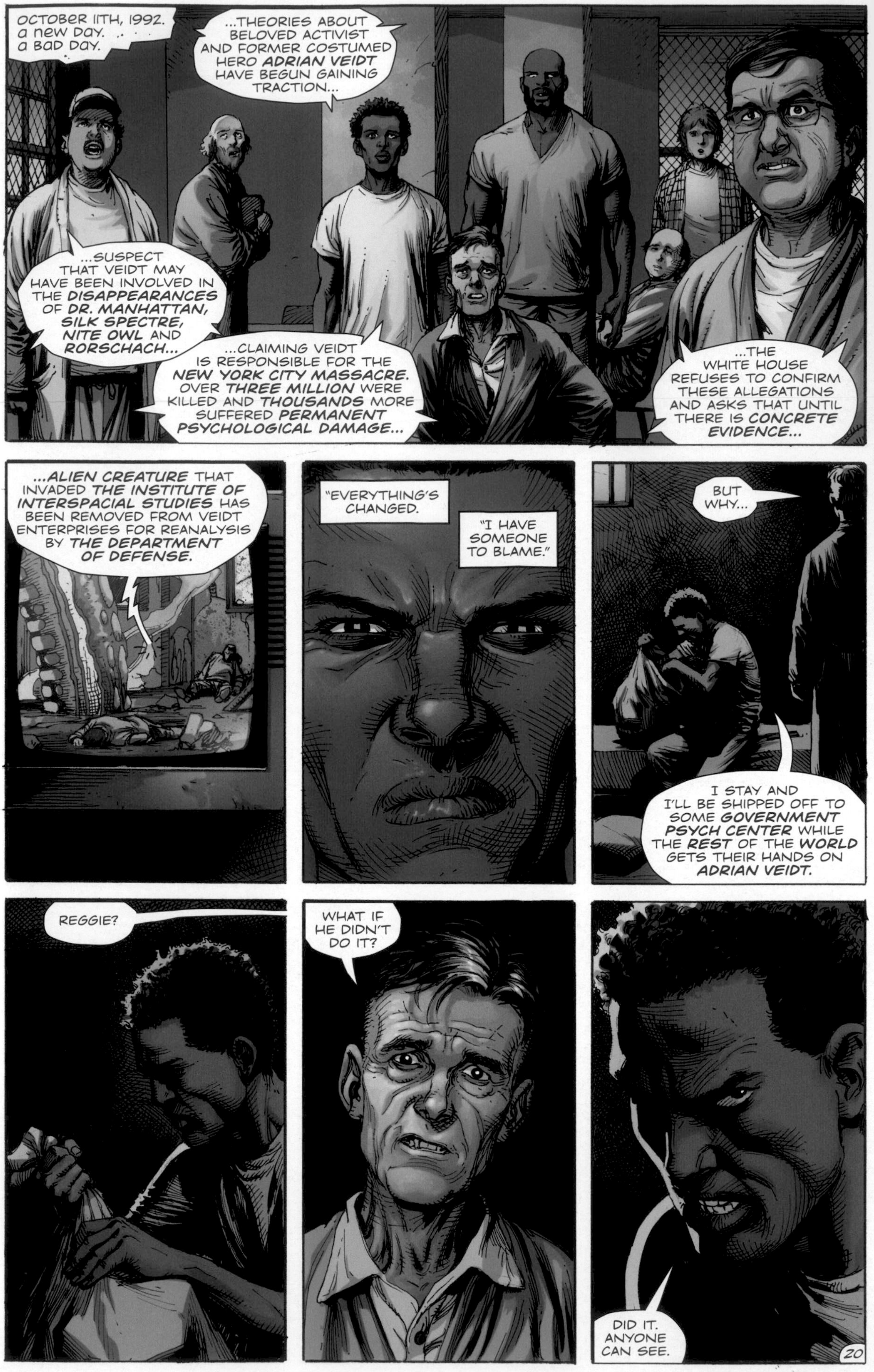

OCTOBER 11TH, 1992. A NEW DAY. A BAD DAY.
...THEORIES ABOUT BELOVED ACTIVIST AND FORMER COSTUMED HERO ADRIAN VEIDT HAVE BEGUN GAINING TRACTION...
...SUSPECT THAT VEIDT MAY HAVE BEEN INVOLVED IN THE DISAPPEARANCES OF DR. MANHATTAN, SILK SPECTRE, NITE OWL AND RORSCHACH...
...CLAIMING VEIDT IS RESPONSIBLE FOR THE NEW YORK CITY MASSACRE. OVER THREE MILLION WERE KILLED AND THOUSANDS MORE SUFFERED PERMANENT PSYCHOLOGICAL DAMAGE...
...THE WHITE HOUSE REFUSES TO CONFIRM THESE ALLEGATIONS AND ASKS THAT UNTIL THERE IS CONCRETE EVIDENCE...
...ALIEN CREATURE THAT INVADED THE INSTITUTE OF INTERSPACIAL STUDIES HAS BEEN REMOVED FROM VEIDT ENTERPRISES FOR REANALYSIS BY THE DEPARTMENT OF DEFENSE.
"EVERYTHING'S CHANGED.
"I HAVE SOMEONE TO BLAME."
BUT WHY...
I STAY AND I'LL BE SHIPPED OFF TO SOME GOVERNMENT PSYCH CENTER WHILE THE REST OF THE WORLD GETS THEIR HANDS ON ADRIAN VEIDT.
REGGIE?
WHAT IF HE DIDN'T DO IT?
DID IT. ANYONE CAN SEE.
20

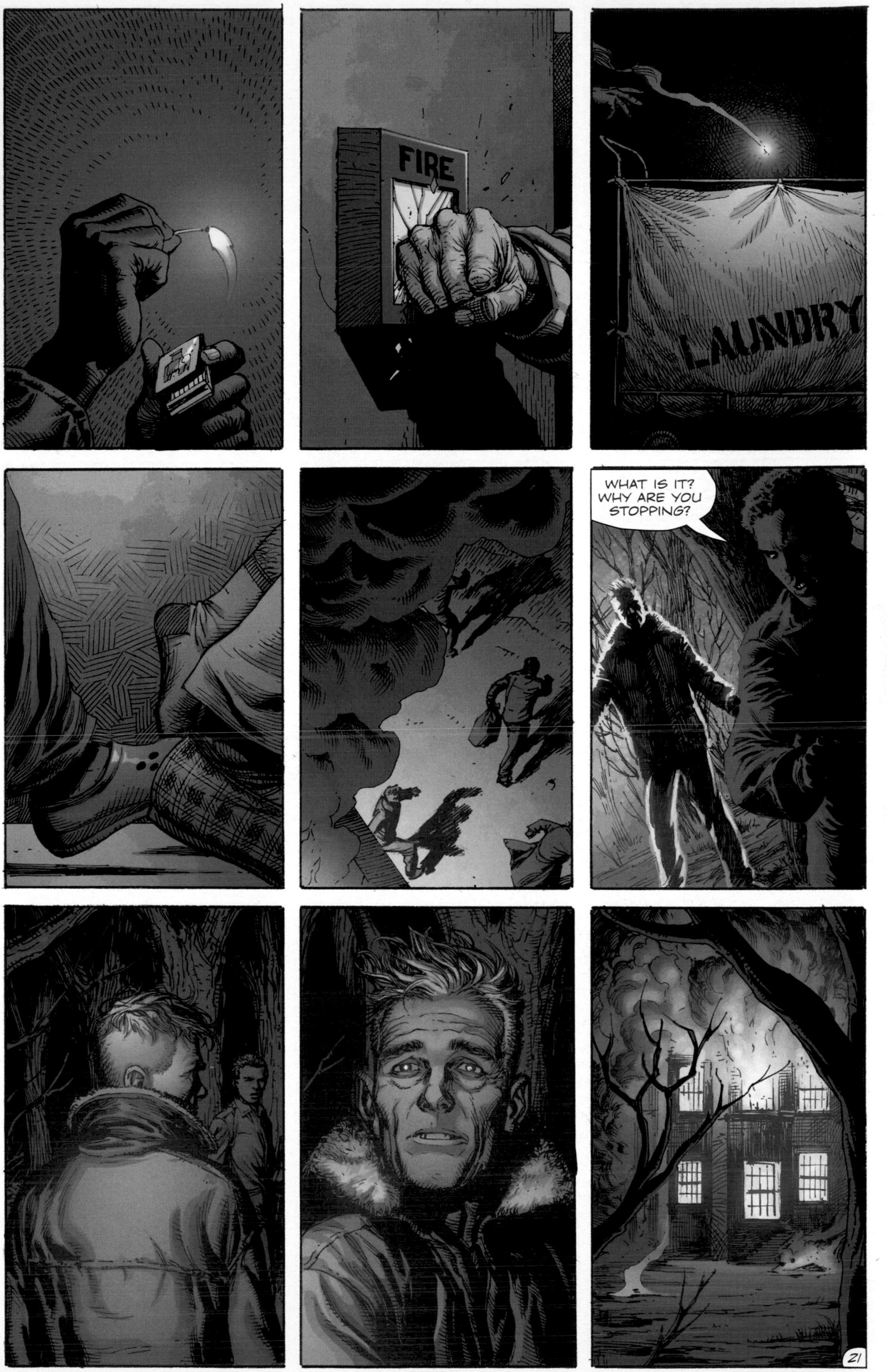

FIRE
LAUNDRY
WHAT IS IT? WHY ARE YOU STOPPING?

HEAT FROM BURNING HELL SCORCHED GROUNDS.

STENCH OF MADNESS FILLED LUNGS.

BYRON?

BUT LIGHT WAS BRIGHT.

IT'S BEEN *CALLING* TO ME.

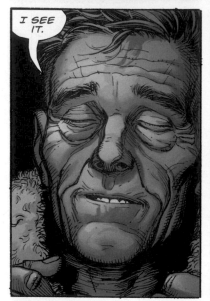

I SEE IT.

SEE WHAT?

BYRON?!

WHAT DO YOU SEE?!

DIDN'T UNDERSTAND.

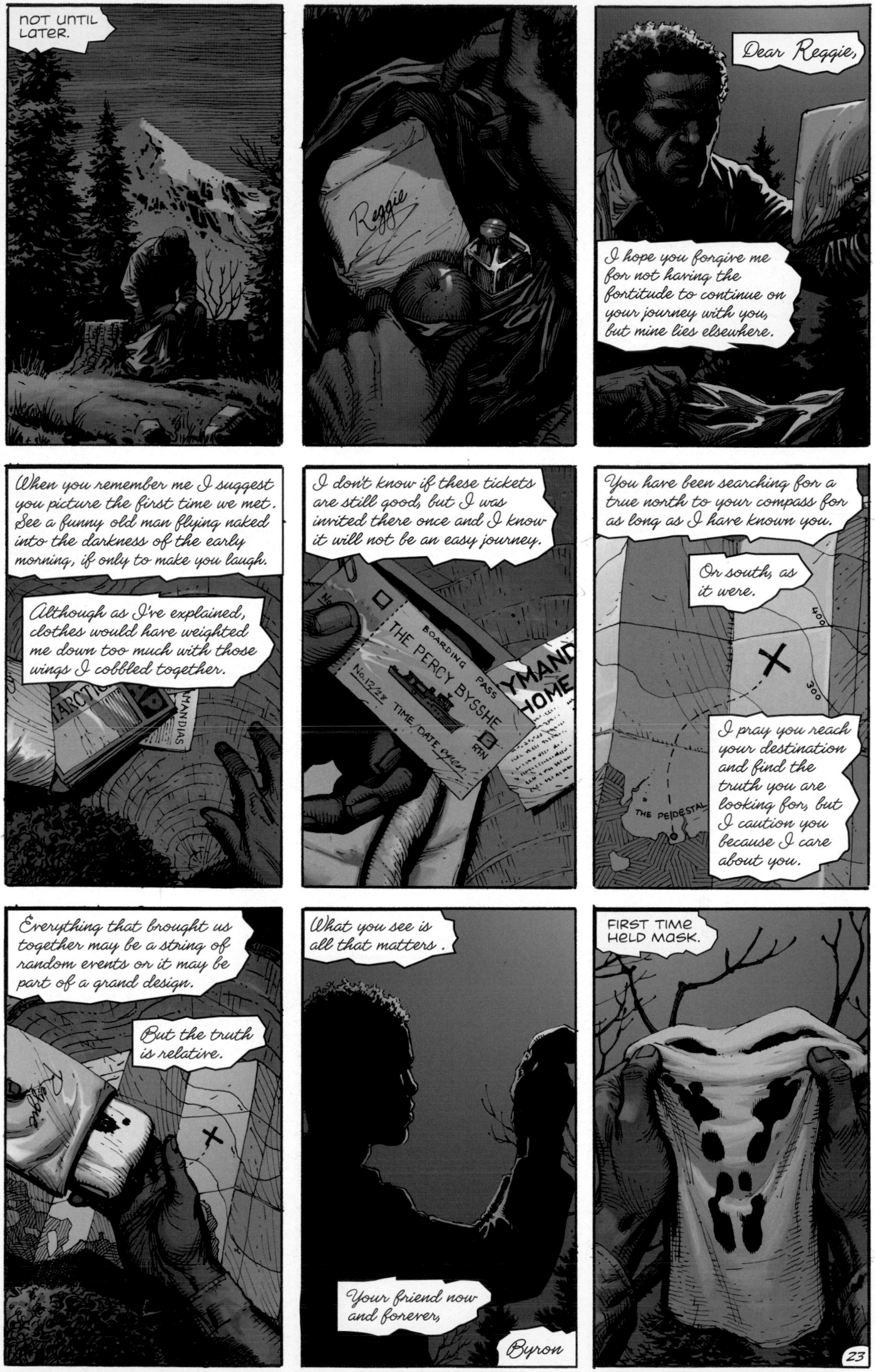
NOT UNTIL LATER.
Reggie
Dear Reggie,
I hope you forgive me for not having the fortitude to continue on your journey with you, but mine lies elsewhere.
When you remember me I suggest you picture the first time we met. See a funny old man flying naked into the darkness of the early morning, if only to make you laugh.
Although as I've explained, clothes would have weighted me down too much with those wings I cobbled together.
I don't know if these tickets are still good, but I was invited there once and I know it will not be an easy journey.
BOARDING PASS
THE PERCY BYSSHE
TIME/DATE open
RTN
You have been searching for a true north to your compass for as long as I have known you.
Or south, as it were.
400
300
THE PEDESTAL
I pray you reach your destination and find the truth you are looking for, but I caution you because I care about you.
Everything that brought us together may be a string of random events or it may be part of a grand design.
But the truth is relative.
What you see is all that matters.
Your friend now and forever,
Byron
FIRST TIME HELD MASK.

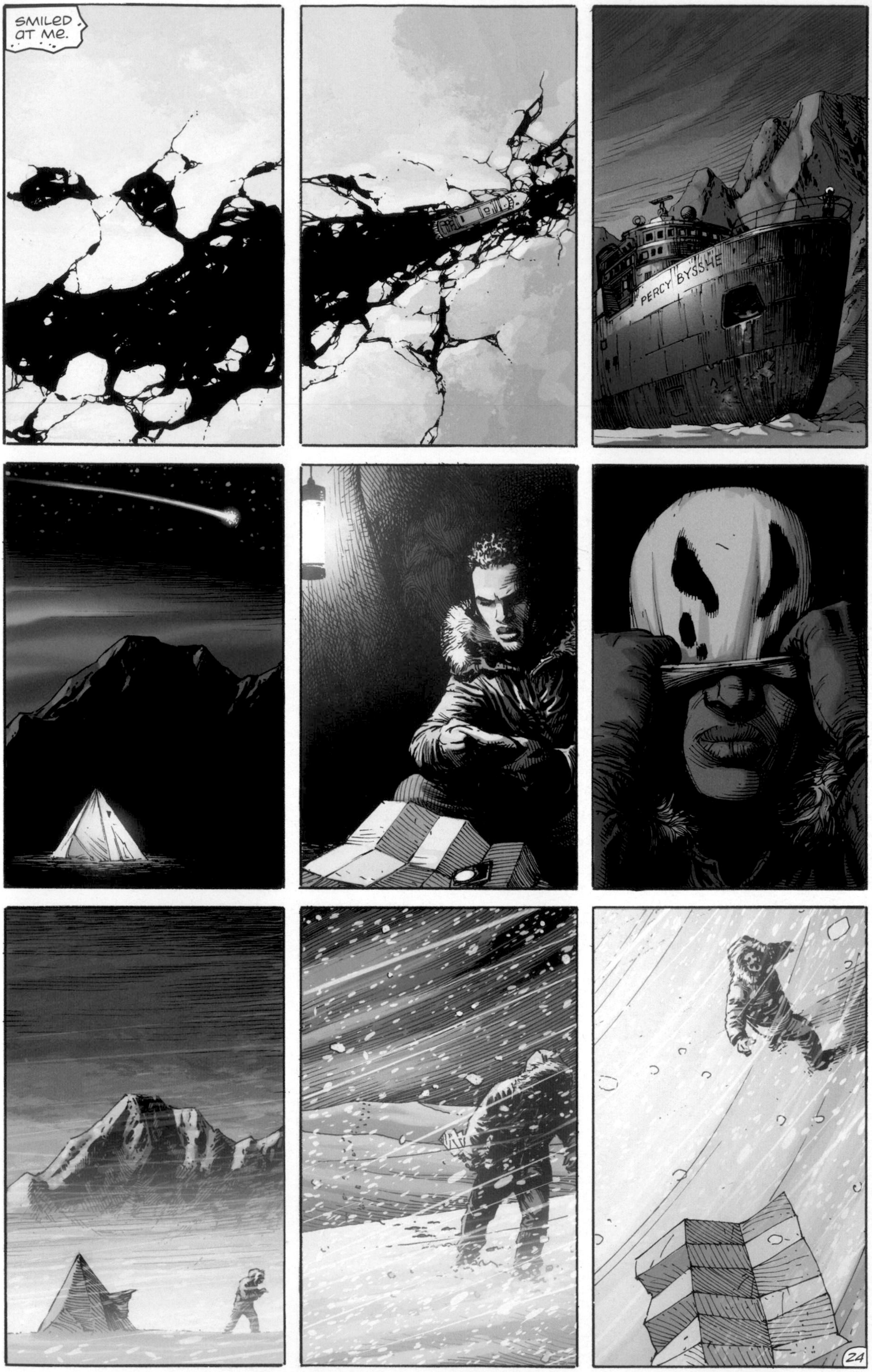
SMILED AT ME.
PERCY BYSSHE

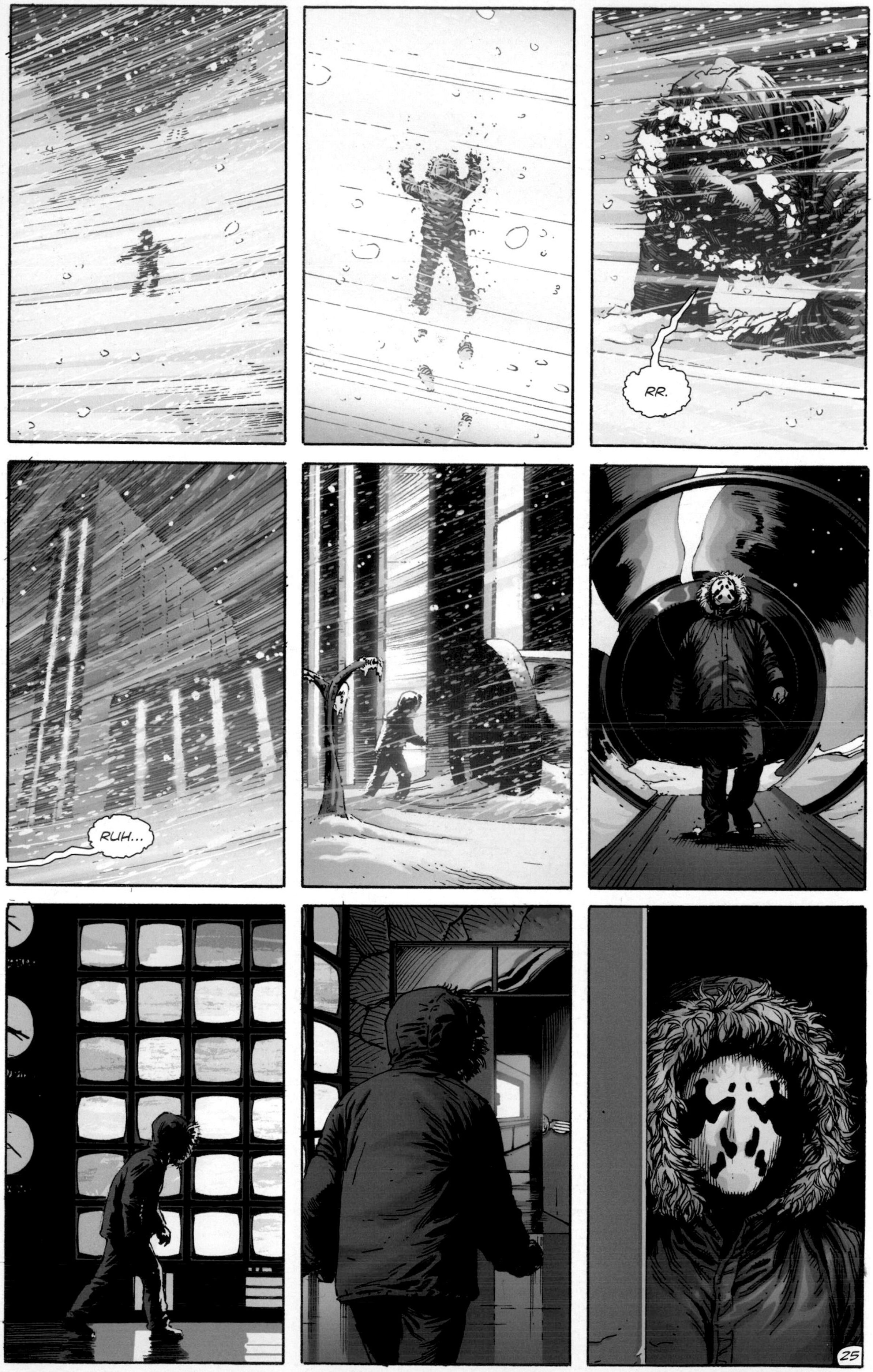
RR.
RUH...

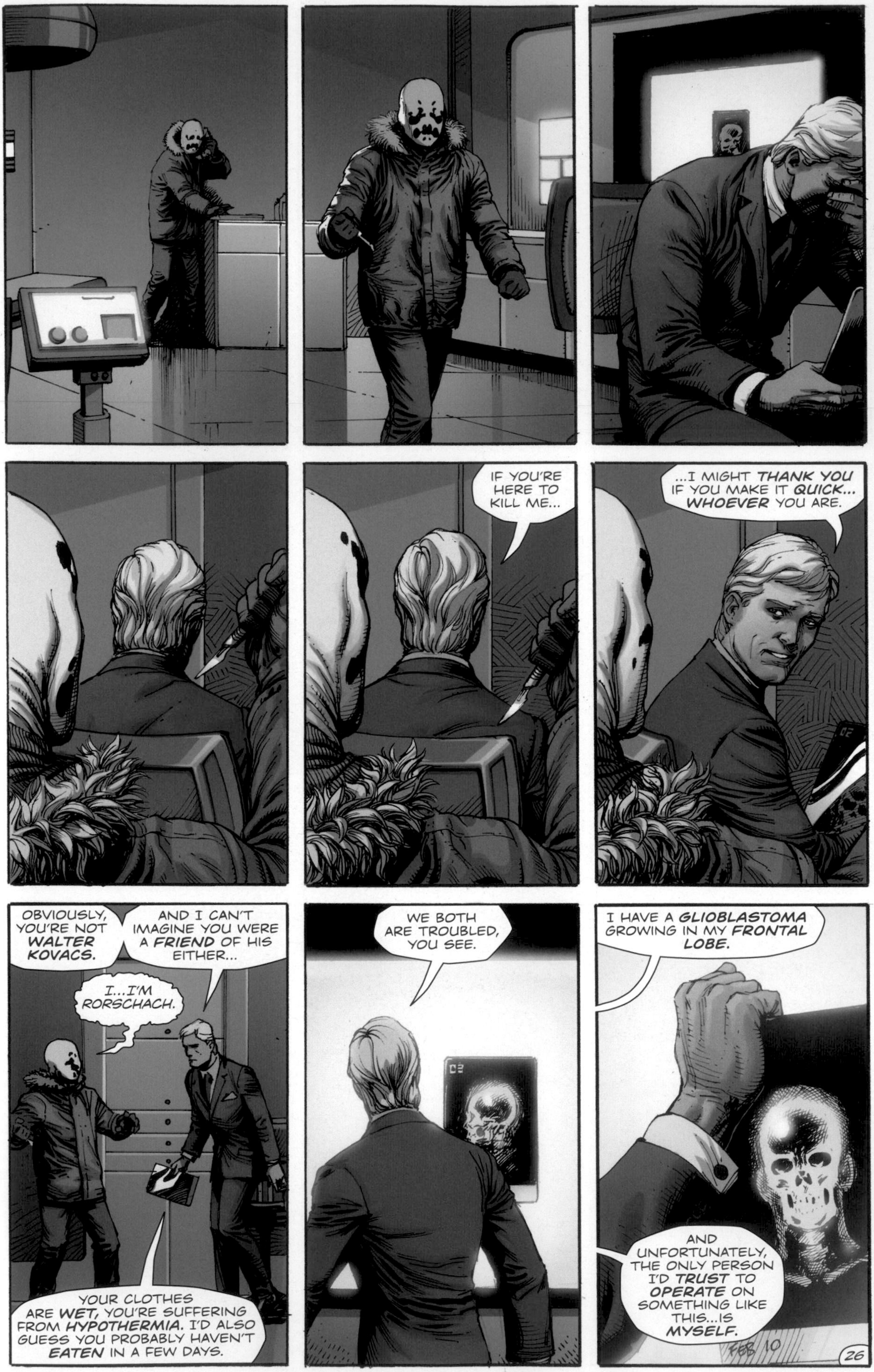
IF YOU'RE HERE TO KILL ME...
...I MIGHT THANK YOU IF YOU MAKE IT QUICK... WHOEVER YOU ARE.
OBVIOUSLY, YOU'RE NOT WALTER KOVACS.
AND I CAN'T IMAGINE YOU WERE A FRIEND OF HIS EITHER...
I...I'M RORSCHACH.
YOUR CLOTHES ARE WET, YOU'RE SUFFERING FROM HYPOTHERMIA. I'D ALSO GUESS YOU PROBABLY HAVEN'T EATEN IN A FEW DAYS.
WE BOTH ARE TROUBLED, YOU SEE.
I HAVE A GLIOBLASTOMA GROWING IN MY FRONTAL LOBE.
AND UNFORTUNATELY, THE ONLY PERSON I'D TRUST TO OPERATE ON SOMETHING LIKE THIS...IS MYSELF.

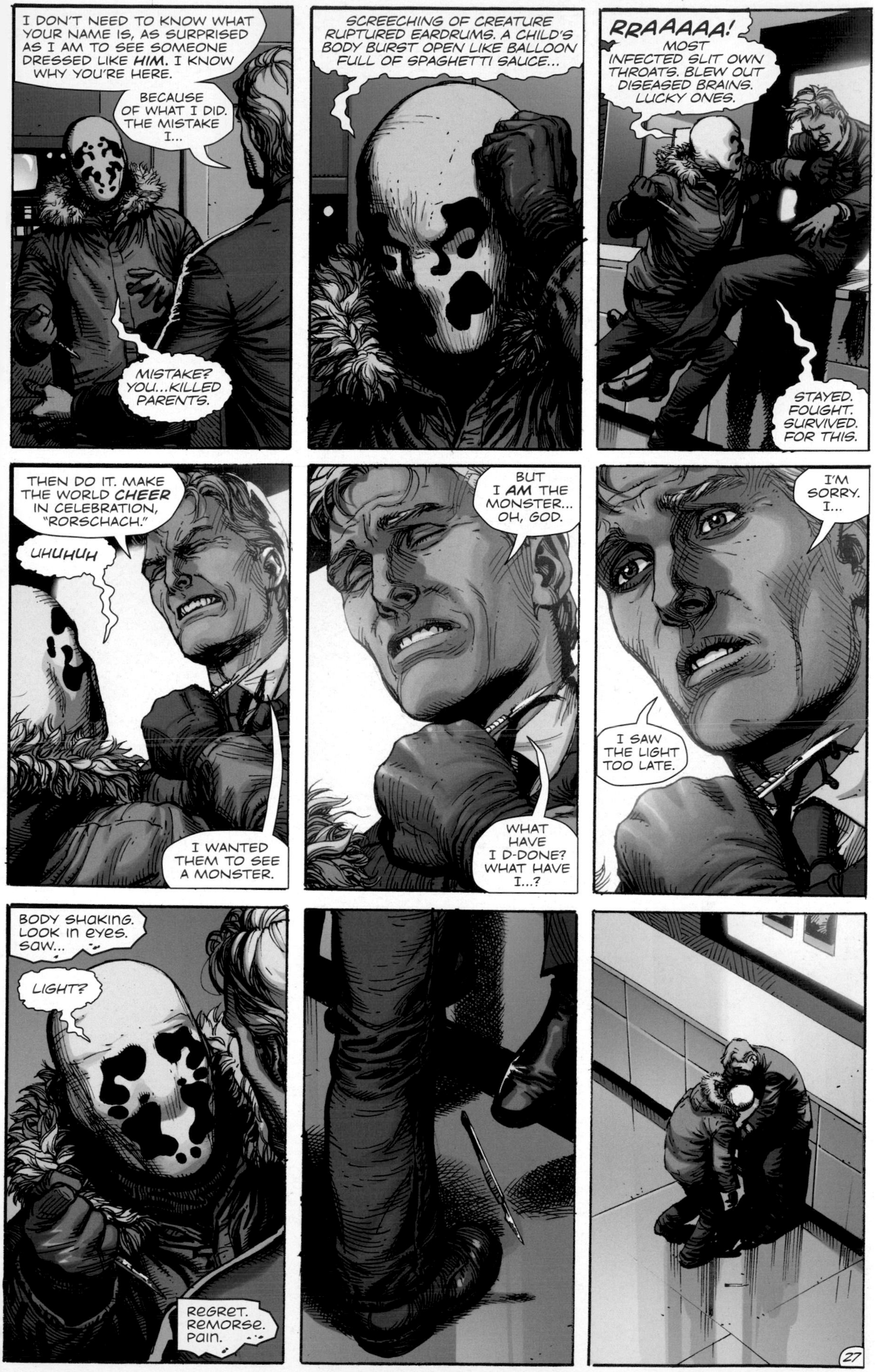
I DON'T NEED TO KNOW WHAT YOUR NAME IS, AS SURPRISED AS I AM TO SEE SOMEONE DRESSED LIKE HIM. I KNOW WHY YOU'RE HERE.
BECAUSE OF WHAT I DID. THE MISTAKE I...
MISTAKE? YOU...KILLED PARENTS.
SCREECHING OF CREATURE RUPTURED EARDRUMS. A CHILD'S BODY BURST OPEN LIKE BALLOON FULL OF SPAGHETTI SAUCE...
RRAAAAA!
MOST INFECTED SLIT OWN THROATS. BLEW OUT DISEASED BRAINS. LUCKY ONES.
STAYED. FOUGHT. SURVIVED. FOR THIS.
THEN DO IT. MAKE THE WORLD CHEER IN CELEBRATION, "RORSCHACH."
UHUHUH
I WANTED THEM TO SEE A MONSTER.
BUT I AM THE MONSTER... OH, GOD.
WHAT HAVE I D-DONE? WHAT HAVE I...?
I'M SORRY. I...
I SAW THE LIGHT TOO LATE.
BODY SHAKING. LOOK IN EYES. SAW...
LIGHT?
REGRET. REMORSE. PAIN.

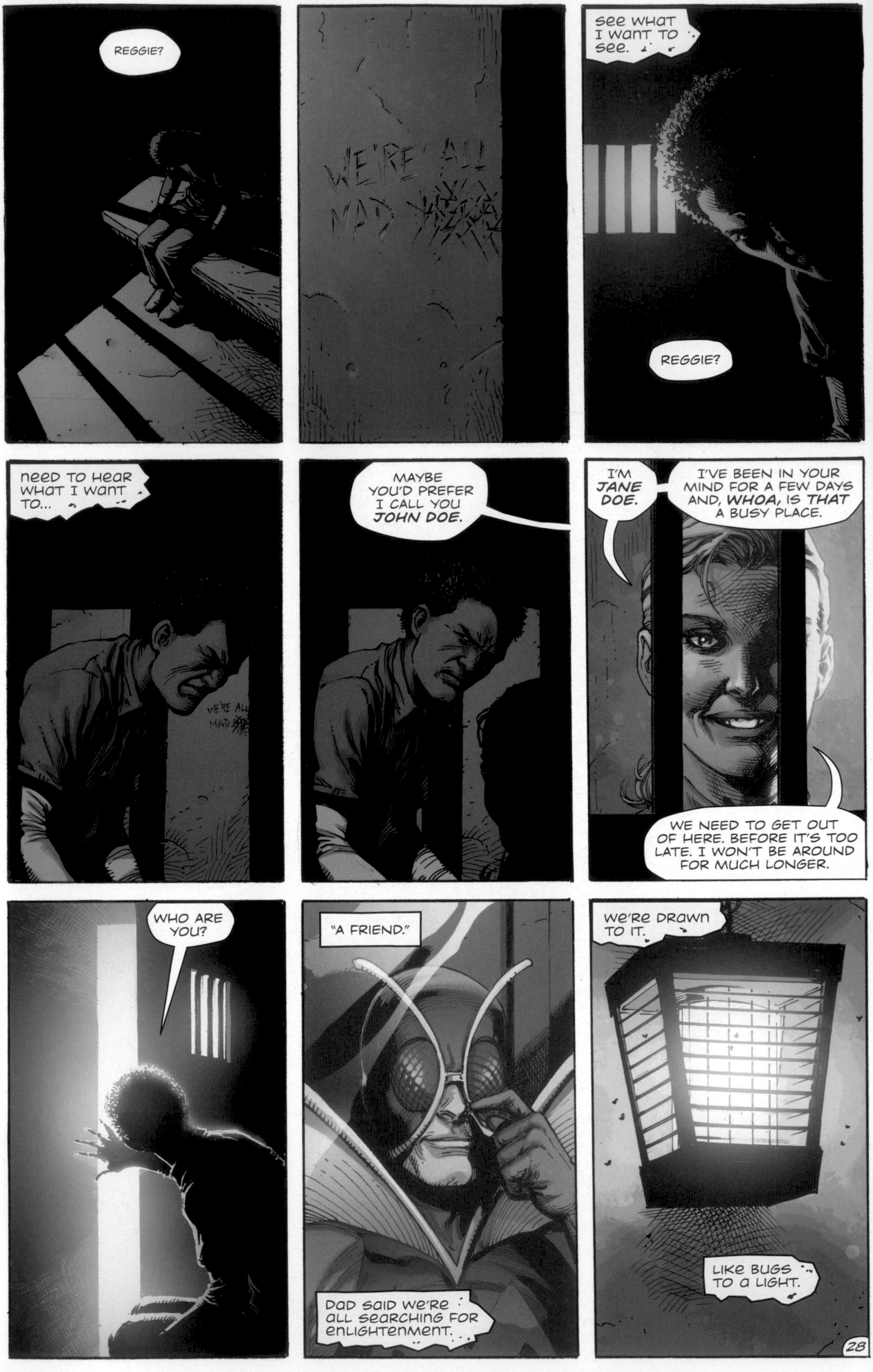
REGGIE?
WE'RE ALL MAD
see what I want to see.
REGGIE?
need to hear what I want to...
MAYBE YOU'D PREFER I CALL YOU JOHN DOE.
I'M JANE DOE.
I'VE BEEN IN YOUR MIND FOR A FEW DAYS AND, WHOA, IS THAT A BUSY PLACE.
WE NEED TO GET OUT OF HERE. BEFORE IT'S TOO LATE. I WON'T BE AROUND FOR MUCH LONGER.
WHO ARE YOU?
"A FRIEND."
Dad said we're all searching for enlightenment.
we're drawn to it.
Like bugs to a light.

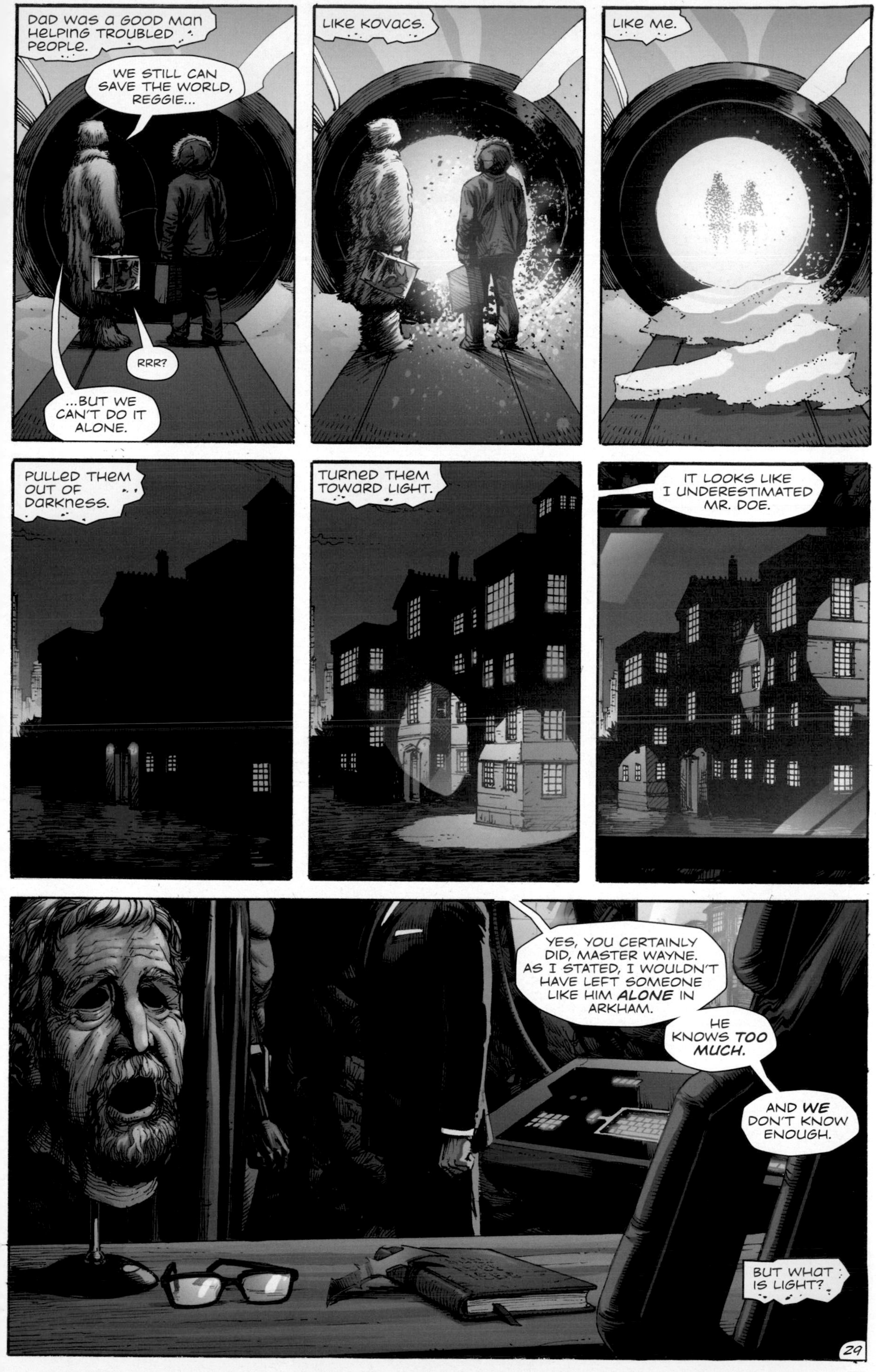
Dad was a good man helping troubled people.
WE STILL CAN SAVE THE WORLD, REGGIE...
RRR?
...BUT WE CAN'T DO IT ALONE.
Like Kovacs.
Like me.
Pulled them out of darkness.
Turned them toward light.
IT LOOKS LIKE I UNDERESTIMATED MR. DOE.
YES, YOU CERTAINLY DID, MASTER WAYNE. AS I STATED, I WOULDN'T HAVE LEFT SOMEONE LIKE HIM ALONE IN ARKHAM.
HE KNOWS TOO MUCH.
AND WE DON'T KNOW ENOUGH.
But what is light?

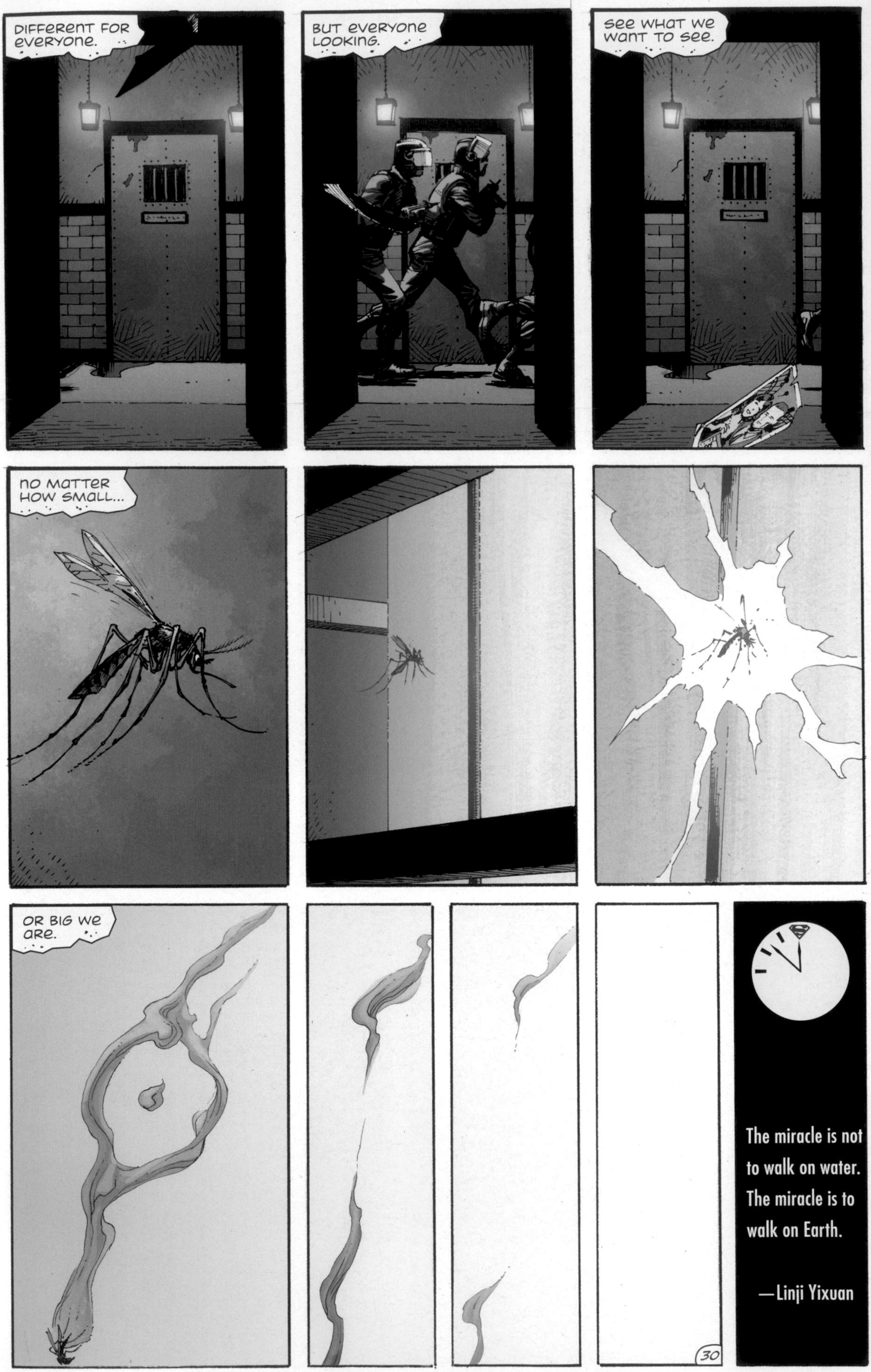
DIFFERENT FOR EVERYONE.
BUT EVERYONE LOOKING.
SEE WHAT WE WANT TO SEE.
NO MATTER HOW SMALL...
OR BIG WE ARE.
30
The miracle is not to walk on water. The miracle is to walk on Earth.
—Linji Yixuan

December 19th, 1962 1965

Dearest Betty,

...continue to write to you with deep love and a desperate hope that you might one day write your older brother in return. I do not know if I have an correct address, if you have thrown away my letters unopened or if you refuse to converse with me out of respect for father's request to "act as if I were dead." Perhaps raising the girls by yourself you simply haven't had the time to get reply. I still mourn Jack's death and am certain he was a wonderful husband and father and I wish I had gotten to know him better. I often wonder if I would have been better off enlisting as he did to make a difference rather than pursuing my own foolish dreams.

I understand from Mr. Grunk that the public exposure of my adventuring and subsequent stay at Fitzgerald has caused our parents and you a great deal of stress. He came to visit yesterday, smelling of tobacco and peppermints as he did when we were children. I agreed to Mr. Grunk's request that father take control of my financial assets as long as you are the beneficiary, once the lawyer fees are accounted for. I assure you, the last thing I ever set out to do was hurt the people I love the most, especially you.

There have been many horrific things said about me in the press since my breakdown. A knot has grown permanently within my stomach. Although I ~~want~~ wish to defend myself from these terrible accusations, I fear there is enough truth within some of them that I have no defense on which to stand. I therefore can only once again apologize for being a disappointment and embarrassment, to you more than anyone else, as you have been the most kind, generous and loving person in my life.

I would hope you find it in your heart to return one of my letters or even come and see me. I'd very much like to apologize in person and see how big the children have gotten. I love you.

Your dearest brother,

Byron

THE FITZGERALD MENTAL HOME
1 FOREST VIEW CIRCLE, WATERVILLE 04, MAINE

November 14th,

Dearest Betty,

As the snow covers the grounds like a cotton blanket outside of my window, I can't help but go back to the Christmas Eve of nearly forty years ago. It was 1927, I was fifteen and you were one week shy of eight. We had just moved into that great house on the hill by the creek. Father was still at the office while Mother was busy unpacking the kitchen. So she sent us into town to pick up a smoked ham. She gave us two dollars to bring back the biggest one we could find. Whatever change was left, we were allowed to spend on whatever we wished. On the way to the market, we made a list in our heads. Of licorice, drawing paper and crayons. We spent the afternoon spoiling our dinner with our favorite sweet treat and coloring pictures. Me of airplanes and you of rainbows they could fly over. Father was not happy when he came home, yelling at Mother and us, angry, we had wasted money on such silly things. They got into an awful fight and he left. Christmas morning, Father came back and admitted to all of us that he had lost his job the day before. The job that was supposed to pay for this great house on the hill by the creek. It was the only time I have ever seen Father cry. He held us tight as he did. All of us. And I remember thinking how lucky we were to be part of such a family.

I often wonder what he might say to me if he came here. Would he scold me for being a dreamer still? Or ~~might~~ would he shed a tear and say he missed me as much as I miss all of you? No matter, I suppose.

Your dearest brother,

Byron

THE FITZGERALD MENTAL HOME
1 FOREST VIEW CIRCLE, WATERVILLE 04, MAINE

June 25th, 1974

Dearest Betty,

I know I missed sending you a letter last week and I wanted to apologize. A friend of mine was killed in a freak automobile accident last Monday that left him decapitated and I was quite shaken. Then on Tuesday, I was forced to attend a new class at Fitzgerald called "Hurting the One You Love" that left me in tears.

I realize that my behavior may have, even now, a negative effect on those closest to me. And despite not seeing or hearing from you in over a decade, there is no one closer to me in my life than my sister. However, as lonely as I am, I want to assure now understand that my letters to you may be unsettling. I would ..., I have nothing but love for you and the rest of the family and I would never do anything to harm you. Perhaps that fear is what has kept you from writing back or seeing me all these years?

Betty, I am also pleased to tell you that you will be contacted soon by an estate lawyer named Mr. Frederick J. Charles. He will be delivering to you a check in the amount of $10,000. I inherited quite a bit from my dear friend who I mentioned above. I had forgotten I loaned him money over the years, but he remembered and had invested it well. I wish I had stayed in touch with him. I never would have guessed he gave me a moment's thought after I was admitted. it gives me hope for us.

If you are so inclined, once you receive the check I am hoping that you might purchase and send me the items listed below under the understanding that you will keep the remaining money for yourself and the girls.

- 78 feet of 3.8 millimeter aluminum alloy tubing
- 40 feet of quarter inch metal cable
- Cable cutters
- 3 rolls, 700 yards each, of polyester cloth (polyethylene terephthalate fabric)
- One pair of goggles

Of course, if this makes you uncomfortable in any way, keep the money for yourself and I will find another way to attain the above.

Truthfully, I don't expect a reply, as I have yet to receive one in the years I've been writing to you, but I hope you keep this letter, and that you have kept all of them, as a reminder of how much you mean to me. If it were not for them, I would surely have lost my mind by now.

Your dearest brother,

Byron

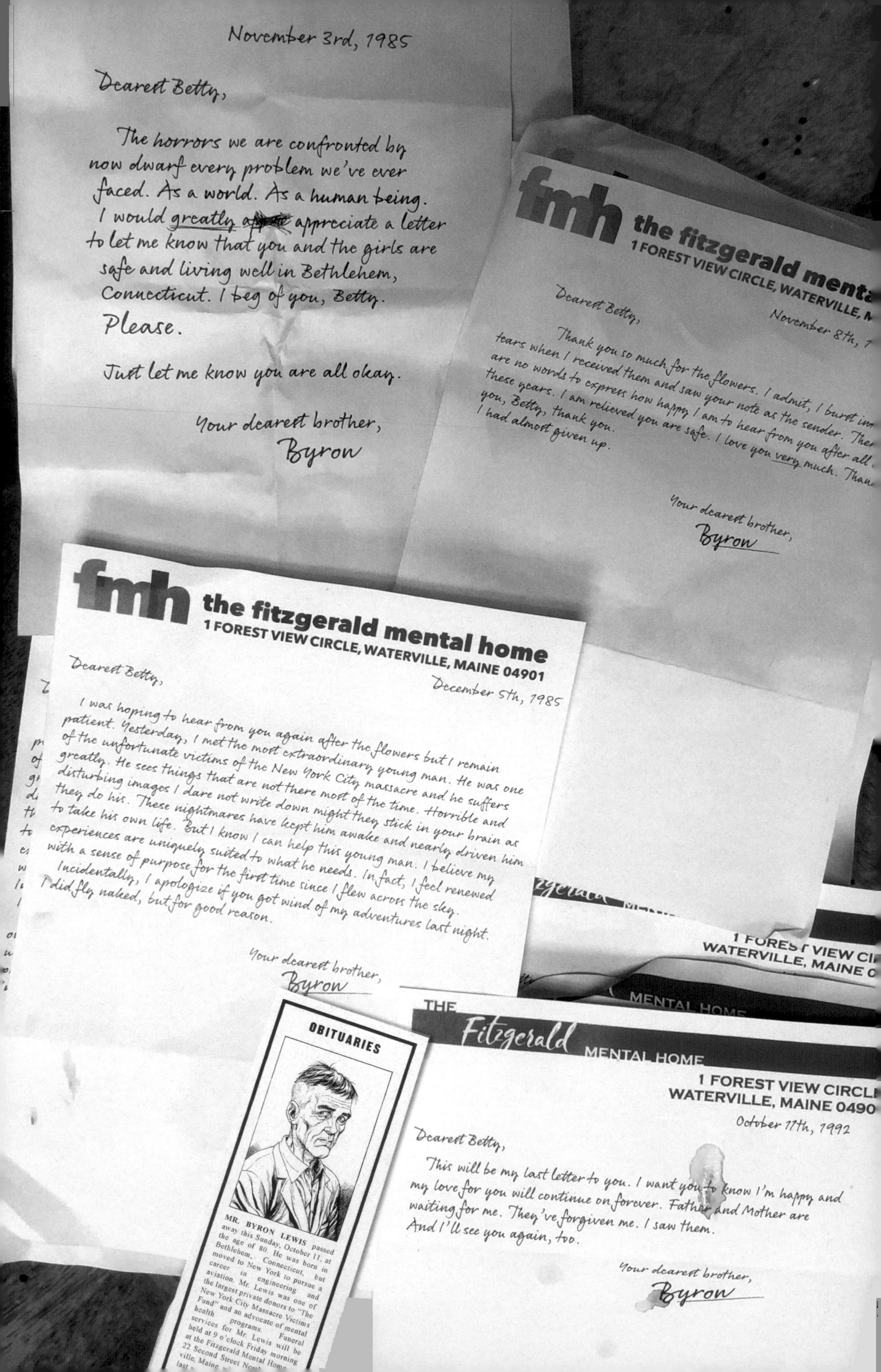
November 3rd, 1985
Dearest Betty,
The horrors we are confronted by now dwarf every problem we've ever faced. As a world. As a human being. I would greatly appreciate a letter to let me know that you and the girls are safe and living well in Bethlehem, Connecticut. I beg of you, Betty.
Please.
Just let me know you are all okay.
Your dearest brother,
Byron
fmh the fitzgerald menta
1 FOREST VIEW CIRCLE, WATERVILLE, M
Dearest Betty,
November 8th,
Thank you so much for the flowers. I admit, I burst in tears when I received them and saw your note as the sender. There are no words to express how happy I am to hear from you after all these years. I am relieved you are safe. I love you very much. Thank you, Betty, thank you.
I had almost given up.
Your dearest brother,
Byron
fmh the fitzgerald mental home
1 FOREST VIEW CIRCLE, WATERVILLE, MAINE 04901
Dearest Betty,
December 5th, 1985
I was hoping to hear from you again after the flowers but I remain patient. Yesterday, I met the most extraordinary young man. He was one of the unfortunate victims of the New York City massacre and he suffers greatly. He sees things that are not there most of the time. Horrible and disturbing images I dare not write down might they stick in your brain as they do his. These nightmares have kept him awake and nearly driven him to take his own life. But I know I can help this young man. I believe my experiences are uniquely suited to what he needs. In fact, I feel renewed with a sense of purpose for the first time since I flew across the sky.
Incidentally, I apologize if you got wind of my adventures last night.
I did fly naked, but for good reason.
Your dearest brother,
Byron
1 FOREST VIEW CI
WATERVILLE, MAINE O
MENTAL HOME
OBITUARIES
MR. BYRON LEWIS passed away this Sunday, October 11, at the age of 80. He was born in Bethlehem, Connecticut, but moved to New York to pursue a career in engineering and aviation. Mr. Lewis was one of the largest private donors to "The New York City Massacre Victims Fund" and an advocate of mental health programs. Funeral services for Mr. Lewis will be held at 9 o'clock Friday morning at the Fitzgerald Mental Home 22 Second Street North ville, Maine
THE Fitzgerald MENTAL HOME
1 FOREST VIEW CIRCL
WATERVILLE, MAINE 0490
October 11th, 1992
Dearest Betty,
This will be my last letter to you. I want you to know I'm happy and my love for you will continue on forever. Father and Mother are waiting for me. They've forgiven me. I saw them.
And I'll see you again, too.
Your dearest brother,
Byron

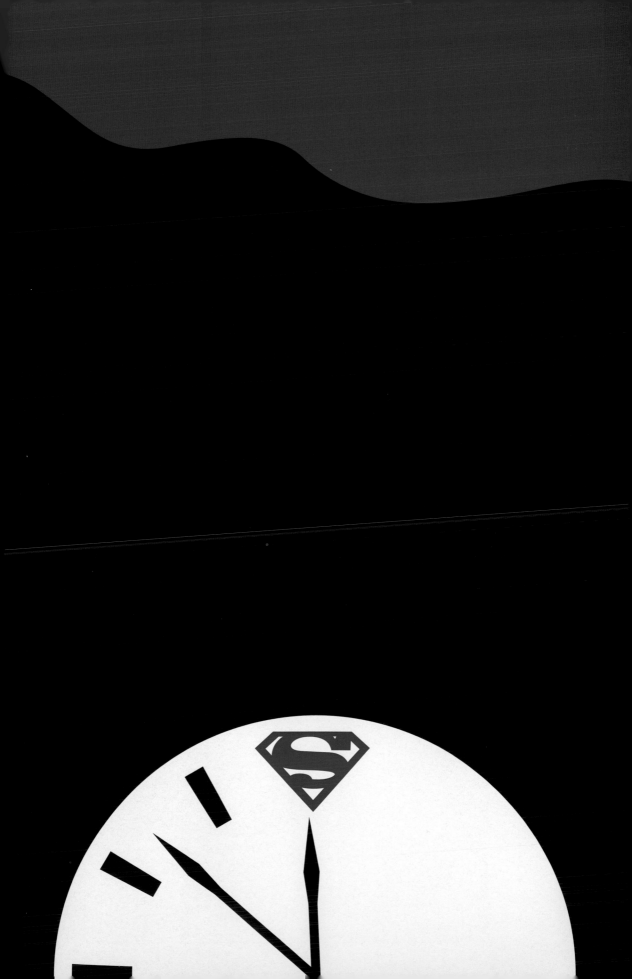

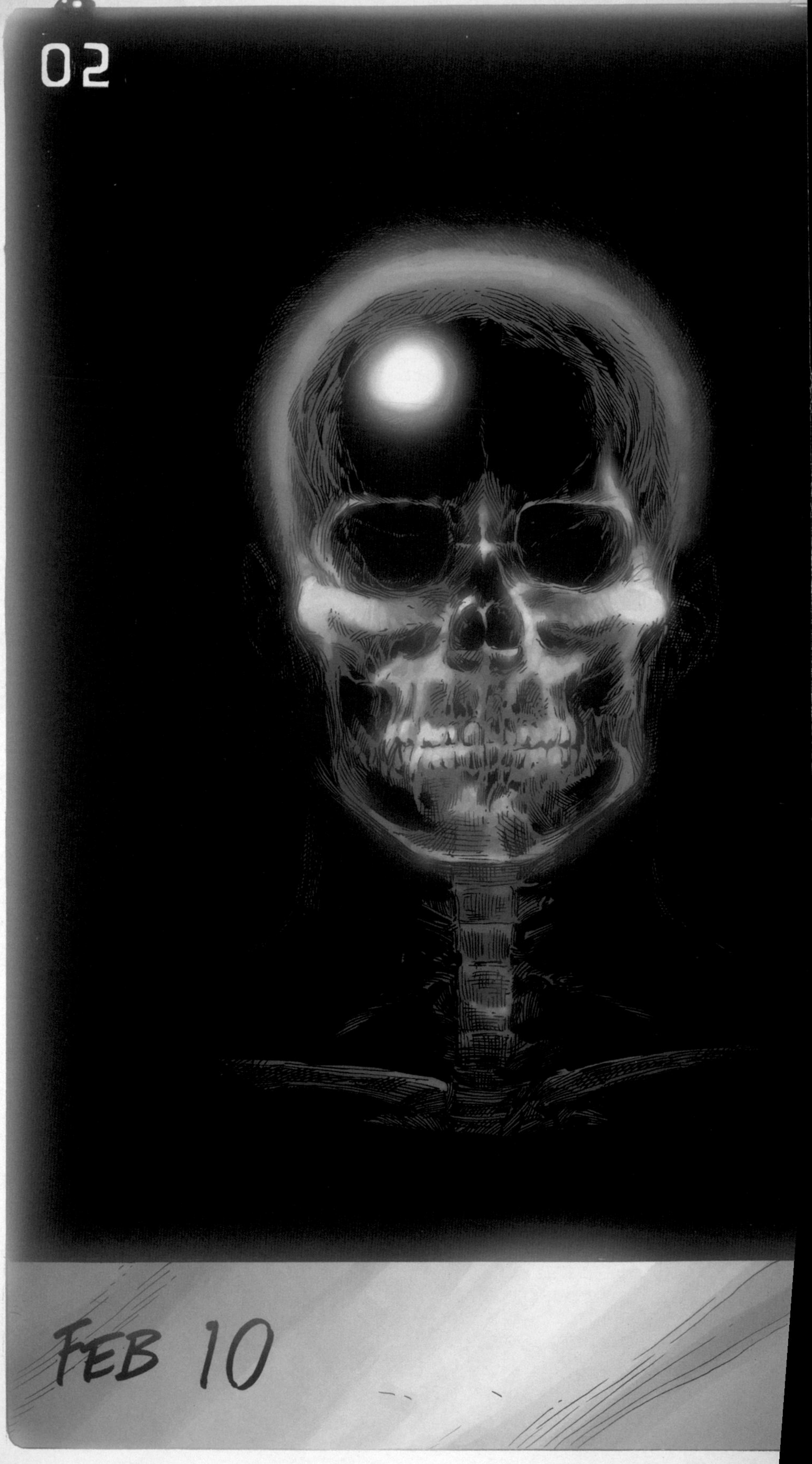

02
FEB 10

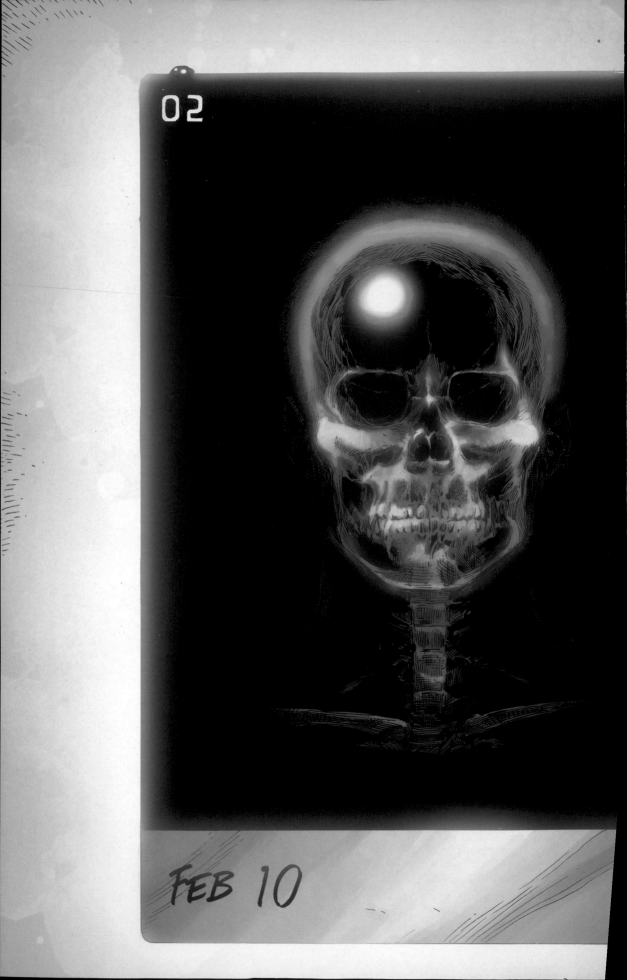

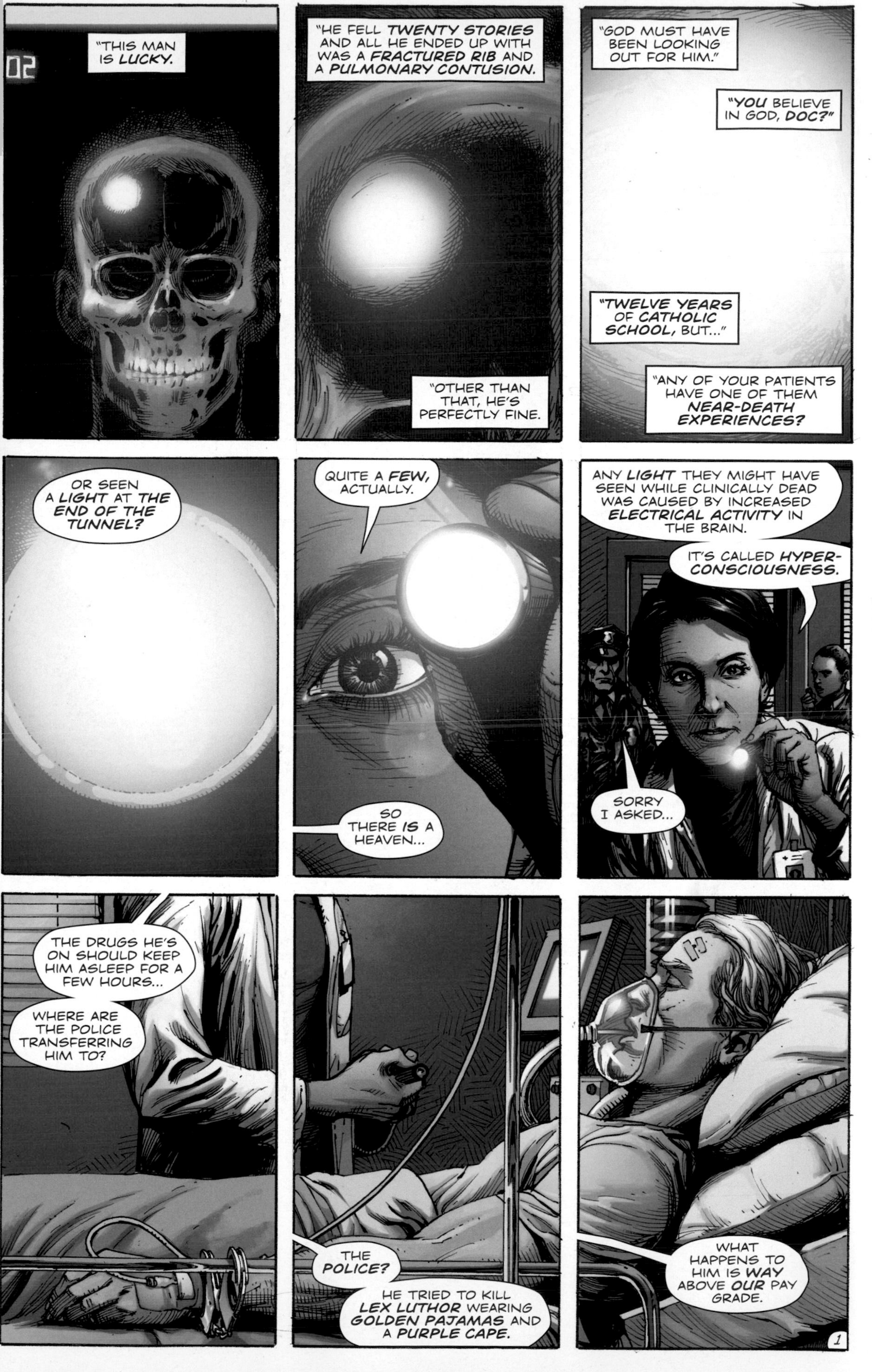

"THIS MAN IS LUCKY.
"HE FELL TWENTY STORIES AND ALL HE ENDED UP WITH WAS A FRACTURED RIB AND A PULMONARY CONTUSION.
"OTHER THAN THAT, HE'S PERFECTLY FINE.
"GOD MUST HAVE BEEN LOOKING OUT FOR HIM."
"YOU BELIEVE IN GOD, DOC?"
"TWELVE YEARS OF CATHOLIC SCHOOL, BUT..."
"ANY OF YOUR PATIENTS HAVE ONE OF THEM NEAR-DEATH EXPERIENCES?
OR SEEN A LIGHT AT THE END OF THE TUNNEL?
QUITE A FEW, ACTUALLY.
SO THERE IS A HEAVEN...
ANY LIGHT THEY MIGHT HAVE SEEN WHILE CLINICALLY DEAD WAS CAUSED BY INCREASED ELECTRICAL ACTIVITY IN THE BRAIN.
IT'S CALLED HYPER-CONSCIOUSNESS.
SORRY I ASKED...
THE DRUGS HE'S ON SHOULD KEEP HIM ASLEEP FOR A FEW HOURS...
WHERE ARE THE POLICE TRANSFERRING HIM TO?
THE POLICE?
HE TRIED TO KILL LEX LUTHOR WEARING GOLDEN PAJAMAS AND A PURPLE CAPE.
WHAT HAPPENS TO HIM IS WAY ABOVE OUR PAY GRADE.

THESE DAYS, EVEN IF YOU *DON'T* HAVE POWERS, YOU WEAR A *HALLOWEEN MASK* AND COMMIT A *CRIME,* YOU'RE A *FEDERAL* PROBLEM...

WANNABES.

YEP. THEY'RE WHY *GOTHAM'S* SUCH A *GODDAMN* MESS.

AND WHY EVERYONE'S IN THE STREETS OVER THERE, *MARCHING* AGAINST *THE BATMAN* AND HIS *GROUPIES.*

LEX LUTHOR SAYS *THE DARK KNIGHT* AND THAT *BAT-SIGNAL* ARE WHAT *DRAW OUT* THE *PAINTED FREAKS* IN THE FIRST PLACE.

LUTHOR'S RIGHT.

THEY SHOULD'VE BROUGHT DOWN *THE BATMAN* AND TURNED OFF HIS *LIGHT* A *LONG* TIME AGO.

THANK *GOD* WE LIVE IN *METROPOLIS.*

SUPERMAN'S THE ONLY THING YOU CAN *BELIEVE* IN ANYMORE.

THERE IS NO GOD

CHRIST, I *HATE* BEING STUCK HERE, BABYSITTING THIS ASSHOLE UNTIL THE *FEDS* SHOW...

I'D RATHER BE *CHAINED* TO MY *DESK.*

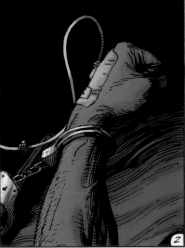

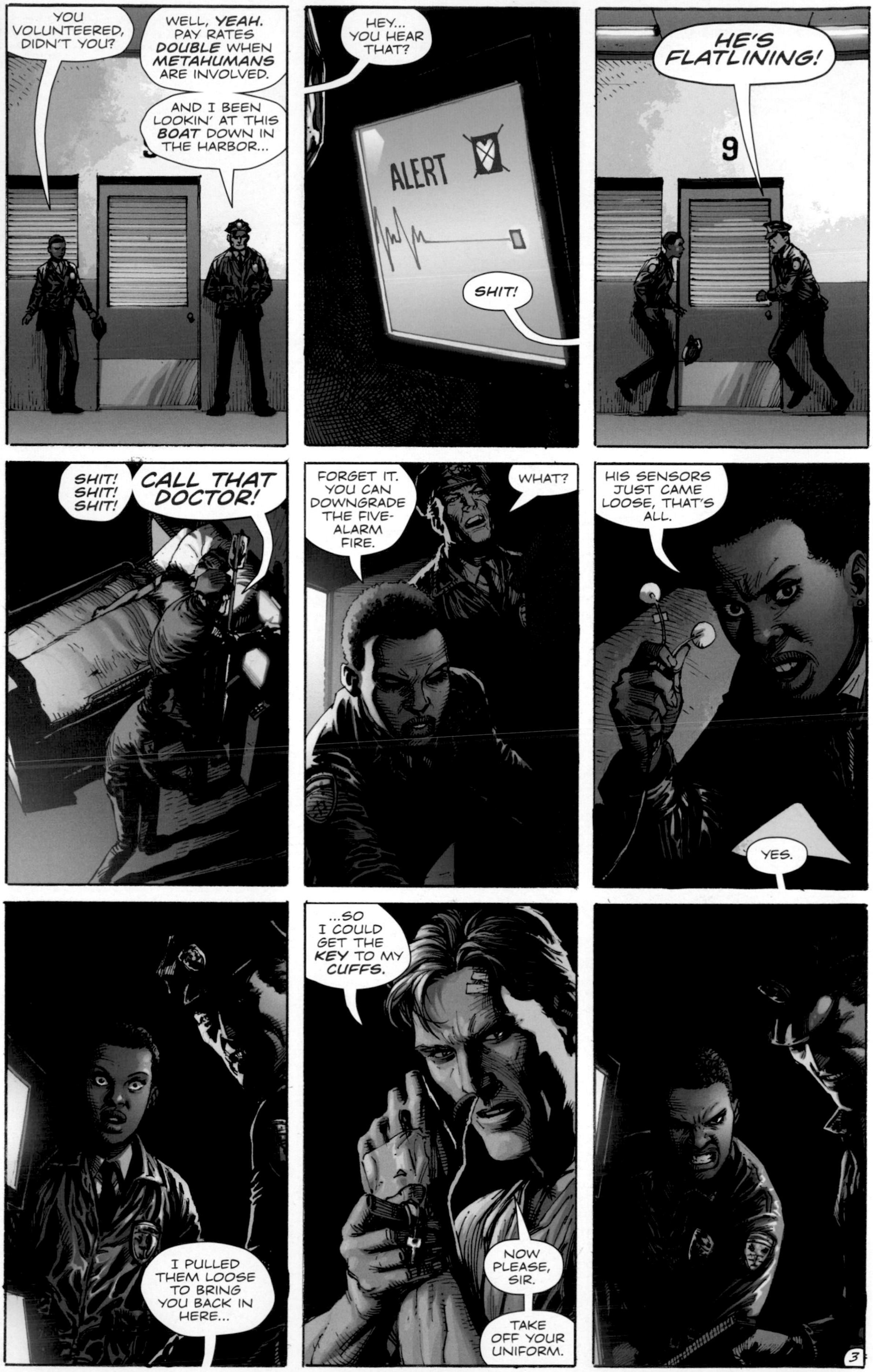
YOU VOLUNTEERED, DIDN'T YOU?
WELL, YEAH. PAY RATES DOUBLE WHEN METAHUMANS ARE INVOLVED.
AND I BEEN LOOKIN' AT THIS BOAT DOWN IN THE HARBOR...
HEY... YOU HEAR THAT?
ALERT
SHIT!
HE'S FLATLINING!
9
SHIT! SHIT! SHIT!
CALL THAT DOCTOR!
FORGET IT. YOU CAN DOWNGRADE THE FIVE-ALARM FIRE.
WHAT?
HIS SENSORS JUST CAME LOOSE, THAT'S ALL.
YES.
I PULLED THEM LOOSE TO BRING YOU BACK IN HERE...
...SO I COULD GET THE KEY TO MY CUFFS.
NOW PLEASE, SIR.
TAKE OFF YOUR UNIFORM.
3

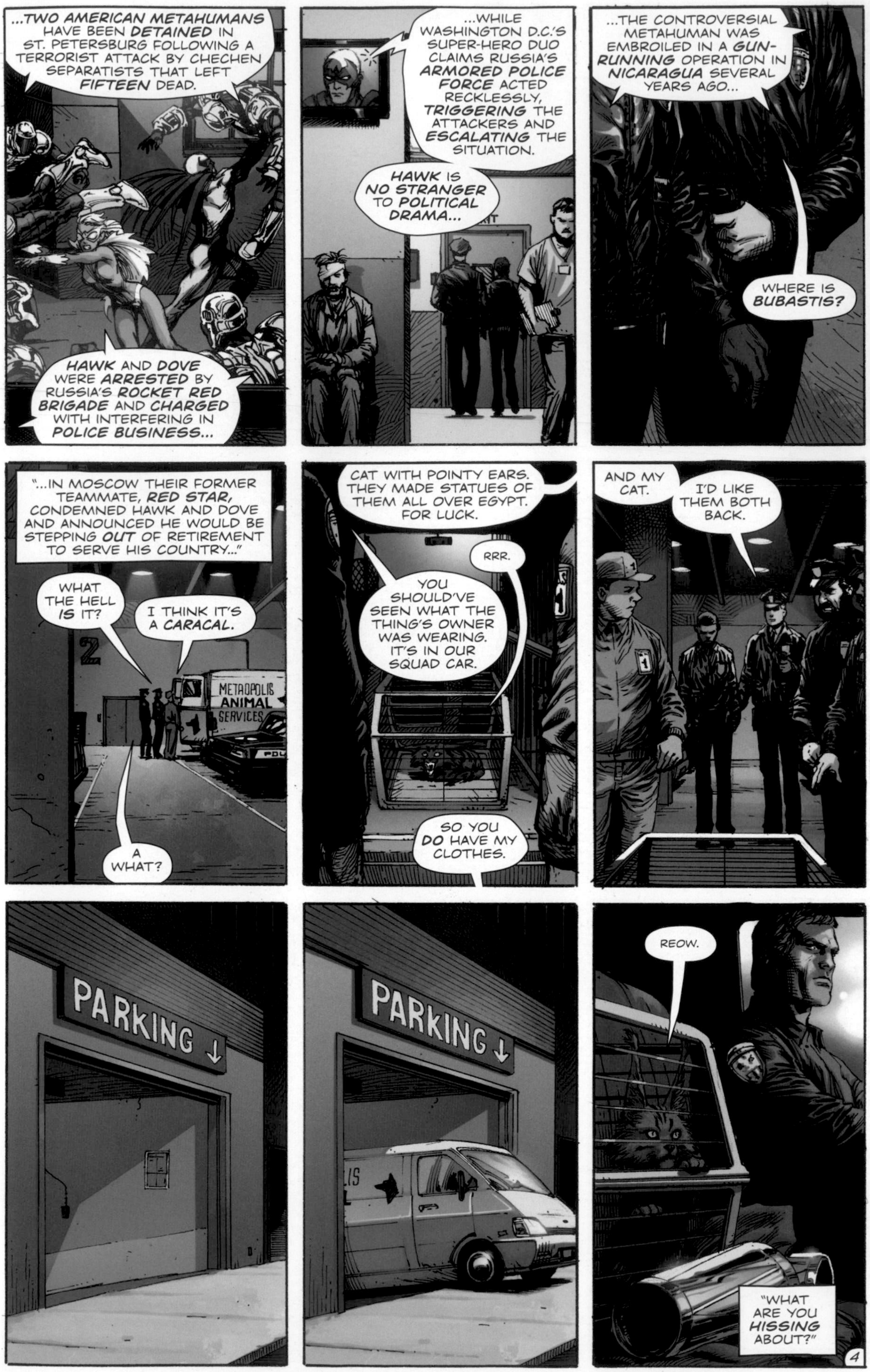
...TWO AMERICAN METAHUMANS HAVE BEEN DETAINED IN ST. PETERSBURG FOLLOWING A TERRORIST ATTACK BY CHECHEN SEPARATISTS THAT LEFT FIFTEEN DEAD.
HAWK AND DOVE WERE ARRESTED BY RUSSIA'S ROCKET RED BRIGADE AND CHARGED WITH INTERFERING IN POLICE BUSINESS...
...WHILE WASHINGTON D.C.'S SUPER-HERO DUO CLAIMS RUSSIA'S ARMORED POLICE FORCE ACTED RECKLESSLY, TRIGGERING THE ATTACKERS AND ESCALATING THE SITUATION.
HAWK IS NO STRANGER TO POLITICAL DRAMA...
...THE CONTROVERSIAL METAHUMAN WAS EMBROILED IN A GUN-RUNNING OPERATION IN NICARAGUA SEVERAL YEARS AGO...
WHERE IS BUBASTIS?
"...IN MOSCOW THEIR FORMER TEAMMATE, RED STAR, CONDEMNED HAWK AND DOVE AND ANNOUNCED HE WOULD BE STEPPING OUT OF RETIREMENT TO SERVE HIS COUNTRY..."
WHAT THE HELL IS IT?
I THINK IT'S A CARACAL.
METROPOLIS ANIMAL SERVICES
A WHAT?
CAT WITH POINTY EARS. THEY MADE STATUES OF THEM ALL OVER EGYPT. FOR LUCK.
RRR.
YOU SHOULD'VE SEEN WHAT THE THING'S OWNER WAS WEARING. IT'S IN OUR SQUAD CAR.
SO YOU DO HAVE MY CLOTHES.
AND MY CAT.
I'D LIKE THEM BOTH BACK.
PARKING ↓
PARKING ↓
REOW.
"WHAT ARE YOU HISSING ABOUT?"

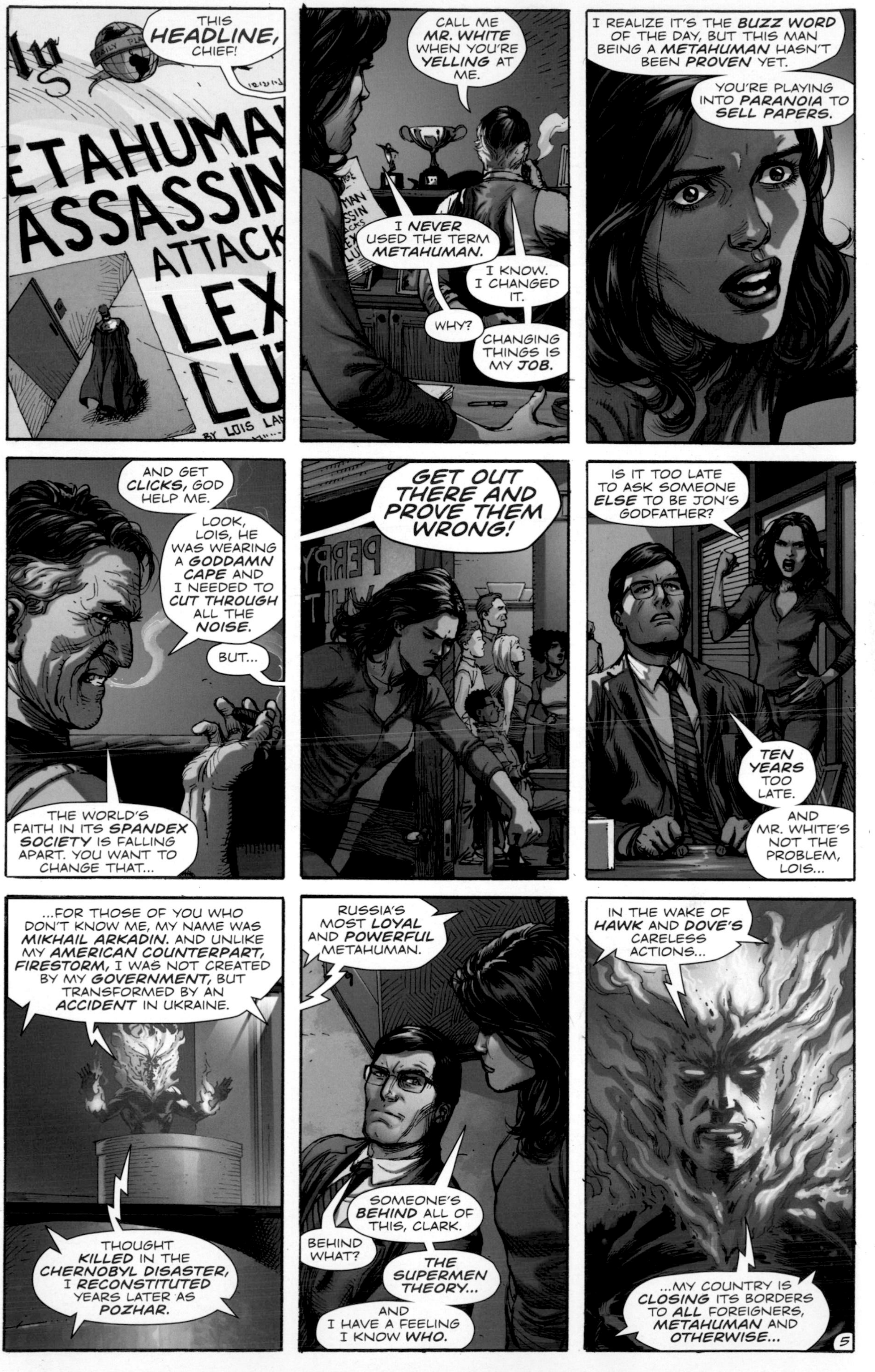
THIS HEADLINE, CHIEF!
ETAHUMA
ASSASSIN
ATTACK
LEX
LU
BY LOIS LA
CALL ME MR. WHITE WHEN YOU'RE YELLING AT ME.
I NEVER USED THE TERM METAHUMAN.
I KNOW. I CHANGED IT.
WHY?
CHANGING THINGS IS MY JOB.
I REALIZE IT'S THE BUZZ WORD OF THE DAY, BUT THIS MAN BEING A METAHUMAN HASN'T BEEN PROVEN YET.
YOU'RE PLAYING INTO PARANOIA TO SELL PAPERS.
AND GET CLICKS, GOD HELP ME.
LOOK, LOIS, HE WAS WEARING A GODDAMN CAPE AND I NEEDED TO CUT THROUGH ALL THE NOISE.
BUT...
THE WORLD'S FAITH IN ITS SPANDEX SOCIETY IS FALLING APART. YOU WANT TO CHANGE THAT...
GET OUT THERE AND PROVE THEM WRONG!
PERRY WHIT
IS IT TOO LATE TO ASK SOMEONE ELSE TO BE JON'S GODFATHER?
TEN YEARS TOO LATE.
AND MR. WHITE'S NOT THE PROBLEM, LOIS...
...FOR THOSE OF YOU WHO DON'T KNOW ME, MY NAME WAS MIKHAIL ARKADIN. AND UNLIKE MY AMERICAN COUNTERPART, FIRESTORM, I WAS NOT CREATED BY MY GOVERNMENT, BUT TRANSFORMED BY AN ACCIDENT IN UKRAINE.
THOUGHT KILLED IN THE CHERNOBYL DISASTER, I RECONSTITUTED YEARS LATER AS POZHAR.
RUSSIA'S MOST LOYAL AND POWERFUL METAHUMAN.
SOMEONE'S BEHIND ALL OF THIS, CLARK.
BEHIND WHAT?
THE SUPERMEN THEORY...
AND I HAVE A FEELING I KNOW WHO.
IN THE WAKE OF HAWK AND DOVE'S CARELESS ACTIONS...
...MY COUNTRY IS CLOSING ITS BORDERS TO ALL FOREIGNERS, METAHUMAN AND OTHERWISE...

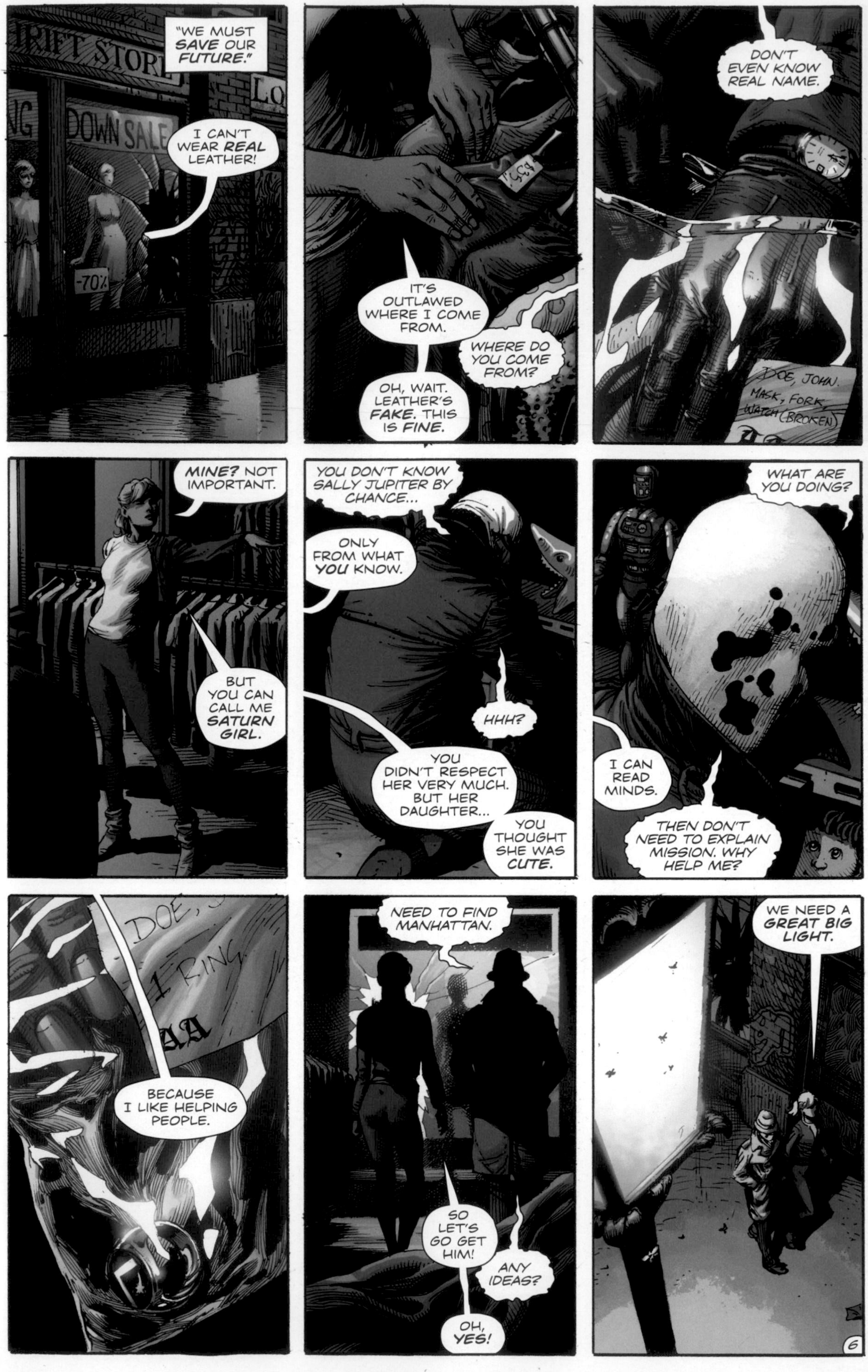
"WE MUST SAVE OUR FUTURE."
IRIFT STORE
DOWN SALE
-70%
I CAN'T WEAR REAL LEATHER!
IT'S OUTLAWED WHERE I COME FROM.
WHERE DO YOU COME FROM?
OH, WAIT. LEATHER'S FAKE. THIS IS FINE.
DON'T EVEN KNOW REAL NAME.
DOE, JOHN.
MASK, FORK
WATCH (BROKEN)
MINE? NOT IMPORTANT.
BUT YOU CAN CALL ME SATURN GIRL.
YOU DON'T KNOW SALLY JUPITER BY CHANCE...
ONLY FROM WHAT YOU KNOW.
HHH?
YOU DIDN'T RESPECT HER VERY MUCH. BUT HER DAUGHTER...
YOU THOUGHT SHE WAS CUTE.
WHAT ARE YOU DOING?
I CAN READ MINDS.
THEN DON'T NEED TO EXPLAIN MISSION. WHY HELP ME?
DOE,
1 RING
BECAUSE I LIKE HELPING PEOPLE.
NEED TO FIND MANHATTAN.
SO LET'S GO GET HIM!
ANY IDEAS?
OH, YES!
WE NEED A GREAT BIG LIGHT.
6

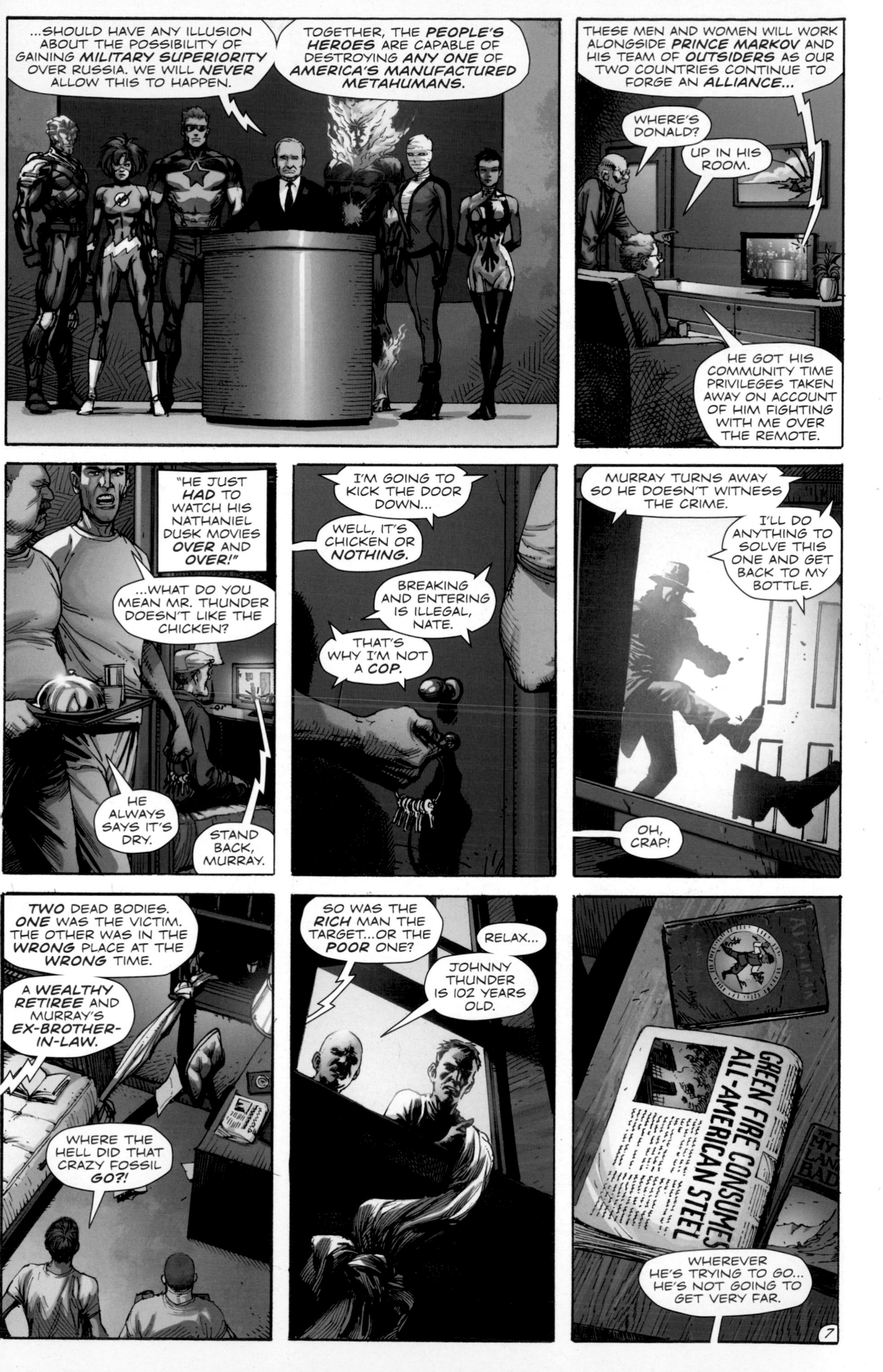
...SHOULD HAVE ANY ILLUSION ABOUT THE POSSIBILITY OF GAINING **MILITARY SUPERIORITY** OVER RUSSIA. WE WILL **NEVER** ALLOW THIS TO HAPPEN.
TOGETHER, THE **PEOPLE'S HEROES** ARE CAPABLE OF DESTROYING **ANY ONE** OF **AMERICA'S MANUFACTURED METAHUMANS.**
THESE MEN AND WOMEN WILL WORK ALONGSIDE **PRINCE MARKOV** AND HIS TEAM OF **OUTSIDERS** AS OUR TWO COUNTRIES CONTINUE TO FORGE AN **ALLIANCE...**
WHERE'S DONALD?
UP IN HIS ROOM.
HE GOT HIS COMMUNITY TIME PRIVILEGES TAKEN AWAY ON ACCOUNT OF HIM FIGHTING WITH ME OVER THE REMOTE.
"HE JUST **HAD** TO WATCH HIS NATHANIEL DUSK MOVIES **OVER** AND **OVER!**"
...WHAT DO YOU MEAN MR. THUNDER DOESN'T LIKE THE CHICKEN?
HE ALWAYS SAYS IT'S DRY.
STAND BACK, MURRAY.
I'M GOING TO KICK THE DOOR DOWN...
WELL, IT'S CHICKEN OR **NOTHING.**
BREAKING AND ENTERING IS ILLEGAL, NATE.
THAT'S WHY I'M NOT A **COP.**
MURRAY TURNS AWAY SO HE DOESN'T WITNESS THE CRIME.
I'LL DO ANYTHING TO SOLVE THIS ONE AND GET BACK TO MY BOTTLE.
OH, CRAP!
TWO DEAD BODIES. **ONE** WAS THE VICTIM. THE OTHER WAS IN THE **WRONG** PLACE AT THE **WRONG** TIME.
A **WEALTHY RETIREE** AND MURRAY'S **EX-BROTHER-IN-LAW.**
WHERE THE HELL DID THAT CRAZY FOSSIL **GO?!**
SO WAS THE **RICH** MAN THE TARGET...OR THE **POOR** ONE?
RELAX...
JOHNNY THUNDER IS 102 YEARS OLD.
GREEN FIRE CONSUMES ALL-AMERICAN STEEL
WHEREVER HE'S TRYING TO GO... HE'S NOT GOING TO GET VERY FAR.

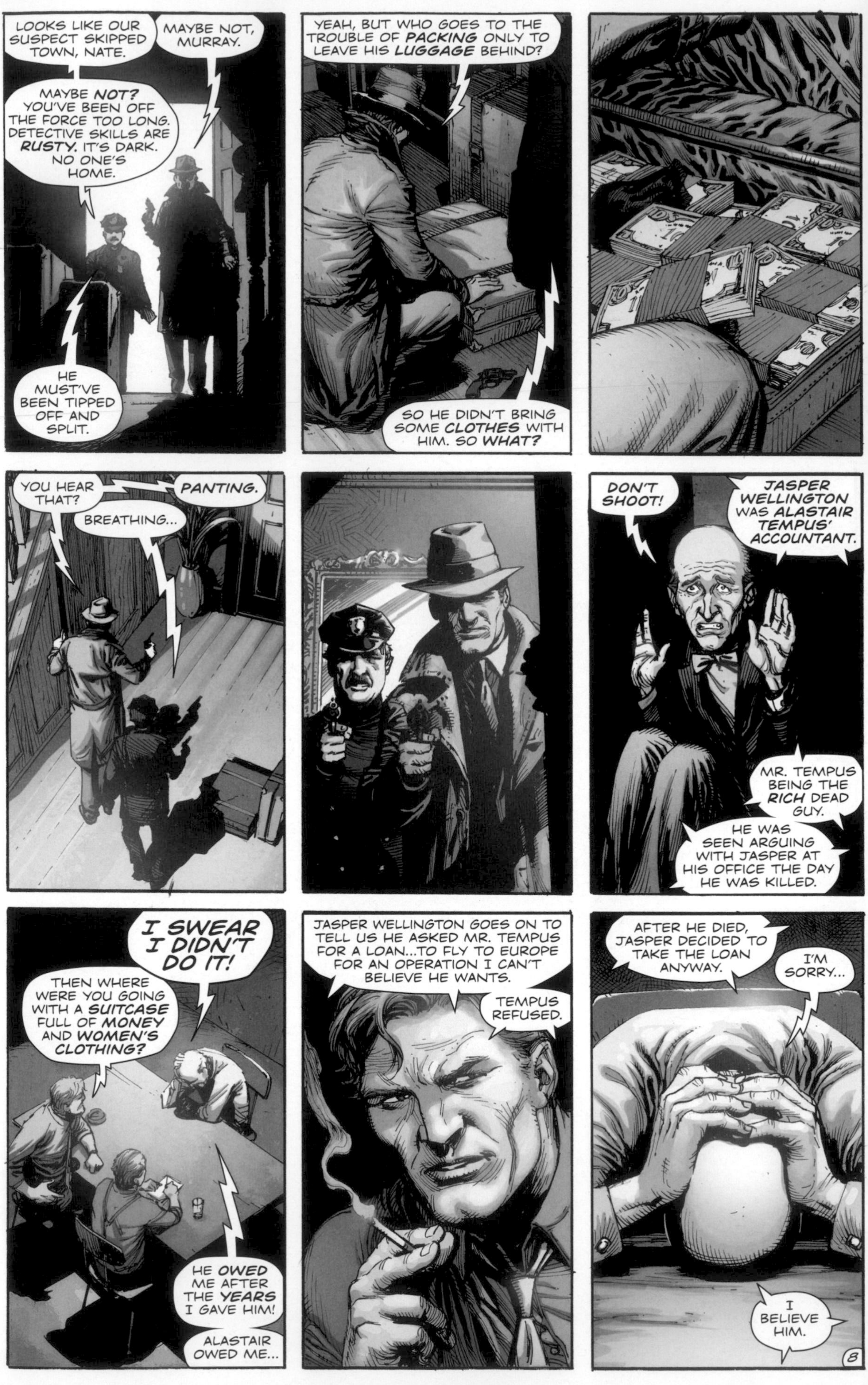
LOOKS LIKE OUR SUSPECT SKIPPED TOWN, NATE.
MAYBE NOT, MURRAY.
MAYBE NOT? YOU'VE BEEN OFF THE FORCE TOO LONG. DETECTIVE SKILLS ARE RUSTY. IT'S DARK. NO ONE'S HOME.
HE MUST'VE BEEN TIPPED OFF AND SPLIT.
YEAH, BUT WHO GOES TO THE TROUBLE OF PACKING ONLY TO LEAVE HIS LUGGAGE BEHIND?
SO HE DIDN'T BRING SOME CLOTHES WITH HIM. SO WHAT?
YOU HEAR THAT?
BREATHING...
PANTING.
DON'T SHOOT!
JASPER WELLINGTON WAS ALASTAIR TEMPUS' ACCOUNTANT.
MR. TEMPUS BEING THE RICH DEAD GUY.
HE WAS SEEN ARGUING WITH JASPER AT HIS OFFICE THE DAY HE WAS KILLED.
I SWEAR I DIDN'T DO IT!
THEN WHERE WERE YOU GOING WITH A SUITCASE FULL OF MONEY AND WOMEN'S CLOTHING?
HE OWED ME AFTER THE YEARS I GAVE HIM!
ALASTAIR OWED ME...
JASPER WELLINGTON GOES ON TO TELL US HE ASKED MR. TEMPUS FOR A LOAN...TO FLY TO EUROPE FOR AN OPERATION I CAN'T BELIEVE HE WANTS.
TEMPUS REFUSED.
AFTER HE DIED, JASPER DECIDED TO TAKE THE LOAN ANYWAY.
I'M SORRY...
I BELIEVE HIM.

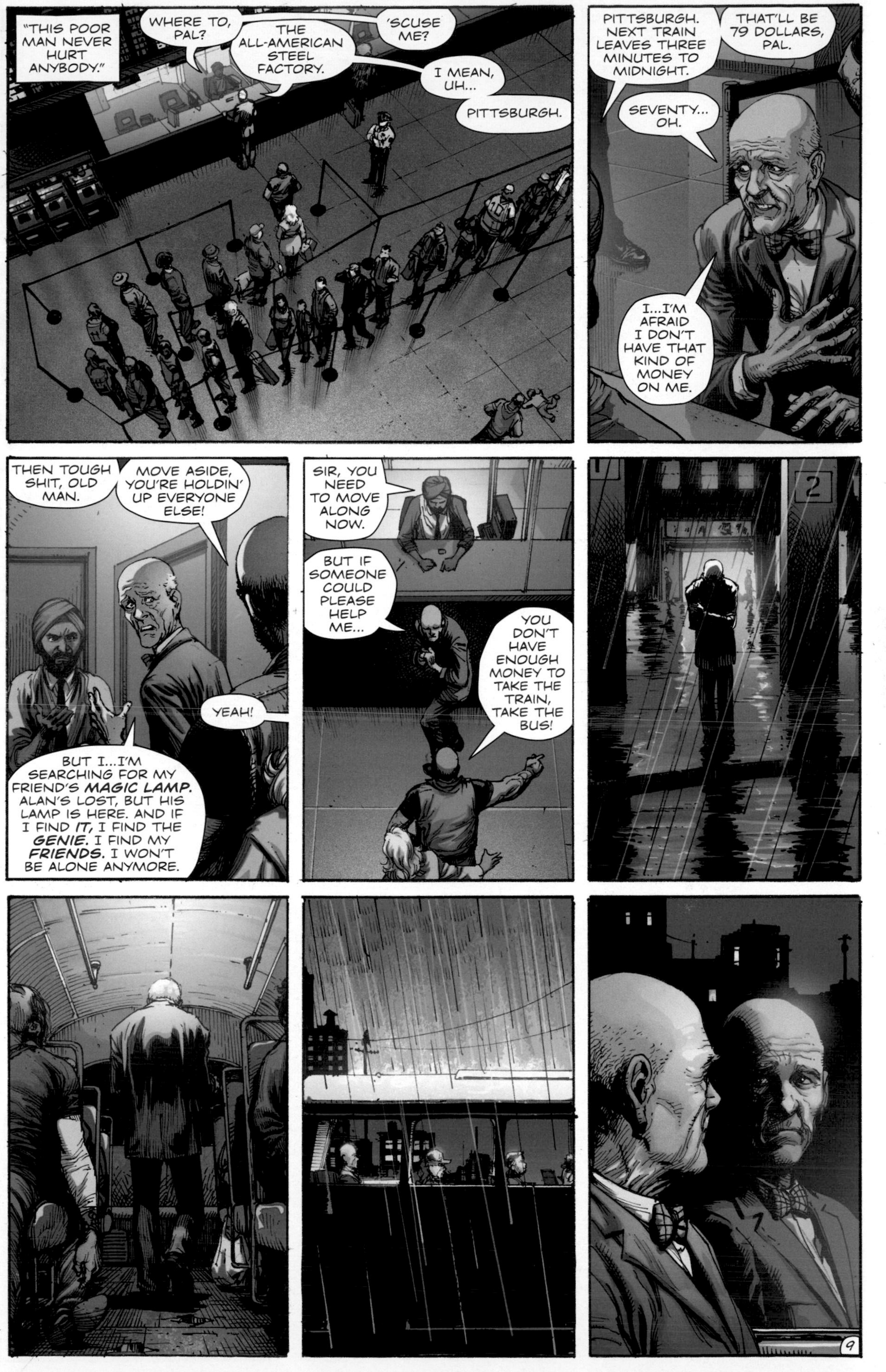
"THIS POOR MAN NEVER HURT ANYBODY."
WHERE TO, PAL?
THE ALL-AMERICAN STEEL FACTORY.
'SCUSE ME?
I MEAN, UH...
PITTSBURGH.
PITTSBURGH. NEXT TRAIN LEAVES THREE MINUTES TO MIDNIGHT.
THAT'LL BE 79 DOLLARS, PAL.
SEVENTY... OH.
I...I'M AFRAID I DON'T HAVE THAT KIND OF MONEY ON ME.
THEN TOUGH SHIT, OLD MAN.
MOVE ASIDE, YOU'RE HOLDIN' UP EVERYONE ELSE!
YEAH!
BUT I...I'M SEARCHING FOR MY FRIEND'S MAGIC LAMP. ALAN'S LOST, BUT HIS LAMP IS HERE. AND IF I FIND IT, I FIND THE GENIE. I FIND MY FRIENDS. I WON'T BE ALONE ANYMORE.
SIR, YOU NEED TO MOVE ALONG NOW.
BUT IF SOMEONE COULD PLEASE HELP ME...
YOU DON'T HAVE ENOUGH MONEY TO TAKE THE TRAIN, TAKE THE BUS!
2
9

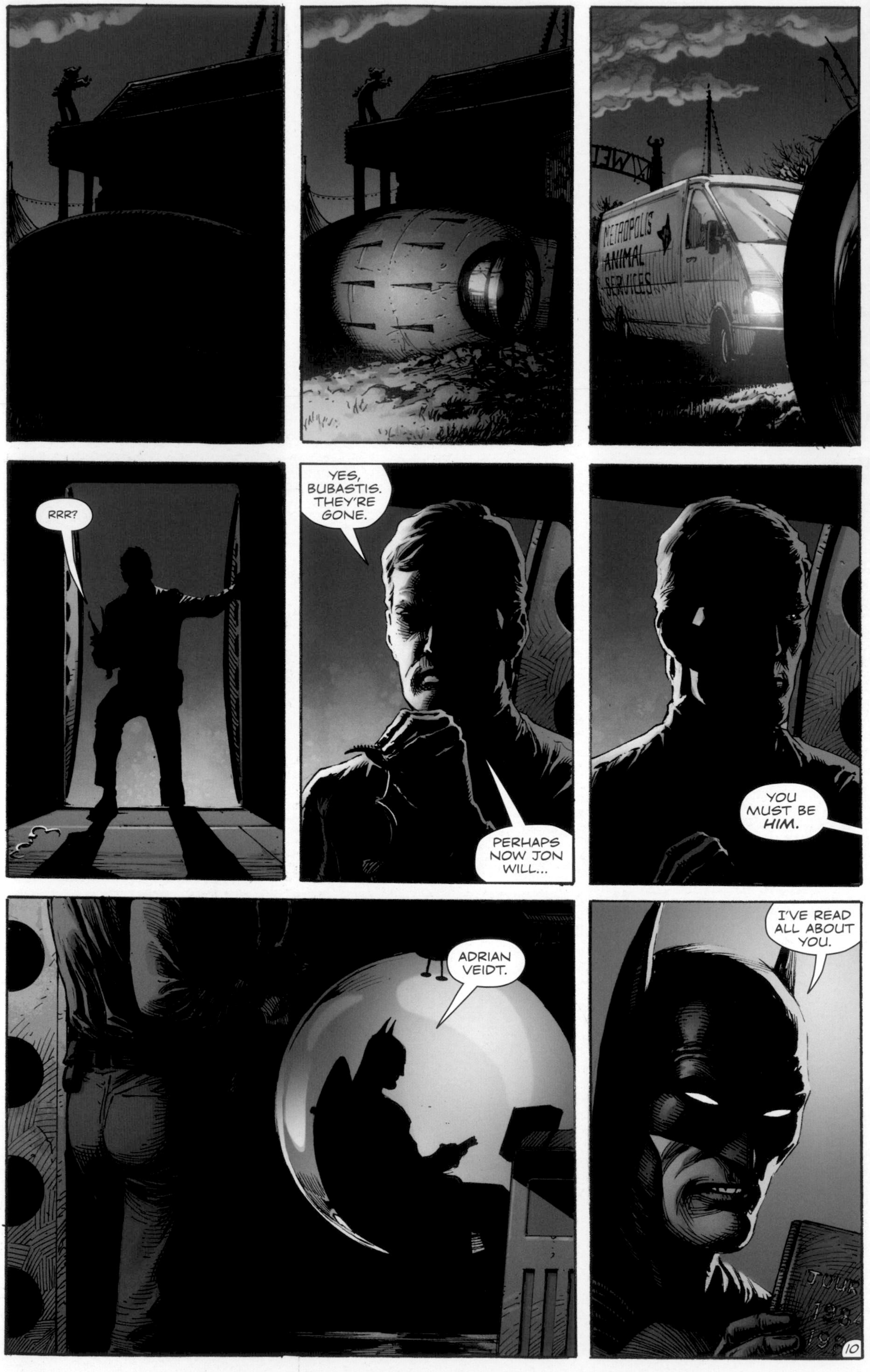
METROPOLIS ANIMAL SERVICES
RRR?
YES, BUBASTIS. THEY'RE GONE.
PERHAPS NOW JON WILL...
YOU MUST BE HIM.
ADRIAN VEIDT.
I'VE READ ALL ABOUT YOU.
10

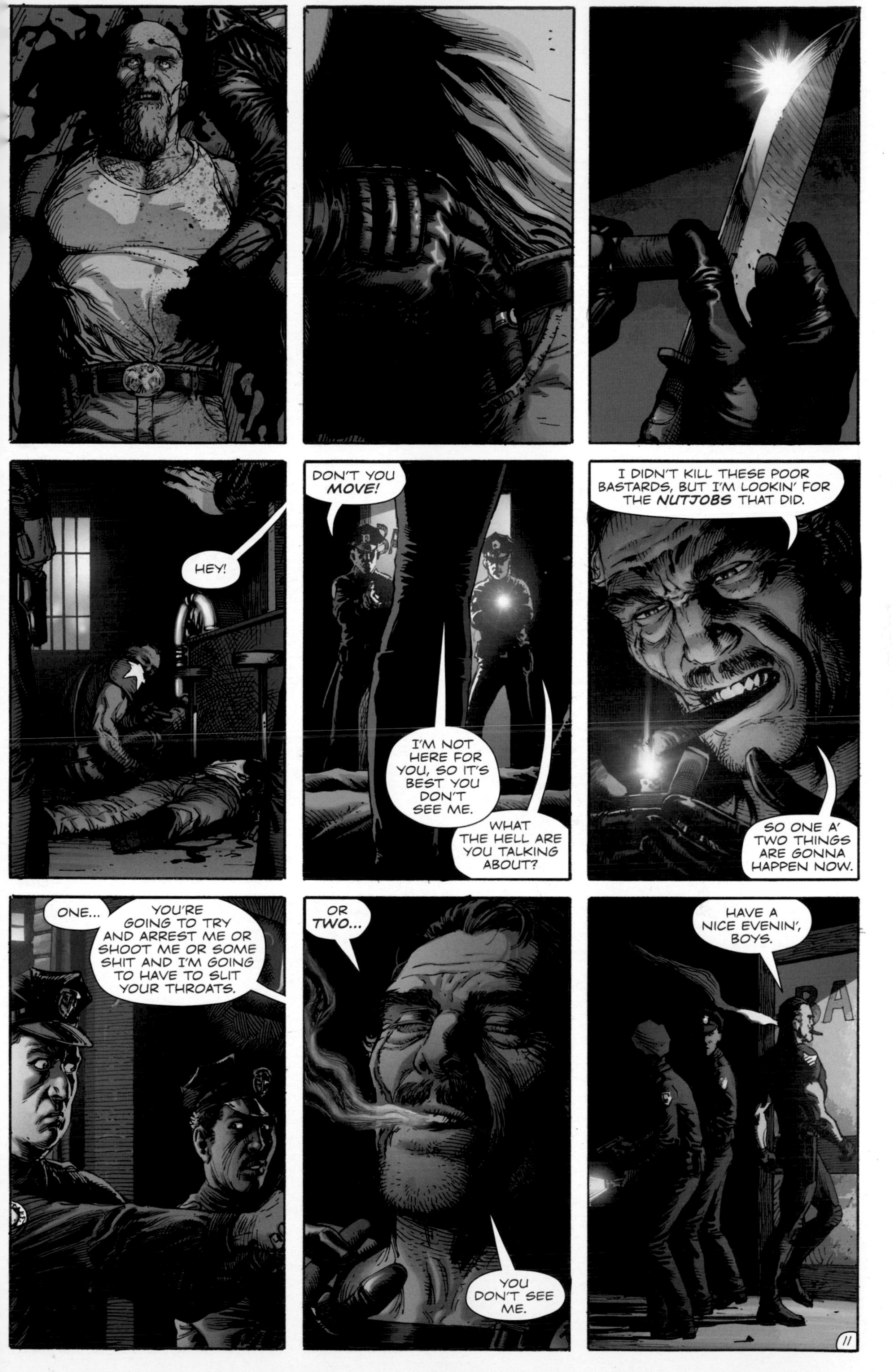
HEY!
DON'T YOU *MOVE!*
I'M NOT HERE FOR YOU, SO IT'S BEST YOU DON'T SEE ME.
WHAT THE HELL ARE YOU TALKING ABOUT?
I DIDN'T KILL THESE POOR BASTARDS, BUT I'M LOOKIN' FOR THE ***NUTJOBS*** THAT DID.
SO ONE A' TWO THINGS ARE GONNA HAPPEN NOW.
ONE...
YOU'RE GOING TO TRY AND ARREST ME OR SHOOT ME OR SOME SHIT AND I'M GOING TO HAVE TO SLIT YOUR THROATS.
OR *TWO...*
YOU DON'T SEE ME.
HAVE A NICE EVENIN', BOYS.

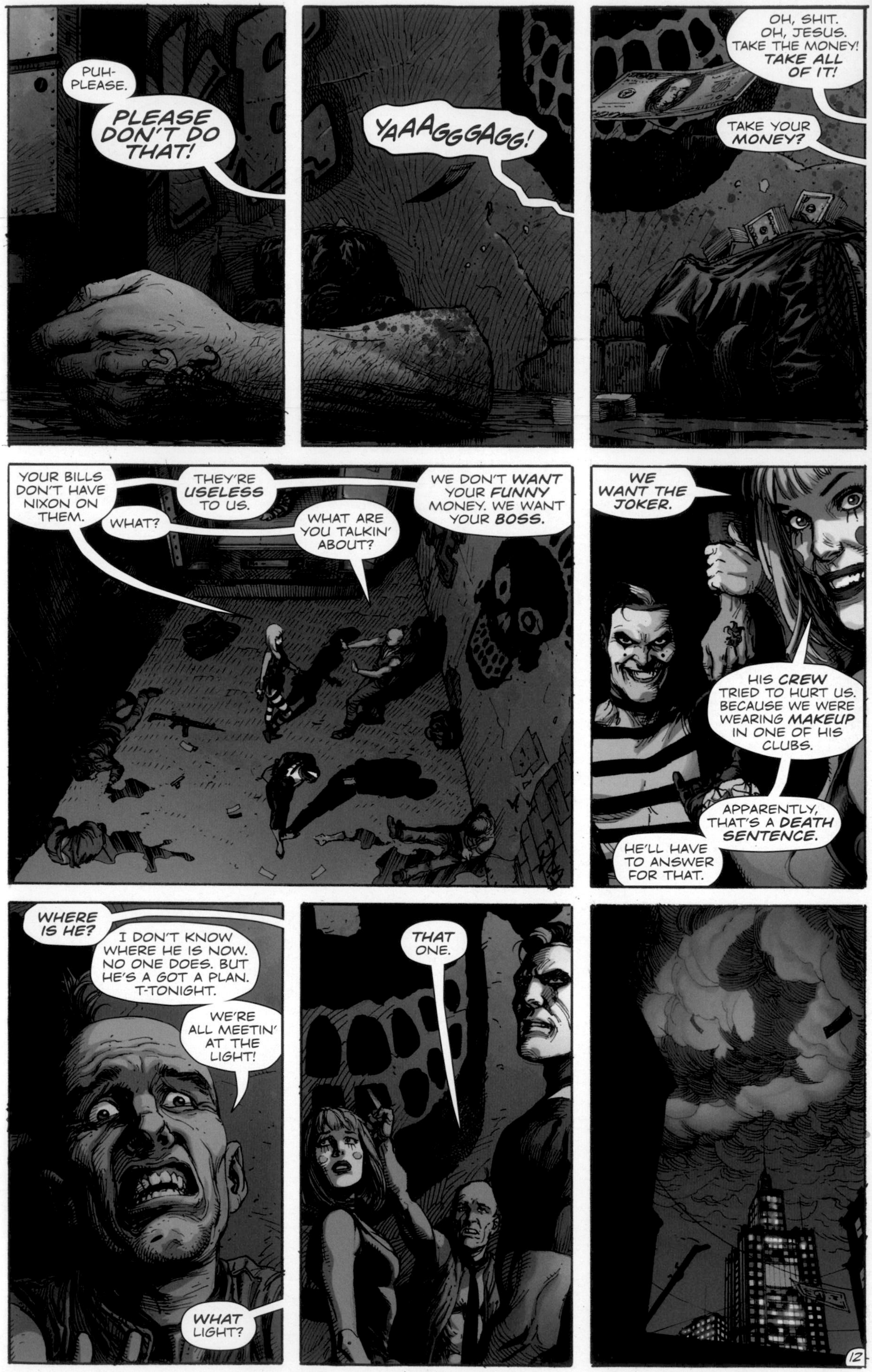
PUH-
PLEASE.
PLEASE DON'T DO THAT!
YAAAGGGAGG!
OH, SHIT. OH, JESUS. TAKE THE MONEY! TAKE ALL OF IT!
TAKE YOUR MONEY?
YOUR BILLS DON'T HAVE NIXON ON THEM.
THEY'RE USELESS TO US.
WHAT?
WHAT ARE YOU TALKIN' ABOUT?
WE DON'T WANT YOUR FUNNY MONEY. WE WANT YOUR BOSS.
WE WANT THE JOKER.
HIS CREW TRIED TO HURT US. BECAUSE WE WERE WEARING MAKEUP IN ONE OF HIS CLUBS.
APPARENTLY, THAT'S A DEATH SENTENCE.
HE'LL HAVE TO ANSWER FOR THAT.
WHERE IS HE?
I DON'T KNOW WHERE HE IS NOW. NO ONE DOES. BUT HE'S A GOT A PLAN. T-TONIGHT.
WE'RE ALL MEETIN' AT THE LIGHT!
WHAT LIGHT?
THAT ONE.

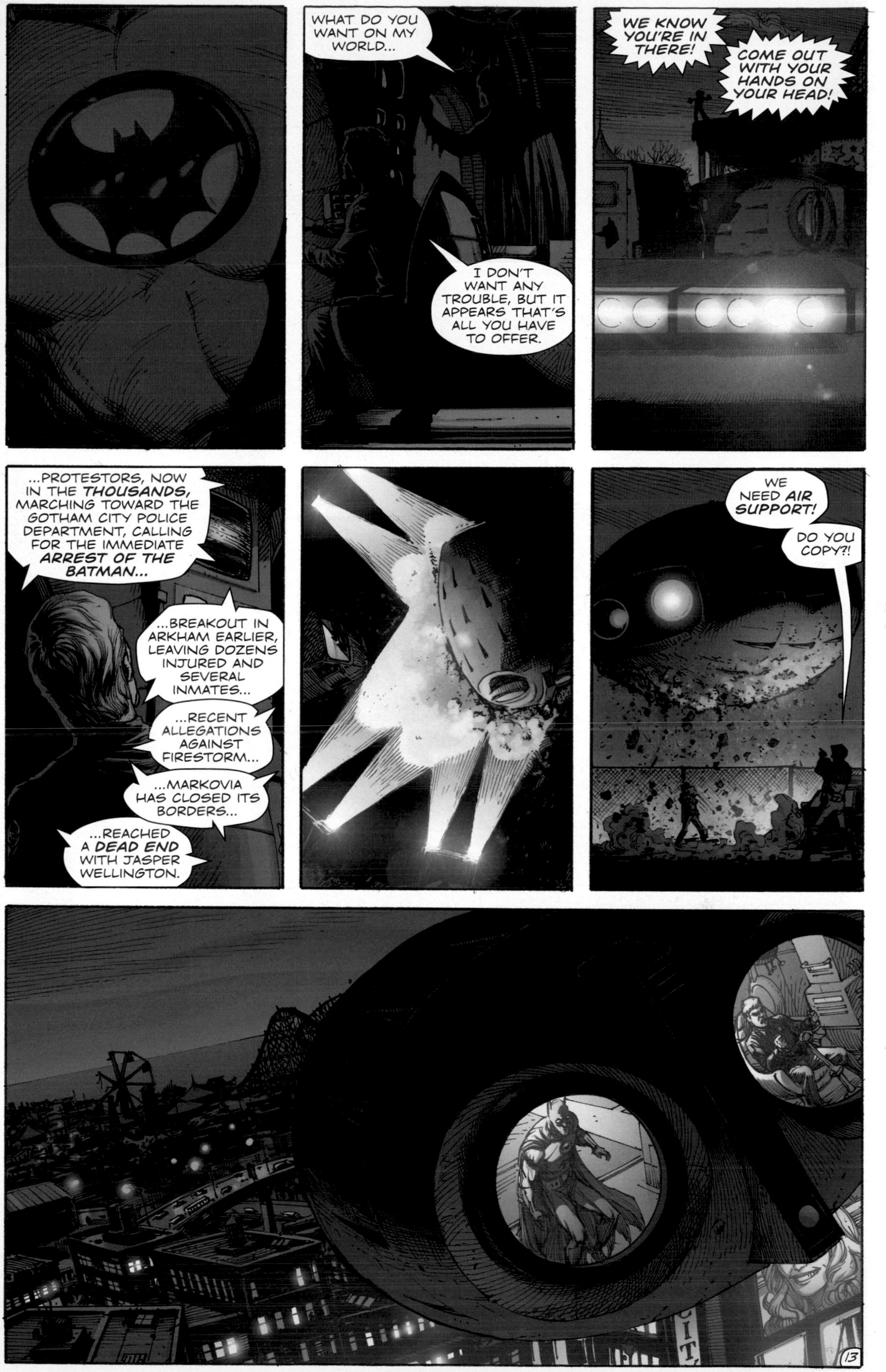
WHAT DO YOU WANT ON MY WORLD...
I DON'T WANT ANY TROUBLE, BUT IT APPEARS THAT'S ALL YOU HAVE TO OFFER.
WE KNOW YOU'RE IN THERE!
COME OUT WITH YOUR HANDS ON YOUR HEAD!
...PROTESTORS, NOW IN THE THOUSANDS, MARCHING TOWARD THE GOTHAM CITY POLICE DEPARTMENT, CALLING FOR THE IMMEDIATE ARREST OF THE BATMAN...
...BREAKOUT IN ARKHAM EARLIER, LEAVING DOZENS INJURED AND SEVERAL INMATES...
...RECENT ALLEGATIONS AGAINST FIRESTORM...
...MARKOVIA HAS CLOSED ITS BORDERS...
...REACHED A DEAD END WITH JASPER WELLINGTON.
WE NEED AIR SUPPORT!
DO YOU COPY?!

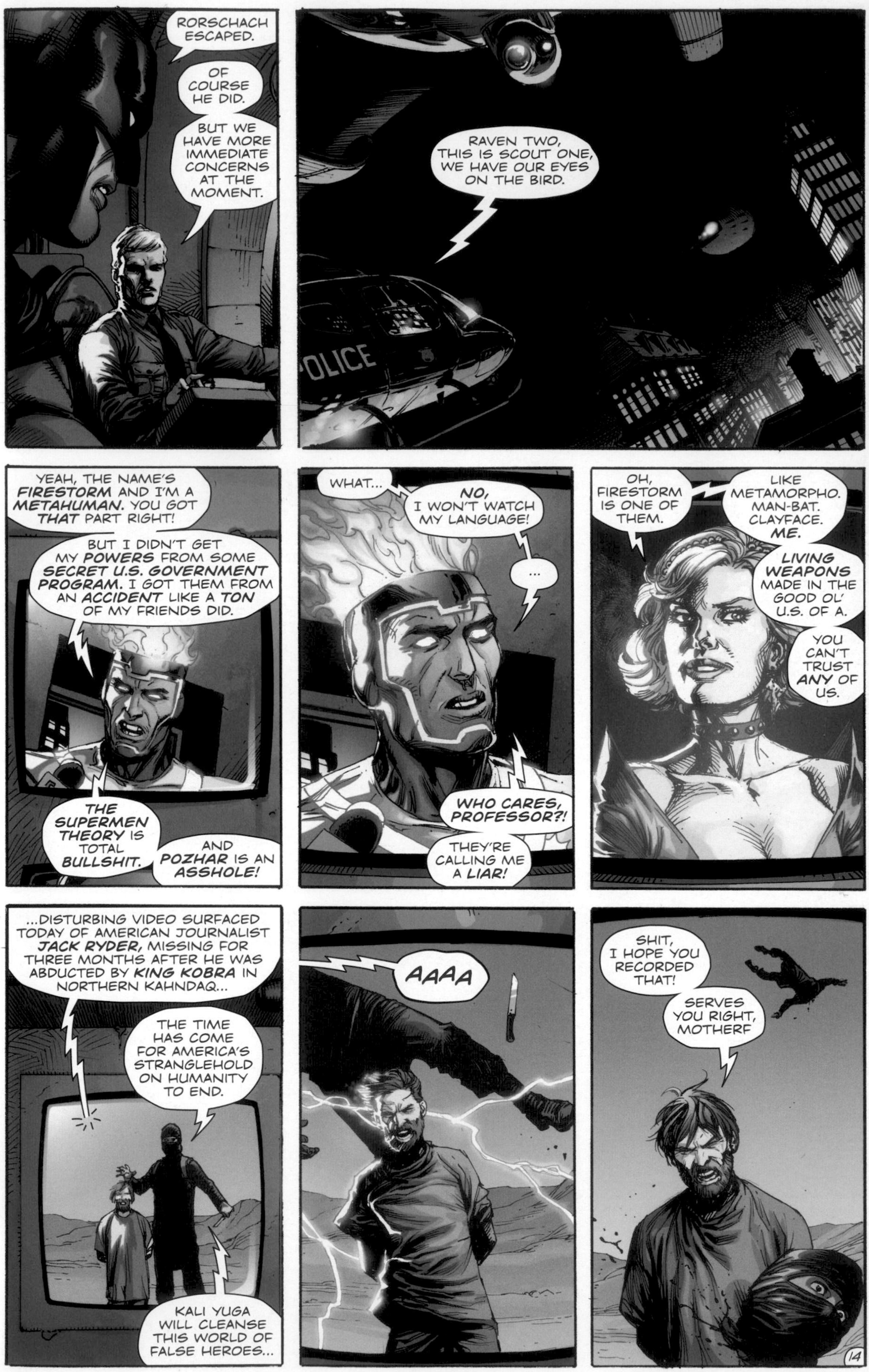
RORSCHACH ESCAPED.
OF COURSE HE DID.
BUT WE HAVE MORE IMMEDIATE CONCERNS AT THE MOMENT.
RAVEN TWO, THIS IS SCOUT ONE, WE HAVE OUR EYES ON THE BIRD.
POLICE
YEAH, THE NAME'S FIRESTORM AND I'M A METAHUMAN. YOU GOT THAT PART RIGHT!
BUT I DIDN'T GET MY POWERS FROM SOME SECRET U.S. GOVERNMENT PROGRAM. I GOT THEM FROM AN ACCIDENT LIKE A TON OF MY FRIENDS DID.
THE SUPERMEN THEORY IS TOTAL BULLSHIT.
AND POZHAR IS AN ASSHOLE!
WHAT...
NO, I WON'T WATCH MY LANGUAGE!
...
WHO CARES, PROFESSOR?!
THEY'RE CALLING ME A LIAR!
OH, FIRESTORM IS ONE OF THEM.
LIKE METAMORPHO. MAN-BAT. CLAYFACE. ME.
LIVING WEAPONS MADE IN THE GOOD OL' U.S. OF A.
YOU CAN'T TRUST ANY OF US.
...DISTURBING VIDEO SURFACED TODAY OF AMERICAN JOURNALIST JACK RYDER, MISSING FOR THREE MONTHS AFTER HE WAS ABDUCTED BY KING KOBRA IN NORTHERN KAHNDAQ...
THE TIME HAS COME FOR AMERICA'S STRANGLEHOLD ON HUMANITY TO END.
KALI YUGA WILL CLEANSE THIS WORLD OF FALSE HEROES...
AAAA
SHIT, I HOPE YOU RECORDED THAT!
SERVES YOU RIGHT, MOTHERF

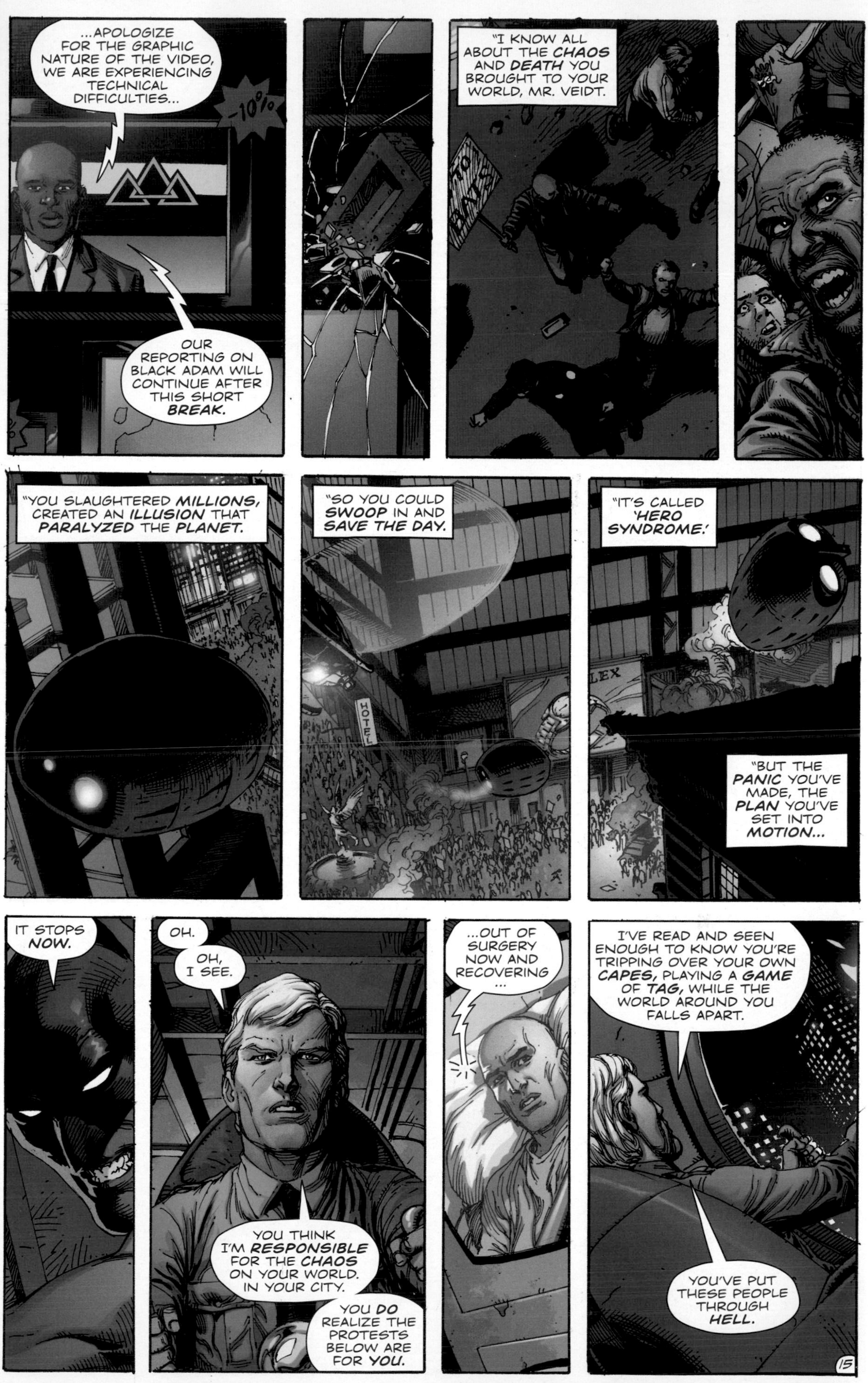
...APOLOGIZE FOR THE GRAPHIC NATURE OF THE VIDEO, WE ARE EXPERIENCING TECHNICAL DIFFICULTIES...
OUR REPORTING ON BLACK ADAM WILL CONTINUE AFTER THIS SHORT BREAK.
-10%
"I KNOW ALL ABOUT THE CHAOS AND DEATH YOU BROUGHT TO YOUR WORLD, MR. VEIDT.
"YOU SLAUGHTERED MILLIONS, CREATED AN ILLUSION THAT PARALYZED THE PLANET.
"SO YOU COULD SWOOP IN AND SAVE THE DAY.
HOTEL
"IT'S CALLED 'HERO SYNDROME.'
"BUT THE PANIC YOU'VE MADE, THE PLAN YOU'VE SET INTO MOTION...
IT STOPS NOW.
OH.
OH, I SEE.
YOU THINK I'M RESPONSIBLE FOR THE CHAOS ON YOUR WORLD. IN YOUR CITY.
YOU DO REALIZE THE PROTESTS BELOW ARE FOR YOU.
...OUT OF SURGERY NOW AND RECOVERING ...
I'VE READ AND SEEN ENOUGH TO KNOW YOU'RE TRIPPING OVER YOUR OWN CAPES, PLAYING A GAME OF TAG, WHILE THE WORLD AROUND YOU FALLS APART.
YOU'VE PUT THESE PEOPLE THROUGH HELL.

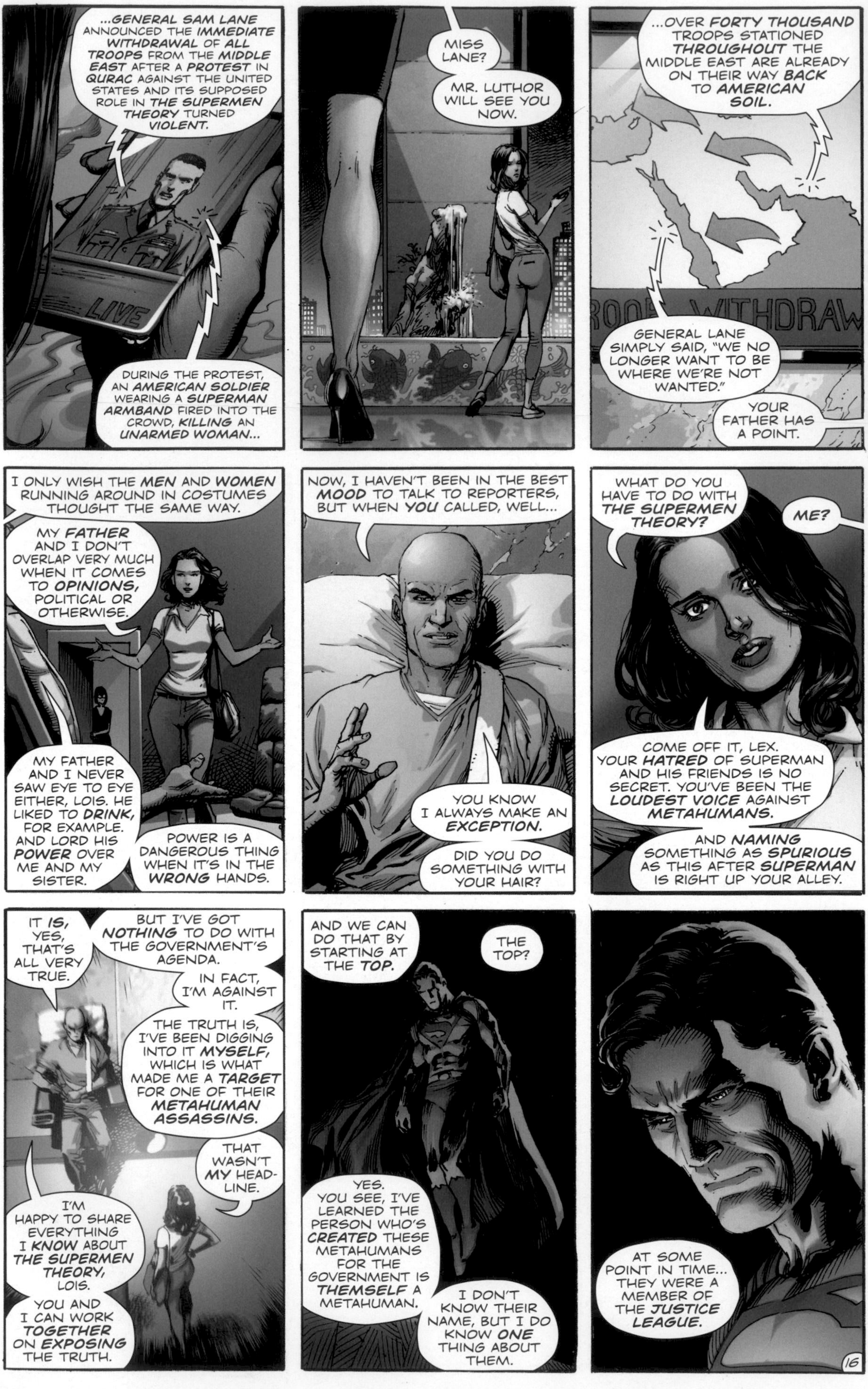

...GENERAL SAM LANE ANNOUNCED THE IMMEDIATE WITHDRAWAL OF ALL TROOPS FROM THE MIDDLE EAST AFTER A PROTEST IN QURAC AGAINST THE UNITED STATES AND ITS SUPPOSED ROLE IN THE SUPERMEN THEORY TURNED VIOLENT.
LIVE
DURING THE PROTEST, AN AMERICAN SOLDIER WEARING A SUPERMAN ARMBAND FIRED INTO THE CROWD, KILLING AN UNARMED WOMAN...
MISS LANE?
MR. LUTHOR WILL SEE YOU NOW.
...OVER FORTY THOUSAND TROOPS STATIONED THROUGHOUT THE MIDDLE EAST ARE ALREADY ON THEIR WAY BACK TO AMERICAN SOIL.
WITHDRAW
GENERAL LANE SIMPLY SAID, "WE NO LONGER WANT TO BE WHERE WE'RE NOT WANTED."
YOUR FATHER HAS A POINT.
I ONLY WISH THE MEN AND WOMEN RUNNING AROUND IN COSTUMES THOUGHT THE SAME WAY.
MY FATHER AND I DON'T OVERLAP VERY MUCH WHEN IT COMES TO OPINIONS, POLITICAL OR OTHERWISE.
MY FATHER AND I NEVER SAW EYE TO EYE EITHER, LOIS. HE LIKED TO DRINK, FOR EXAMPLE. AND LORD HIS POWER OVER ME AND MY SISTER.
POWER IS A DANGEROUS THING WHEN IT'S IN THE WRONG HANDS.
NOW, I HAVEN'T BEEN IN THE BEST MOOD TO TALK TO REPORTERS, BUT WHEN YOU CALLED, WELL...
YOU KNOW I ALWAYS MAKE AN EXCEPTION.
DID YOU DO SOMETHING WITH YOUR HAIR?
WHAT DO YOU HAVE TO DO WITH THE SUPERMEN THEORY?
ME?
COME OFF IT, LEX. YOUR HATRED OF SUPERMAN AND HIS FRIENDS IS NO SECRET. YOU'VE BEEN THE LOUDEST VOICE AGAINST METAHUMANS.
AND NAMING SOMETHING AS SPURIOUS AS THIS AFTER SUPERMAN IS RIGHT UP YOUR ALLEY.
IT IS, YES, THAT'S ALL VERY TRUE.
BUT I'VE GOT NOTHING TO DO WITH THE GOVERNMENT'S AGENDA.
IN FACT, I'M AGAINST IT.
THE TRUTH IS, I'VE BEEN DIGGING INTO IT MYSELF, WHICH IS WHAT MADE ME A TARGET FOR ONE OF THEIR METAHUMAN ASSASSINS.
THAT WASN'T MY HEAD-LINE.
I'M HAPPY TO SHARE EVERYTHING I KNOW ABOUT THE SUPERMEN THEORY, LOIS.
YOU AND I CAN WORK TOGETHER ON EXPOSING THE TRUTH.
AND WE CAN DO THAT BY STARTING AT THE TOP.
THE TOP?
YES. YOU SEE, I'VE LEARNED THE PERSON WHO'S CREATED THESE METAHUMANS FOR THE GOVERNMENT IS THEMSELF A METAHUMAN.
I DON'T KNOW THEIR NAME, BUT I DO KNOW ONE THING ABOUT THEM.
AT SOME POINT IN TIME... THEY WERE A MEMBER OF THE JUSTICE LEAGUE.

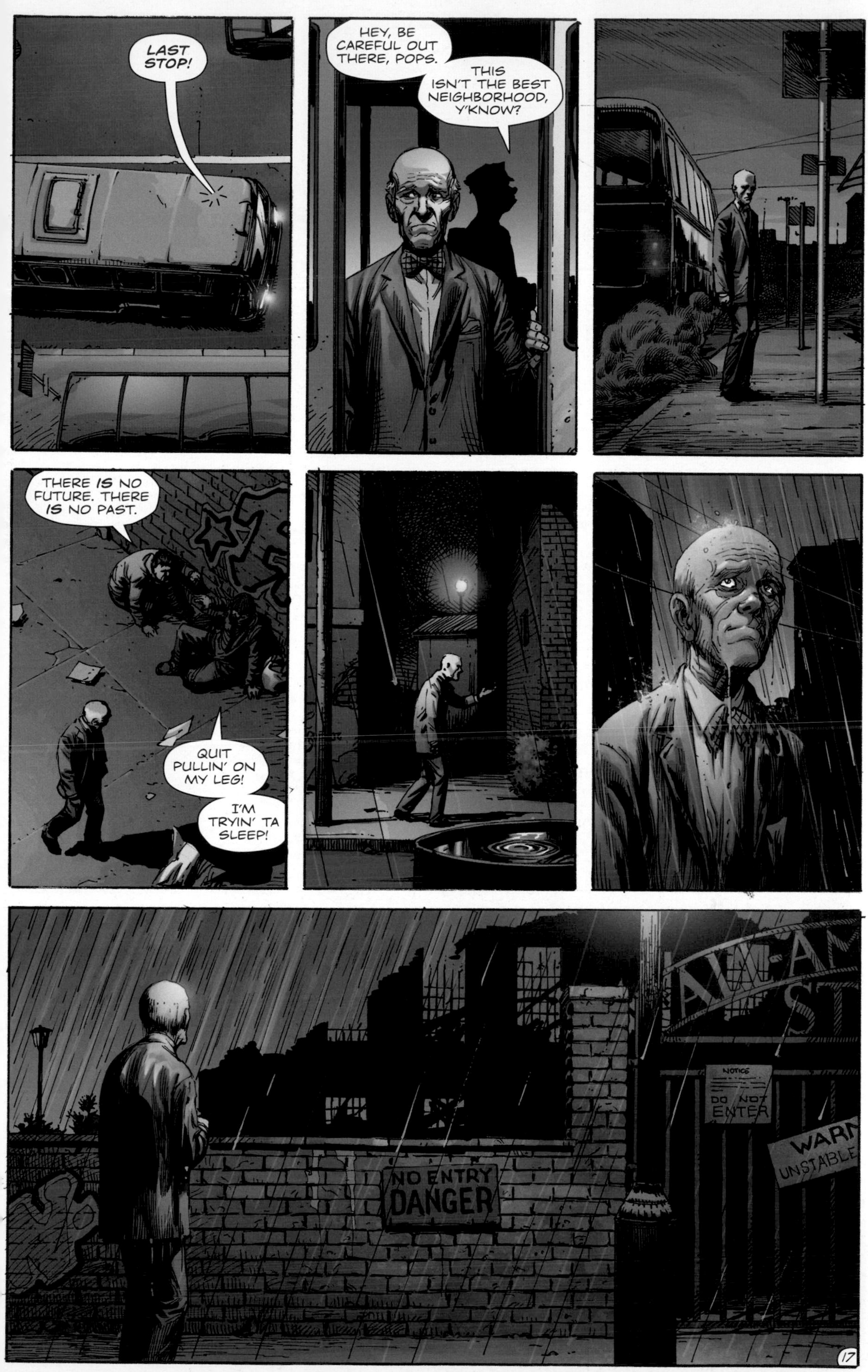
LAST STOP!
HEY, BE CAREFUL OUT THERE, POPS.
THIS ISN'T THE BEST NEIGHBORHOOD, Y'KNOW?
THERE IS NO FUTURE. THERE IS NO PAST.
QUIT PULLIN' ON MY LEG!
I'M TRYIN' TA SLEEP!
NO ENTRY
DANGER
NOTICE
DO NOT ENTER
WARN
UNSTABLE

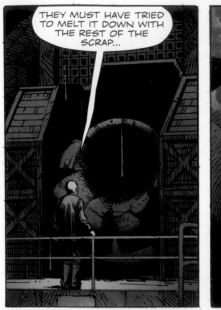

THEY MUST HAVE TRIED TO MELT IT DOWN WITH THE REST OF THE SCRAP...

THIS PLACE IS LOADED!

WE CAN SELL THIS SHIT. GET SOME CASH.

HAHAHAHA.

YEAH!

HEY, WAIT A SECOND!

WHO'S THAT?

HE SECURITY?

SECURITY? NAW. HE'S LOST.

MAYBE HE'S GOT SOMETHIN'!

YEAH! YOU GOT SOMETHIN', OLD MAN?!

NO. I'M SEARCHING FOR SOMETHING.

I'M LOOKING FOR MY FRIENDS.

GIMME WHAT YOU GOT!

GIMME YOUR WALLET BEFORE I POKE OUT YOUR EYES!

AAA!

PLEASE! PLEASE, LEAVE ME ALONE!

HELP!

LOOKIT THE OLD FART GO!

HAHAHA!

WE'LL GIVE YOU A FIVE-SECOND LEAD!

18

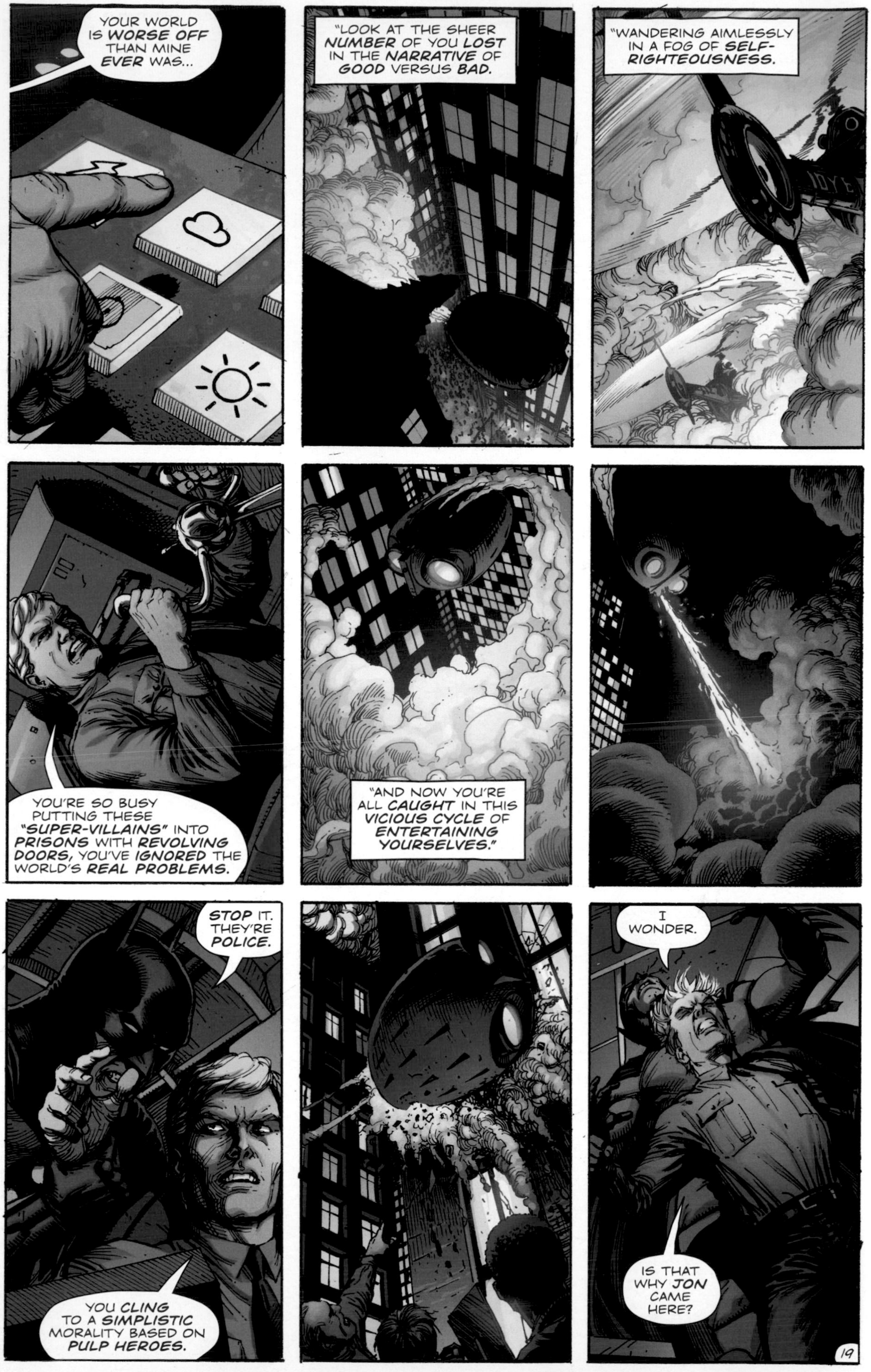

YOUR WORLD IS WORSE OFF THAN MINE EVER WAS...
"LOOK AT THE SHEER NUMBER OF YOU LOST IN THE NARRATIVE OF GOOD VERSUS BAD.
"WANDERING AIMLESSLY IN A FOG OF SELF-RIGHTEOUSNESS.
YOU'RE SO BUSY PUTTING THESE "SUPER-VILLAINS" INTO PRISONS WITH REVOLVING DOORS, YOU'VE IGNORED THE WORLD'S REAL PROBLEMS.
"AND NOW YOU'RE ALL CAUGHT IN THIS VICIOUS CYCLE OF ENTERTAINING YOURSELVES."
STOP IT. THEY'RE POLICE.
YOU CLING TO A SIMPLISTIC MORALITY BASED ON PULP HEROES.
I WONDER.
IS THAT WHY JON CAME HERE?

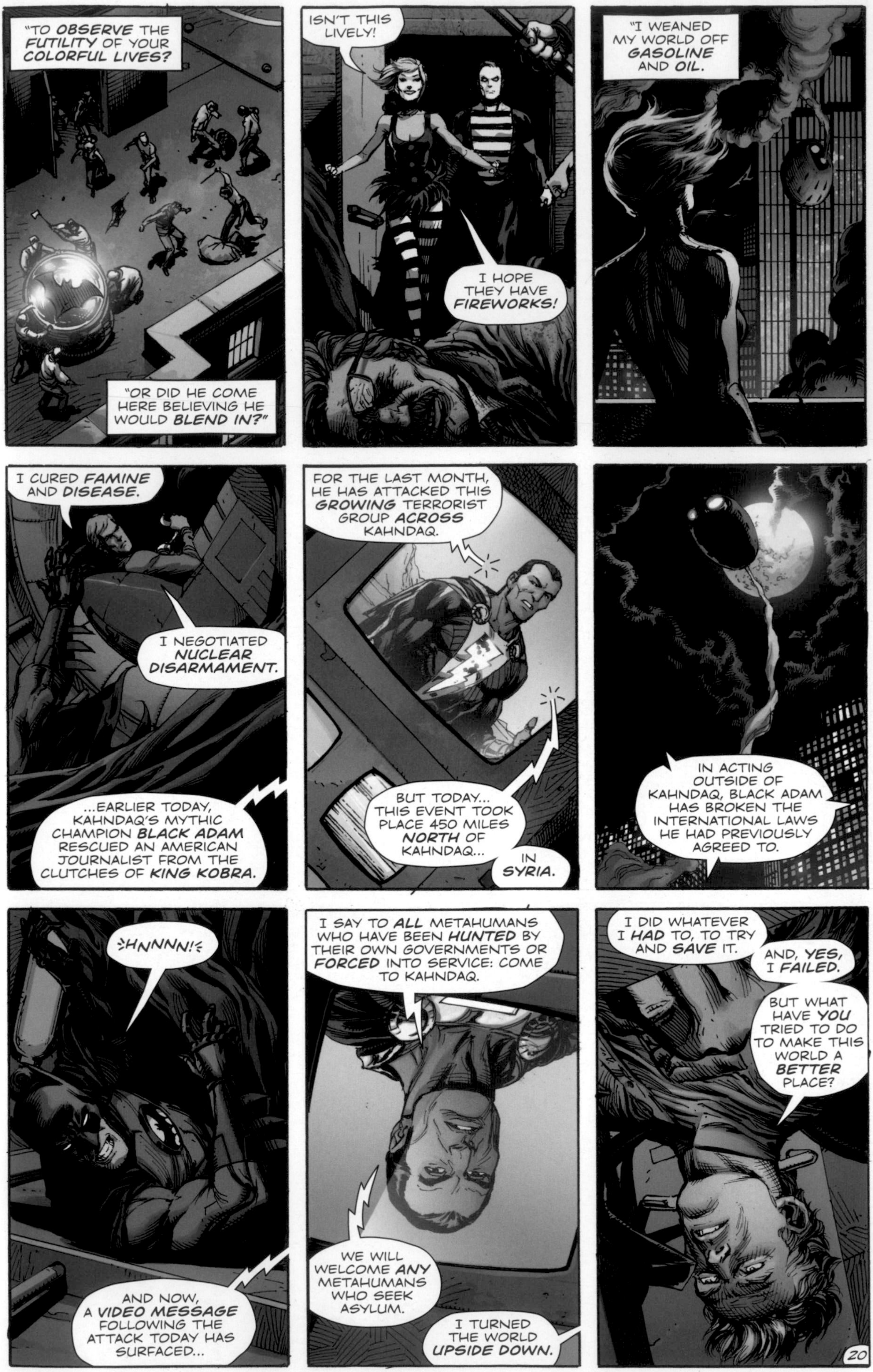

"TO OBSERVE THE FUTILITY OF YOUR COLORFUL LIVES?
"OR DID HE COME HERE BELIEVING HE WOULD BLEND IN?"
ISN'T THIS LIVELY!
I HOPE THEY HAVE FIREWORKS!
"I WEANED MY WORLD OFF GASOLINE AND OIL.
I CURED FAMINE AND DISEASE.
I NEGOTIATED NUCLEAR DISARMAMENT.
...EARLIER TODAY, KAHNDAQ'S MYTHIC CHAMPION BLACK ADAM RESCUED AN AMERICAN JOURNALIST FROM THE CLUTCHES OF KING KOBRA.
FOR THE LAST MONTH, HE HAS ATTACKED THIS GROWING TERRORIST GROUP ACROSS KAHNDAQ.
BUT TODAY... THIS EVENT TOOK PLACE 450 MILES NORTH OF KAHNDAQ...
IN SYRIA.
IN ACTING OUTSIDE OF KAHNDAQ, BLACK ADAM HAS BROKEN THE INTERNATIONAL LAWS HE HAD PREVIOUSLY AGREED TO.
HNNNN!
AND NOW, A VIDEO MESSAGE FOLLOWING THE ATTACK TODAY HAS SURFACED...
I SAY TO ALL METAHUMANS WHO HAVE BEEN HUNTED BY THEIR OWN GOVERNMENTS OR FORCED INTO SERVICE: COME TO KAHNDAQ.
WE WILL WELCOME ANY METAHUMANS WHO SEEK ASYLUM.
I TURNED THE WORLD UPSIDE DOWN.
I DID WHATEVER I HAD TO, TO TRY AND SAVE IT.
AND, YES, I FAILED.
BUT WHAT HAVE YOU TRIED TO DO TO MAKE THIS WORLD A BETTER PLACE?

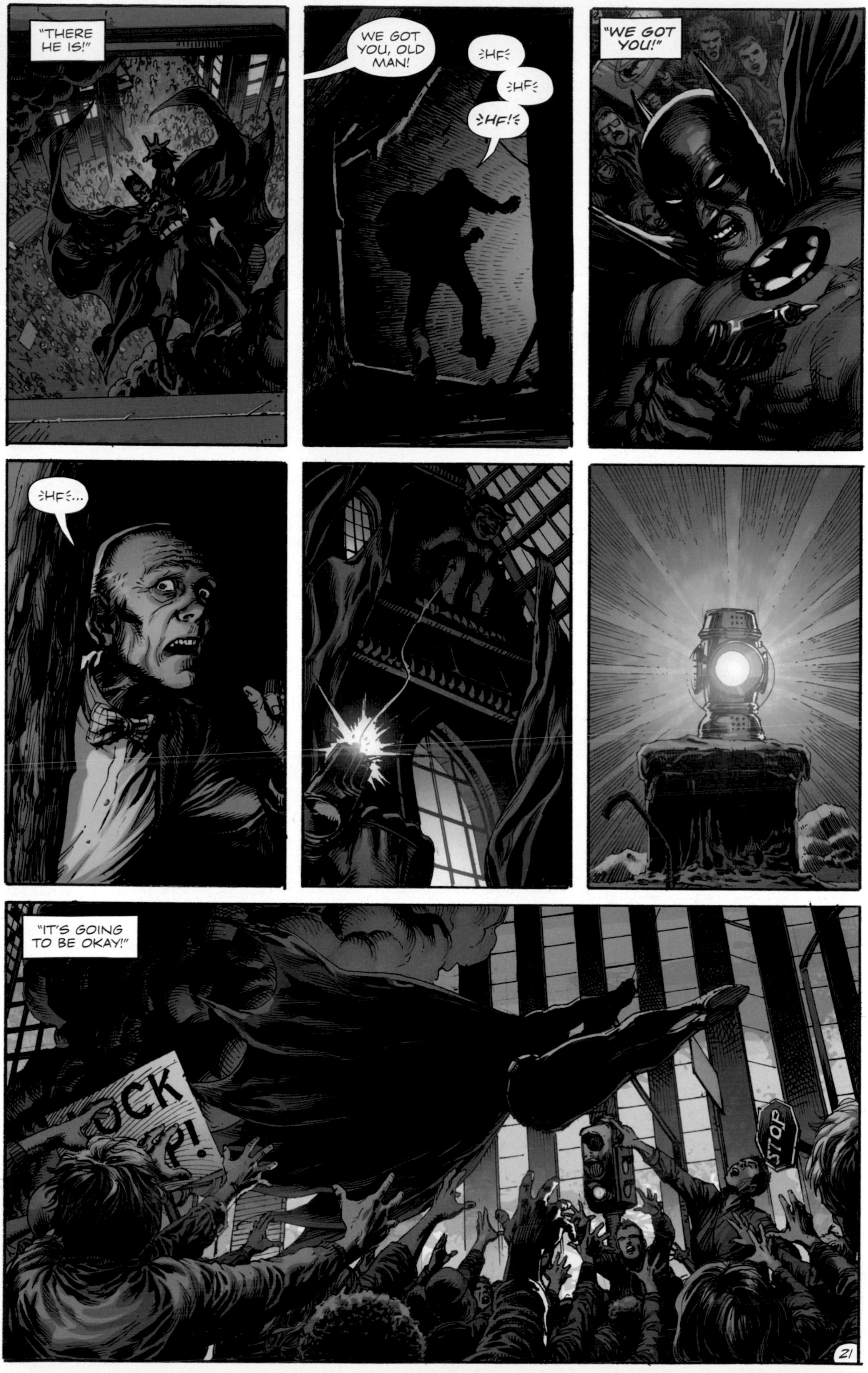
"THERE HE IS!"
WE GOT YOU, OLD MAN!
HF
HF
HF!
"WE GOT YOU!"
HF...
"IT'S GOING TO BE OKAY!"
OCK
P!
STOP

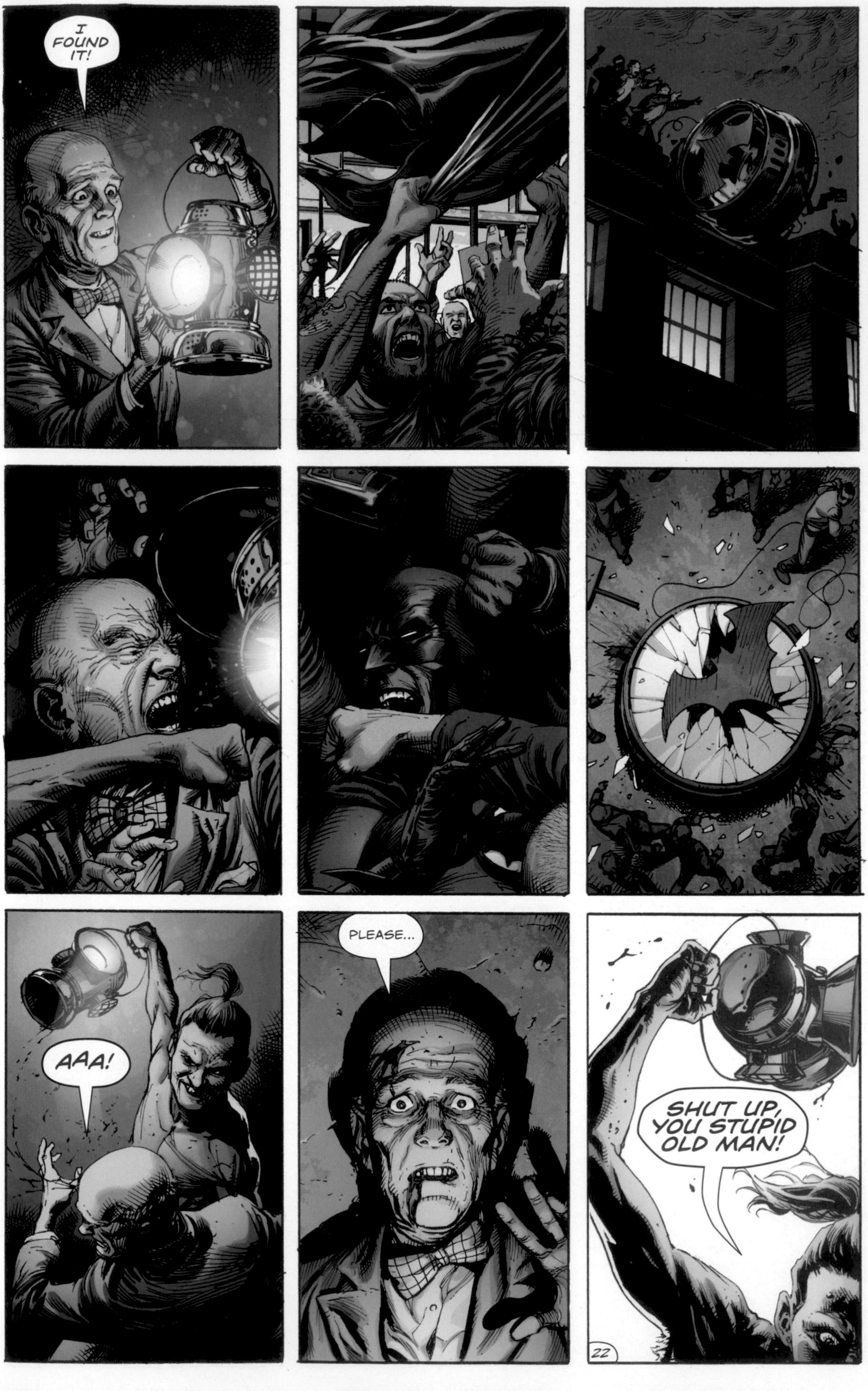
I FOUND IT!
AAA!
PLEASE...
SHUT UP, YOU STUPID OLD MAN!
22

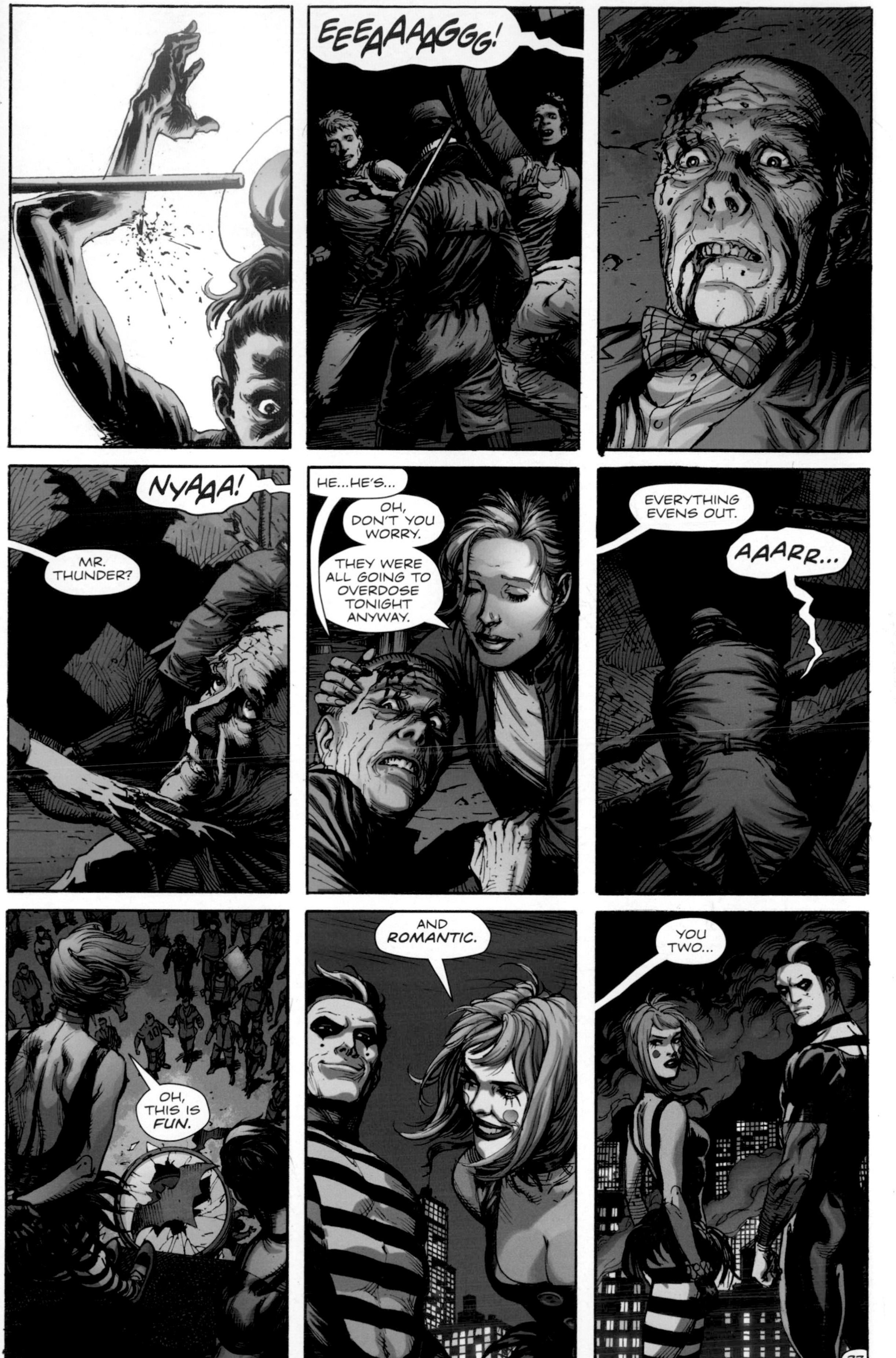
EEEAAAAGGG!
NYAAA!
MR. THUNDER?
HE...HE'S...
OH, DON'T YOU WORRY.
THEY WERE ALL GOING TO OVERDOSE TONIGHT ANYWAY.
EVERYTHING EVENS OUT.
AAARR...
OH, THIS IS FUN.
AND ROMANTIC.
YOU TWO...
23

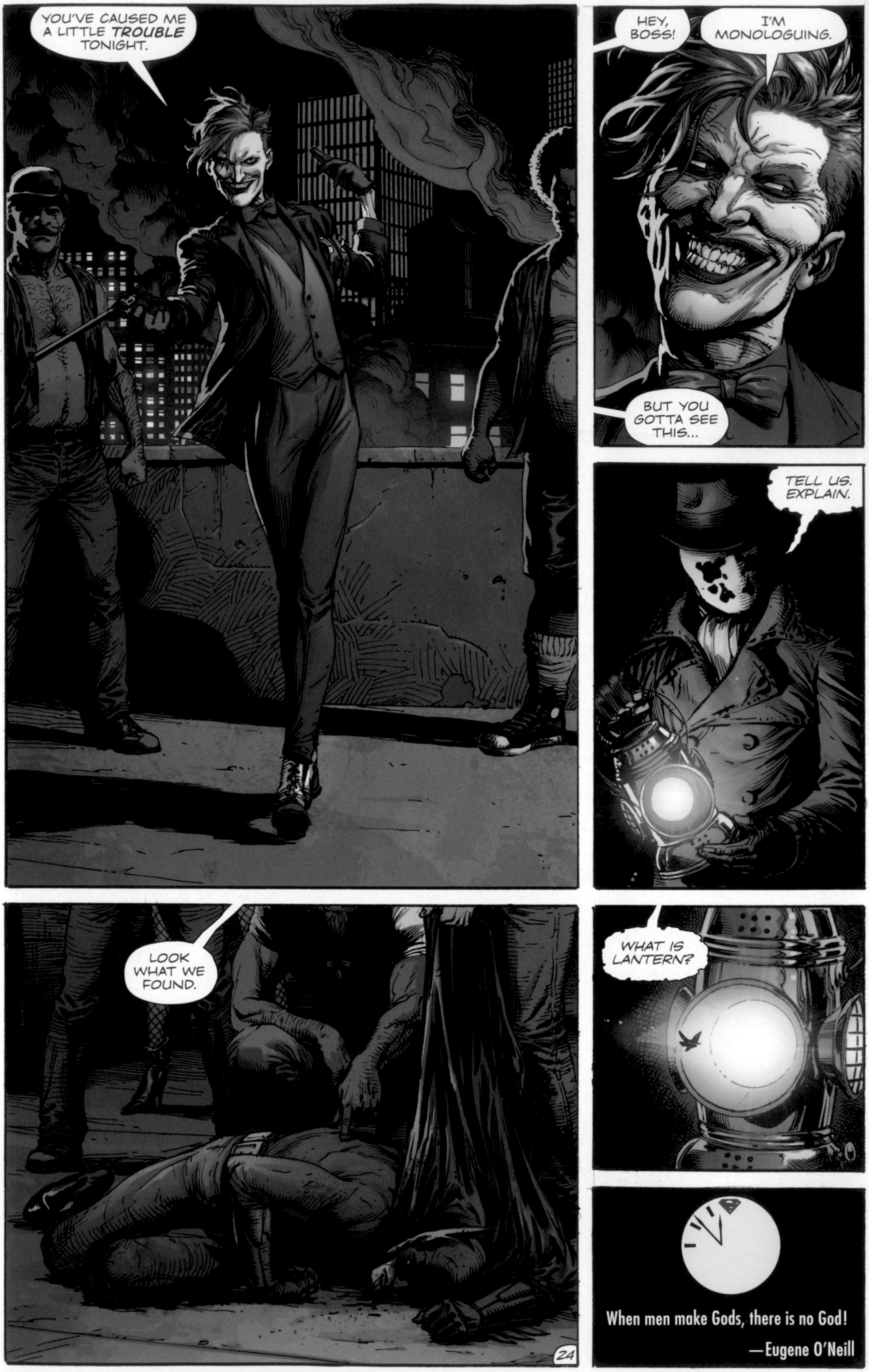
YOU'VE CAUSED ME A LITTLE TROUBLE TONIGHT.
HEY, BOSS!
I'M MONOLOGUING.
BUT YOU GOTTA SEE THIS...
TELL US. EXPLAIN.
LOOK WHAT WE FOUND.
WHAT IS LANTERN?
When men make Gods, there is no God!
—Eugene O'Neill

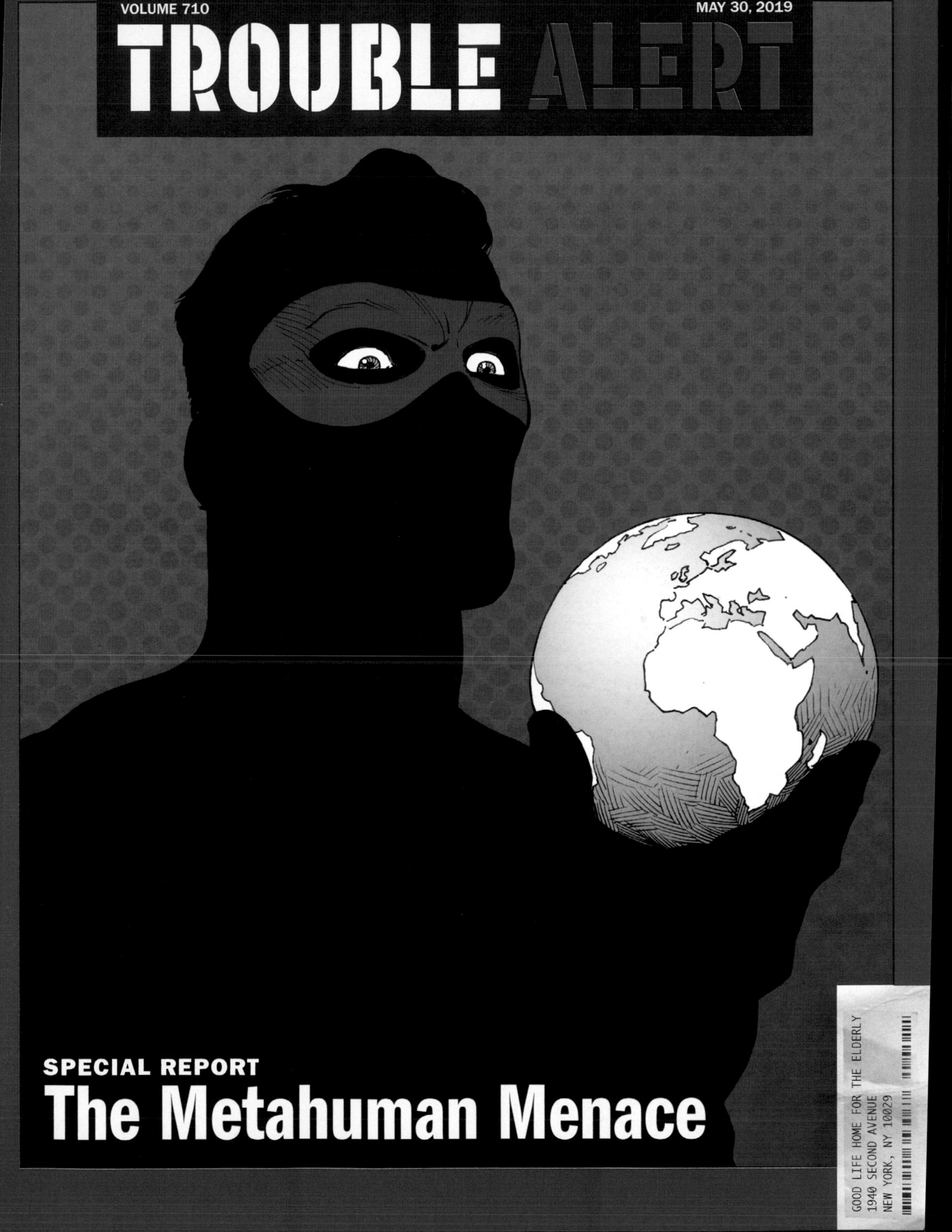
VOLUME 710
MAY 30, 2019
TROUBLE ALERT
SPECIAL REPORT
The Metahuman Menace
GOOD LIFE HOME FOR THE ELDERLY
1940 SECOND AVENUE
NEW YORK, NY 10029

The Rise of the Metahuman-American

Is it true there can be too much of a good thing? Over 97 percent of the world's metahumans identify themselves as American. The Supermen Theory proposes that the United States government, inspired by Superman, established the Department of Metahuman Affairs and began a decade-long program to create their own superhuman soldiers. The Department identified those with a metagene (labeled meta-positive) and put these test subjects through acts of "distress" in hopes of triggering their metagene. Once transformed, these metahumans are assigned to a scripted "super-hero and super-villain" narrative, training in plain sight, but ready to be called into action by the U.S. government at any time. The President has continued to deny these accusations, recently calling the Supermen Theory "total trash." However, many metahumans have already stepped forward and admitted their involvement. TROUBLE ALERT continues its running tally.

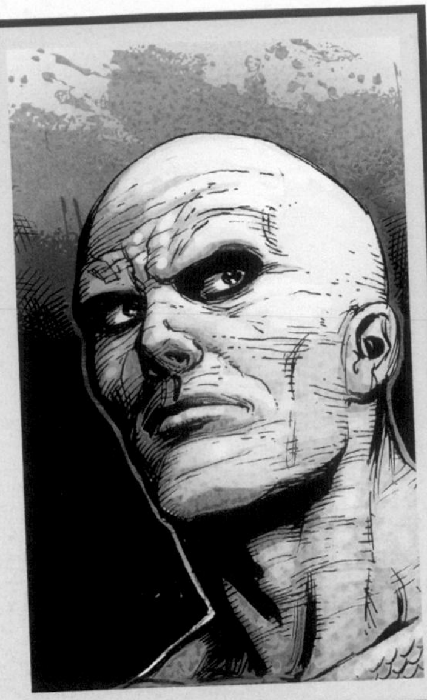

METAMORPHO

During a tax fraud investigation into industrialist Simon Stagg, government documents from the Department of Metahuman Affairs leaked to the public revealing an elaborate ruse: Soldier-for-hire Rex Mason was identified as meta-positive by the department and purposely exposed to an ancient energy source in an attempt to trigger his metamorphosis into a metahuman. Dubbed **Metamorpho**, Mason is considered the first manufactured super-hero. Found guilty of tax fraud, Simon Stagg fled the country and is currently missing, along with Metamorpho.

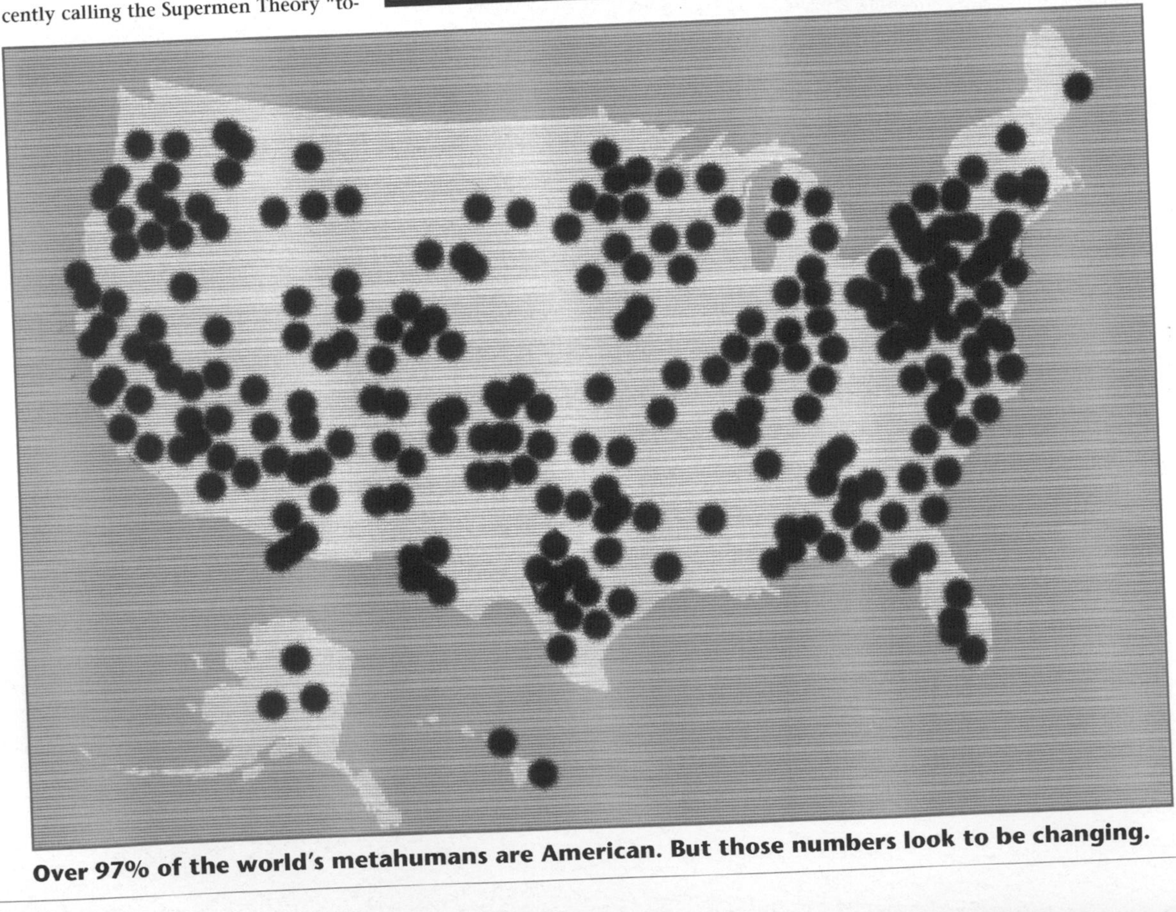

Over 97% of the world's metahumans are American. But those numbers look to be changing.

DOC DREAD

According to government documents, one of the members of Metamorpho's rogues gallery was in fact Rex Mason's childhood friend, Bobby Fradon. Recruited to play the part of a super-villain, Fradon donned the garb of **"Doc Dread"** and wielded a variety of chemical weapons.

ELEMENT GIRL

Agent Urania "Rainie" Blackwell was a spy for the United States, recruited by the Department of Metahuman Affairs after they discovered she was meta-positive. Exposed to the same ancient energy source as Rex Mason, Blackwell was transformed into **Element Girl**. Revealed to be unstable, she was discharged from her position. She later committed suicide.

STINGAREE

Element Girl's former lover, Agent Samuel Reese, was recruited to play the role of a crime lord to battle Metamorpho. He died in a helicopter crash not long after.

LADY CLAYFACE

Sondra Fuller was a member of a cell of the terrorist group King Kobra. Later recruited as a double agent by the Department of Metahuman Affairs, Fuller underwent what she says were horrific experiments in order to trigger her metagene.

MAN-BAT

Dr. Kirk Langstrom's research was funded by the Department of Metahuman Affairs. Transforming into the monstrous **Man-Bat**, Dr. Langstrom vanished after he went public with his connection to the Supermen Theory.

FIRESTORM

His secret origin unrevealed, **Firestorm** has denied any ties to the Department of Metahuman Affairs or the Supermen Theory. Like his Russian counterpart, Pozhar, Firestorm is a being of immense power, the limits of which are unknown.

KILLER FROST

Dr. Louise Lincoln recently stepped forward, claiming both she and her "enemy" Firestorm were created by the Department of Metahuman Affairs. She has continued to identify several other metahumans as part of the Department's program, including Captain Atom, Firehawk, Moonbow and Typhoon.

47

The Metahuman A

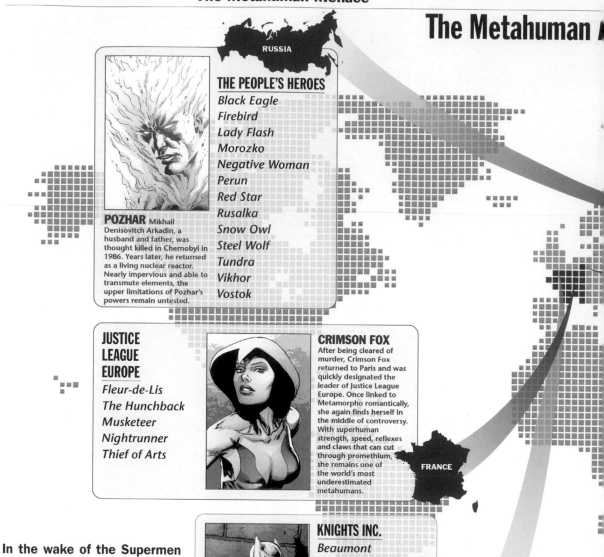

RUSSIA

THE PEOPLE'S HEROES

Black Eagle
Firebird
Lady Flash
Morozko
Negative Woman
Perun
Red Star
Rusalka
Snow Owl
Steel Wolf
Tundra
Vikhor
Vostok

POZHAR Mikhail Denisovitch Arkadin, a husband and father, was thought killed in Chernobyl in 1986. Years later, he returned as a living nuclear reactor. Nearly impervious and able to transmute elements, the upper limitations of Pozhar's powers remain untested.

JUSTICE LEAGUE EUROPE

Fleur-de-Lis
The Hunchback
Musketeer
Nightrunner
Thief of Arts

CRIMSON FOX

After being cleared of murder, Crimson Fox returned to Paris and was quickly designated the leader of Justice League Europe. Once linked to Metamorpho romantically, she again finds herself in the middle of controversy. With superhuman strength, speed, reflexes and claws that can cut through promethium, she remains one of the world's most underestimated metahumans.

FRANCE

In the wake of the Supermen

Theory, countries across the world have turned their attention and resources away from nuclear arsenals and toward building metahuman armies. World leaders are aggressively pursuing and recruiting metahumans. Some are even scanning their populace, thanks to new technology by Lexcorp, in hopes of finding those rare few with a metagene. Once identified meta-positive, the subjects are put through "traumatic events" in an attempt to trigger metamorphosis into a metahuman. The metahumans listed here do not represent every foreign metahuman, but those known to be aligned with their government.

THE KNIGHT Little is known of the newest person to take on the identity of the Knight save that she is the first female to do so. Ordained by the Queen, Knights Inc. has rapidly grown, protecting the borders of the United Kingdom.

KNIGHTS INC.

Beaumont
Canterbury Cricket
Crusader
Godiva
Golden Pharaoh
The Hood
Jack O'Lantern
Looking Glass
Lionheart
Mrs. Hyde
Ridge
Silent Knight
The Squire
Templar

UNITED KINGDOM

Race Heats Up

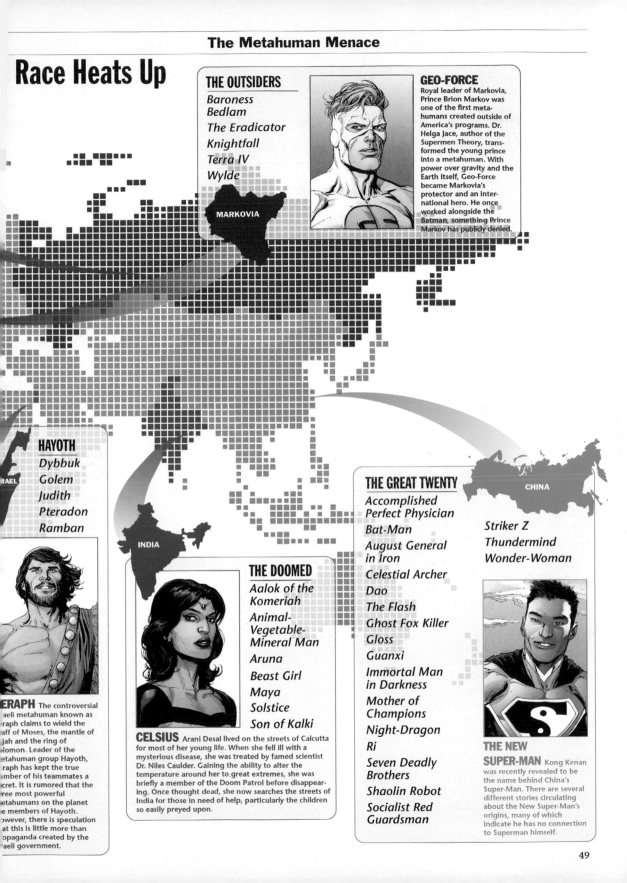

THE OUTSIDERS

Baroness
Bedlam
The Eradicator
Knightfall
Terra IV
Wylde

MARKOVIA

GEO-FORCE

Royal leader of Markovia, Prince Brion Markov was one of the first meta-humans created outside of America's programs. Dr. Helga Jace, author of the Supermen Theory, transformed the young prince into a metahuman. With power over gravity and the Earth itself, Geo-Force became Markovia's protector and an international hero. He once worked alongside the Batman, something Prince Markov has publicly denied.

HAYOTH

Dybbuk
Golem
Judith
Pteradon
Ramban

RAEL

INDIA

ERAPH The controversial aeli metahuman known as raph claims to wield the aff of Moses, the mantle of jah and the ring of olomon. Leader of the etahuman group Hayoth, raph has kept the true cret. It is rumored that the ree most powerful etahumans on the planet e members of Hayoth. owever, there is speculation at this is little more than opaganda created by the aeli government.

THE DOOMED

Aalok of the Komeriah
Animal-Vegetable-Mineral Man
Aruna
Beast Girl
Maya
Solstice
Son of Kalki

CELSIUS Arani Desai lived on the streets of Calcutta for most of her young life. When she fell ill with a mysterious disease, she was treated by famed scientist Dr. Niles Caulder. Gaining the ability to alter the temperature around her to.great extremes, she was briefly a member of the Doom Patrol before disappearing. Once thought dead, she now searches the streets of India for those in need of help, particularly the children so easily preyed upon.

THE GREAT TWENTY

Accomplished Perfect Physician
Bat-Man
August General in Iron
Celestial Archer
Dao
The Flash
Ghost Fox Killer
Gloss
Guanxi
Immortal Man in Darkness
Mother of Champions
Night-Dragon
Ri
Seven Deadly Brothers
Shaolin Robot
Socialist Red Guardsman

CHINA

Striker Z
Thundermind
Wonder-Woman

THE NEW SUPER-MAN

Kong Kenan was recently revealed to be the name behind China's Super-Man. There are several different stories circulating about the New Super-Man's origins, many of which indicate he has no connection to Superman himself.

49

The Troubled Past—and Future—of Kahndaq

Once the most dangerous nation in the world, Kahndaq now appears to be the safest. At least for those who live within it. Located on the southern tip of the Sinai Peninsula, Kahndaq has been plagued for centuries by dictators, civil wars and genocide...until an ancient myth, that of the Mighty Adam, became a reality.

Confirmed satellite sightings of unregistered metahumans in Kahndaq

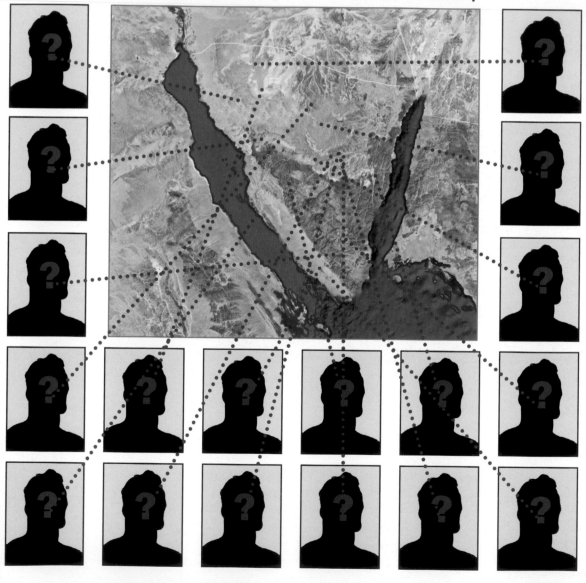

A "Super" Invitation

In a recent message that surfaced online, Black Adam offered asylum to metahumans from across the world. Concern grows as to what Adam's true intentions are. Is he creating a metahuman army of his own? Do his actions in Syria indicate a desire to act outside of Kahndaq? And with all of the tension in the world focused on the Metahuman Arms Race, will there be anyone there to stop him? And the most controversial question of them all: If Kahndaq has indeed become a place of peace and prosperity under his rule...should they?

BLACK ADAM, SAVIOR OR SINNER?

There is a legend in Kahndaq about a magical champion called the Mighty Adam who helped free the people from slavery and the rule of Prince Ahk-Ton. But their freedom was short-lived as the Mighty Adam disappeared soon after. Thousands of years later, a man claiming to be the Mighty Adam, now calling himself Black Adam, reappeared. He battled the Shazam family in Philadelphia before returning to Kahndaq where he confronted and slaughtered the then-dictator and his army. In confrontations with more of America's metahumans, Adam agreed to stay within the borders of Kahndaq, a country where he was celebrated as a hero. However, the day the U.S. and Russian militaries began to withdraw from the Middle East, Adam entered Syria to confront King Kobra.

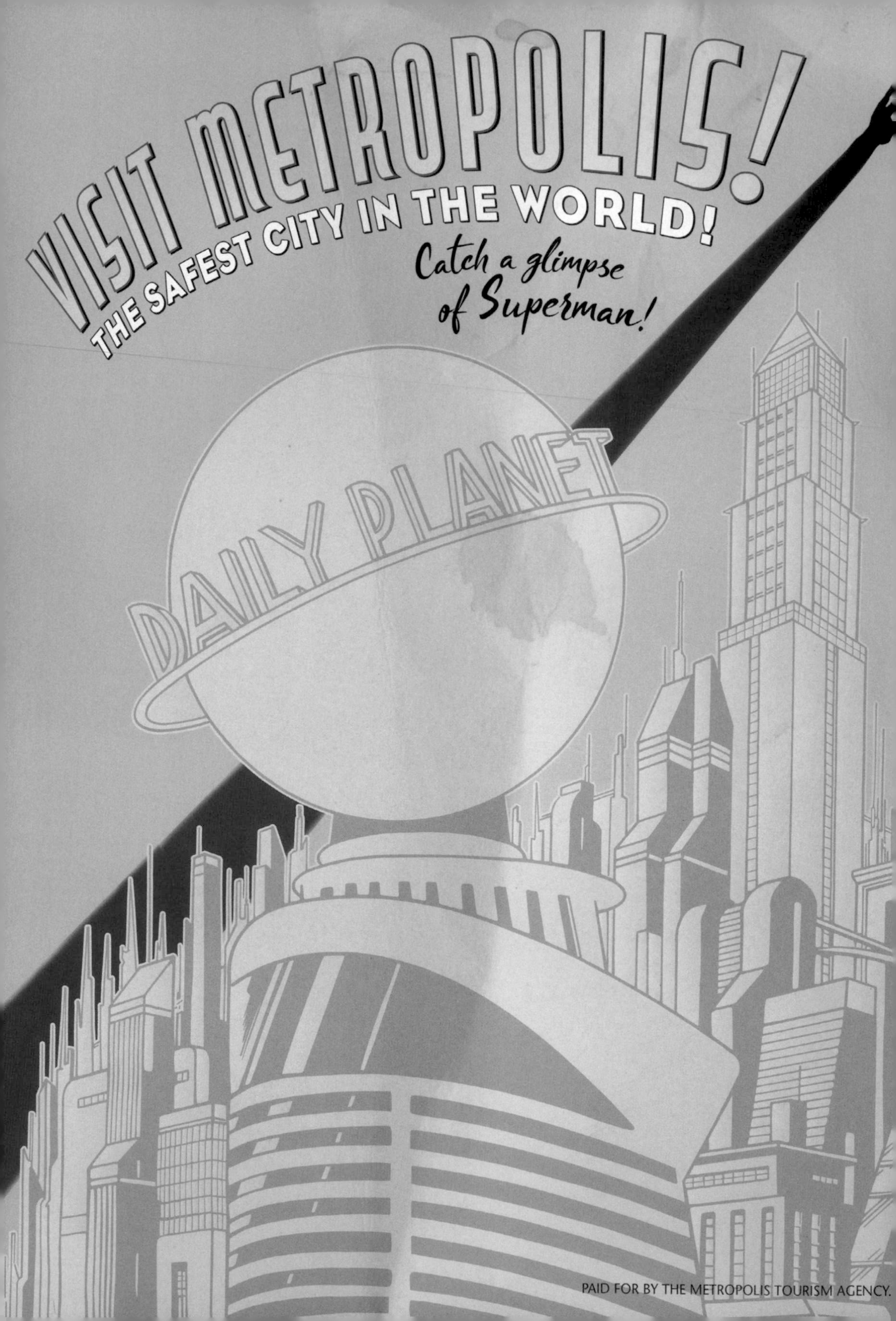
VISIT METROPOLIS!
THE SAFEST CITY IN THE WORLD!
Catch a glimpse of Superman!
DAILY PLANET
PAID FOR BY THE METROPOLIS TOURISM AGENCY.

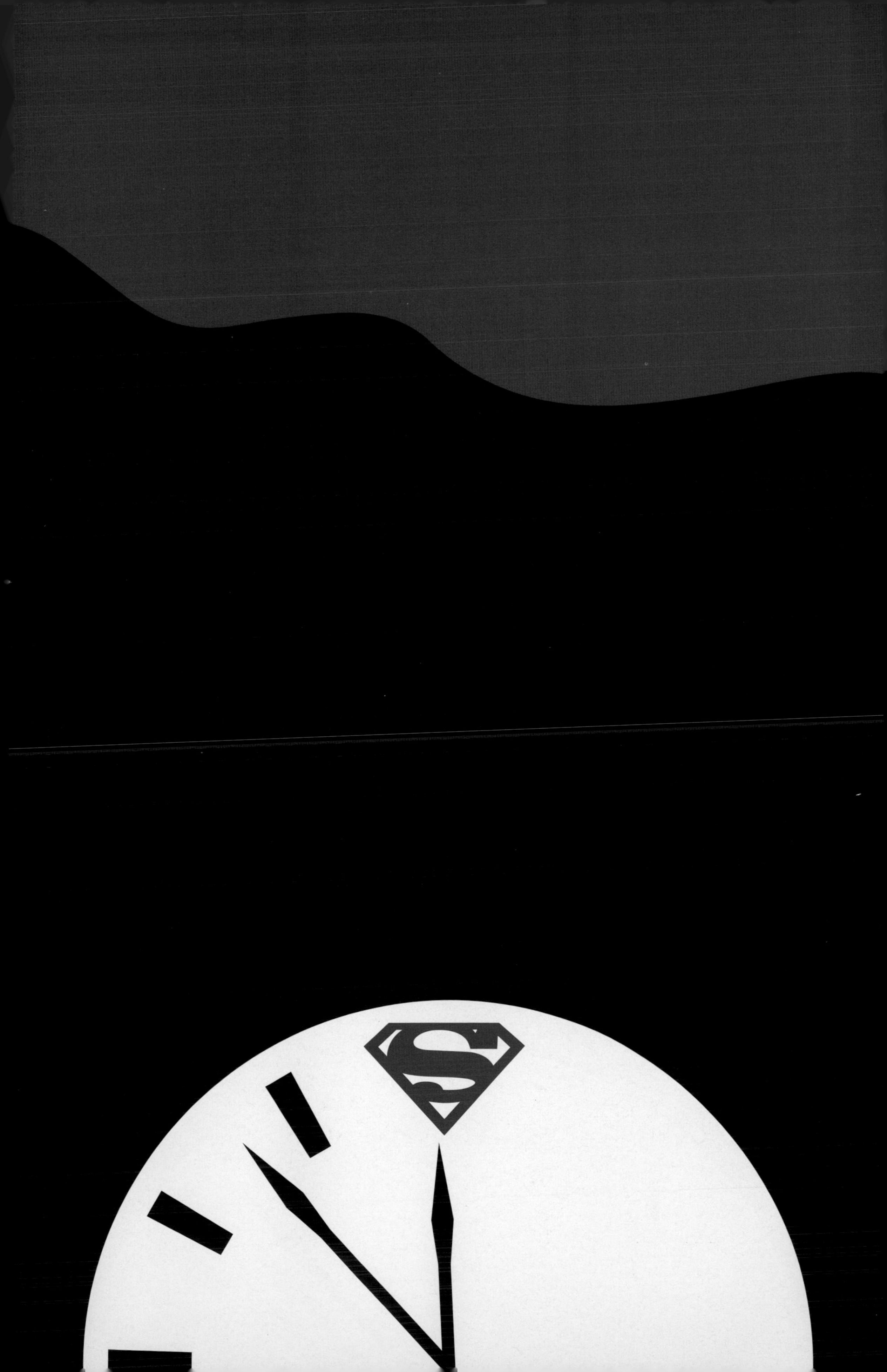

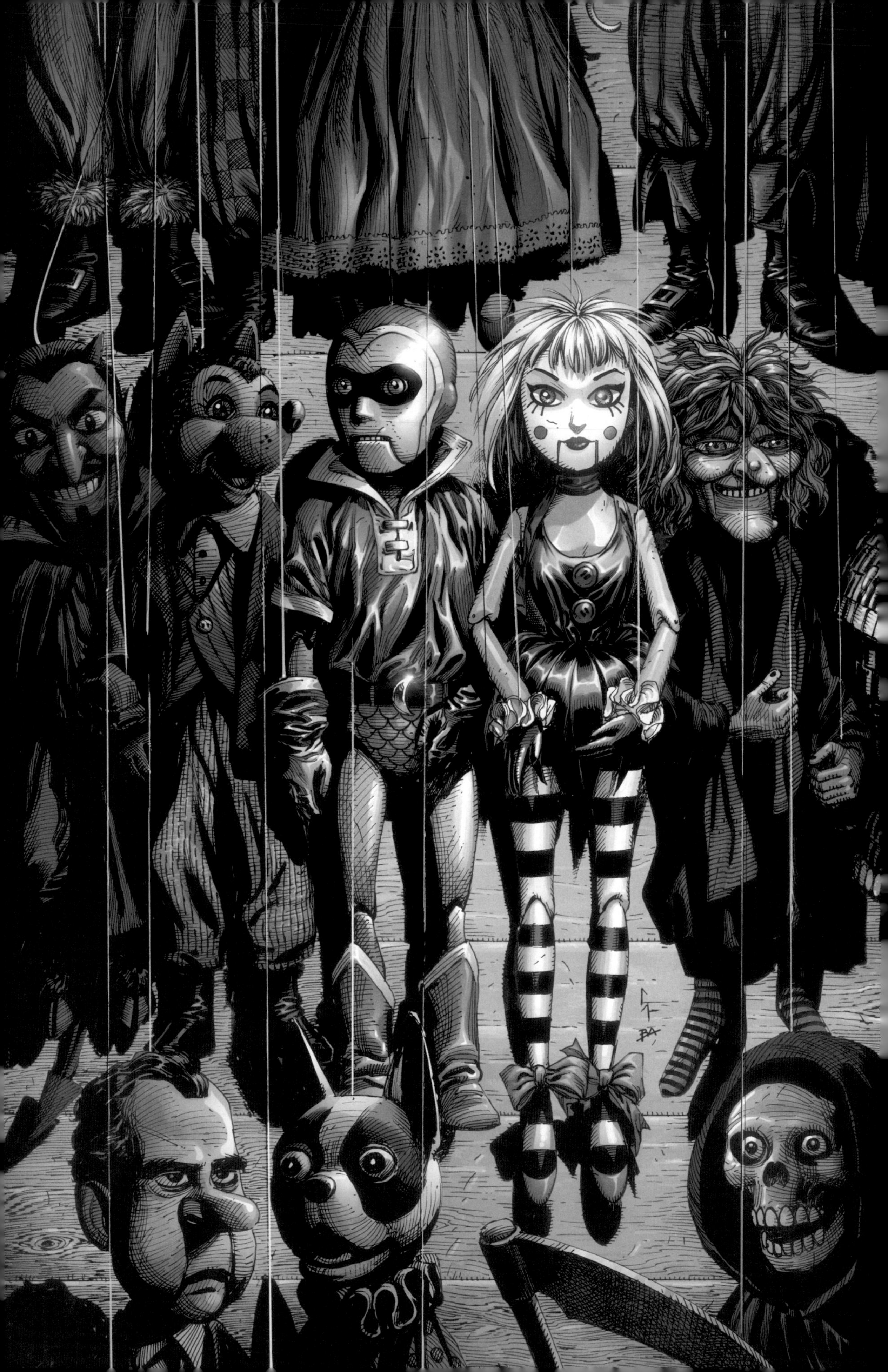

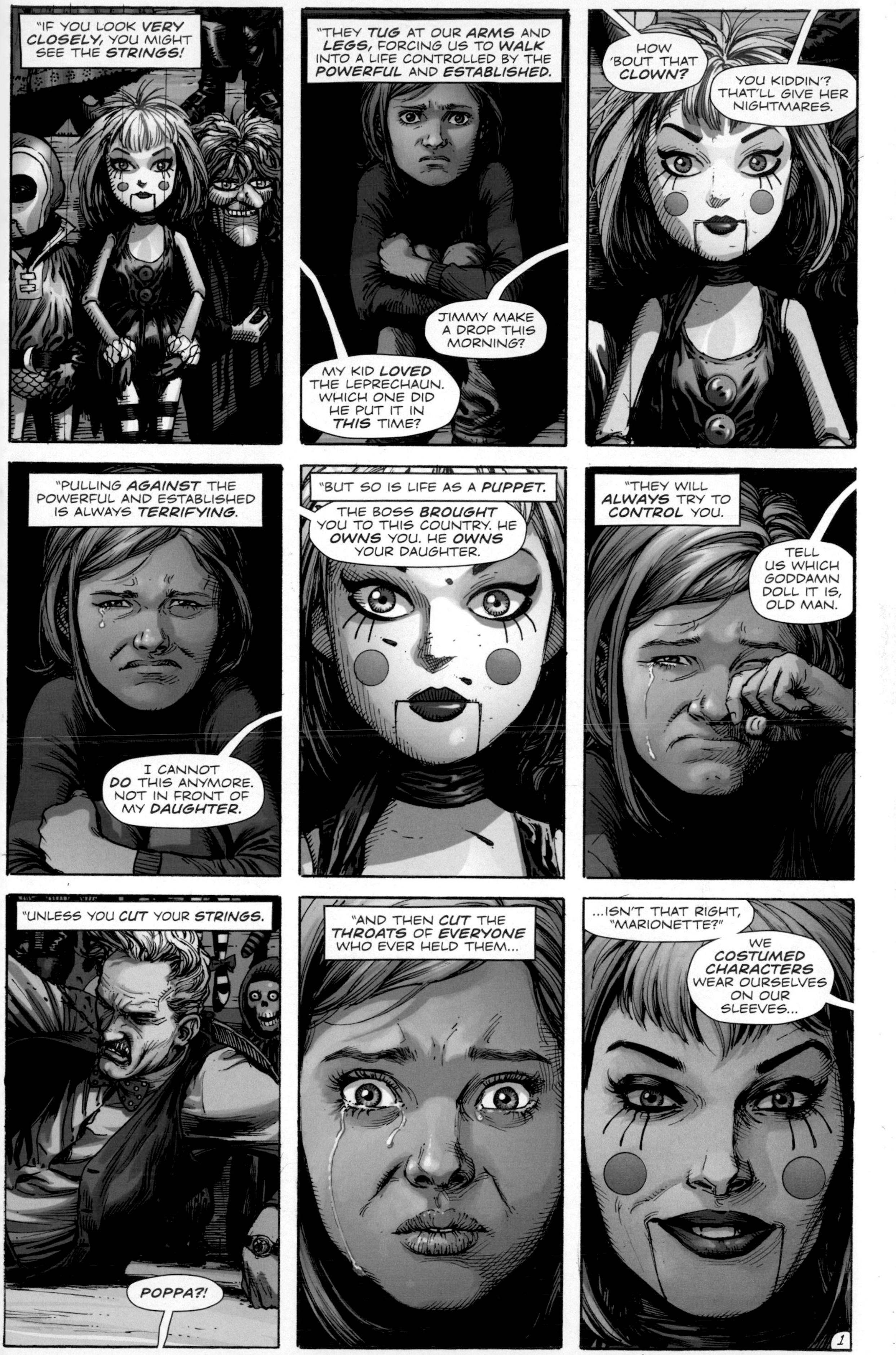
"IF YOU LOOK VERY CLOSELY, YOU MIGHT SEE THE STRINGS!
"THEY TUG AT OUR ARMS AND LEGS, FORCING US TO WALK INTO A LIFE CONTROLLED BY THE POWERFUL AND ESTABLISHED.
JIMMY MAKE A DROP THIS MORNING?
MY KID LOVED THE LEPRECHAUN. WHICH ONE DID HE PUT IT IN THIS TIME?
HOW 'BOUT THAT CLOWN?
YOU KIDDIN'? THAT'LL GIVE HER NIGHTMARES.
"PULLING AGAINST THE POWERFUL AND ESTABLISHED IS ALWAYS TERRIFYING.
I CANNOT DO THIS ANYMORE. NOT IN FRONT OF MY DAUGHTER.
"BUT SO IS LIFE AS A PUPPET.
THE BOSS BROUGHT YOU TO THIS COUNTRY. HE OWNS YOU. HE OWNS YOUR DAUGHTER.
"THEY WILL ALWAYS TRY TO CONTROL YOU.
TELL US WHICH GODDAMN DOLL IT IS, OLD MAN.
"UNLESS YOU CUT YOUR STRINGS.
POPPA?!
"AND THEN CUT THE THROATS OF EVERYONE WHO EVER HELD THEM...
...ISN'T THAT RIGHT, "MARIONETTE?"
WE COSTUMED CHARACTERS WEAR OURSELVES ON OUR SLEEVES...
1

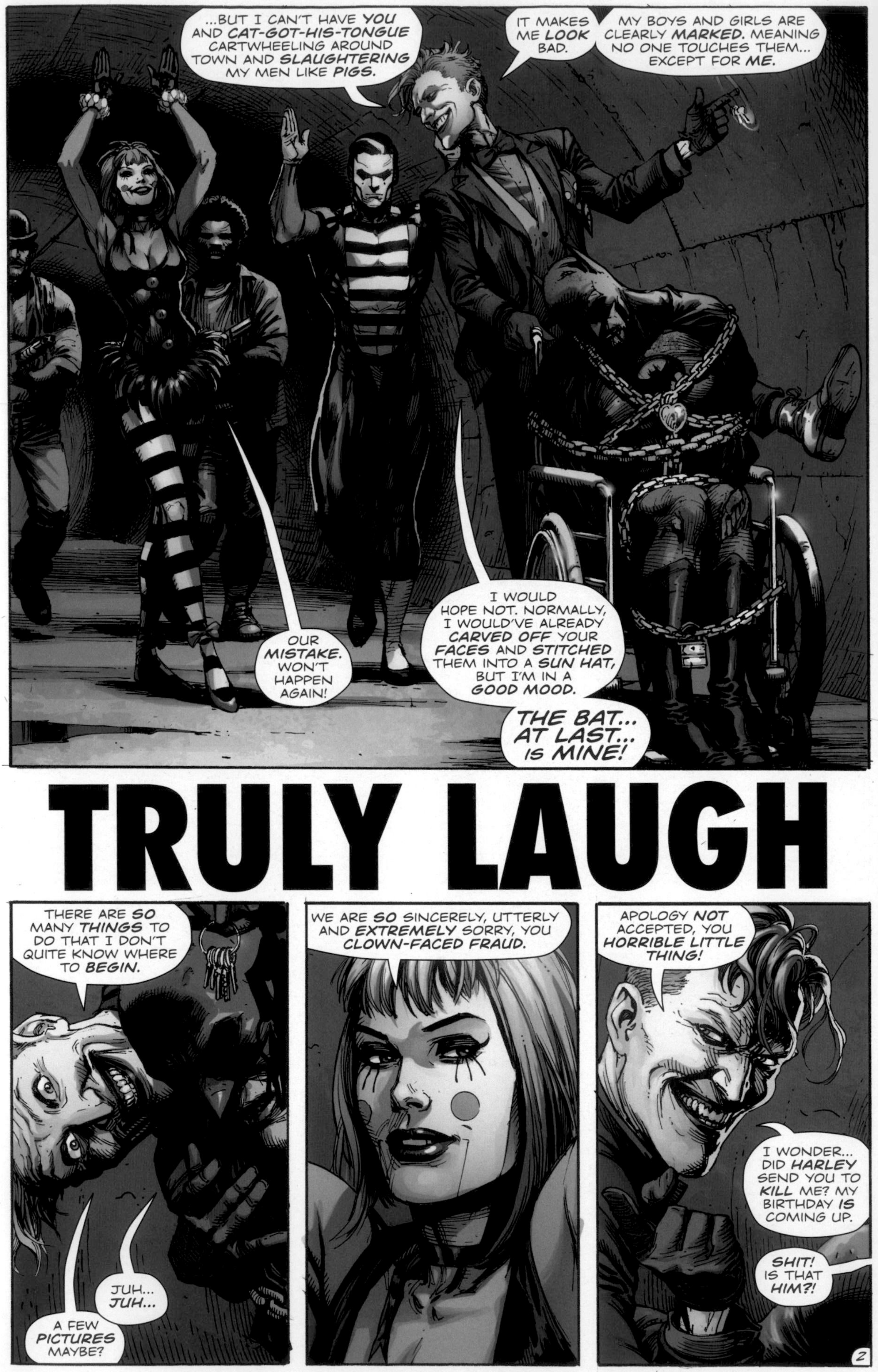
...BUT I CAN'T HAVE YOU AND CAT-GOT-HIS-TONGUE CARTWHEELING AROUND TOWN AND SLAUGHTERING MY MEN LIKE PIGS.
IT MAKES ME LOOK BAD.
MY BOYS AND GIRLS ARE CLEARLY MARKED. MEANING NO ONE TOUCHES THEM... EXCEPT FOR ME.
OUR MISTAKE. WON'T HAPPEN AGAIN!
I WOULD HOPE NOT. NORMALLY, I WOULD'VE ALREADY CARVED OFF YOUR FACES AND STITCHED THEM INTO A SUN HAT, BUT I'M IN A GOOD MOOD.
THE BAT... AT LAST... IS MINE!
TRULY LAUGH
THERE ARE SO MANY THINGS TO DO THAT I DON'T QUITE KNOW WHERE TO BEGIN.
JUH... JUH...
A FEW PICTURES MAYBE?
WE ARE SO SINCERELY, UTTERLY AND EXTREMELY SORRY, YOU CLOWN-FACED FRAUD.
APOLOGY NOT ACCEPTED, YOU HORRIBLE LITTLE THING!
I WONDER... DID HARLEY SEND YOU TO KILL ME? MY BIRTHDAY IS COMING UP.
SHIT! IS THAT HIM?!

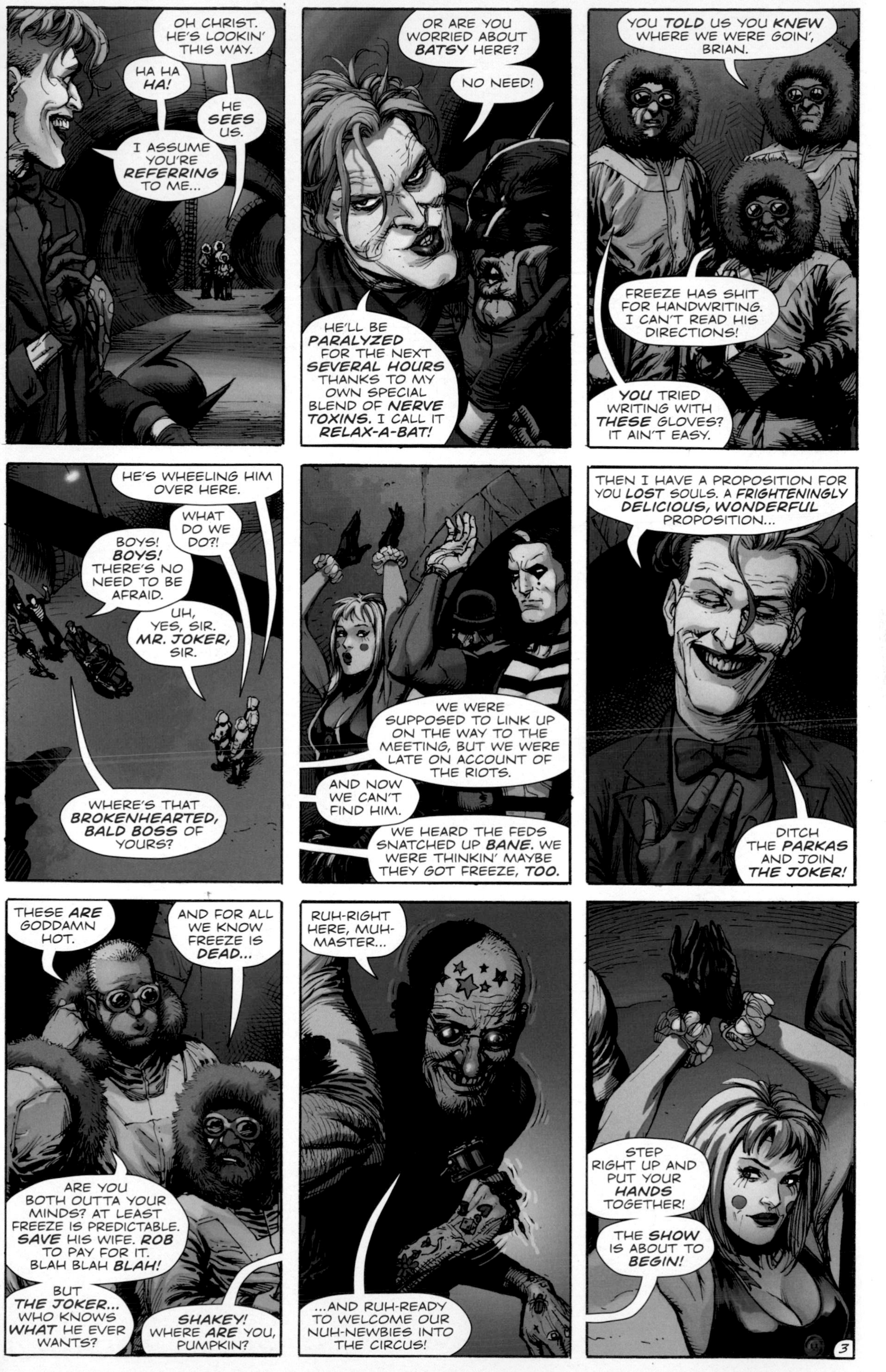

OH CHRIST. HE'S LOOKIN' THIS WAY.
HA HA HA!
HE SEES US.
I ASSUME YOU'RE REFERRING TO ME...
OR ARE YOU WORRIED ABOUT BATSY HERE?
NO NEED!
HE'LL BE PARALYZED FOR THE NEXT SEVERAL HOURS THANKS TO MY OWN SPECIAL BLEND OF NERVE TOXINS. I CALL IT RELAX-A-BAT!
YOU TOLD US YOU KNEW WHERE WE WERE GOIN', BRIAN.
FREEZE HAS SHIT FOR HANDWRITING. I CAN'T READ HIS DIRECTIONS!
YOU TRIED WRITING WITH THESE GLOVES? IT AIN'T EASY.
HE'S WHEELING HIM OVER HERE.
WHAT DO WE DO?!
BOYS! BOYS! THERE'S NO NEED TO BE AFRAID.
UH, YES, SIR. MR. JOKER, SIR.
WHERE'S THAT BROKENHEARTED, BALD BOSS OF YOURS?
WE WERE SUPPOSED TO LINK UP ON THE WAY TO THE MEETING, BUT WE WERE LATE ON ACCOUNT OF THE RIOTS.
AND NOW WE CAN'T FIND HIM.
WE HEARD THE FEDS SNATCHED UP BANE. WE WERE THINKIN' MAYBE THEY GOT FREEZE, TOO.
THEN I HAVE A PROPOSITION FOR YOU LOST SOULS. A FRIGHTENINGLY DELICIOUS, WONDERFUL PROPOSITION...
DITCH THE PARKAS AND JOIN THE JOKER!
THESE ARE GODDAMN HOT.
AND FOR ALL WE KNOW FREEZE IS DEAD...
ARE YOU BOTH OUTTA YOUR MINDS? AT LEAST FREEZE IS PREDICTABLE. SAVE HIS WIFE. ROB TO PAY FOR IT. BLAH BLAH BLAH!
BUT THE JOKER... WHO KNOWS WHAT HE EVER WANTS?
SHAKEY! WHERE ARE YOU, PUMPKIN?
RUH-RIGHT HERE, MUH-MASTER...
...AND RUH-READY TO WELCOME OUR NUH-NEWBIES INTO THE CIRCUS!
STEP RIGHT UP AND PUT YOUR HANDS TOGETHER!
THE SHOW IS ABOUT TO BEGIN!

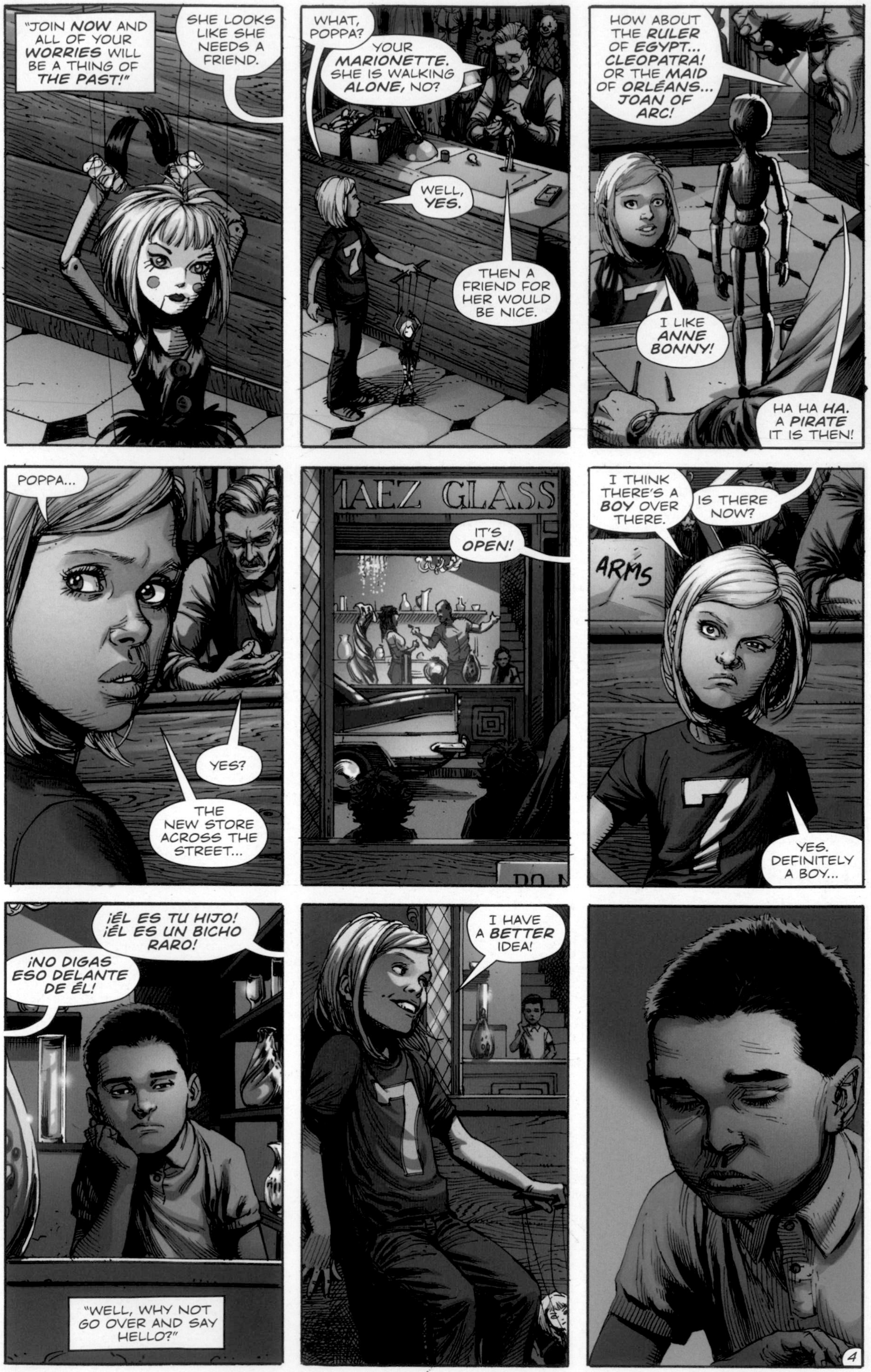
"JOIN NOW AND ALL OF YOUR WORRIES WILL BE A THING OF THE PAST!"
SHE LOOKS LIKE SHE NEEDS A FRIEND.
WHAT, POPPA?
YOUR MARIONETTE. SHE IS WALKING ALONE, NO?
WELL, YES.
THEN A FRIEND FOR HER WOULD BE NICE.
HOW ABOUT THE RULER OF EGYPT... CLEOPATRA! OR THE MAID OF ORLÉANS... JOAN OF ARC!
I LIKE ANNE BONNY!
HA HA HA. A PIRATE IT IS THEN!
POPPA...
YES?
THE NEW STORE ACROSS THE STREET...
MAEZ GLASS
IT'S OPEN!
I THINK THERE'S A BOY OVER THERE.
IS THERE NOW?
ARMS
YES. DEFINITELY A BOY...
¡ÉL ES TU HIJO! ¡ÉL ES UN BICHO RARO!
¡NO DIGAS ESO DELANTE DE ÉL!
"WELL, WHY NOT GO OVER AND SAY HELLO?"
I HAVE A BETTER IDEA!

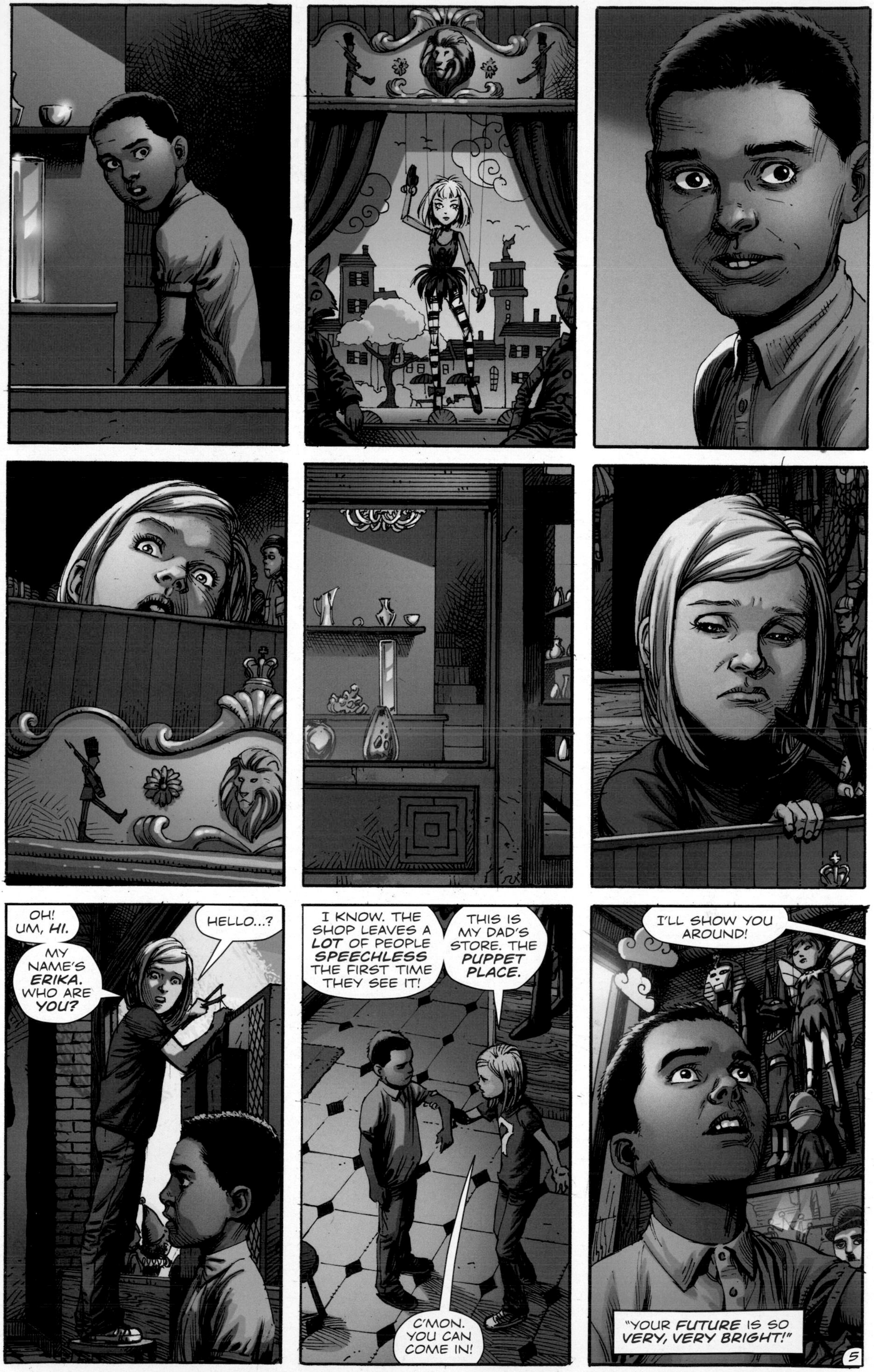
OH! UM, HI.
MY NAME'S ERIKA. WHO ARE YOU?
HELLO...?
I KNOW. THE SHOP LEAVES A LOT OF PEOPLE SPEECHLESS THE FIRST TIME THEY SEE IT!
THIS IS MY DAD'S STORE. THE PUPPET PLACE.
C'MON. YOU CAN COME IN!
I'LL SHOW YOU AROUND!
"YOUR FUTURE IS SO VERY, VERY BRIGHT!"
5

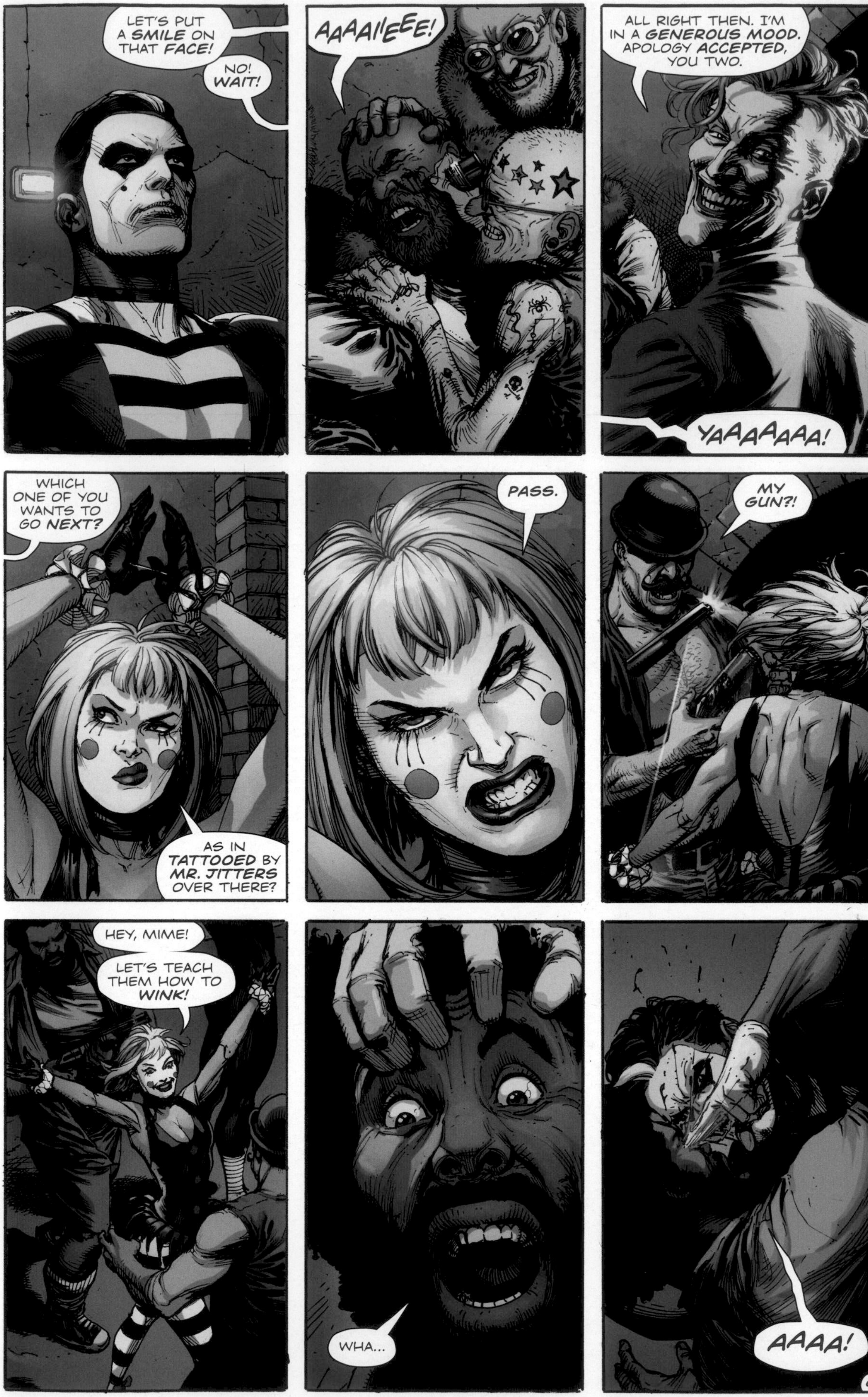
LET'S PUT A SMILE ON THAT FACE!
NO! WAIT!
AAAAII'EEE!
ALL RIGHT THEN. I'M IN A GENEROUS MOOD. APOLOGY ACCEPTED, YOU TWO.
YAAAAAAA!
WHICH ONE OF YOU WANTS TO GO NEXT?
AS IN TATTOOED BY MR. JITTERS OVER THERE?
PASS.
MY GUN?!
HEY, MIME!
LET'S TEACH THEM HOW TO WINK!
WHA...
AAAA!

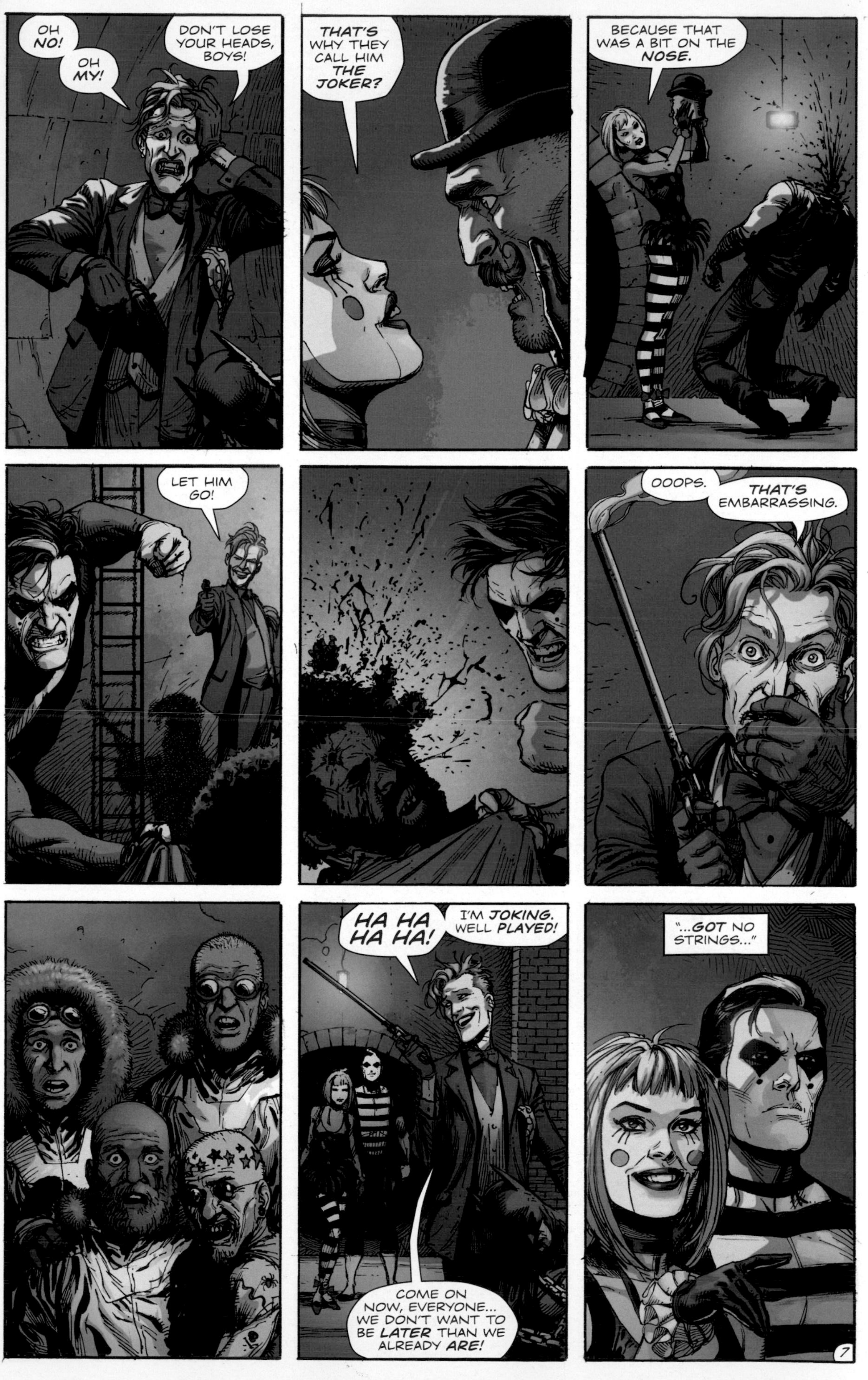
OH NO!
OH MY!
DON'T LOSE YOUR HEADS, BOYS!
THAT'S WHY THEY CALL HIM THE JOKER?
BECAUSE THAT WAS A BIT ON THE NOSE.
LET HIM GO!
OOOPS.
THAT'S EMBARRASSING.
HA HA HA HA!
I'M JOKING. WELL PLAYED!
COME ON NOW, EVERYONE... WE DON'T WANT TO BE LATER THAN WE ALREADY ARE!
"...GOT NO STRINGS..."
7

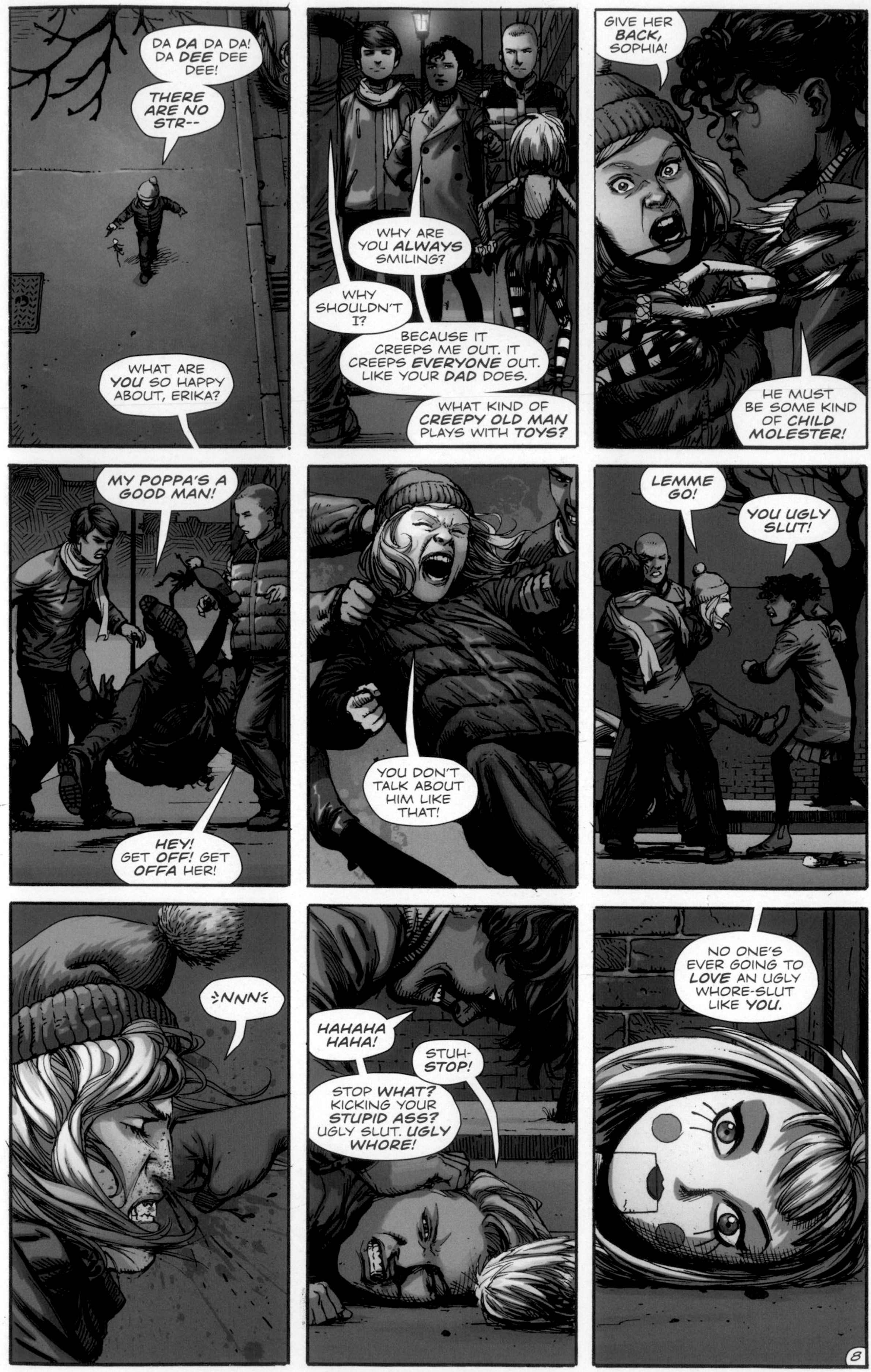
DA DA DA DA! DA DEE DEE DEE!
THERE ARE NO STR--
WHAT ARE YOU SO HAPPY ABOUT, ERIKA?
WHY ARE YOU ALWAYS SMILING?
WHY SHOULDN'T I?
BECAUSE IT CREEPS ME OUT. IT CREEPS EVERYONE OUT. LIKE YOUR DAD DOES.
WHAT KIND OF CREEPY OLD MAN PLAYS WITH TOYS?
GIVE HER BACK, SOPHIA!
HE MUST BE SOME KIND OF CHILD MOLESTER!
MY POPPA'S A GOOD MAN!
HEY! GET OFF! GET OFFA HER!
YOU DON'T TALK ABOUT HIM LIKE THAT!
LEMME GO!
YOU UGLY SLUT!
NNN
HAHAHA HAHA!
STUH-STOP!
STOP WHAT? KICKING YOUR STUPID ASS? UGLY SLUT. UGLY WHORE!
NO ONE'S EVER GOING TO LOVE AN UGLY WHORE-SLUT LIKE YOU.

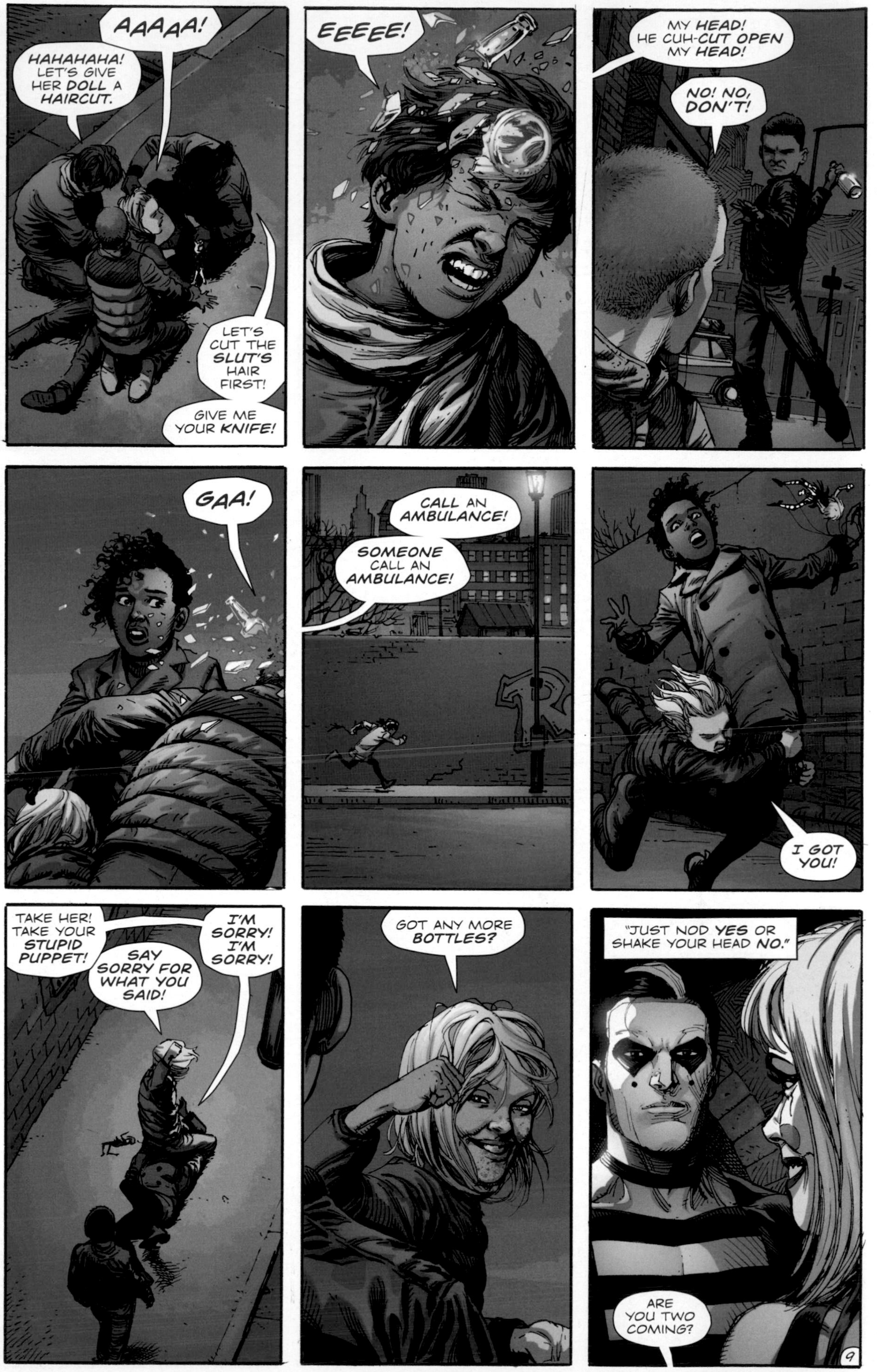
AAAAA!
HAHAHAHA! LET'S GIVE HER DOLL A HAIRCUT.
LET'S CUT THE SLUT'S HAIR FIRST!
GIVE ME YOUR KNIFE!
EEEEE!
MY HEAD! HE CUH-CUT OPEN MY HEAD!
NO! NO, DON'T!
GAA!
CALL AN AMBULANCE!
SOMEONE CALL AN AMBULANCE!
I GOT YOU!
TAKE HER! TAKE YOUR STUPID PUPPET!
I'M SORRY! I'M SORRY!
SAY SORRY FOR WHAT YOU SAID!
GOT ANY MORE BOTTLES?
"JUST NOD YES OR SHAKE YOUR HEAD NO."
ARE YOU TWO COMING?
9

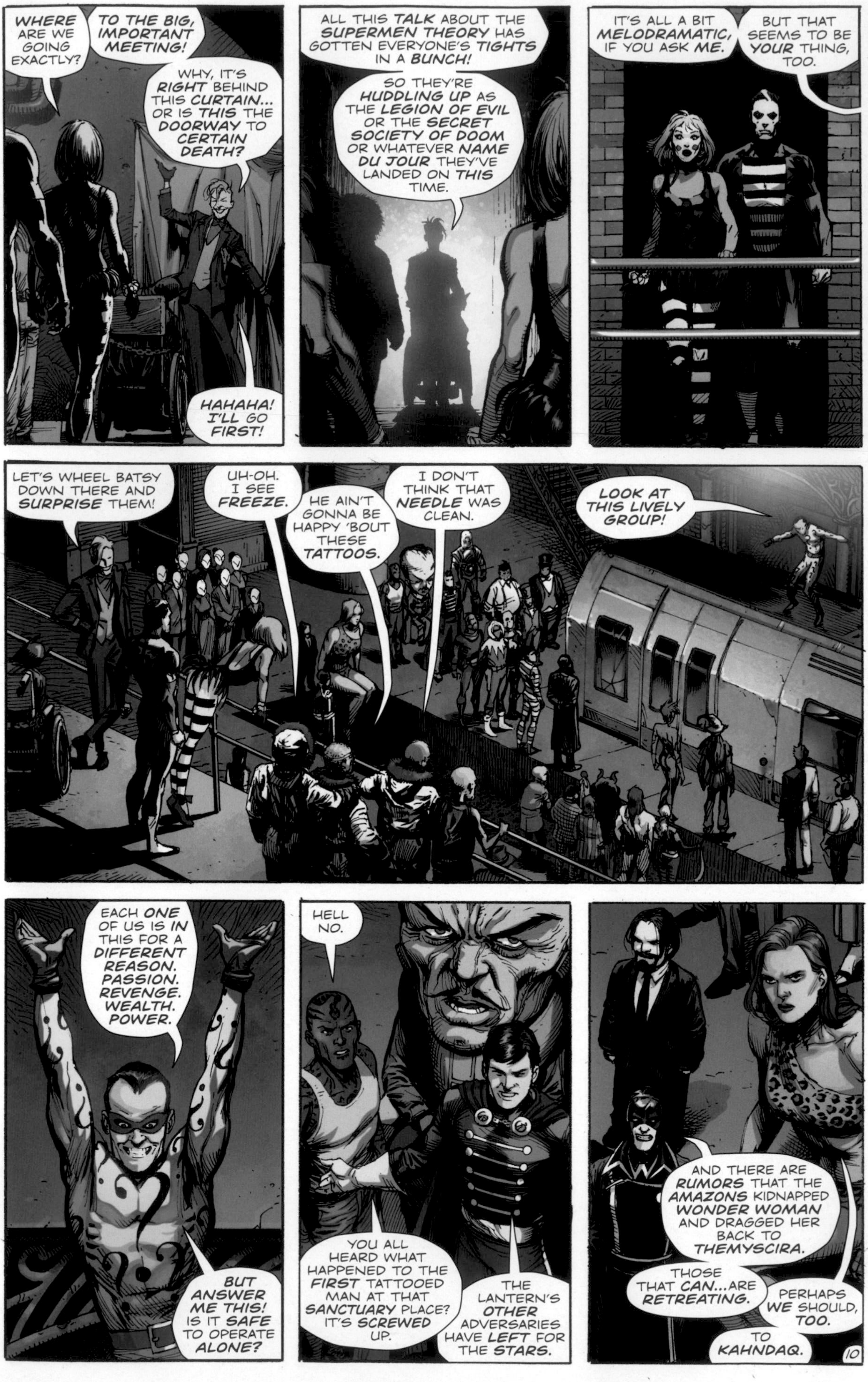
WHERE ARE WE GOING EXACTLY?
TO THE BIG, IMPORTANT MEETING!
WHY, IT'S RIGHT BEHIND THIS CURTAIN... OR IS THIS THE DOORWAY TO CERTAIN DEATH?
HAHAHA! I'LL GO FIRST!
ALL THIS TALK ABOUT THE SUPERMEN THEORY HAS GOTTEN EVERYONE'S TIGHTS IN A BUNCH!
SO THEY'RE HUDDLING UP AS THE LEGION OF EVIL OR THE SECRET SOCIETY OF DOOM OR WHATEVER NAME DU JOUR THEY'VE LANDED ON THIS TIME.
IT'S ALL A BIT MELODRAMATIC, IF YOU ASK ME.
BUT THAT SEEMS TO BE YOUR THING, TOO.
LET'S WHEEL BATSY DOWN THERE AND SURPRISE THEM!
UH-OH. I SEE FREEZE.
HE AIN'T GONNA BE HAPPY 'BOUT THESE TATTOOS.
I DON'T THINK THAT NEEDLE WAS CLEAN.
LOOK AT THIS LIVELY GROUP!
EACH ONE OF US IS IN THIS FOR A DIFFERENT REASON. PASSION. REVENGE. WEALTH. POWER.
BUT ANSWER ME THIS! IS IT SAFE TO OPERATE ALONE?
HELL NO.
YOU ALL HEARD WHAT HAPPENED TO THE FIRST TATTOOED MAN AT THAT SANCTUARY PLACE? IT'S SCREWED UP.
THE LANTERN'S OTHER ADVERSARIES HAVE LEFT FOR THE STARS.
AND THERE ARE RUMORS THAT THE AMAZONS KIDNAPPED WONDER WOMAN AND DRAGGED HER BACK TO THEMYSCIRA.
THOSE THAT CAN...ARE RETREATING.
PERHAPS WE SHOULD, TOO.
TO KAHNDAQ.
10

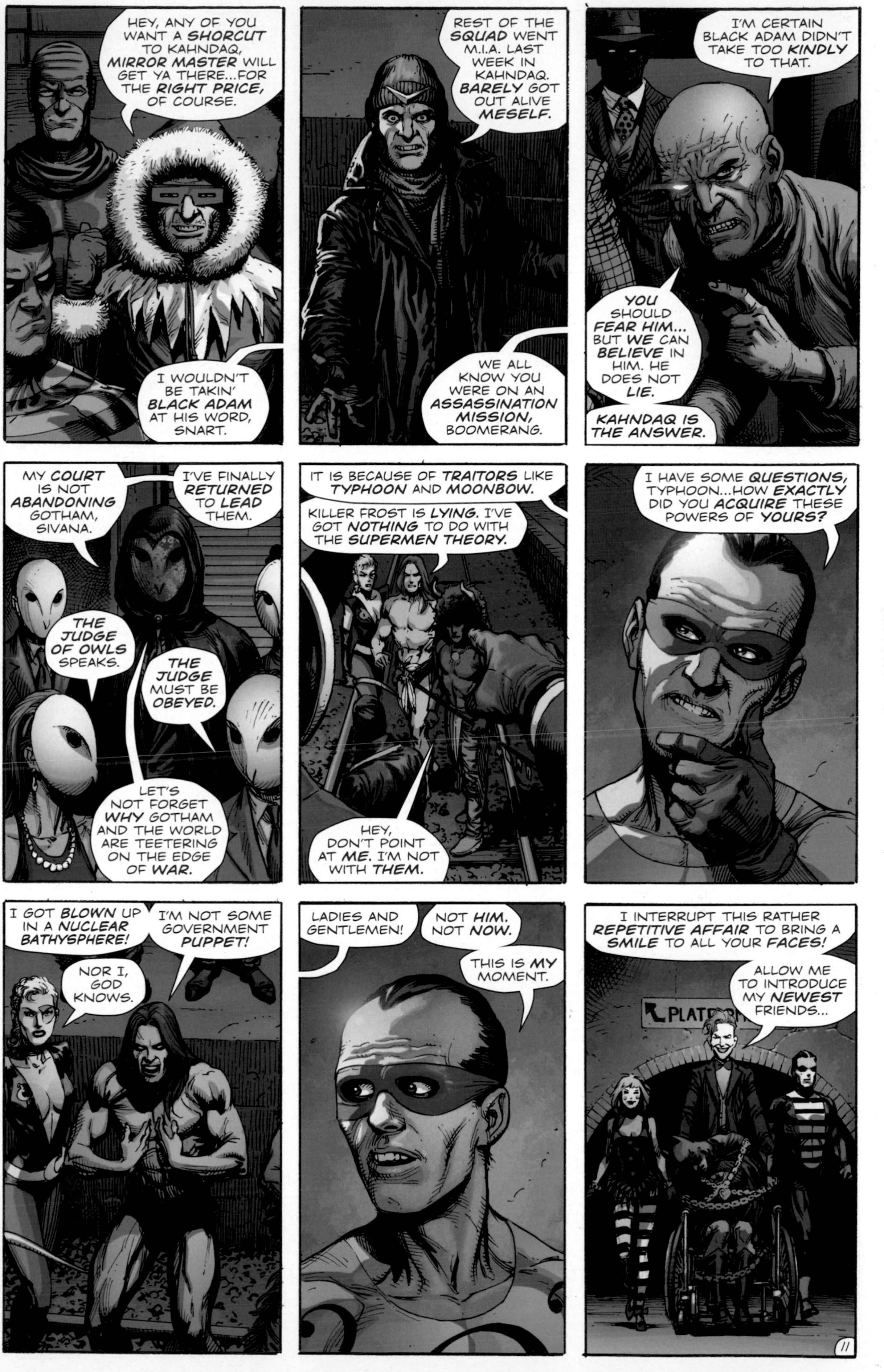
HEY, ANY OF YOU WANT A SHORCUT TO KAHNDAQ, MIRROR MASTER WILL GET YA THERE...FOR THE RIGHT PRICE, OF COURSE.
I WOULDN'T BE TAKIN' BLACK ADAM AT HIS WORD, SNART.
REST OF THE SQUAD WENT M.I.A. LAST WEEK IN KAHNDAQ. BARELY GOT OUT ALIVE MESELF.
WE ALL KNOW YOU WERE ON AN ASSASSINATION MISSION, BOOMERANG.
I'M CERTAIN BLACK ADAM DIDN'T TAKE TOO KINDLY TO THAT.
YOU SHOULD FEAR HIM... BUT WE CAN BELIEVE IN HIM. HE DOES NOT LIE.
KAHNDAQ IS THE ANSWER.
MY COURT IS NOT ABANDONING GOTHAM, SIVANA.
I'VE FINALLY RETURNED TO LEAD THEM.
THE JUDGE OF OWLS SPEAKS.
THE JUDGE MUST BE OBEYED.
LET'S NOT FORGET WHY GOTHAM AND THE WORLD ARE TEETERING ON THE EDGE OF WAR.
IT IS BECAUSE OF TRAITORS LIKE TYPHOON AND MOONBOW.
KILLER FROST IS LYING. I'VE GOT NOTHING TO DO WITH THE SUPERMEN THEORY.
HEY, DON'T POINT AT ME. I'M NOT WITH THEM.
I HAVE SOME QUESTIONS, TYPHOON...HOW EXACTLY DID YOU ACQUIRE THESE POWERS OF YOURS?
I GOT BLOWN UP IN A NUCLEAR BATHYSPHERE!
I'M NOT SOME GOVERNMENT PUPPET!
NOR I, GOD KNOWS.
LADIES AND GENTLEMEN!
NOT HIM. NOT NOW.
THIS IS MY MOMENT.
I INTERRUPT THIS RATHER REPETITIVE AFFAIR TO BRING A SMILE TO ALL YOUR FACES!
ALLOW ME TO INTRODUCE MY NEWEST FRIENDS...
PLATF

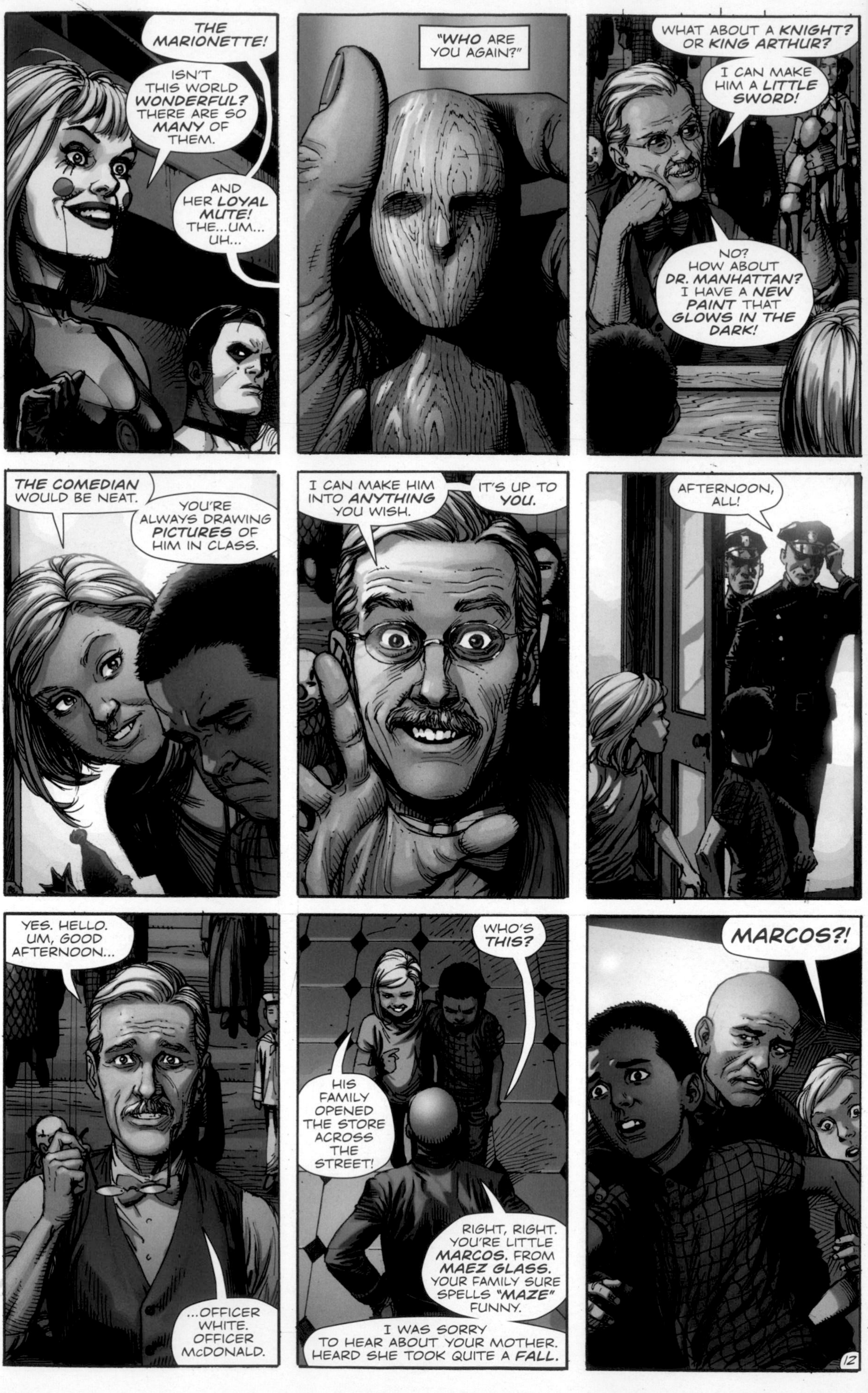

THE MARIONETTE!
ISN'T THIS WORLD WONDERFUL? THERE ARE SO MANY OF THEM.
AND HER LOYAL MUTE! THE...UM... UH...
"WHO ARE YOU AGAIN?"
WHAT ABOUT A KNIGHT? OR KING ARTHUR?
I CAN MAKE HIM A LITTLE SWORD!
NO? HOW ABOUT DR. MANHATTAN? I HAVE A NEW PAINT THAT GLOWS IN THE DARK!
THE COMEDIAN WOULD BE NEAT.
YOU'RE ALWAYS DRAWING PICTURES OF HIM IN CLASS.
I CAN MAKE HIM INTO ANYTHING YOU WISH.
IT'S UP TO YOU.
AFTERNOON, ALL!
YES. HELLO. UM, GOOD AFTERNOON...
...OFFICER WHITE. OFFICER McDONALD.
WHO'S THIS?
HIS FAMILY OPENED THE STORE ACROSS THE STREET!
RIGHT, RIGHT. YOU'RE LITTLE MARCOS. FROM MAEZ GLASS. YOUR FAMILY SURE SPELLS "MAZE" FUNNY.
I WAS SORRY TO HEAR ABOUT YOUR MOTHER. HEARD SHE TOOK QUITE A FALL.
MARCOS?!

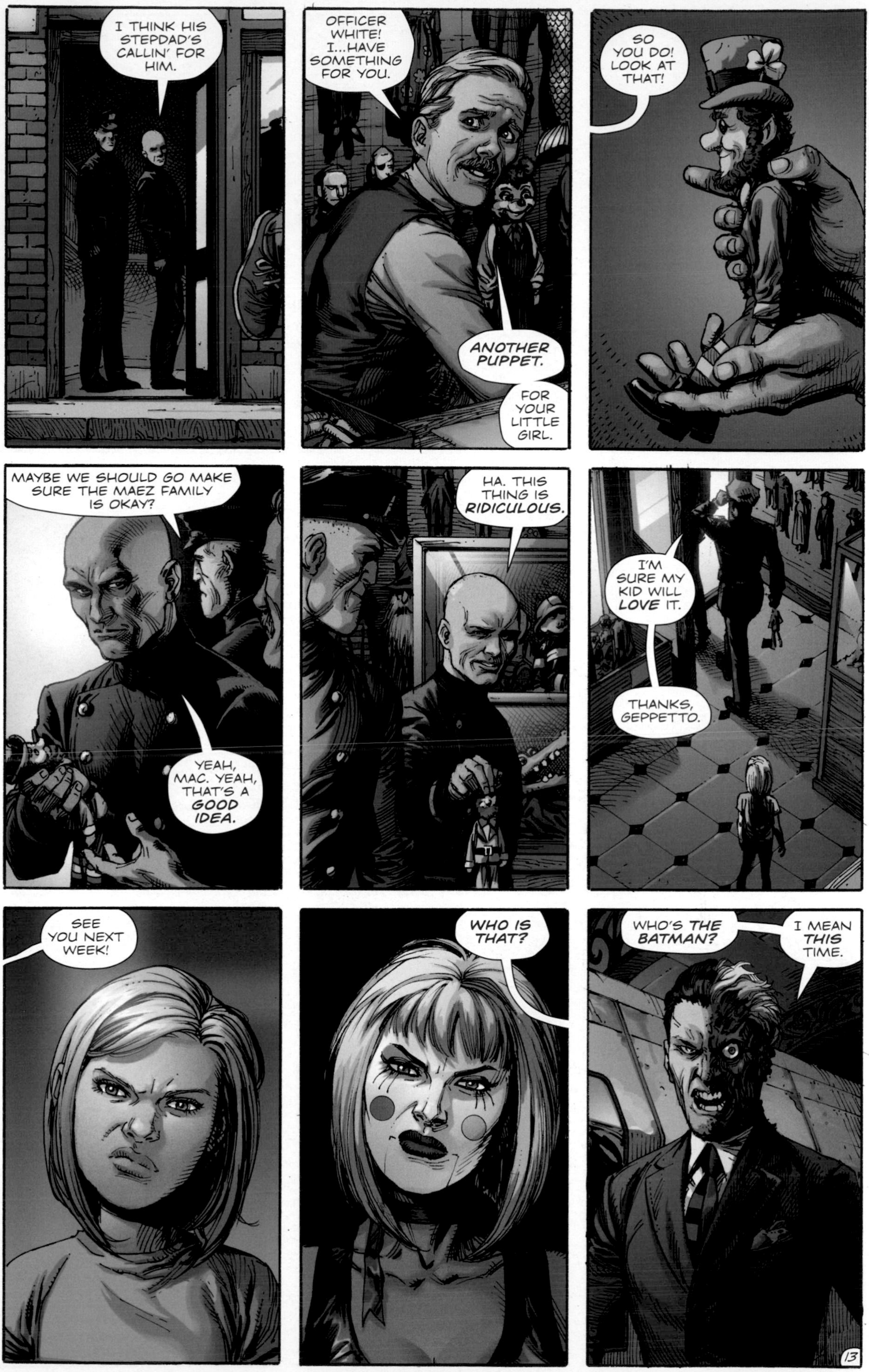
I THINK HIS STEPDAD'S CALLIN' FOR HIM.
OFFICER WHITE! I...HAVE SOMETHING FOR YOU.
ANOTHER PUPPET.
FOR YOUR LITTLE GIRL.
SO YOU DO! LOOK AT THAT!
MAYBE WE SHOULD GO MAKE SURE THE MAEZ FAMILY IS OKAY?
YEAH, MAC. YEAH, THAT'S A GOOD IDEA.
HA. THIS THING IS RIDICULOUS.
I'M SURE MY KID WILL LOVE IT.
THANKS, GEPPETTO.
SEE YOU NEXT WEEK!
WHO IS THAT?
WHO'S THE BATMAN?
I MEAN THIS TIME.
13

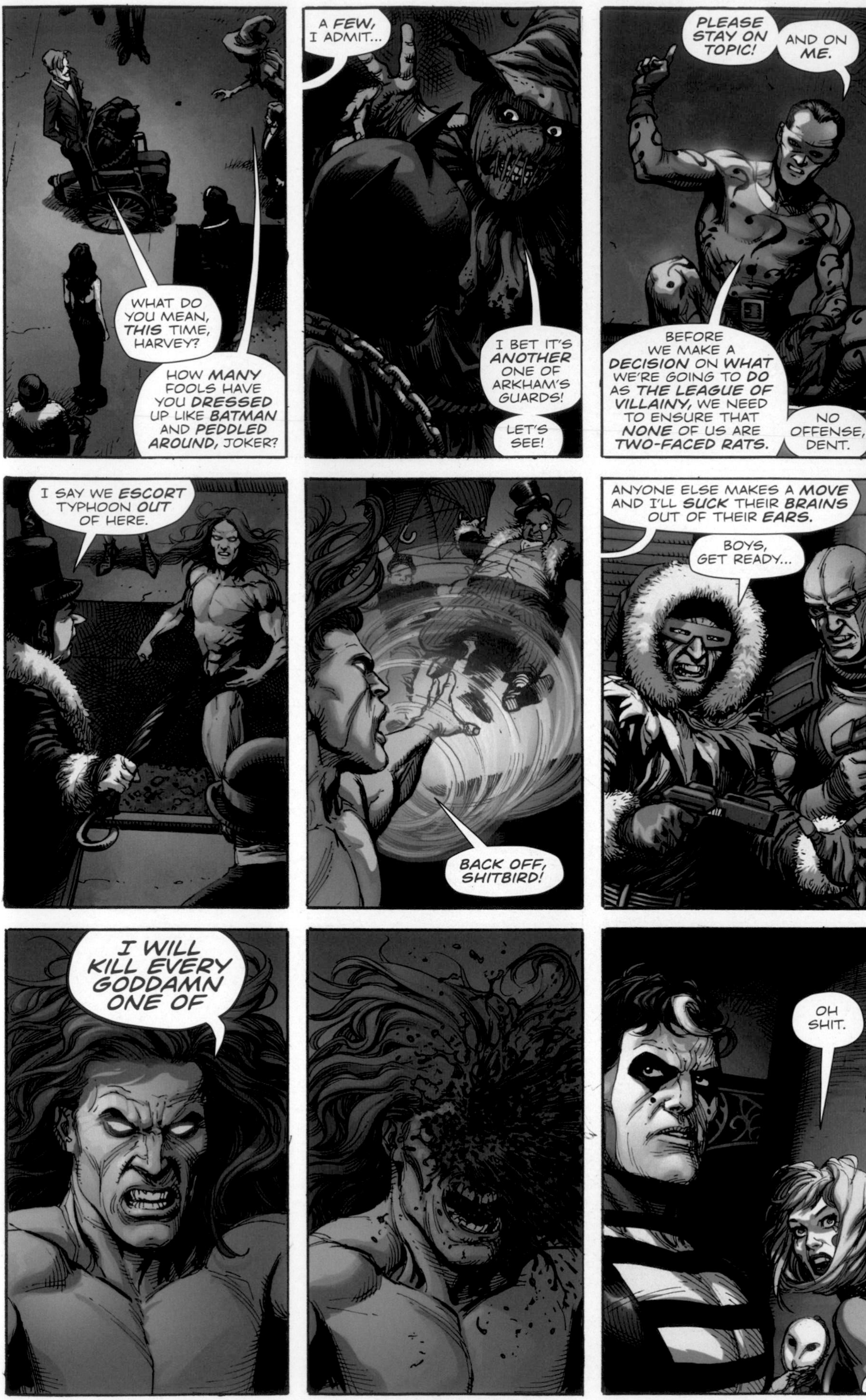
WHAT DO YOU MEAN, THIS TIME, HARVEY?
HOW MANY FOOLS HAVE YOU DRESSED UP LIKE BATMAN AND PEDDLED AROUND, JOKER?
A FEW, I ADMIT...
I BET IT'S ANOTHER ONE OF ARKHAM'S GUARDS!
LET'S SEE!
PLEASE STAY ON TOPIC!
AND ON ME.
BEFORE WE MAKE A DECISION ON WHAT WE'RE GOING TO DO AS THE LEAGUE OF VILLAINY, WE NEED TO ENSURE THAT NONE OF US ARE TWO-FACED RATS.
NO OFFENSE, DENT.
I SAY WE ESCORT TYPHOON OUT OF HERE.
BACK OFF, SHITBIRD!
ANYONE ELSE MAKES A MOVE AND I'LL SUCK THEIR BRAINS OUT OF THEIR EARS.
BOYS, GET READY...
I WILL KILL EVERY GODDAMN ONE OF
OH SHIT.

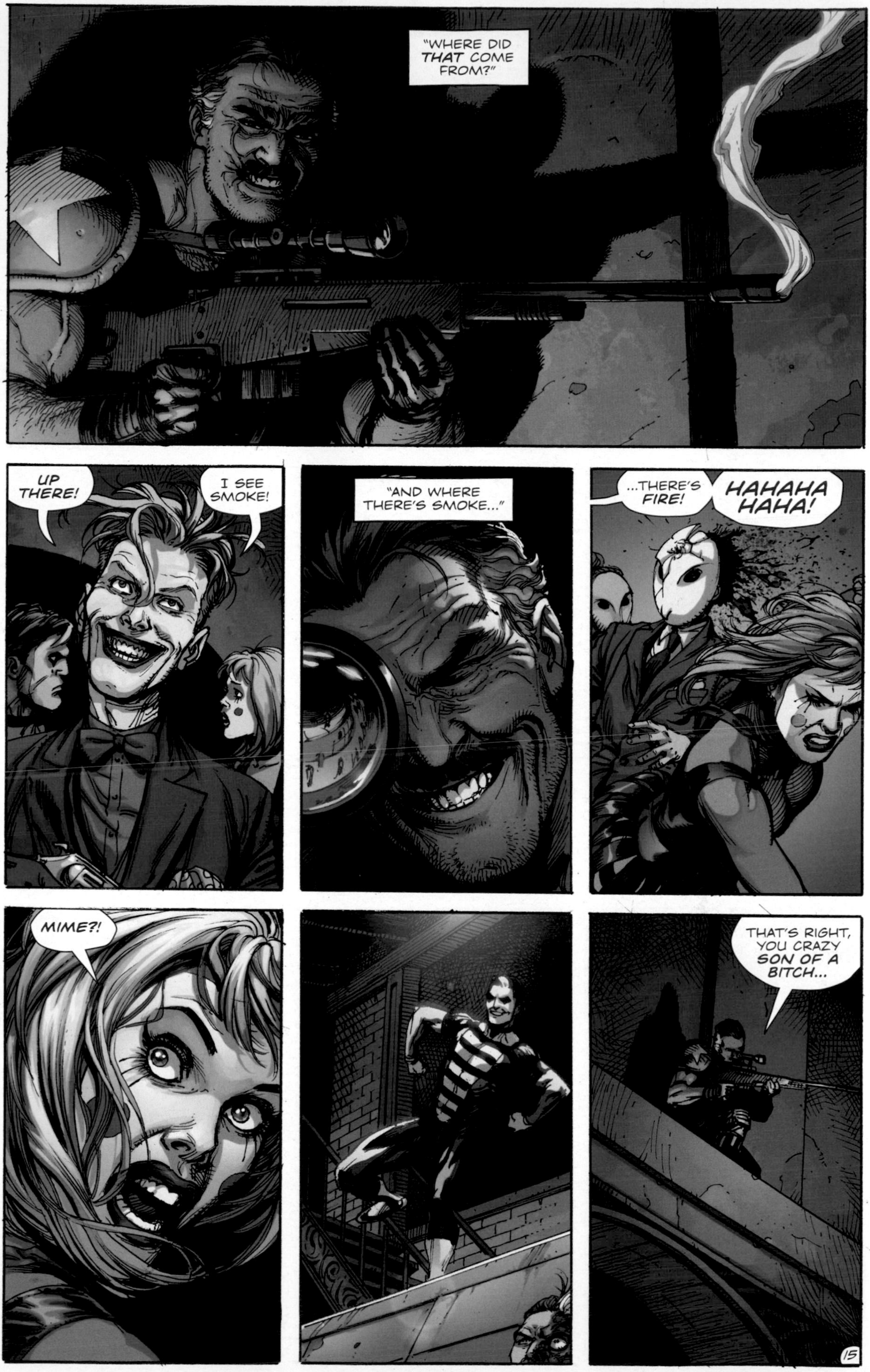
"WHERE DID THAT COME FROM?"
UP THERE!
I SEE SMOKE!
"AND WHERE THERE'S SMOKE..."
...THERE'S FIRE!
HAHAHA HAHA!
MIME?!
THAT'S RIGHT, YOU CRAZY SON OF A BITCH...
15

SAY CHEESE.

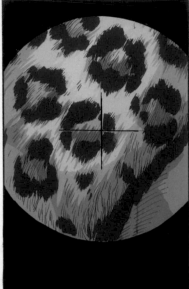

WHAT THE FUH...

KK!

WELL, SHIT. HERE WE GO.

AAAA!

BOSS?!

LET'S GO, DANCING MAN!

WE'RE LEAVING.

YES, NOW.

YOU! STOP RIGHT TH...

EEY!!AAA!

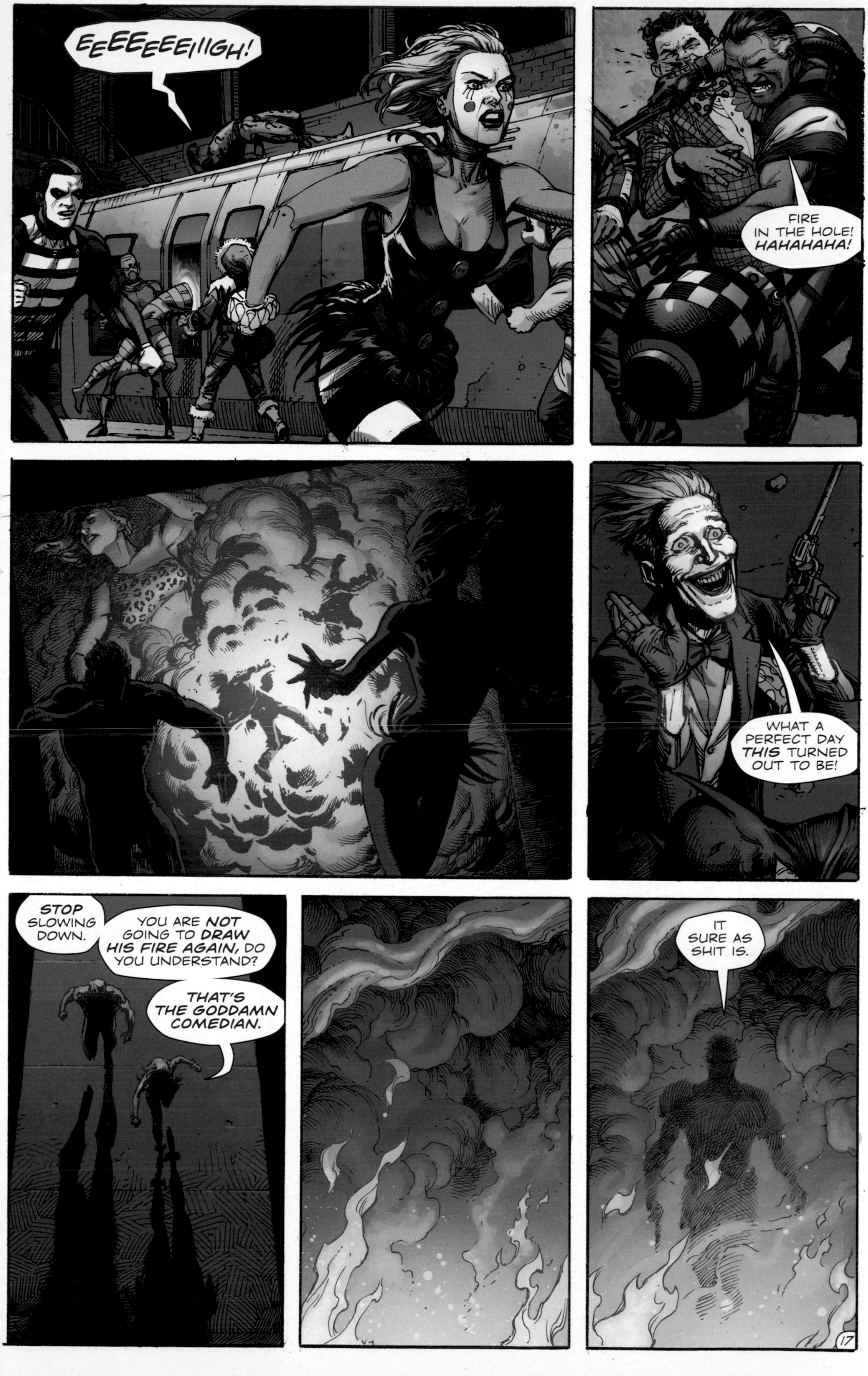
EEEEEEEEIIIGH!
FIRE IN THE HOLE! HAHAHAHA!
WHAT A PERFECT DAY THIS TURNED OUT TO BE!
STOP SLOWING DOWN.
YOU ARE NOT GOING TO DRAW HIS FIRE AGAIN, DO YOU UNDERSTAND?
THAT'S THE GODDAMN COMEDIAN.
IT SURE AS SHIT IS.

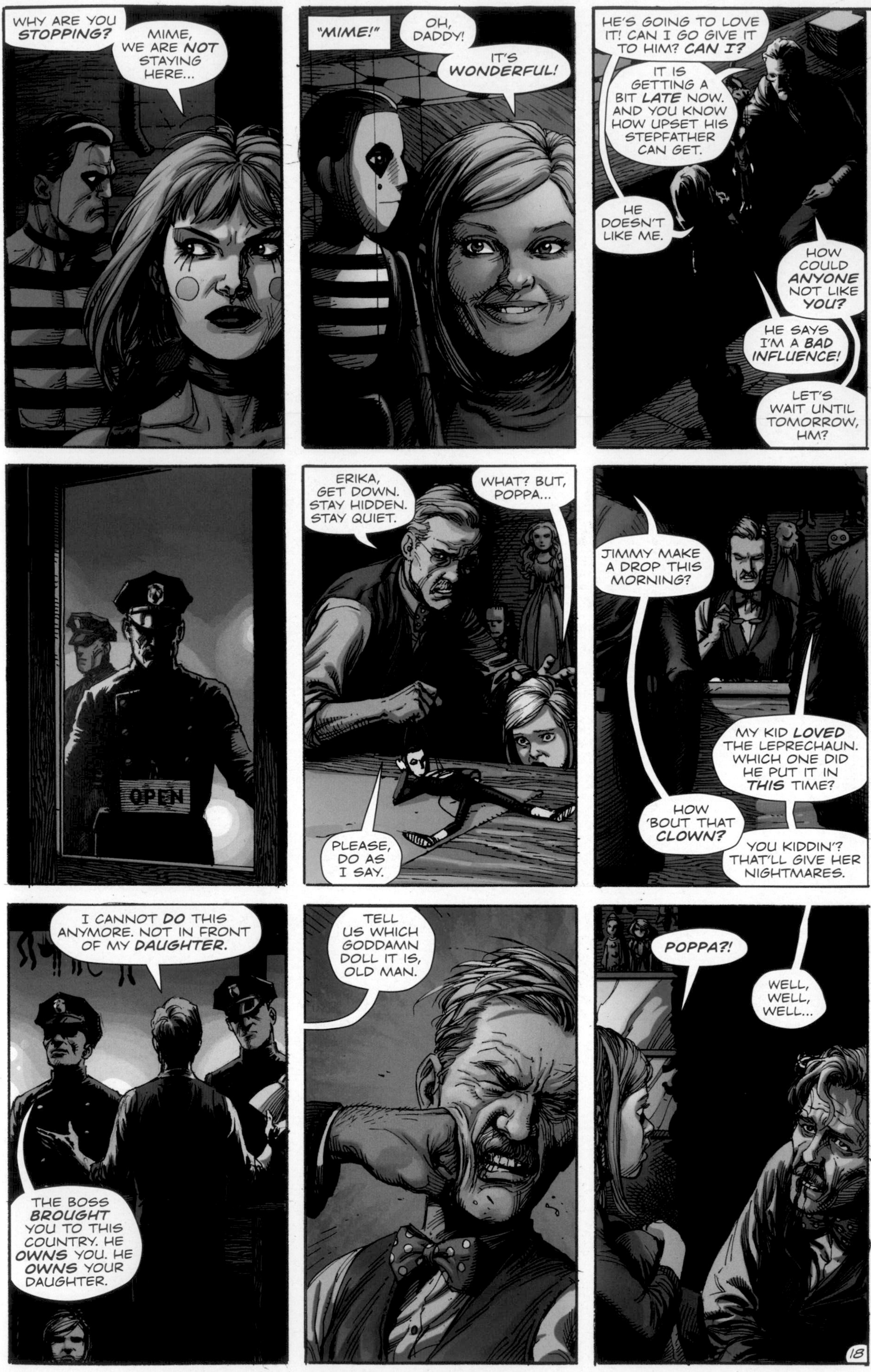

WHY ARE YOU STOPPING?
MIME, WE ARE NOT STAYING HERE...
"MIME!"
OH, DADDY!
IT'S WONDERFUL!
HE'S GOING TO LOVE IT! CAN I GO GIVE IT TO HIM? CAN I?
IT IS GETTING A BIT LATE NOW. AND YOU KNOW HOW UPSET HIS STEPFATHER CAN GET.
HE DOESN'T LIKE ME.
HOW COULD ANYONE NOT LIKE YOU?
HE SAYS I'M A BAD INFLUENCE!
LET'S WAIT UNTIL TOMORROW, HM?
OPEN
ERIKA, GET DOWN. STAY HIDDEN. STAY QUIET.
WHAT? BUT, POPPA...
PLEASE, DO AS I SAY.
JIMMY MAKE A DROP THIS MORNING?
MY KID LOVED THE LEPRECHAUN. WHICH ONE DID HE PUT IT IN THIS TIME?
HOW 'BOUT THAT CLOWN?
YOU KIDDIN'? THAT'LL GIVE HER NIGHTMARES.
I CANNOT DO THIS ANYMORE. NOT IN FRONT OF MY DAUGHTER.
THE BOSS BROUGHT YOU TO THIS COUNTRY. HE OWNS YOU. HE OWNS YOUR DAUGHTER.
TELL US WHICH GODDAMN DOLL IT IS, OLD MAN.
POPPA?!
WELL, WELL, WELL...

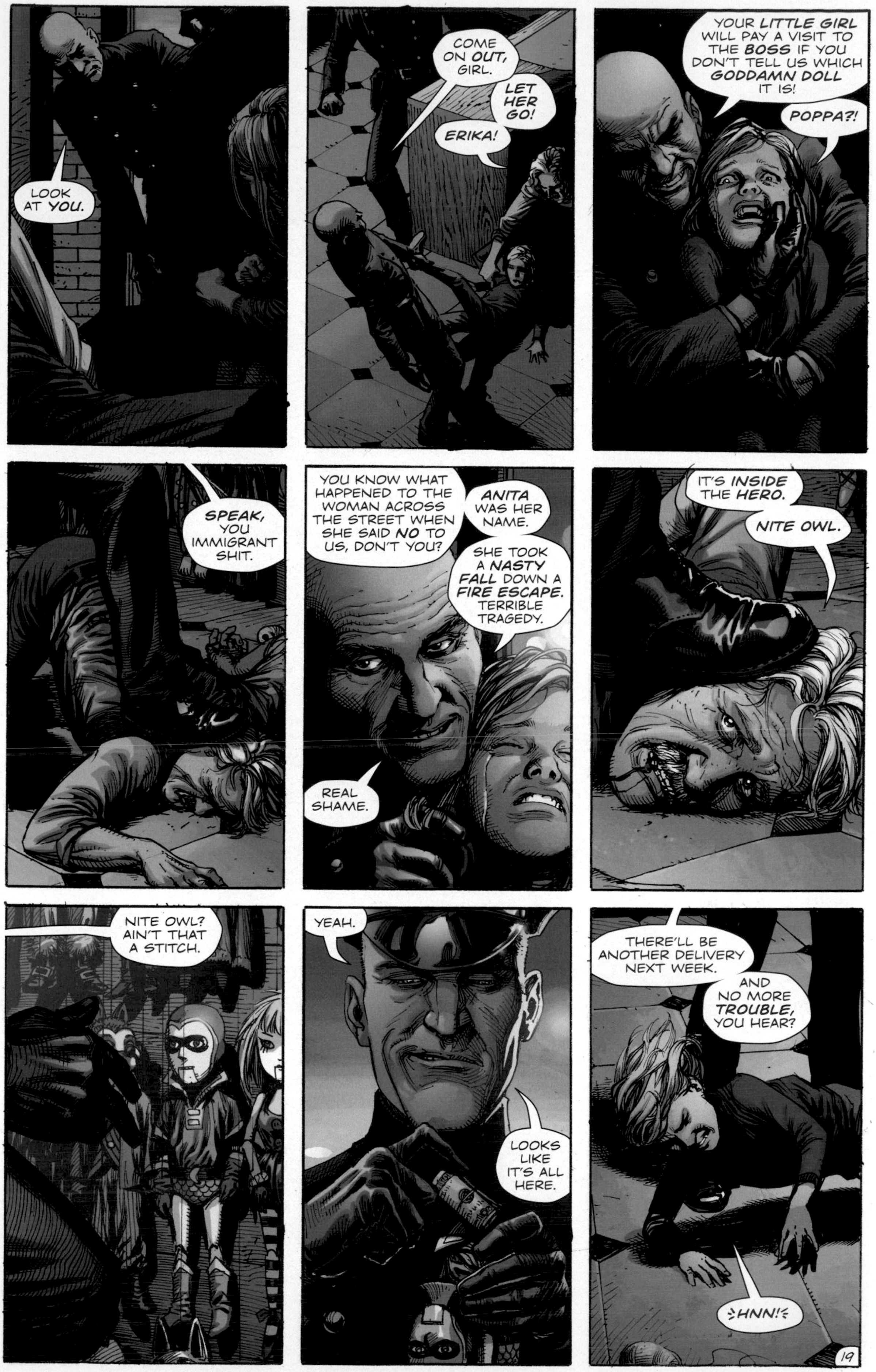
LOOK AT YOU.
COME ON OUT, GIRL.
LET HER GO!
ERIKA!
YOUR LITTLE GIRL WILL PAY A VISIT TO THE BOSS IF YOU DON'T TELL US WHICH GODDAMN DOLL IT IS!
POPPA?!
SPEAK, YOU IMMIGRANT SHIT.
YOU KNOW WHAT HAPPENED TO THE WOMAN ACROSS THE STREET WHEN SHE SAID NO TO US, DON'T YOU?
ANITA WAS HER NAME.
SHE TOOK A NASTY FALL DOWN A FIRE ESCAPE. TERRIBLE TRAGEDY.
REAL SHAME.
IT'S INSIDE THE HERO.
NITE OWL.
NITE OWL? AIN'T THAT A STITCH.
YEAH.
LOOKS LIKE IT'S ALL HERE.
THERE'LL BE ANOTHER DELIVERY NEXT WEEK.
AND NO MORE TROUBLE, YOU HEAR?
HNN!
19

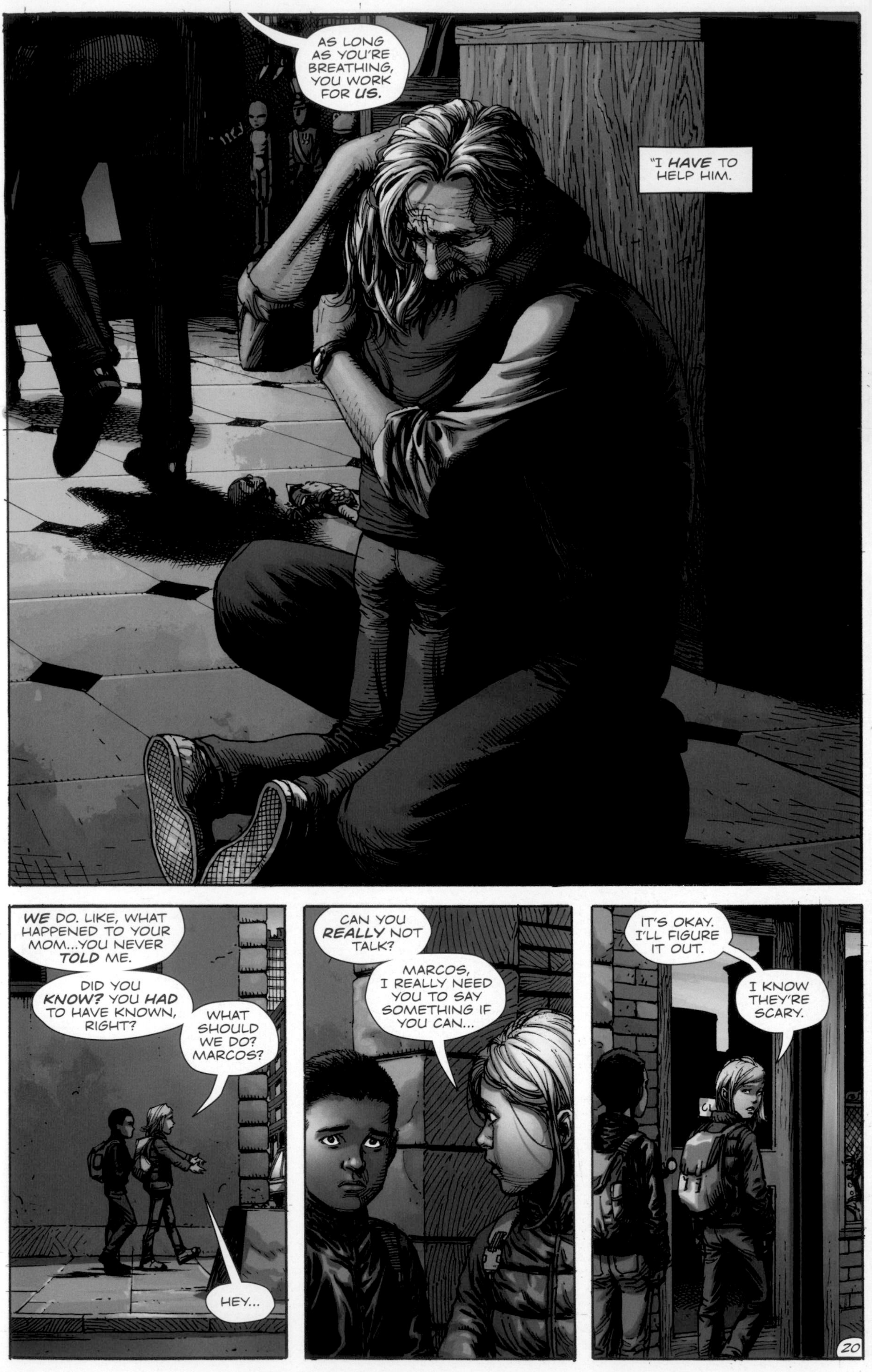
AS LONG AS YOU'RE BREATHING, YOU WORK FOR US.
"I HAVE TO HELP HIM.
WE DO. LIKE, WHAT HAPPENED TO YOUR MOM...YOU NEVER TOLD ME.
DID YOU KNOW? YOU HAD TO HAVE KNOWN, RIGHT?
WHAT SHOULD WE DO? MARCOS?
HEY...
CAN YOU REALLY NOT TALK?
MARCOS, I REALLY NEED YOU TO SAY SOMETHING IF YOU CAN...
IT'S OKAY. I'LL FIGURE IT OUT.
I KNOW THEY'RE SCARY.
20

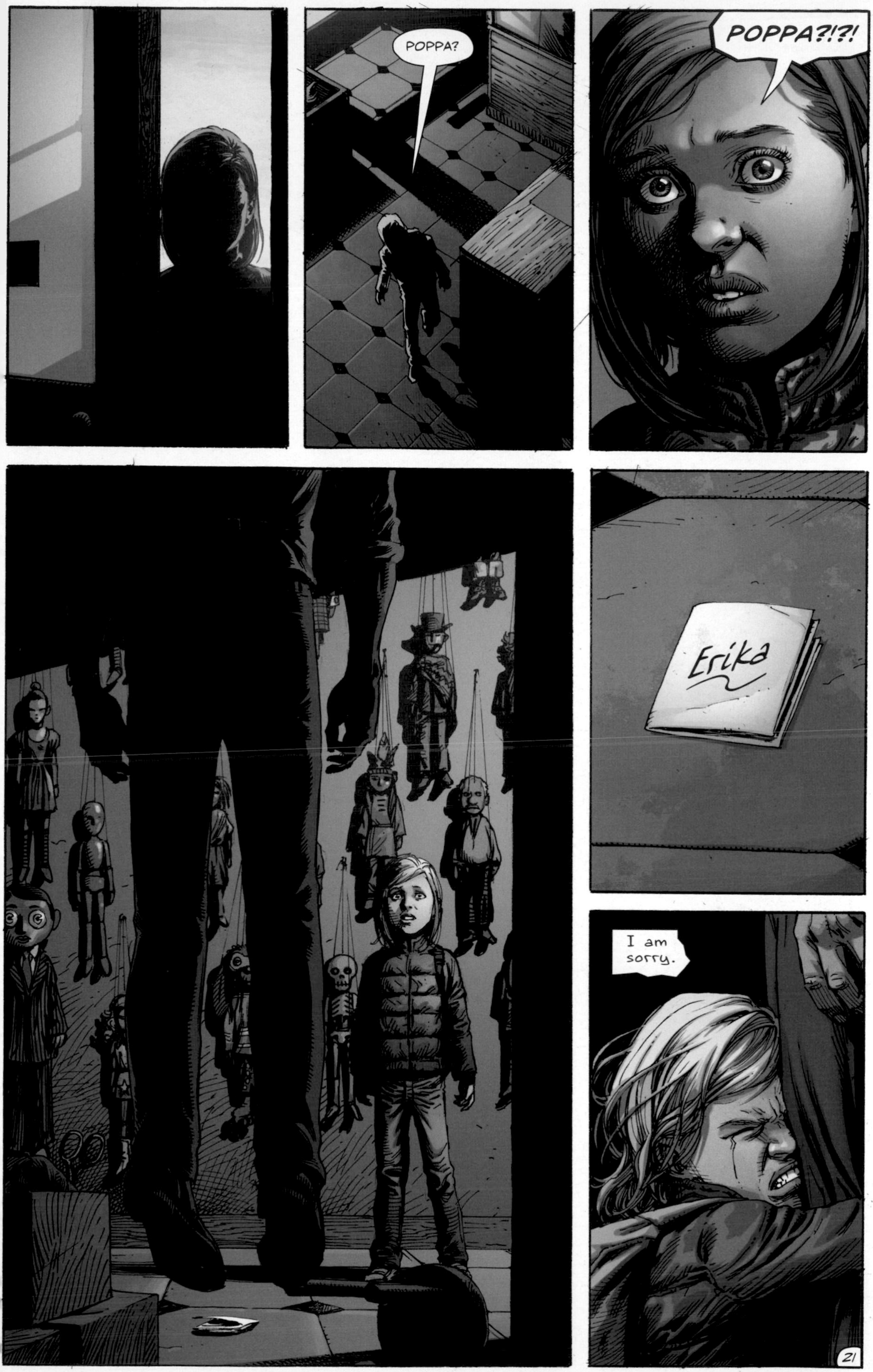
POPPA?
POPPA?!?!
Erika
I am sorry.

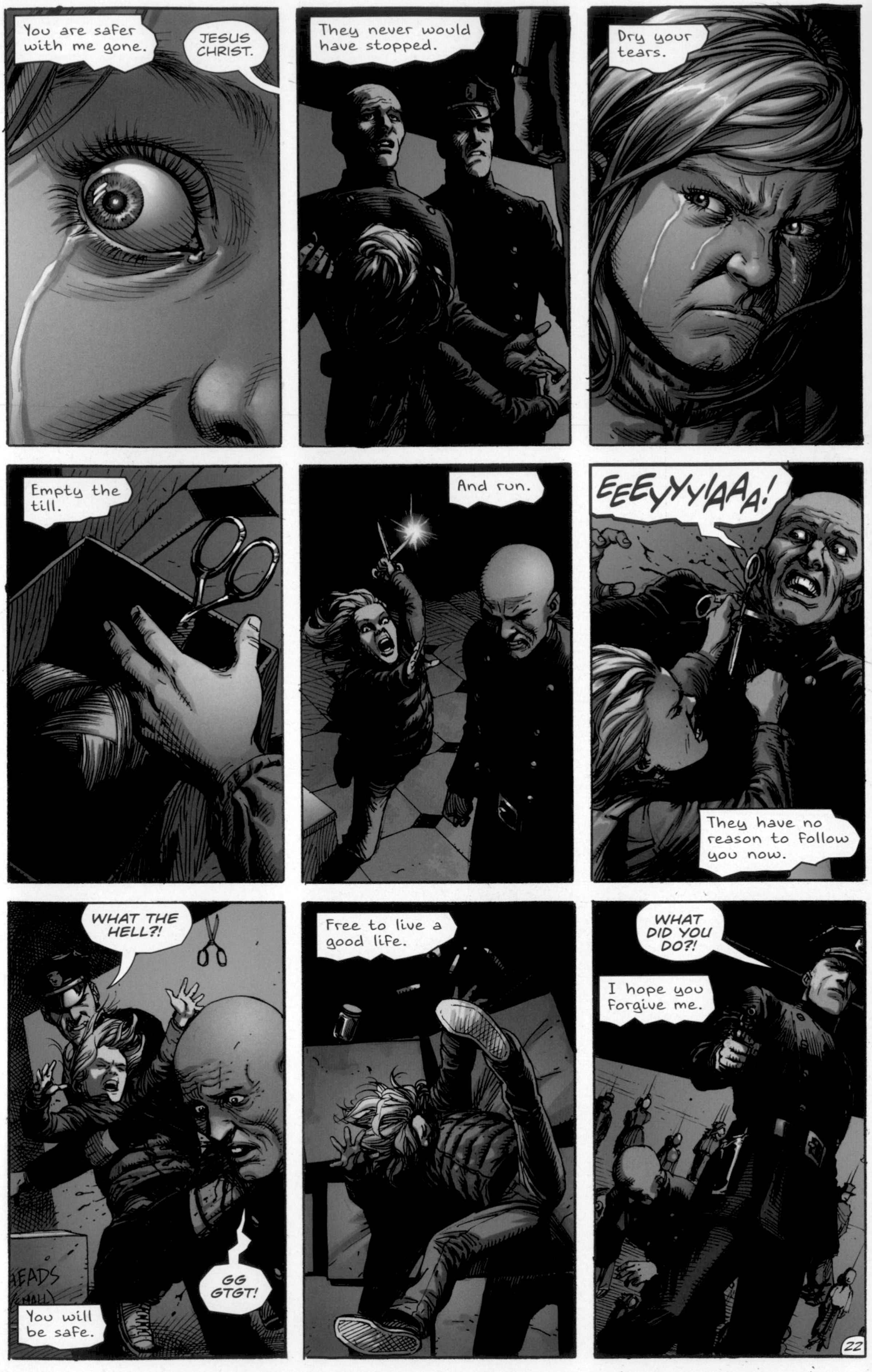
You are safer with me gone.
JESUS CHRIST.
They never would have stopped.
Dry your tears.
Empty the till.
And run.
EEEYYYIAAAA!
They have no reason to follow you now.
WHAT THE HELL?!
GG GTGT!
You will be safe.
Free to live a good life.
WHAT DID YOU DO?!
I hope you forgive me.

One day you will make your own family.

RRAAAA!

And when that day comes, I hope you understand.

YOU DUMB KID! I'LL KILL YOU!

I'LL SNAP YOUR GODDAMN NECK!

The lengths a parent will go to protect their child.

:KKT!:

I only wish I had more to give you than my life.

G-GET... GT...

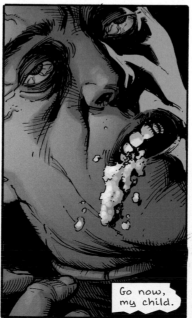

Go now, my child.

And be who you want to be.

Love,

Poppa

WHERE DO YOU THINK YOU'RE GOING?

23

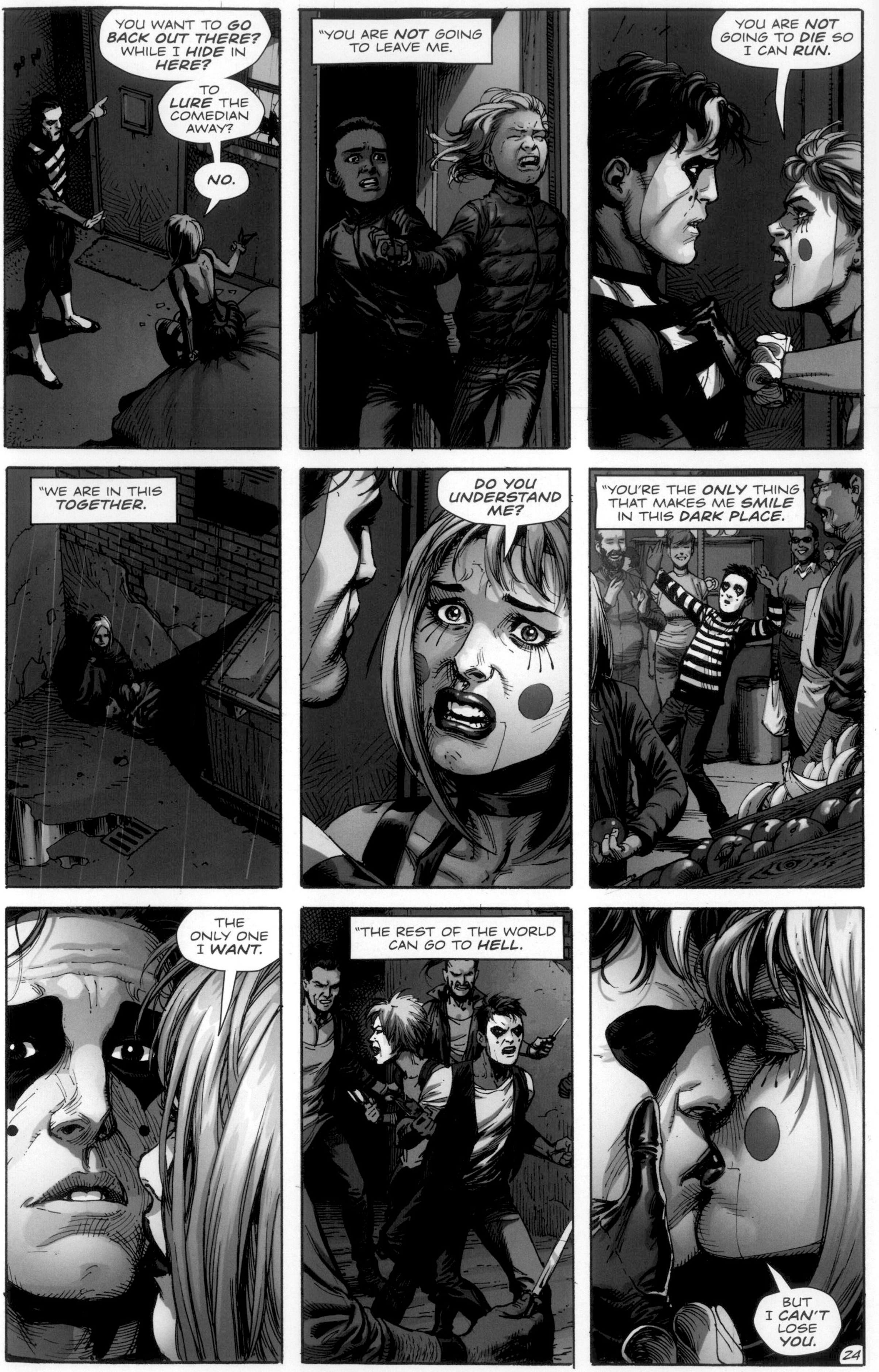
YOU WANT TO GO BACK OUT THERE? WHILE I HIDE IN HERE?
TO LURE THE COMEDIAN AWAY?
NO.
"YOU ARE NOT GOING TO LEAVE ME.
YOU ARE NOT GOING TO DIE SO I CAN RUN.
"WE ARE IN THIS TOGETHER.
DO YOU UNDERSTAND ME?
"YOU'RE THE ONLY THING THAT MAKES ME SMILE IN THIS DARK PLACE.
THE ONLY ONE I WANT.
"THE REST OF THE WORLD CAN GO TO HELL.
BUT I CAN'T LOSE YOU.

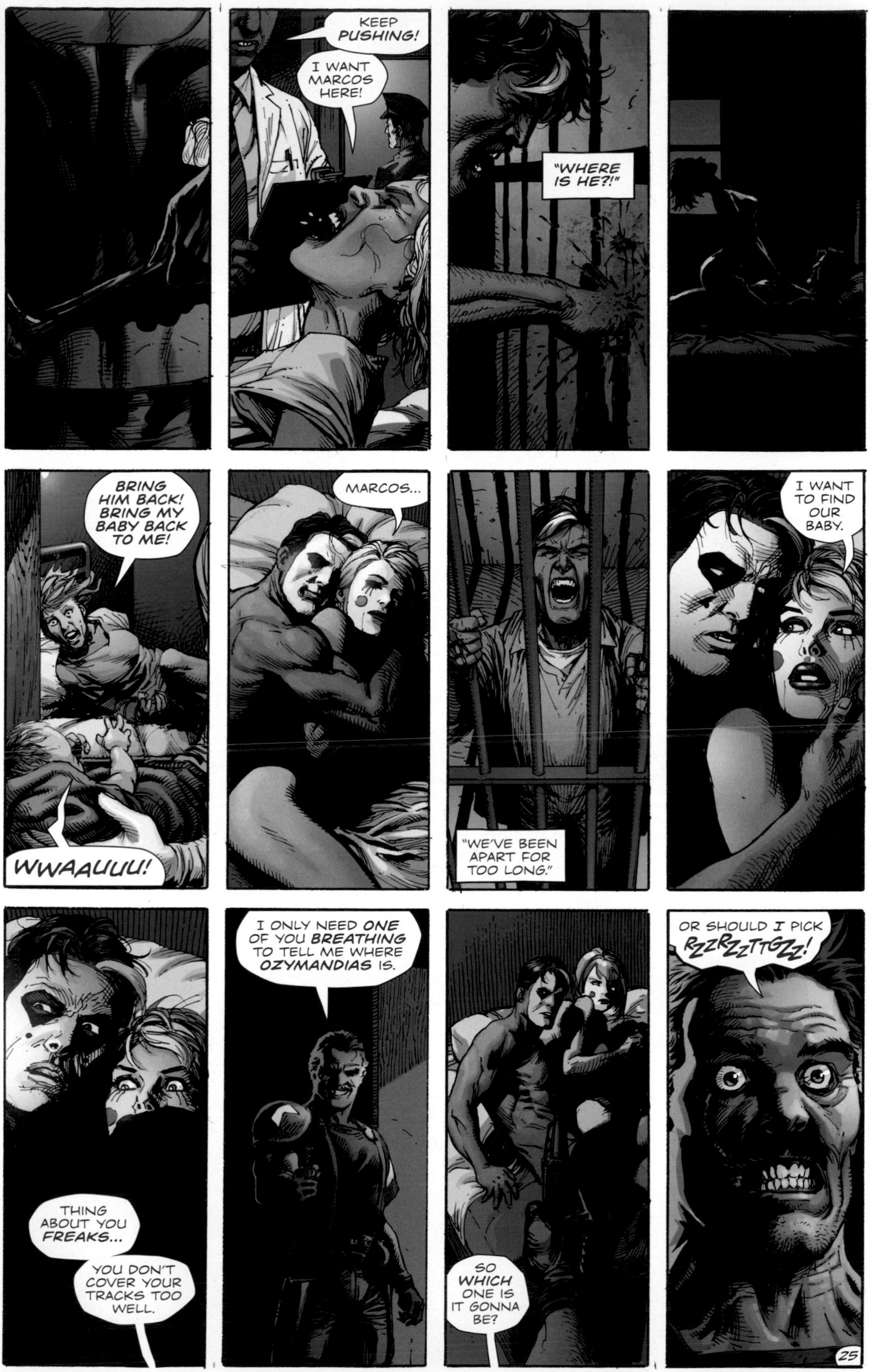
KEEP PUSHING!
I WANT MARCOS HERE!
"WHERE IS HE?!"
BRING HIM BACK! BRING MY BABY BACK TO ME!
WWAAUUU!
MARCOS...
"WE'VE BEEN APART FOR TOO LONG."
I WANT TO FIND OUR BABY.
THING ABOUT YOU FREAKS...
YOU DON'T COVER YOUR TRACKS TOO WELL.
I ONLY NEED ONE OF YOU BREATHING TO TELL ME WHERE OZYMANDIAS IS.
SO WHICH ONE IS IT GONNA BE?
OR SHOULD I PICK RZZRZZTTGZZ!

HAHAHAHAHA!

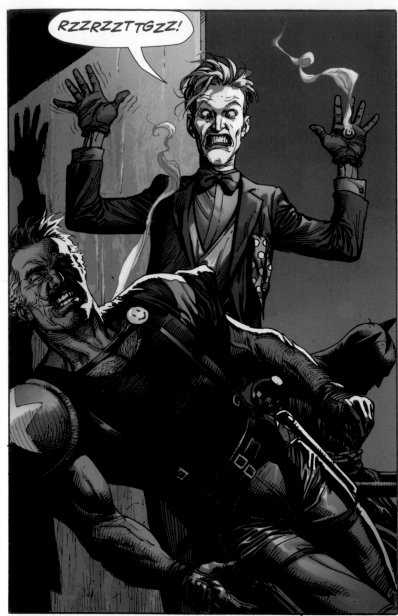

RZZRZZTTGZZ!

OH, *JOY.*

I *LIKE* YOU TWO. YOU MAKE ME *LAUGH.*

I WAS JUST THINKING...

...I BET *THE COMEDIAN* KNOWS WHERE *DR. MANHATTAN* IS.

DR. MANHATTAN? WHO'S THAT?

I COULD *USE* A GOOD DENTIST.

IT *HURTS* WHEN I *SMILE.*

To truly laugh, you must be able to take your pain, and play with it.

—Charlie Chaplin

26

CONFIDENTIAL

DMA

DEPARTMENT OF METAHUMAN AFFAIRS

AGENT DAVID DRAKE

A.K.A. TYPHOON

FL294-1981

DEPARTMENT OF METAHUMAN AFFAIRS

ASSIGNMENT APPROVAL FORM

AGENT NUMBER #FL294-1981

NAME David Matthew Drake

ASSIGNED ALIAS Typhoon

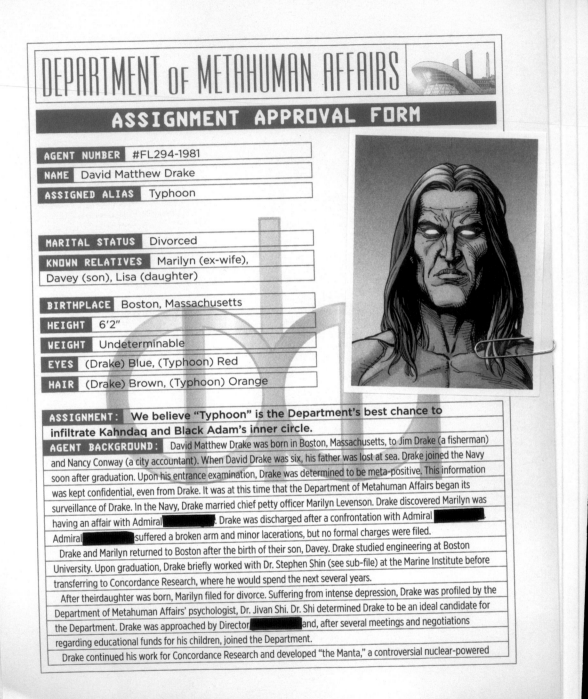

MARITAL STATUS Divorced

KNOWN RELATIVES Marilyn (ex-wife), Davey (son), Lisa (daughter)

BIRTHPLACE Boston, Massachusetts

HEIGHT 6′2″

WEIGHT Undeterminable

EYES (Drake) Blue, (Typhoon) Red

HAIR (Drake) Brown, (Typhoon) Orange

ASSIGNMENT: **We believe "Typhoon" is the Department's best chance to infiltrate Kahndaq and Black Adam's inner circle.**

AGENT BACKGROUND: David Matthew Drake was born in Boston, Massachusetts, to Jim Drake (a fisherman) and Nancy Conway (a city accountant). When David Drake was six, his father was lost at sea. Drake joined the Navy soon after graduation. Upon his entrance examination, Drake was determined to be meta-positive. This information was kept confidential, even from Drake. It was at this time that the Department of Metahuman Affairs began its surveillance of Drake. In the Navy, Drake married chief petty officer Marilyn Levenson. Drake discovered Marilyn was having an affair with Admiral [redacted]. Drake was discharged after a confrontation with Admiral [redacted]. Admiral [redacted] suffered a broken arm and minor lacerations, but no formal charges were filed.

Drake and Marilyn returned to Boston after the birth of their son, Davey. Drake studied engineering at Boston University. Upon graduation, Drake briefly worked with Dr. Stephen Shin (see sub-file) at the Marine Institute before transferring to Concordance Research, where he would spend the next several years.

After theirdaughter was born, Marilyn filed for divorce. Suffering from intense depression, Drake was profiled by the Department of Metahuman Affairs' psychologist, Dr. Jivan Shi. Dr. Shi determined Drake to be an ideal candidate for the Department. Drake was approached by Director [redacted] and, after several meetings and negotiations regarding educational funds for his children, joined the Department.

Drake continued his work for Concordance Research and developed "the Manta," a controversial nuclear-powered

ASSIGNMENT APPROVAL FORM

CONTINUED bathysphere that has since revolutionized deep-sea exploration. On board Concordance's research ship, the *Neptune Explorer*, Drake was seemingly killed after he was exposed to the nuclear core of the bathysphere. However, in reality this was a "controlled accident" designed and carried out by the Department of Metahuman Affairs. Drake survived the explosion and his metagene was triggered.

Drake's appearance was drastically altered. He gained the ability to create various meteorological storms centered around him. At the center of these storms, Drake wielded telekinetic control over wind, water and lightning. He was also able to "ride" these storms, mimicking flight.

Dubbed "Typhoon" by Director [redacted], Drake was assigned to play the role of "super-villain" in public in order to test and master his new powers. In his first outing he came into contact with Firestorm. Typhoon used his various confrontations with Firestorm to gain control over his abilities and make contacts in the criminal metahuman underworld. Unfortunately, Drake made contact with his ex-wife and children on several occasions. In one instance, Drake attacked his ex-wife's new husband. In another, Drake was reprimanded for revealing the truth behind his origins to his son. A cover story was quickly put into place, blaming Drake for a Category 1 hurricane that struck the coast of Florida and left 25 dead, later referred to as Hurricane Drake. Drake's relationship with his ex-wife and children ended after that. Drake struggled with alcohol and drugs and often sought out confrontations with Firestorm against the Department's orders. During one of his episodes, Drake hunted down and nearly killed Agent # GL1-1960, Jordan Weir a.k.a. the Puppet Master a.k.a. the Puppeteer, after learning of the role he played in Drake's psychological reconditioning.

Despite these various setbacks, Drake has been an invaluable agent to the Department. He was instrumental in the recruitment of Agent #FI43-1986, who continues to be an exemplary part of the Department and has kept Drake focused and responsible. We expect their work together to continue to have a significant impact on the Department's gathering of intel from within the criminal metahuman community.

We anxiously await the Director's approval of this next step for Agent Drake.

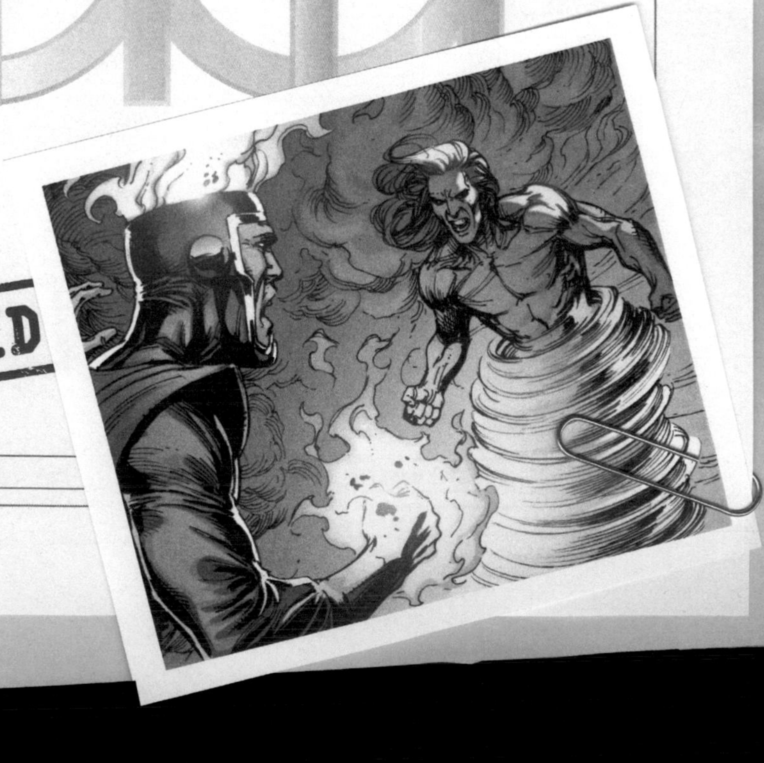

APPROVED

AGENT NUMBER #FL294-1981

DEPARTMENT of METAHUMAN AFFAIRS

REPORT FORM

REPORTING AGENT
David Matthew Drake, Typhoon

Agent Brandon and I will be infiltrating the Riddler's gathering tonight, which he is calling "the League of Villainy." Although Agent Brandon will remain stateside, the plan continues to be for me to travel into Kahndaq with the other volunteers and join Black Adam's army in order to report back. As of today we have identified three metahumans who have already committed themselves to Black Adam's cause.

METAHUMAN: The Creeper TRUE NAME: Jack Ryder

Reporter Jack Ryder was rescued from King Kobra by Black Adam in Syria. His identity as the Creeper is not known publicly, but he has crossed paths with both the Batman and the Justice League. He appears to be mentally unstable, and it is my opinion that the Department should consider the Creeper a liability for Black Adam should he remain in Kahndaq. The exact nature and extent of the Creeper's abilities remain unknown, though he has demonstrated super-agility and enhanced strength.

METAHUMAN: Giganta TRUE NAME: Dr. Doris Zeul

We have been monitoring ongoing communications between Dr. Zeul and Kahndaq. Dr. Zeul is expected to be a voice of support for Kahndaq among the criminal underworld tonight. The origins of her newfound loyalty to Black Adam have yet to be determined. As the world knows, Dr. Zeul gained the ability to increase her size and mass after performing experiments on herself and triggering her metagene, all of which I witnessed firsthand during the Crime Syndicate's invasion (see report).

METAHUMAN: Sandstorm TRUE NAME: Unknown

We know very little about the metahuman from Syria. There are reports of Sandstorm uncovering and destroying terrorist cells with a focus on freeing children held captive, but consequently he has been seen attacking Syrian soldiers, also with a focus on protecting children. We have confirmation that he is now working alongside Black Adam. It is said he has command over the entire desert.

`FOR DEPARTMENTAL USE ONLY`

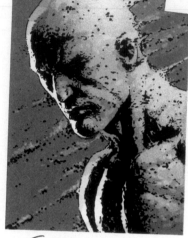

SANDSTORM

GIGANTA

THE CREEPER

THE MET

BIG MG
Gorai
Hamr
Judon
Naiac
Ram
Samu

Rising Sun Izumi Yasunari was a foun
Japan's superhero team Big Action Science
Japan's most powerful metahuman. Able t
of the sun. Rising Sun now leads a new te
Action, inheriting the duty of Ultimon, w
Japan from the kaiju that threatened it du
Wars." Big Monster Action is now capturi
these creatures.

THE EL
The B
of Teh
Mant
The P
Siroc
Super

IRAN

THE

Sayeh
peering
though
exactly
unclea
leading
metah
search
first to
War" s
endga
arms t
inven
it" re
Sayeh
what
inten
meta

BLACK ADAM has
opened the borders of
Kahndaq to any metahuman
seeking asylum. The number
of metahumans who have
joined him are said to be in
the dozens already, but their
identities remain a mystery.
With both America and Russia
withdrawing their troops
from the Middle East, Black
Adam has promised to bring
stability to the region.

DEPARTMENT OF METAHUMAN AFFAIRS

REPORT OF DEATH

NAME David Matthew Drake

AGENT NUMBER FL294-1981

DATE OF DEATH 7/25

PLACE OF DEATH Gotham

PERSON OR OFFICIAL RESPONSIBLE FOR CU

NAME Marilyn Levenson

ADDRESS 13 Hanger Way Salem, MA 01970

RELATIONSHIP ex-wife

DATE CONTACTED by Gotham PD 7/26

DISPOSITION OF REMAINS being held in Gotham City Morgue awaiting instructions

CIRCUMSTANCES (TO REMAIN CONFIDENTIAL) My colleague Agent David Drake was killed last night by an unknown assailant under the streets of Gotham. He was shot in the head. I pulled his body from the ensuing fire and, per Department protocol, vacated the scene.

As his longtime colleague, I respectfully request that Agent David Drake be cleared of any involvement in the deaths caused by Hurricane Drake and publicly recognized by the Department as the American hero we know he was. His children deserve to hear the truth about their father.

His soul is with God now. Do the right thing and one day yours will be, too.

Respectfully

B Brandon

SIGNATURE OF AGENT

AGENT NUMBER F143-1986

NAME Brittany Brandon / Moonbow

UMAN ARMS RACE CONTINU

R ACTION

t Zero-X

JAPAN

ember of believed to be ss the power d Big Monster protected "Monster domesticating

ASU

mith

nt One

yk

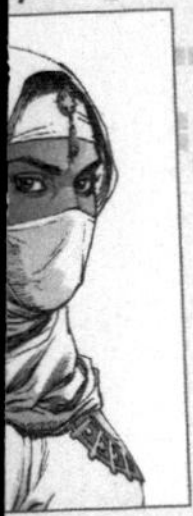

ER

er is capable of the future, far ahead she can nto tomorrow is h is currently owing group of s across Iran in ers. She was the the term "Super referring to the the metahuman Whether she e phrase or "saw to be clarified. ince been silent on seen but remains onsolidating Iran's ns.

DREAMER

Betty Clawman is an Australian metahuman able to move through dreams. Throughout the last month, world leaders and foreign metahumans have claimed to have been confronted by Dreamer and her team in their sleep. The Australian government has denied these accusations.

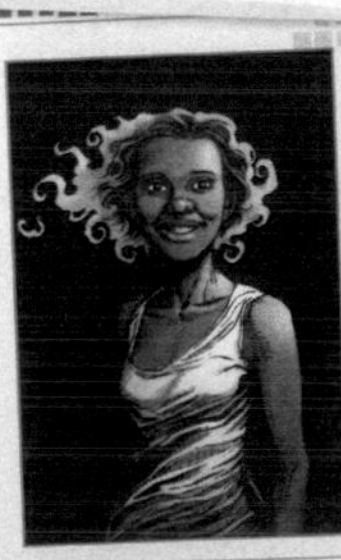

AUSTRALIA

THE SLEEPING SOLDIERS

The Argonaut
Dark Ranger
Miss Midnight
The Tasmanian Devil
Umbaluru

DEPARTMENT of METAHUMAN AFFAIRS

FOR GENERAL RELEASE

DAVID DRAKE died Wednesday, July 25, at the age of 43. There will be no funeral service. Donations for those affected by his criminal actions can be made to the Metahuman Victims Fund, 555 5th Street NW, #109, Washington D.C. 20001. Drake leaves behind a son, David, and daughter, Lisa.

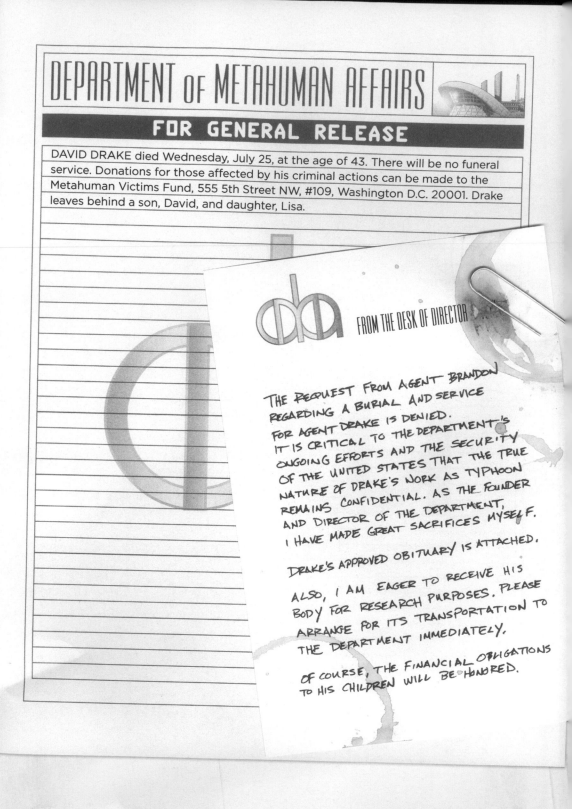

FROM THE DESK OF DIRECTOR

THE REQUEST FROM AGENT BRANDON REGARDING A BURIAL AND SERVICE FOR AGENT DRAKE IS DENIED. IT IS CRITICAL TO THE DEPARTMENT'S ONGOING EFFORTS AND THE SECURITY OF THE UNITED STATES THAT THE TRUE NATURE OF DRAKE'S WORK AS TYPHOON REMAINS CONFIDENTIAL. AS THE FOUNDER AND DIRECTOR OF THE DEPARTMENT, I HAVE MADE GREAT SACRIFICES MYSELF.

DRAKE'S APPROVED OBITUARY IS ATTACHED.

ALSO, I AM EAGER TO RECEIVE HIS BODY FOR RESEARCH PURPOSES. PLEASE ARRANGE FOR ITS TRANSPORTATION TO THE DEPARTMENT IMMEDIATELY.

OF COURSE, THE FINANCIAL OBLIGATIONS TO HIS CHILDREN WILL BE HONORED.

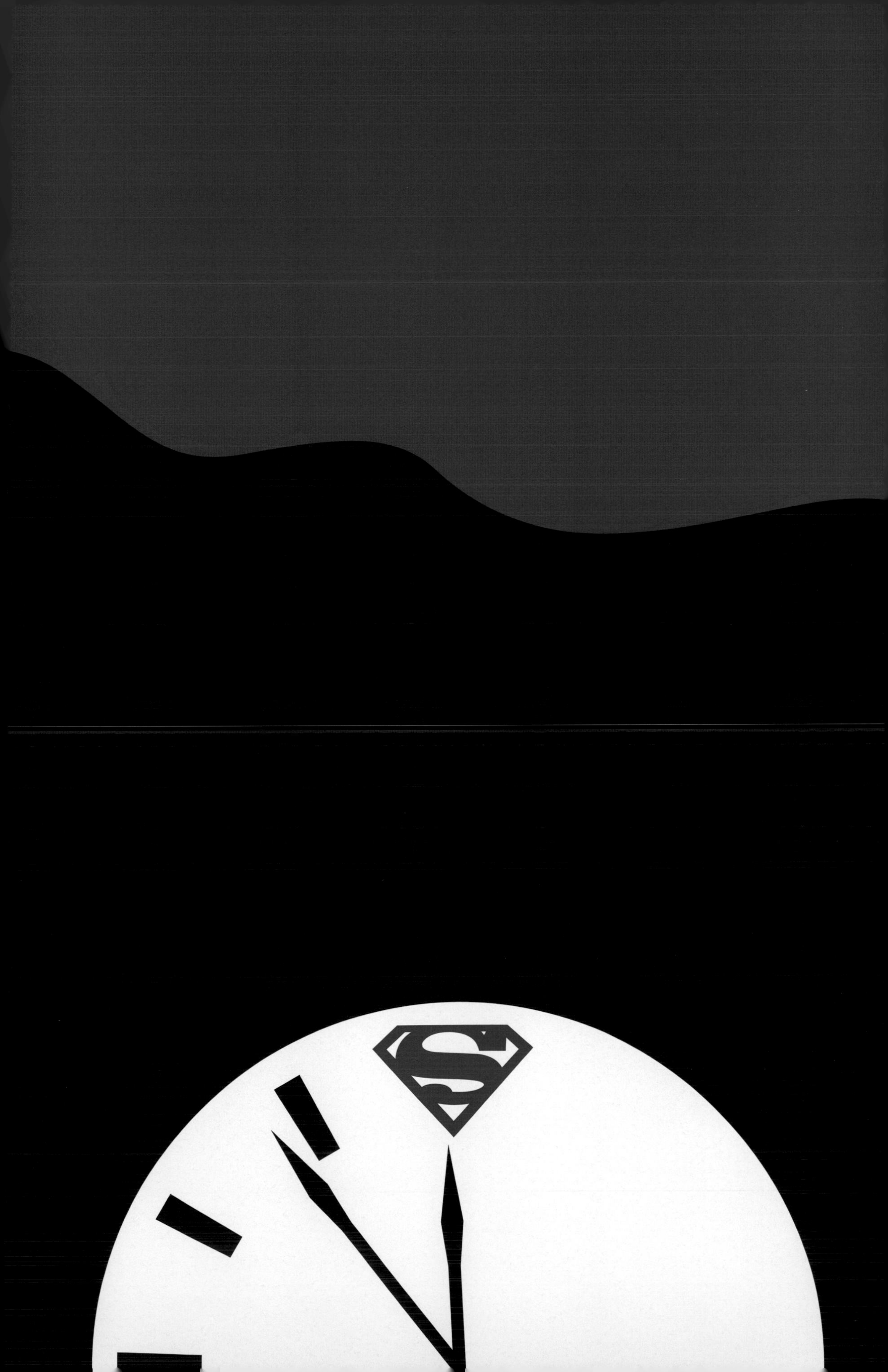

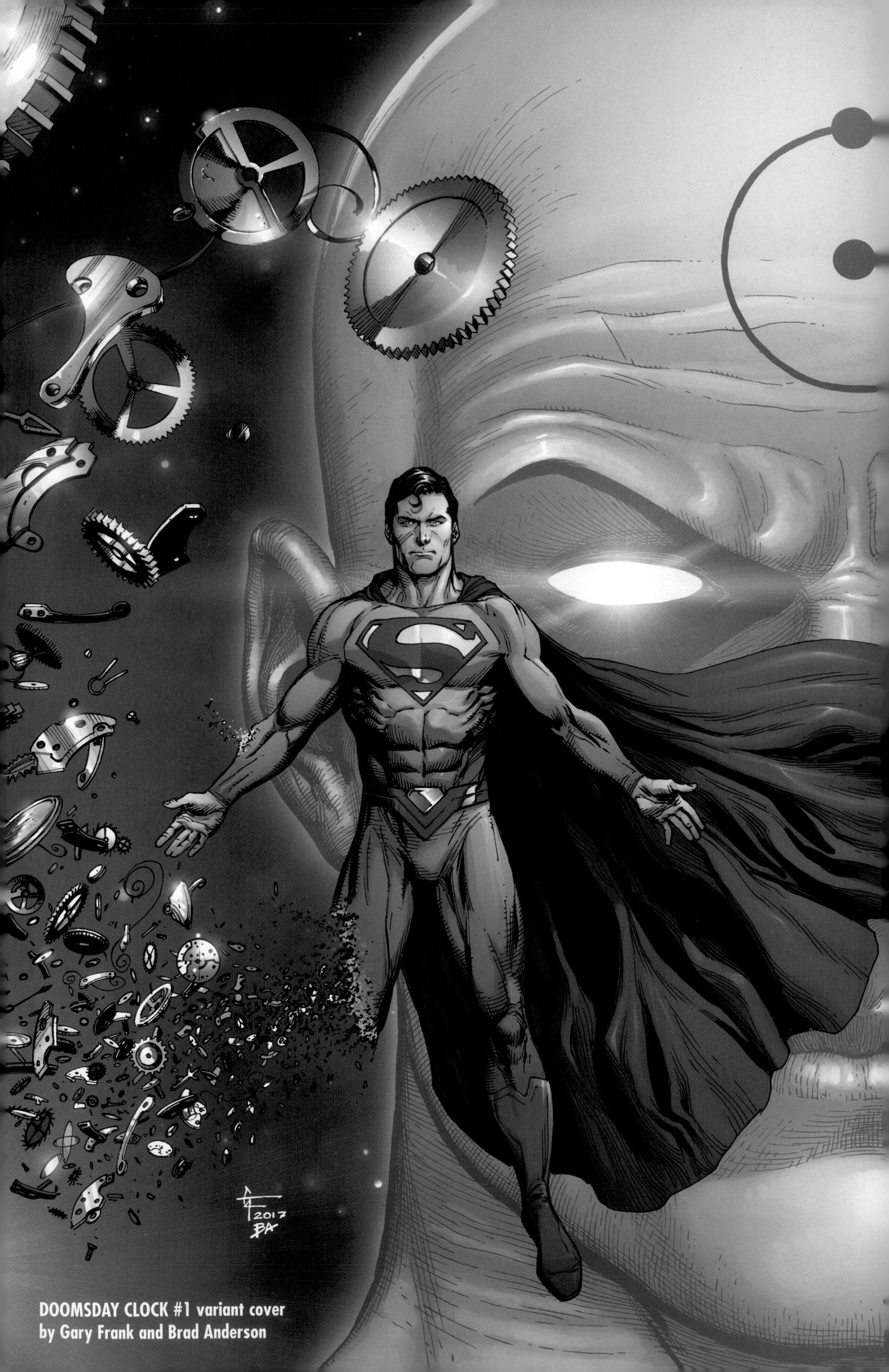

DOOMSDAY CLOCK #1 variant cover
by Gary Frank and Brad Anderson

DOOMSDAY CLOCK #2 variant cover
by Gary Frank and Brad Anderson

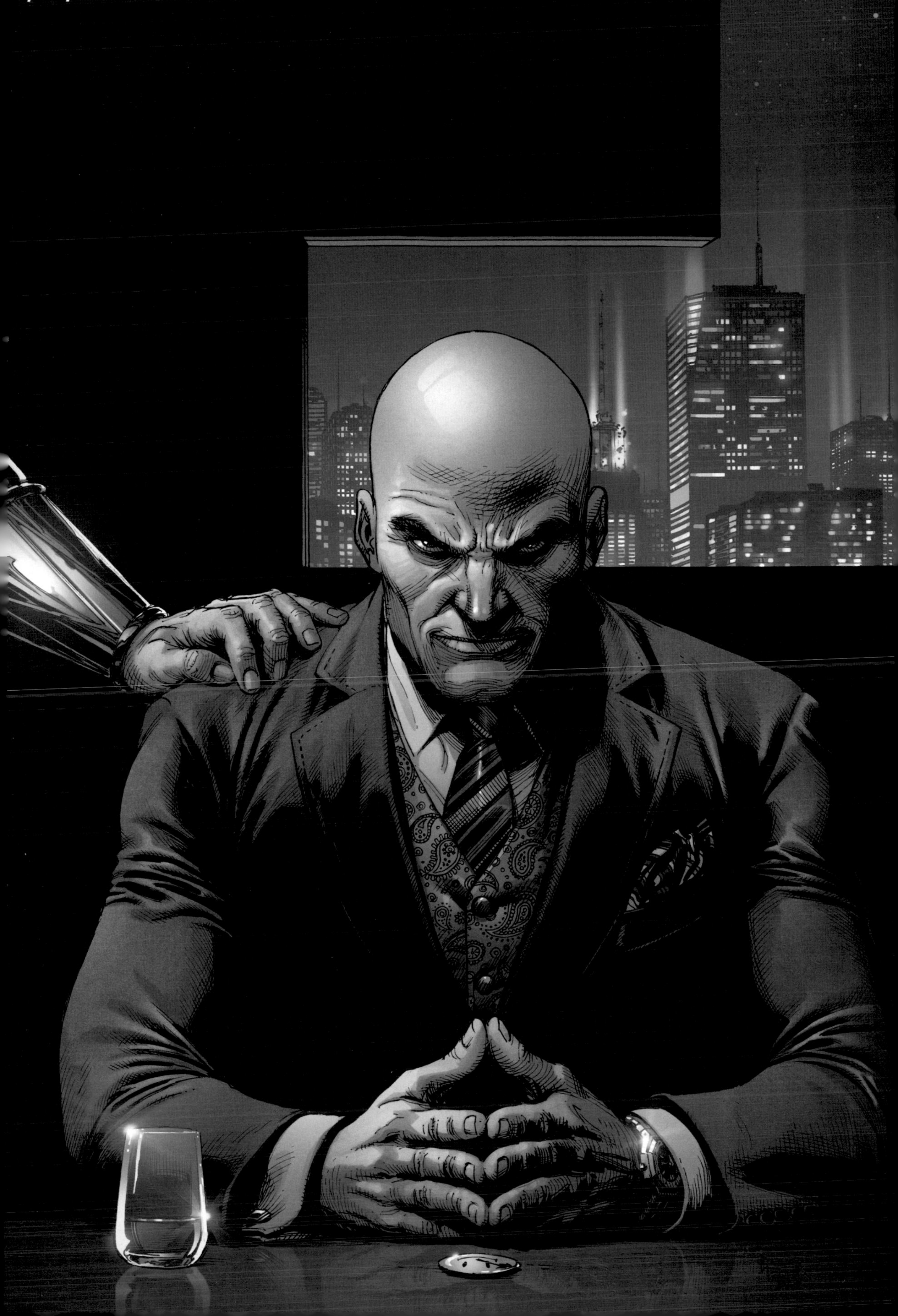

DOOMSDAY CLOCK #3 variant cover
by Gary Frank and Brad Anderson

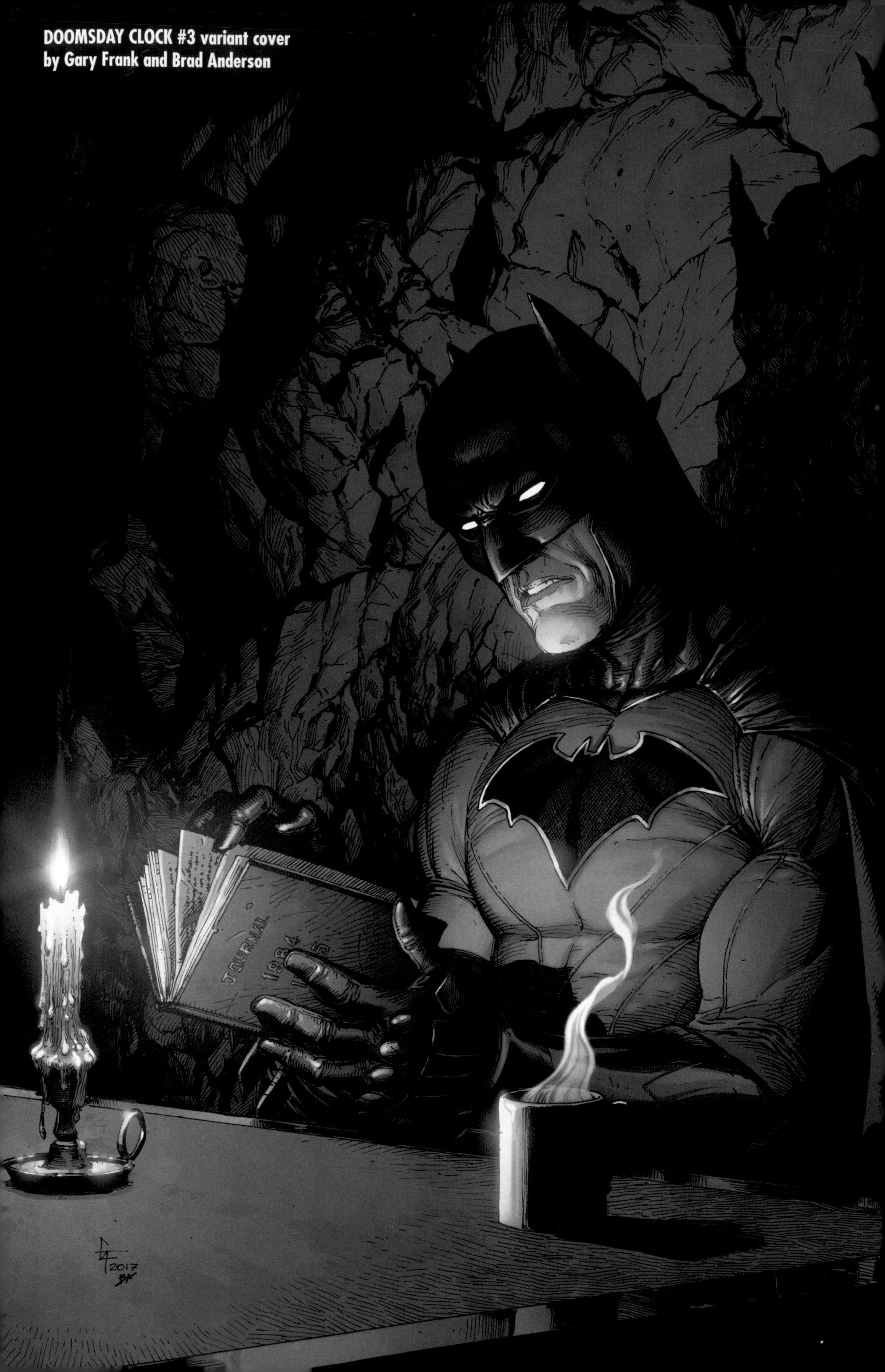

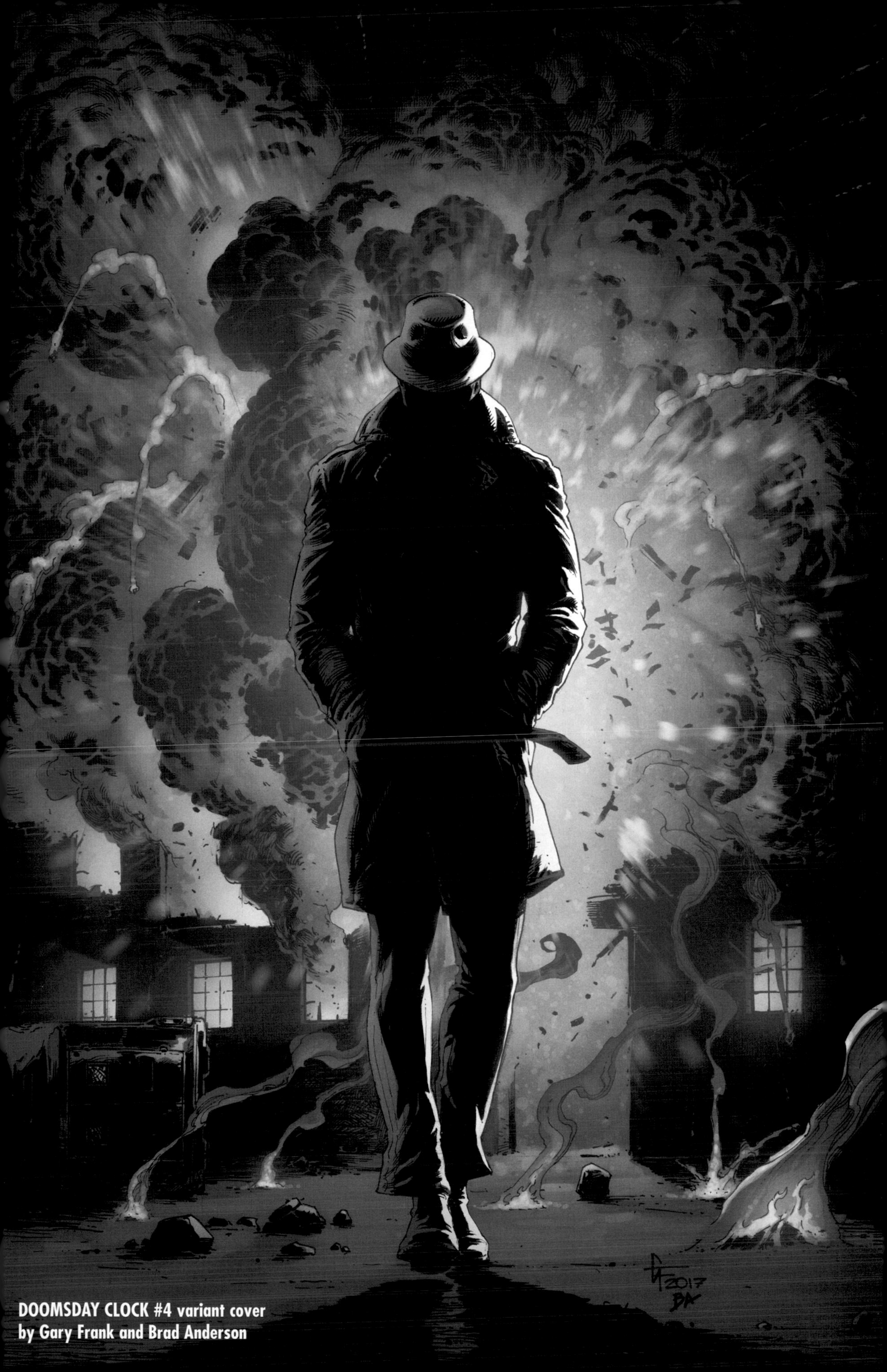

DOOMSDAY CLOCK #4 variant cover
by Gary Frank and Brad Anderson

DOOMSDAY CLOCK #5 variant cover
by Gary Frank and Brad Anderson

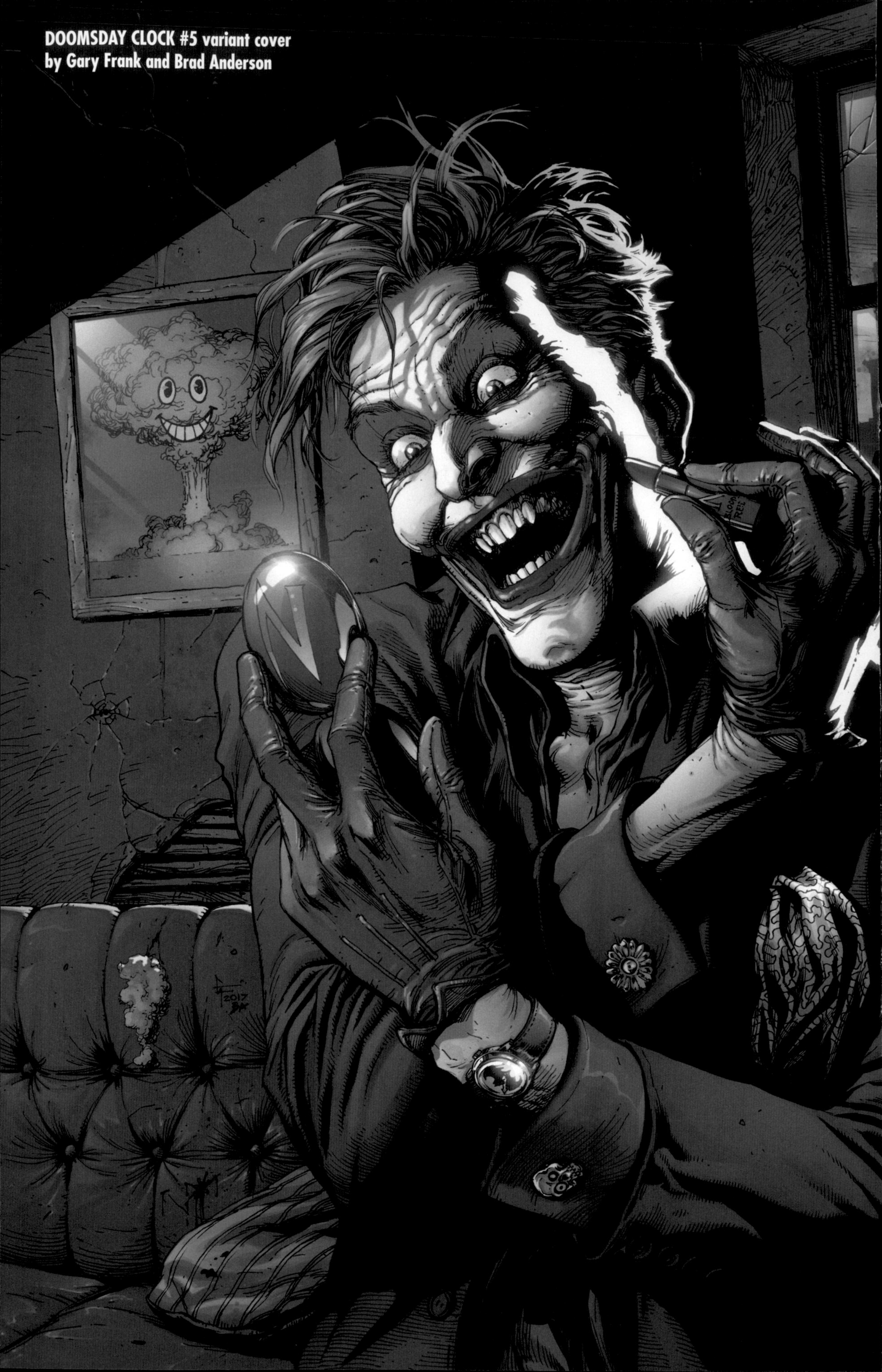

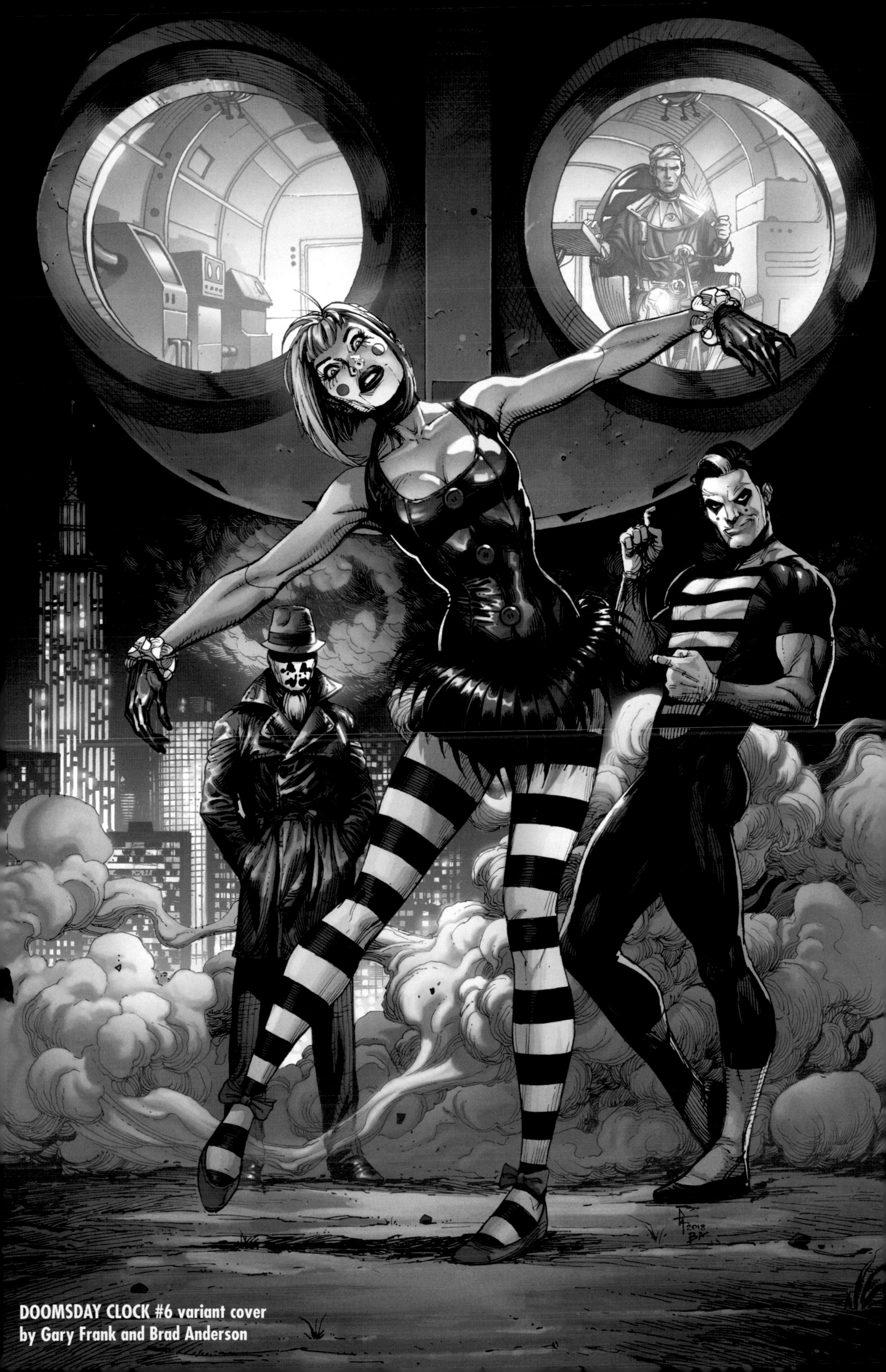

DOOMSDAY CLOCK #6 variant cover
by Gary Frank and Brad Anderson

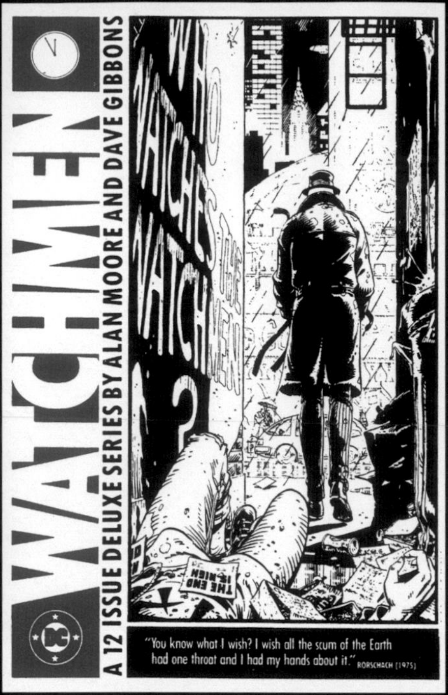
WATCHMEN
A 12 ISSUE DELUXE SERIES BY ALAN MOORE AND DAVE GIBBONS
"You know what I wish? I wish all the scum of the Earth had one throat and I had my hands about it." RORSCHACH (1975)

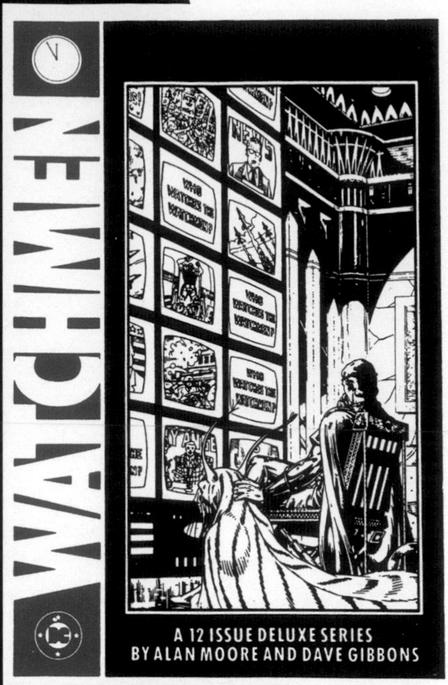
WATCHMEN
A 12 ISSUE DELUXE SERIES
BY ALAN MOORE AND DAVE GIBBONS

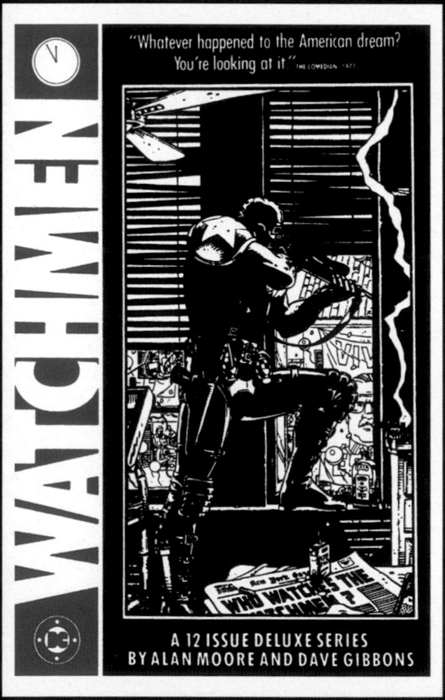
WATCHMEN
"Whatever happened to the American dream?
You're looking at it." THE COMEDIAN
WHO WATCHES THE WATCHMEN?
A 12 ISSUE DELUXE SERIES
BY ALAN MOORE AND DAVE GIBBONS

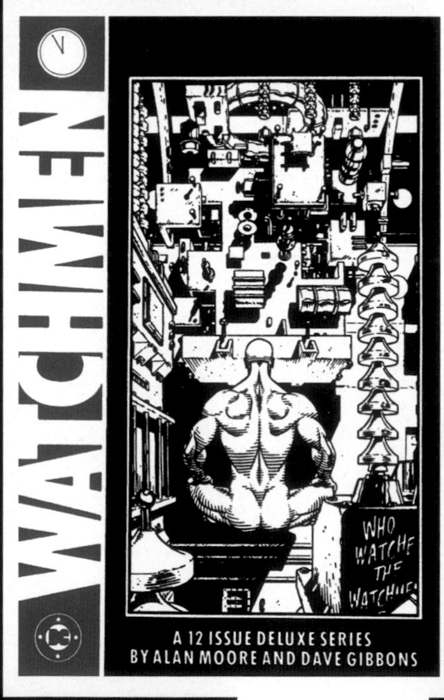
WATCHMEN
A 12 ISSUE DELUXE SERIES
BY ALAN MOORE AND DAVE GIBBONS

When WATCHMEN #1 hit stands in 1988, it was accompanied by a series of ominous black-and-white advertisements featuring the primary characters (above, art by Dave Gibbons). For DOOMSDAY CLOCK, the series' variant covers were repurposed into a similar campaign as an homage to the

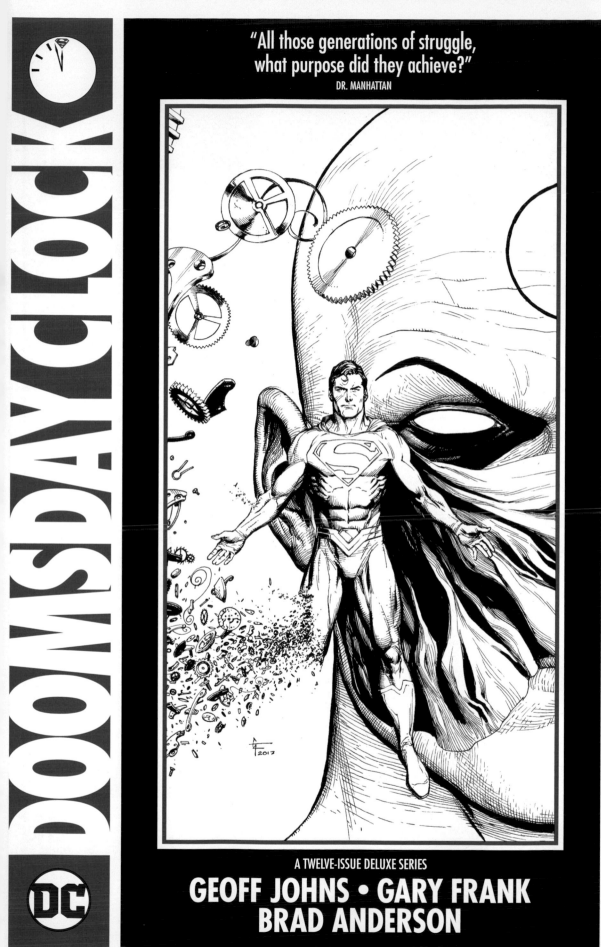

"All those generations of struggle,
what purpose did they achieve?"

DR. MANHATTAN

DOOMSDAY CLOCK

A TWELVE-ISSUE DELUXE SERIES

GEOFF JOHNS • GARY FRANK
BRAD ANDERSON

TM & © DC Comics.

"I hope you'll forgive me while I warm up.
I haven't done this in a while."

OZYMANDIAS

A TWELVE-ISSUE DELUXE SERIES

GEOFF JOHNS • GARY FRANK
BRAD ANDERSON

DOOMSDAY CLOCK

"If reading this now, whether I am alive or dead, you will know truth."

RORSCHACH

JOURNAL
1984

A TWELVE-ISSUE DELUXE SERIES

GEOFF JOHNS • GARY FRANK

BRAD ANDERSON

DC

"Go on. Tell me what you really see."
DR. MALCOLM LONG

A TWELVE-ISSUE DELUXE SERIES
GEOFF JOHNS • GARY FRANK
BRAD ANDERSON

"What's so goddamned funny? I don't get it.
Somebody explain it to me."
THE COMEDIAN

A TWELVE-ISSUE DELUXE SERIES
GEOFF JOHNS • GARY FRANK
BRAD ANDERSON

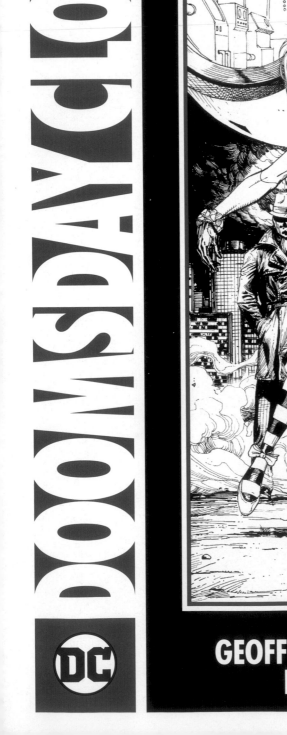

"We're all puppets, Laurie.
I'm just a puppet who can see the strings."

DR. MANHATTAN

A TWELVE-ISSUE DELUXE SERIES

GEOFF JOHNS • GARY FRANK
BRAD ANDERSON